COMMUNICATE!

Rudolph F. Verderber

Distinguished Teaching Professor of Communication
University of Cincinnati

8th edition

Wadsworth Publishing Company
I T P™ **An International Thomson Publishing Company**

Belmont · Albany · Boston · Cincinnati · Detroit · London · Madrid · Melbourne
Mexico City · New York · Paris · San Francisco · Singapore · Tokyo · Toronto · Washington

Editor	**Katherine Hartlove**
Communication Studies Editor	**Todd R. Armstrong**
Development Editor	**Sherry Symington**
Editorial Assistant	**Jessica Monday**
Project Development Editor	**Lewis De Simone**
Production Services Coordinator	**Debby Kramer**
Production Editor	**Cecile Joyner, The Cooper Company**
Interior and Cover Designers	**Cloyce Wall & Scott Williams**
Print Buyer	**Barbara Britton**
Permissions Editor	**Robert Kauser**
Copy Editor	**Margaret C. Tropp**
Photo Researcher	**Terri Wright**
Interior Illustrator	**Seventeenth Street Studios**
Cover Illustrator	**Lisa Berman**
Compositor	**Monotype Composition Company**
Printer	**R.R. Donnelly & Sons**
Photo Credits	**See Page iii**

Library of Congress Cataloging-in-Publication Data

Verderber, Rudolph F.
 Communicate! / Rudolph F. Verderber. — 8th ed.
  p. cm.
 Includes bibliographical references and index.
 ISBN: 0-534-25812-3
 1. Communication.   I. Title
P90.V43   1995   95-15056
302.2—dc20

**For more information,
contact Wadsworth Publishing Company:**

Wadsworth Publishing Company
10 Davis Drive
Belmont, California 94002, USA

International Thomson Publishing Europe
Berkshire House 168-173
High Holborn
London, WC1V 7AA, England

Thomas Nelson Australia
102 Dodds Street
South Melbourne 3205
Victoria, Australia

Nelson Canada
1120 Birchmount Road
Scarborough, Ontario
Canada M1K 5G4

International Thomson Editores
Campos Eliseos 385, Piso 7
Col. Polanco
11560 México D.F. México

International Thomson Publishing GmbH
Königswinterer Strasse 418
53227 Bonn, Germany

International Thomson Publishing Asia
221 Henderson Road
#05-10 Henderson Building
Singapore 0315

International Thomson Publishing Japan
Hirakawacho Kyowa Building, 3F
2-2-1 Hirakawacho
Chiyoda-ku, Tokyo 102, Japan

B RIEF CONTENTS

C ONTENTS

SELF-ANALYSIS
Interpersonal Communication   213

four Group Communication   215

Public Speaking   263

PERSPECTIVES

P

Instructors bring different approaches to teaching communication. Some tend to emphasize theory and research, whereas others focus on skills acquisition and practice. In this eighth edition of *Communicate!* I have tried to impart conceptual understanding of relevant theory and research, but I also believe such understanding is incomplete unless students can translate it into genuine communication competence. Further, achieving communication competence is a goal that students of all ages and backgrounds can relate to and aspire to—something I try to acknowledge by treating readers with respect and using a diversity of examples.

With a combination of theory, skills practice, and competency evaluation, students (1) learn to understand the major concepts from communication theory and research, (2) become able to recognize how these concepts and theories provide a basis for communication skills, (3) have access to a range of communication skills, and (4) begin to apply what they learn in class to real-life situations, thus increasing communication competence in all settings.

Goals of This Edition

The primary goal of this edition is to continue to present the elements of communication competence in a way that is appealing to both the student learning the skills and to the instructor who is guiding that learning. A major challenge is to be sensitive to the burgeoning research in communication while still providing a manageable, coherent introduction that makes a real difference to the development of students' skills.

This revision emphasizes current trends in the field while preserving the qualities that previous users have said they find valuable:

- *Competency-based orientation* that shows students how to translate theory and research into communication behaviors.

- *A reliable learning model* that gives instructors and students alike a consistent way to approach each new topic.
- *A clear, concise writing style.*
- *Ample examples.*
- *Numerous suggestions for practice integrated within chapters.*

For those of you who are teaching from this book for the first time, I believe you will find that the book supports its coverage of the fundamental issues with a pedagogical framework that helps make your job easier. In short, this edition provides sound contemporary content presented in the style that has made *Communicate!* a leader in the field and an eminently teachable text.

This eighth edition has been revised with the following goals in mind: (1) to increase emphasis on gender and cross-cultural issues; (2) to increase emphasis on skills that cross all communication settings; (3) to put greater emphasis on public speaking and increase the audience-centered approach; (4) to increase documentation and update sources; and (5) to add more examples that speak to a wide range of contemporary students.

Features of the Text

Today's students demand that everything in a text be purposeful and a genuine aid to learning. Although I hope the following features add to the interest value of this book, their primary purpose is to enable readers to translate theory and research into communication behaviors, recognize and practice their communication skills, and extend their learning outside the classroom.

The Learning Model.   The material in this book is specifically arranged to help students learn and practice new skills and become comfortable using them in real-life situations. To help maximize what students can accomplish, this book uses a systematic learning model that consists of six integrated steps.

1. *Theoretical understanding.*   Learning new skills begins with an understanding of how and why certain skills are effective. This book presents communication theories that provide the foundation for specific skills.

2. *Examples.*   The second step of the learning model is the study of concrete examples of communication behavior that help bridge the gap between theory and practice. Specific examples enable students to identify effective skill usage.

3. *Steps involved in the performance of skills.*   The third step of the learning model involves breaking down complex behaviors so that students can see the individual components of the skills. Thus when a new skill is presented, the text describes the essential steps students will need to master in order to perform that skill.

4. *Practice in using skills.*   The fourth step of the learning model involves putting the students' new-found knowledge of skills into practice. Throughout this book, exercises are presented that encourage students to try out the skills in familiar situations. In some of the exercises, individuals will practice alone; in other exercises, students are encouraged to practice the skills in interactions with members of the class, friends, or family members.

5. *Self-assessment.*   The fifth step of the learning model involves a focus on self and commitment to change. To improve communication skills, students must first evaluate how well they currently perform. For each skill an individual selects to work on, he or she is invited to prepare a communication improvement goal statement that specifies a realistic plan for improvement. The elements of the goals statements are introduced in Chapter 1. Then at the end of each of the four major sections, or Parts, of the book, students are encouraged to write a goal statement to help them with their mastery of a key skill within that Part. Self-evaluation checklists help the students identify skills to work on.

6. *Review.*   The final step of the learning model involves reviewing what has been learned. A summary of the chapter's content is provided at the end of each chapter.

Focus on Gender and Culture.   I have targeted gender and cultural issues for significant expansion in this edition. Rather than segregating these issues in separate chapters, they are woven throughout the book wherever they are especially relevant to the theory or application of skills. In addition, a few of the Perspectives (guest essays) highlight these topics.

Perspectives.   Ten guest essays, called "Perspectives," provide thoughtful reflections and helpful advice on contemporary topics such as how "assertive" American speakers might offend people from other cultures and why the speaking style of women sometimes puts them at a disadvantage in groups. These essays reinforce and extend the core lessons of the text.

Practices.   Any study of fundamental skills calls not only for clear explanation but also for well-conceived ideas to help students put those fundamentals into practice. Throughout the text, realistic, workable exercises are included for practice of the skills discussed. This edition features many revisions of exercises and a number of newly created exercises. In each exercise a specific behavioral objective, such as writing well-phrased perception checks, is sought.

Many practice sessions include "By Yourself" sections: suggestions for analysis that allow students to reflect on personal experiences relevant to the material covered in that section and to analyze whether and how they have used the skills they have learned. Other exercises are designed to be done in class—some with pairs of students, some in small groups, and some as a whole class.

Through the analysis, observation, and practice models, instructors can help students learn quickly and efficiently. You will also find exercises that provide practical applications of the various communication skills. Thirteen speech preparation exercises carry students through the steps necessary to prepare their first speech.

Suggested Readings.   At the end of each chapter is an annotated list of books, both popular and scholarly, that provides supplemental analysis of the material covered in the chapter.

Major Changes in the Eighth Edition

For those who are familiar with or have used the previous edition of *Communicate!*, here is a brief summary of the most significant changes, chapter by chapter.

Part One, Introduction, continues to provide a broad perspective on the discipline. Chapter 1 has an expanded section on communication contexts, and "The Learning Contract" has been refined to "Communication Improvement Goal Statements."

Part Two, Establishing a Communication Foundation, has been revised so that the student sees perception, verbal communication, and nonverbal communication as fundamental to all types of communication. In this section of the book there is far more emphasis on gender and cultural differences. In addition, the self-concept section has been considerably revised in Chapter 2, Perception of Self and Others.

Part Three, Interpersonal Communication, has more emphasis on specific skills that lead to interpersonal competence. The part has a much more comprehensive chapter on relationships than the previous edition. Chapter 8, "Communication in Relationships," features a new section on the "Life Cycle" of relationships and also includes information on "Climates" in the section on "Stabilizing Relationships."

Part Four, Group Communication, has an increased amount of information on cultural differences.

Part Five, Public Speaking, has undergone major revision. The five introductory chapters are now all built upon six Action Steps to speech preparation. In keeping with the increased emphasis on an audience-centered approach, Part Five also includes a new chapter on audience adaptation. Both Chapter 16 "Informative Speaking" and Chapter 17 "Persuasive Speaking" emphasize the concept of the speech plan that is introduced in Chapter 13, "Adapting to Audiences." Chapter 17, "Persuasive Speaking" also features new sections on informative and persuasive speaking contrasts and analyzing audiences. In addition, theoretical material has been better integrated into the Principles of Persuasive Speaking.

Supplementary Materials

As a user of this text you also have access to supplementary materials developed at Wadsworth. For more information, call your local sales representative.

- *Instructor's Resource Manual.* The *Instructor's Resource Manual* for *Communicate!* includes role-playing exercises, experiential learning exercises, discussion questions, written assignments, possible course schedules, exam questions (multiple choice and essay) with page references and answer keys, and transparency masters.
- *Transparency Acetates.* This package includes diagrams, figures, and illustrations that will help you demonstrate important topics in the class.
- *Computerized Testing.* All test questions in the *Instructor's Resource Manual* are available on disk for the IBM PC and compatibles and the Macintosh.
- *Videotapes.* There are videotapes available that cover selected topics from the text.

Acknowledgments

The eighth edition could not have been completed without the help of many people. Mostly, I would like to acknowledge the help of my colleagues at various colleges and universities who offered prerevision suggestions or who read the completed manuscript for the eighth edition and offered many valuable suggestions: Lori J. Carrell, University of Wisconsin—Oshkosh; Virginia Thigpen, Volunteer State Community College; Robert Bohlken, Northwest Missouri State University; Janice Stuckey, University of Montevallo; and Stephen A. March, Pima Community College/University of Arizona.

C O M M U N I C A T E !

How you can learn the most from this book and
communicate more effectively in your everyday life.

Each day presents you with many different opportunities to communicate—with a friend or a coworker, in a class discussion or group meeting, and in public speaking situations. *Communicate!* helps you rise to each occasion confident in your ability to communicate effectively.

To reach your goal of skilled communication, you'll need a combination of conceptual knowledge and practical technique. *Communicate!* is specifically designed to help you build a solid knowledge base and transfer that knowledge into actual practice. At every stage, this book provides you with the clear explanations and tools you need to learn actively, gradually, and thoroughly. The following pages give you an advance look at these features. I hope you'll find that reviewing this learning guide gives you a head start on your way to better communication.

Best wishes,

Rudolph F. Verderber

---------------- COMMUNICATE! gives you a clear, hands-on approach to learning the process and skills of interpersonal, group, and public communication. For instance, in Part Two you'll actively learn the steps involved in improving your interpersonal communication. Likewise, Part Four shows you the action steps to take toward effective public speaking. You will also discover how particular skills cross over into different communication genres. Each of the following features of *Communicate!* is designed to help you develop these practical skills on the basis of a strong conceptual understanding and ultimately apply them to your own life. As you review the following features, consider how they can aid your overall process of development as a communicator.

The learning model

To guide you in your learning process, Communicate! *adopts a learning model (described in the Preface) that is consistent with its integrated, practical approach. Broken out into six steps, this flexible model helps you approach the material in a cohesive and manageable way. A strong grasp of this model will enable you to gain a deeper understanding of the ideas in each chapter and how they relate to everyday interactions.*

Occasion and Setting Analysis

1. Complete the following questions about the occasion and setting:

   a. How large will the audience be? _____

   b. When will the speech be given? _____

   c. Where in the program does the speech occur? _____

   d. What are the time limits for the speech? _____

   e. What are the specific assignments and expectations for the speech? _____

   _____

   f. Where will the speech be given? _____

   g. What facilities are necessary to give the speech? _____

   _____

2. What effect will the occasion and setting have on your speech? _____

   _____

3. What is the most important factor you must take into account to meet the demands of the setting?

   _____

   _____

Checklists

You will find analysis checklists included at strategic points throughout Communicate! *These checklists, like this one on audience analysis, give you a clear, step-by-step guideline for assessing specific factors affecting your communication. Completing these checklists will give you valuable insights on the communication process and highlight ways you can enhance your skills.*

Chapter objectives and summaries

Each chapter in Communicate! *begins with a short list of objectives. These objectives tell you what you can expect to learn from the chapter, making it easier to see the importance of the chapter material to your own communication skills. The summary at the end of each chapter will help you confirm that you have understood the key concepts and achieved your objectives.*

Objectives

After you have read this chapter, you should be able to:

Explain ways of determining emotional states of others

Question for information

Paraphrase information

Support positive and negative feelings

Give alternative interpretations

Praise

Give and receive constructive criticism

Eliminate inappropriate responses

Practice in Preparing Informative Speeches

By Yourself

1. Prepare an informative speech. An outline and a bibliography are required. Criteria for evaluation include means of generating audience interest, conveying understanding, ensuring retention, and building credibility. As an addendum to the outline, you may wish to write a plan for adapting the speech to your audience based on predictions you made using the audience analysis checklist on page 275. In the plan include four short sections discussing strategies for (1) building credibility, (2) getting and maintaining interest, (3) facilitating understanding, and (4) increasing retention. You may wish to discuss how you will use your creativity to ensure that the speech will be perceived as intellectually stimulating, relevant, clear, and memorable. When and deliver tive speech.

Some suitable topics are as follows: Gateway Arch, a fisherman's skein, racing ice skates, Golden Gate Bridge, a ballet dancer, a college professor.

2. Pr thing is dor topic; selec presentatio lows: how spinach sou helicopter,

4. Prepare an extended definition of a word. Evaluation will focus on the definition's clarity and on the organization and quality of the developmental material. Examples of the kinds of general or abstract words for which extended definitions are appropriate are as follows: expressionism, rhetoric, logic, existentialism, Epicurean, acculturation, myth, fossil, extrasensory perception, and epistemology.

3. Pr Evaluation

5. Prepare a report on some aspect of communication in a specific culture or on an individual speaker from that culture. Topics in the area of culture and communication might include Native Americans: language and culture; storytelling as public speaking in Jewish culture; call and response in public speaking in African-American culture; Japanese–American business relations: communication differences. Examples of individual speakers might include Barbara Jordan, Sagoyewatha, Sojourner Truth, Malcolm X, Elie Wiesel.

6. Write a critique of at least one of the informative speeches you hear in class. Outline the speech. As you outline, answer the questions on the informative speech checklist (Figure 16.2).

Opportunities for practice

There's no question that improving your communication skills takes both knowledge and hands-on practice. Right from the start, Communicate! *gives you many opportunities to try first-hand the principles and techniques you're reading about. Throughout the book, you'll find "Practice" sections carefully designed to give you vital experience in individual, group, or public communication contexts.*

Interpersonal Conversation and Analysis

Dating

Sheila and Susan talk about the advantages and disadvantages of dating exclusively within one's own religion. Read the conversation aloud in its entirety. After you have considered its merits, read it again, this time noting the analysis in the right-hand column.

Conversation	Analysis
Susan: How are you and Bill getting along these days?	*Susan introduces the subject with a question.*
Sheila: Not too well. I think you could say our relationship is coming to an end. The feelings just aren't there, and so many problems have been building up.	*Sheila's answer is neither as specific nor as concrete as it could have been.*
Susan: I get the impression from the expression on your face that you're having problems. Is there one specific problem?	*Susan responds with a perception check wording; she's responding both to Sheila's spoken words and to what she is implying. A feelings paraphrase wording would be better: "From the way you're talking, I get the impression that you're very sad about the outcome of the relationship."*
Sheila: Well, there are a lot, but one that I didn't think would make such a difference at the beginning of the relationship that's made a difference now is the fact that we're from different religions. I'm Jewish and he isn't, and at first I never thought it would affect me, but it does make a difference.	*Sheila says, "It really does make a difference," but she doesn't go on to say what the difference is. We would expect Susan to ask about the difference.*
Susan: I think I was kind of lucky, well, lucky in the long run. When I was in high school, my parents wouldn't allow me to go out with anybody who wasn't Jewish. I really resented that at first, but now I'm kind of glad since I'm thinking about the future now. And as my parents said, you don't know what could come out of a high-school relationship.	*Susan assumes she understands. She needs a question or a content paraphrase here. Instead, she changes the emphasis to her own experience. Now, apparently, the conversation will focus on Susan and an implied contrast in upbringing.*

SOURCE: Conversation presented in Interpersonal Communication class, University of Cincinnati. Reprinted by permission of Sheila Slone and Susan Lautman.

Samples for analysis

Communicate! *features a diverse range of sample speeches, conversations, and other forms of communication. At the back of the book, you'll find a number of more extensive samples with accompanying analyses. Studying these samples and analyses will give you extra practice in assessing the qualities of effective communication.*

Self-analysis questionnaires

Parts Two through Five in Communicate! *conclude with a self-analysis questionnaire. The questionnaires, like this one on interpersonal communication, ask you to rate your skill and effectiveness in key areas of communication. These self-analysis tools help you get a clear picture of where you are now as a communicator and assist you in creating learning goals specifically tailored to your needs.*

Communication improvement goal statements

Improving your communication abilities in diverse situations is quite a challenge. Setting goals for yourself during the learning process will help you meet that challenge with much greater success. On page 24 of Communicate!, *you'll find a goal-setting process that many students find useful in formulating their own goals. It clearly describes the steps you need to take to structure achievable and valuable learning goals, from stating the goal and describing the problem to creating an action plan and assessing your progress.*

Self-Analysis

Interpersonal Communication
Chapters 5–8

What kind of an interpersonal communicator are you? The following analysis looks at specific behaviors that are characteristic of effective interpersonal communicators. On the line provided for each statement, indicate the response that best captures your behavior: 1, never; 2, rarely; 3, occasionally; 4, often; 5, almost always.

_____ In conversation, I am able to make relevant contributions without interrupting others. (Ch. 5)

_____ I describe objectively to others my negative feelings about their behavior toward me without withholding or blowing up. (Ch. 5)

_____ I change the way I listen depending on the purpose of my listening. (Ch. 6)

_____ I listen attentively, regardless of my interest in the person or the ideas. (Ch. 6)

_____ I am able to remember names, telephone numbers, and other specific information that I have heard only once. (Ch. 6)

_____ When I'm not sure whether I understand, I seek clarification. (Ch. 7)

_____ I am quick to praise people for doing things well. (Ch. 7)

_____ I criticize people for their mistakes only when they ask for criticism. (Ch. 7)

_____ I am able to maintain a positive communication climate by speaking in ways that others perceive as descriptive, provisional, and nonmanipulative. (Ch. 8)

_____ When I find myself in conflict with another person, I am able to discuss the issue openly without withdrawing or appearing competitive or aggressive. (Ch. 8)

Based on your responses, select the interpersonal communication behavior that you would most like to change. Write a communication improvement goal statement similar to the sample goal statement in Chapter 1 (page 24). If you would like verification of your self-analysis before you write a goal statement, have a friend or coworker complete this same analysis for you.

Goal Statement

Problem:
Usually, when I get up to speak in class or in the student senate, I find myself burying my head in my notes or looking at the ceiling or the walls.

Goal:
To look at people more directly when I'm giving a speech.

Procedure:
I will take time to practice oral presentations aloud in my room. (1) I will stand up just as I do in class or in the student senate. (2) I will pretend various objects in the room are people, and I will consciously attempt to look at those objects as I am talking. (3) In giving a speech, I will try to be aware of when I am looking at my audience and when I'm not.

Test of Achieving Goal:
This goal will be considered achieved when I am maintaining eye contact with my audience most of the time.

Signed:

Dated:

Witnessed by:

It's Her Idea, and He Gets the Credit. Why?

In group meetings, your style of speaking can make the difference in whether you are heard, no matter how good your ideas are. Certain communication habits often put women at a disadvantage in groups.

Cynthia was a member of a committee to raise funds for a political candidate. Most of the committee members were focused on canvassing local businesses for support. When Cynthia suggested that they write directly to a list of former colleagues, friends, and supporters of the candidate, inviting them to join an honorary board (and inviting them to contribute), her suggestion was ignored. Later the same suggestion was made by another committee member, Barry. Suddenly, the group came alive, enthusiastically embracing and planning to implement "Barry's idea."

Some of the men I spoke to—and just about every woman—told me of the experience of saying something at a meeting and having it ignored, then hearing the same comment taken up when it is repeated by someone else (nearly always a man).

Many people (especially women) try to avoid seeming presumptuous at meetings by prefacing their statements with a disclaimer such as, "I don't know if this will work, but . . ." or "You've probably already thought of this, but. . . ." Such disclaimers are even found on e-mail—the electronic conversation medium. An example given by linguist Susan Herring to illustrate the tone of messages typical of women who took part in an on-line discussion began, "This may be a silly naive question, but. . . ."

Some speakers (again, including many women) may also speak at a lower volume, and try to be succinct so as not to take up more meeting time than necessary. Barbara and Gene Eakins examined tape recordings of seven university faculty meetings and found that, with one exception, the men spoke more often and, without exception, spoke longer. The men's turns ranged from 10.66 to 17.07 seconds, the women's from 3 to 10 seconds. The longest contribution by a woman was still shorter than the shortest contribution by a man.

Herring found the same situation in electronic meetings. In the e-mail discussion she analyzed, she found that men's messages were twice as long, on average, as women's. And their voices sounded very different. All but one of the five women used an "attenuated/personal" voice: "I am intrigued by your comment . . . Could you say a bit more?" The tone adopted by the men who dominated discussion was assertive ("It is obvious that . . ."; "Note that . . .").

All these aspects of how one speaks at a meeting mean that when two people say "the same thing," they probably say it very differently. They may speak with or without a disclaimer, loudly or softly, in a self-deprecating or declamatory way, briefly or at length, and tentatively or without apparent certainty. They may initiate ideas or support or argue against ideas raised by others. When dissenting, they may adopt a conciliatory tone, mitigating the disagreement, or an adversarial one, emphasizing it.

Before women decide to change their styles, though, they must realize the double bind they face. Geraldine Ferraro was called by Barbara Bush "the word that rhymes with witch." Ferraro's speech style was influenced by her Italian heritage, her New York City upbringing, and her working-class roots. Any woman who tries to become more "assertive" runs a risk of being sanctioned for being "too aggressive," just as men from the South may be seen as not masculine enough.

On the other hand, it may also be wise to decide that being seen as aggressive is a price worth paying for being listened to. Finally, we can all hope that if enough women adjust their styles, expectations of how a feminine woman speaks may gradually change as a result. ■

SOURCE: Deborah Tannen, *Talking From 9 to 5* (New York: William Morrow, 1994), pp. 277–289. © 1994 by Deborah Tannen, Ph. D. Reprinted by permission of William Morrow & Company, Inc.

Perspectives

Throughout the book, "Perspectives" let you share in the experiences and insights of many different communicators. Their stories give you diverse perspectives on communication, bringing to life the ideas, challenges, and practices you're learning in this book.

Module A

Interviewing for Information

"Ramsey, I just got a call from Parker at City Hall saying that the police are planning to extend the experimental program at the Garden Projects—the cooperative program between police and residents for moving drug pushers out of the area. I want you to find out all you can about this. I want to know how well the experimental project is working, what happens to the pushers, what the residents think about the effectiveness of the program, and anything else you can think of."

The Interview Plan

Interviews are more likely to achieve the desired result if they are carefully planned. Creating and implementing an interviewing plan involves clearly defining the purpose of the interview, selecting the best person to interview, planning a procedure for the interview, and conducting the interview.

Defining the Purpose of the Interview

Too often, interviewers go into an informative interview without a clearly identified purpose. A clear purpose is a specific goal that can be summarized in one sentence. Without such a statement of purpose, the interviewer's questions more than likely will have no direction, and the information derived from the interview may not fit together well.

Suppose you wish to obtain information about the food service in your dormitory. Possible specific purposes would be:

1. To determine the criteria for selecting the food catering service.

2. To determine the most efficient means of setting up a cafeteria line.

3. To determine the major elements a dietitian must take into account in order to plan dormitory meals.

Notice that each of these covers an entirely different aspect of food service. Your choice, then, would depend on the nature of the information you wish to get.

Selecting the Best Person to Interview

Somewhere on campus or in the larger community there are people who have or who can direct you to the information you want. How do you find out whom you should interview? If you are pursuing the third purpose, "To determine the major elements a dietitian must take into account in order to plan dormitory meals," one of the kitchen employees can tell you who is in charge of the dining hall. Or you could phone your student center and inquire about who

Special sections on interviewing

Communicate! includes two special sections on interviewing: one on interviewing for information and another on job interviewing. These modules include specific discussions of the unique principles and practices of interviewing— a skill most of us find critical to our lives beyond the classroom.

one

Introduction

Although your primary goal in college is to broaden your educational horizons, these years are also the time for you to ask questions about how you want to spend the rest of your life. Whatever your aspirations, you will discover the importance of effective communication in helping you achieve your goals. This one-chapter unit gives insight into the communication process and ways of improving your communication competence.

1

*Communication
Perspective*

3

**After you have read
this chapter, you
should be able to:**

Define communication

*List and show the interrela-
tionships among the elements
of the communication process*

*Explain five underlying prin-
ciples of communication*

*Explain the six functions of
communication*

*Explain four aspects of com-
munication competence*

*Identify the goals of interper-
sonal communication, group
communication, and public
speaking*

*Write communication goal
statements*

Communication
Perspective

A s the selection committee deliberated, they felt they had four viable candidates for the position. "They all look good on paper," Carson said, "but I must admit I was especially impressed with the way Corrie Jackson presented herself to us. Not only did she have a clear vision for where we need to be five years from now, but also she explained that vision with precise, concrete statements. I was really convinced that she was on the right track. She gets my vote."

Your presence in this course may be far more important to you than you imagined when you chose (or were required) to take it, for communication effectiveness is vital to success in nearly every walk of life. For instance, of the 17 factors most important in helping graduating college students obtain employment, Curtis, Winsor, and Stephens found oral communication, listening ability, and enthusiasm (all of which are basic to this book) first, second, and third, respectively.[1] So, whether you aspire to a career in business, industry, government, education, or almost any other field you can name, communication skills are likely to be a prerequisite to your success.

Becoming a more competent communicator involves both an understanding of basic communication theory and the acquisition of specific skills. In this chapter, we define communication, explain the process, consider underlying principles, discuss the functions it serves, and finally, consider means for increasing competence.

Communication Defined

Communication is the transactional process of creating meaning. Three concepts are key in this definition. First, when we say communication is a *process* we are acknowledging that it is a systematic series of behaviors with a purpose that occur over some period of time. A five-minute talk with a friend, a nod of assent when the leader of a group asks whether members agree with a statement, and a 45-minute speech by a candidate for public office are all examples of the process of communication.

Second, during any communication process meaning is occurring. *Meaning* is the content, intention, and significance that is assigned to communication behavior. *Content* is the specific information conveyed in the behavior—the "what" of communication. *Intention* is the speaker's reason for doing the behavior—the "why" of the communication. *Significance* is the value of the communication—"how important" the communication is.

Third, the process of creating meaning is transactional. By *transactional* we mean that those communicating are *mutually* responsible for the meaning that each internalizes during and after the interaction. For example, suppose Joe says to his brother, "Go upstairs and get the thingamajig off my whatchamacallit." The shared meaning that has been created, or the extent to which this message is effective, depends on what happens next. If his brother says, "OK," runs upstairs, and returns with the object that Joe seeks, then one of many shared meanings will have been successfully created. If, however, Joe's brother responds, "Go get it yourself. I'm not your slave," a different shared meaning of Joe's request will have been created.

In public speaking, the transactional nature of communication is less obvious, but it still exists. When Rachel says, "The problem with the current system is that it is unfair," the members of the audience will each provide their own meanings for "unfair," some of which may be quite different from the one Rachel intended. If she then elaborates on her meaning or offers examples of unfairness, her listeners either will have their interpretation of her meaning reinforced or will modify it accordingly. Even in public speaking, then, meaning is created jointly by the participants in a communication transaction.

The Complex Process of Communication

Because you have been communicating for as long as you can remember, the process may seem to be almost second nature. But in reality, competent communication is difficult to achieve because communication is a complex process. To get a mental picture of the complexity, envision yourself as a salesperson attending the Monday morning staff meeting. At these meetings, it's customary for Elizabeth, the sales manager, to speak to the staff. But from the time the people enter the meeting room, communication takes place. This communication process involves the following interrelated elements: the context of the communication, the participants, the messages being communicated, the channels through which the communication occurs, the presence or absence of "noise," and the verbal and nonverbal responses known as feedback.

Context

The context of communication affects the expectations of the participants, the meaning these participants receive, and their subsequent behavior. The communication context includes the (1) physical, (2) social, (3) historical, (4) psychological, and (5) cultural circumstances that surround a communication episode.

Physical Context. The physical context of a communication episode includes factors such as the location of the episode; environmental factors such as heat, lighting, and noise; the physical distance between communicators; seating arrangements; and the time of day. Each of these factors can affect the communication. Physical context helps to define what behaviors or messages will be seen as socially appropriate and thus indicates to the participant what type of conversation to expect. The formality of the conference room in which Elizabeth is giving her Monday morning speech to the sales staff establishes a different context than does the lunchroom in the same office. The seating arrangement may encourage passive listening or, if the chairs are arranged in a circle, active group discussion. Lighting, the time of day, and the distance between Elizabeth and the staff create a different atmosphere for communication than would a table for two in a candlelit restaurant. In Chapter 4 you will learn more about how the physical context may affect the expectations of participants and the meanings they receive.

Social Context. The social context is determined by whether the communication episode takes place among family members, friends, acquaintances, work associates, or strangers. In some cases competent communication in a family context differs from competent communication in a work or friendship context. For example, Darren may understand that his brother is showing affection when he calls him "Dunderhead" at home, but would interpret the same behavior as a demeaning put-down if Elizabeth used that expression in front of his coworkers at the sales meeting. Why? Because the social context is different.

Historical Context. The historical context is derived both from general historical events and from the meanings created during previous communication episodes between the particular participants. For instance, if Elizabeth says, "We've got to approach all of our customers the way Manley did," a new salesperson unacquainted with Manley's approach would have no idea what Elizabeth means.

Psychological Context.   Psychological context refers to the moods and feelings each person brings to a communication episode. For example, suppose that Elizabeth is feeling pressured because her secretary is out sick and her paperwork is piling up. If at the start of her speech she sounds out of sorts, one staff member might simply perceive Elizabeth as unusually cranky this morning, whereas another might perceive her as being upset with the staff.

Cultural Context.   The cultural context includes the shared beliefs, values, and norms that affect the behaviors of a relatively large group of people.[2] In the United States there is a dominant European-American culture. But there are also many other cultures, including African-American, Mexican-American, Native American, Spanish-American, and Asian-American, as well as such nonethnic cultures as gay, middle-class, and corporate, to name only a few. Moreover, within each of these cultural categories several more specific cultures exist as well. Some researchers refer to people who, while living in the dominant culture, have membership in another culture as *subcultures* or *co-cultures*.[3] Since nearly all of the sub- or co-cultures have different cultures within them (for instance, neither all African-American nor all Asian-American people are of one culture), in this text we will just say that within the dominant culture of the United States many other cultures exist. Regardless of number or types, as Peter Andersen points out, culture is an inseparable part of the communication process.[4]

Although shared beliefs and values are important characteristics of culture, it is the communication rules (or norms) of a culture that affect the context in which people interact. *Rules* are the unwritten underlying guidelines for what is viewed as "acceptable communication behavior" within a particular culture. These unwritten rules give us clues as to what kinds of messages and behavior are proper in a given physical or social context or with a particular person or group of people, and they also provide us with a framework in which to interpret the behavior of others. If a regional manager is attending the Monday morning sales meeting, a person who heckles or speaks out of turn might be stared down by everyone else in the group. Sometimes we don't know the rules; we have to learn them from experience. Thus, a new member of the staff might be taken aback when the group begins heckling Elizabeth during the regular sales meeting.

The Monday morning sales meeting is an example of a specific business culture. Whether the culture we are referring to is the dominant European-American culture or a particular African-American, Asian-American, or Mexican-American culture, each one has its own set of rules that affect the communication among members of that culture. At various places in this text, we consider different cultural rules and how they affect communication.

Usually we learn the communication rules of a culture through direct experience. Children whose native culture encourages spontaneous expression and tolerates interrupting others may find it difficult to attend a school where the accepted rule is to sit quietly and raise your hand to be recognized. When we communicate with people of a different race, gender, nationality, religion, political affiliation, class, organization, or group, effective communication is likely to be more difficult than when we communicate with people from our own culture.

In summary, the physical, social, historical, psychological, and cultural contexts all have a significant impact on how we communicate.

Participants

The participants in a communication transaction play the roles of sender and receiver, sometimes—as in interpersonal communication—simultaneously. As senders, we form messages and attempt to communicate them to others through verbal and nonverbal symbols. As receivers, we process the messages sent to us and react to them both verbally and nonverbally.

Each of us is a product of our individual experiences, feelings, ideas, moods, occupation, religion, culture, and so forth. As a result, the meaning sent and the meaning received in a communication transaction may not be exactly the same. For instance, when Elizabeth speaks of a "good sale," she may mean one in which she makes a maximum profit; by contrast, Gordon, one of her salespersons, might view a good sale as one that leaves the customer with such a good feeling that the customer is likely to buy another product from him later on. Whether the setting is a speech, group discussion, or friendly conversation, communicators who neglect such individual differences in experience and attitudes may find that the meanings they have communicated are not the ones they intended.

While people obviously differ in an infinite number of ways, the differences that are particularly important to communication can be grouped into five major categories: (1) physical traits, (2) psychological attributes, (3) social experiences, (4) knowledge and skills, and (5) gender and culture.

Physical Traits.   People's physical differences, including race, sex, age, and level of physical ability, are likely to have a significant effect on their communication. We more easily identify with and understand those with whom we share similar physical characteristics.[5] The more similar two people are, the better either person is able to predict the behavior of the other. When we encounter strangers of the opposite sex, or of a different race or age group or level of physical ability, these differences are likely to provide significant challenges to us in interpersonal, group, or public speaking settings.

Psychological Attributes.   People's psychological differences, including personality, self-confidence, attitudes, and values, are likely to affect their communication. For example, most people feel some nervousness in communication settings. Some people are quite uncomfortable when they first enter a room full of total strangers. Efforts at making friends may be quite difficult. Others feel most nervous in public-speaking settings. On the other hand, some people look at all new communication situations with enthusiasm—they enjoy encountering people they don't know or may be highly motivated when given a chance to give a speech to strangers. Since nervousness is most intense for most people in public-speaking settings, we'll consider the subject of communication apprehension in the public-speaking part of this text.

Social Experiences.   Differences in people's social relationships are likely to affect their communication. Friends usually have greater latitude in how they can say something in order to be understood correctly than do strangers or adversaries. That is one reason communication between a public speaker and an audience differs qualitatively from communication between friends or colleagues. For example, when Elizabeth speaks to a consumer activist group about the meaning of automobile sticker prices, she will probably have to choose her words and monitor her nonverbal behavior more carefully than she does when she is addressing her coworkers at the weekly sales meeting.

Knowledge and Skills.   Differences in people's knowledge and skills are likely to affect their communication. Through educational experiences people have the opportunity to acquire language and communication skills that can enable them to express a wide variety of ideas and feelings. Thus, more widely read and better educated people are likely to express themselves far differently from less widely read and educated people.

Gender and Culture.   People's gender and cultural differences result in different perspectives and life experiences that affect their communication. When we are aware of such differences, we tend to see them as barriers to communication. The more one person differs from another, the less either person is able to predict the other's behavior. When people do not believe they know how another person will behave, fear often results. Some people respond to their fear by withdrawing or becoming compliant, whereas others mask their fear with aggressive behavior. Throughout this text, we consider differences between males and females and people from different cultures that affect skill usage.

Messages

Communication takes place through the sending and receiving of messages. It is easy to think of messages as simply the words transmitted from one person to another. Actually, messages are far more complex. They include the elements of meanings, symbols, encoding and decoding, and form or organization.

Meaning and Symbols.   The pure ideas and feelings that exist in a person's mind represent *meanings*. You may have ideas about how to study for your next exam, what your career goal is, and whether taxes should be raised or lowered; you also may have feelings such as jealousy, anger, and love. The meanings you have within you, however, cannot be transferred magically into another's mind. To share these ideas and feelings, you form messages comprising both verbal and nonverbal symbols. *Symbols* are words, sounds, and actions that represent specific content meaning. As you speak, you choose words to convey your meaning. At the same time, facial expressions, eye contact, gestures, and tone of voice—all nonverbal cues—accompany your words and also affect the meaning your listener receives from the symbols you use. As you listen, you use both the verbal symbols and the nonverbal cues and assign meanings to them.

Encoding and Decoding.   The cognitive thinking process of transforming ideas and feelings into symbols and organizing them into a message is called *encoding* a message; the process of transforming messages of another back into one's own ideas and feelings is called *decoding*. You have been communicating for so long that most of the time you probably don't think consciously about either the encoding or the decoding process. Only when a difficulty in communication arises do you become aware of them. For example, if you are giving a speech and you see puzzled frowns suggesting that your audience is not understanding your point, you may go through a conscious encoding process to select expressions that better convey your meaning. Likewise, you may become aware of the decoding process when you must figure out the meaning of an unfamiliar word based on its use in a particular sentence.

The encoding and decoding processes include nonverbal cues, which significantly affect the meaning created between the participants in a communication transaction. Even when we consciously encode verbal messages designed to create specific meanings, our less controllable nonverbal behaviors can create unintended and conflicting meanings. Unintended meanings are created when the decoding person receives a meaning unrelated to what the encoder thought he or she was communicating. For instance, if your boss looks directly at you when he says that some members of the department just aren't pulling their own weight, you are likely to be upset because you are unaware that he looked at you purposely to avoid calling attention to the people he was really talking about. Conflicting meanings are created when the verbal symbols are contradicted by the nonverbal cues. For instance, if a coworker says, "Yes, I'm very interested in the way you arrived at that decision," the meaning you decode will be very different if the person leans forward and looks interested or yawns and looks away.

The processes of encoding and decoding messages are at the heart of communication. For this reason, many of the skills presented in this book relate directly to improving how we form and interpret messages.

Form or Organization.   When meaning is complex, we may need to communicate it in sections or in a certain order—that is, in a particular form. In this case, the meaning must be organized. Message form is especially important in public speaking when one person talks without interruption for a relatively long time. Elizabeth's coworkers will derive much more meaning from her Monday morning pep talk if her thoughts are organized than if she rambles on, randomly expressing whatever comes to mind. Even in the give-and-take of interpersonal conversation, form can affect the understanding of messages. For instance, when Yolanda's husband tells her about the apartment he looked at yesterday, she is likely to have a clearer picture if his description moves logically from room to room than if she has to piece together impressions communicated in haphazard order.

Channels

A channel is both the route traveled by the message and the means of transportation. Messages are transmitted through sensory channels. Face-to-face communication has two basic channels: sound (verbal symbols) and light (nonverbal cues).

However, people can and do communicate by any of the five sensory channels. A fragrant scent or a firm handshake may contribute as much to meaning as what is seen or heard. In general, the more channels used to carry a message, the more likely it is that the communication will succeed.

Noise

Noise is any stimulus, external or internal to the participants, that interferes with the sharing of meaning. Much of our success as communicators depends on how we cope with external, internal, and semantic noises, each of which can create blocks in the sensory channels and interfere with the decoding process.

External Noise.   Sights, sounds, and other stimuli in the environment that draw people's attention away from intended meaning are known as *external noise.* For instance, while listening to directions on how to work a new food processor, your attention may be drawn to the sound of the doorbell or the sight of your child perching precariously on a kitchen stool. Such distractions constitute external noise no matter which sensory channel is involved.

Internal Noise.   Thoughts and feelings that interfere with the communication process are known as *internal noise.* Have you ever found yourself daydreaming during a lecture? Perhaps your mind wanders to thoughts of the dance you attended last night or to the argument you had with a friend this morning. Because of this internal noise, chances are you won't receive all the meaning intended by your professor. The same applies if, for example, feelings of anger or anxiety, stereotyping, or prejudice cause you to misinterpret what a friend is trying to tell you.

Semantic Noise.   Unintended meanings aroused by certain verbal symbols can inhibit the accuracy of decoding. This kind of linguistic "static" is known as *semantic noise.* Suppose a friend describes a forty-year-old secretary as "the girl in the office." If you think of "girl" as a condescending term for a forty-year-old woman, you might not even hear what your friend has to say about her because you're distracted by the chauvinistic meaning such a verbal symbol has for you. Symbols that are derogatory to a person or group, such as ethnic slurs, often cause semantic noise; profanity and value-laden words can have the same effect. More generally, because the meanings we assign to words depend on our own experience, other people may at times decode a word or phrase differently from the way we intend. This, too, is semantic noise.

Feedback

As receivers attempt to decode the meaning of messages, they are likely to give some kind of verbal or nonverbal response. This response, called *feedback,* tells the sender whether the message has been heard, seen, or understood. Feedback is another reason communication is transactional. If the feedback tells the sender that the communication was not received or was misinterpreted, the person can send the message again, perhaps in a different way, until the listener receives the meaning the sender intends. For example, if, when you say "Wilson's policy isn't really fair" your listener cocks his head and squints, you may sense that what you said wasn't clear. Instead of going on as you intended, you might adjust and say, "I'm speaking specifically of his practice of not allowing a person to make up a speech even when the person had a doctor's excuse for missing class."

During this course, you will be involved in different kinds of communication situations that will determine the amount and type of response communicators can give one another. But in any situation, paying attention to both verbal and nonverbal feedback allows us to behave in ways that increase understanding of our messages. In all of our communication, whether interpersonal, small-group, or public-speaking, we want to stimulate as much feedback as the situation will allow.

A Model of the Process

Let's look at a pictorial representation to see how the elements of communication interrelate. Figure 1.1 illustrates the transactional communication process in an interpersonal communication relationship. In the minds of the participants are meanings—thoughts or feelings that they intend to share. Those thoughts or feelings are created, shaped, and affected by the participants' total field of experience, including such specific factors as values, culture, environment, experiences, occupation, gender, interests, knowledge, and attitudes. To turn meaning into messages, participants encode a thought or feeling into words and actions and send it via sending channels—in this case, sound (speech) and light (nonverbal behavior). For instance, Doris might say, "I'm really concerned about the test." At the same time Doris is sending such a message, she is also receiving messages from Paul—that is, she is conscious of Paul's nonverbal and verbal reactions.

Meanings that have been encoded into symbols are turned back into meaning by participants through the decoding process. This decoding process is affected by the participants' total field of experience—that is, by all the same factors that shape the encoding process.

The area around the participants represents the physical, social, historical, psychological, and cultural context, which includes the formal and informal rules in operation during the communication and the participants' prior relationships. During the entire transaction, external, internal, and semantic noise may be occurring at various points that affect the ability of participants to share meanings.

In a group or public-speaking situation, all these elements of communication operate simultaneously—and differently—for everyone present. As a result, communication in these settings is especially complex. Whereas some people focus on the speaker's message, others may be distracted by noise—whether external (the hum of the air conditioning), internal (preoccupation with personal matters), or semantic (a reaction to the speaker's choice of words). Furthermore, all the participants bring their unique perspectives to the communication transaction. Less skillful communicators are oblivious to such factors and plunge ahead regardless of whether they are being understood or even heard. Skillful communicators attend to verbal and nonverbal feedback and adapt their words and nonverbal behavior until they are confident that their listeners have received the meanings they intend to share.

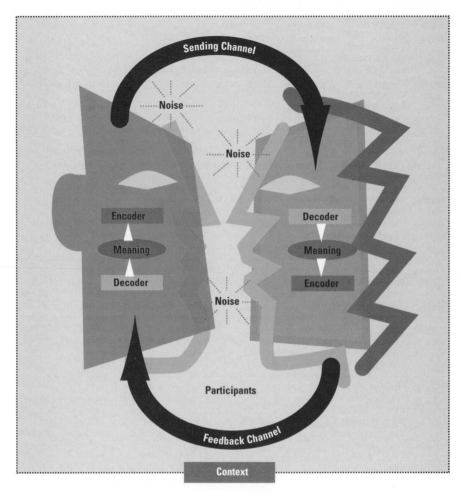

Figure 1.1 *A model of communication between two individuals*

By Yourself

1. For the following episode, identify the context, participants, channel, message, noise, and feedback.

Maria and her daughter Tina are shopping. As they walk through an elegant dress shop, Tina, who is feeling particularly happy, sees a dress she wants. With a look of great anticipation and excitement Tina says, "That's a beautiful dress—can I have it? Please, Mom!" Maria, who is thinking about how difficult it has been to make ends meet, frowns, shrugs her shoulders, and says distractedly, "Well—yes—I guess so." Tina, noticing her mother's hesitation, continues, "And it's only fifty dollars!" Suddenly, Maria relaxes, smiles, and says, "Yes, it is a beautiful dress—try it on. If it fits, let's buy it."

2. Think of two recent communication episodes that you participated in. One should be an episode that you thought went really well. The other should be one that you felt went poorly. Compare the episodes. Describe the context in which the episodes occurred, the participants, the rules that seemed to govern your behavior and that of the other participants, the messages that were used to create the meaning, the channels used, any noise that interfered with the transaction, the feedback that was shared, and the result.

Communication Principles

Now that we have seen the elements that comprise the communication transaction, we can turn to the principles that underlie communication. Five of these principles that have the greatest impact on our ability to communicate effectively are that (1) communication has purpose, (2) communication is continuous, (3) communication messages vary in conscious encoding, (4) communication is relational, and (5) communication is learned.

Communication Has Purpose

When people communicate with one another, they have a purpose for doing so. As Kathy Kellermann, a leading researcher on interpersonal contexts, puts it, all communication is goal-directed,[6] whether or not the purpose is conscious. The purpose of a given transaction may be serious or trivial, but one way to evaluate the success of the communication is to ask whether it achieves its purpose. When Beth calls Leah to ask whether she'd like to join her for lunch to discuss a project they are working on, her purpose may be to resolve a misunderstanding, to encourage Leah to work more closely with her, or simply to establish a cordial atmosphere. When Kareem shares statistics he has found with other members of student government to show the extent of drug abuse on campuses, his purpose may be to contribute information to a group discussion or to plead a case for confronting the problem of drug abuse. Depending on the speaker's purpose, even an apparently successful transaction may fail to achieve its goal. And of course, different purposes call for different communication strategies.

Speakers may not always be aware of their purpose. For instance, when Jamal passes Tony on the street and says lightly, "Tony—what's happening?" Jamal probably doesn't consciously think, "I haven't talked with Tony for a while. I hope (1) that Tony is aware that I recognize him, (2) that he realizes the lines of communication between us are still open, and (3) that he understands I don't have the time to talk with him right now." In this case the social obligation to recognize Tony is met spontaneously with the first acceptable expression that comes to Jamal's mind. Regardless of whether Jamal consciously thinks about the purpose, it still motivates his behavior. In this case Jamal will have achieved his goal if Tony responds with an equally casual greeting.

Frank & Ernest reprinted by permission of NEA, Inc.

Communication Is Continuous

Because communication is nonverbal as well as verbal, we are always sending behavioral messages from which others draw inferences or meaning. Even silence or absence are communication behaviors if another person infers meaning from them. Why? Because your nonverbal behavior represents reactions to your environment and to the people around you. If you are cold, you shiver; if you are hot or nervous, you perspire; if you are bored, happy, or confused, your face or body language probably will show it. As skilled communicators, we need to be aware of the messages, whether explicit or implicit, we are constantly sending to others. In Chapter 4, we will consider nonverbal behavior in greater detail.

Communication Messages Vary in Conscious Encoding

As we discussed earlier in this chapter, sharing meanings with another person involves encoding messages into verbal and nonverbal symbols. The amount of conscious preparation time, however, varies considerably. This encoding process may occur spontaneously, may be based on a "script" that you have learned or rehearsed, or may be carefully considered based on your understanding of the situation in which you find yourself.[7]

For each of us there are times when our interpersonal communication reflects a spontaneous expression of emotion. When this happens, our messages are encoded without much conscious thought. For example, when you burn your finger, you may blurt out "Ouch," or some such expression. When something goes right, you may break out in a broad smile. In this sense, much of our communication is spontaneous and natural. However, not all spontaneous communication is appropriate. For instance, if someone accidentally stepped on your toe and you blurted out, "Watch what you're doing, butthead," the receiver would likely become defensive. In Chapter 5 we will suggest more appropriate ways of communicating negative feelings.

At other times, however, our communication is "scripted." R. P. Abelson defines a *script* as a "highly stylized sequence of typical events in a well-understood situation."[8] Thus, in some communication episodes we use conversational phrases that we have learned from our past encounters and judge to be appropriate to the present situation. To use scripted reactions effectively, we learn or practice them until they become automatic. Many of these scripts are learned in childhood. For example, when you want the sugar bowl but cannot reach it, you may say "Please pass the sugar," followed by "Thank you" when someone complies. This conversational sequence comes from the "table manners script" that you may have had drilled into you at home. Scripts enable us to use messages that are appropriate to the situation and are likely to increase our effectiveness of communication. Because scripts are based on past experiences, many are culturally bound. That is, they are appropriate for a particular relationship in a certain situation within a specific culture. One goal of this text is to acquaint you with general scripts (or skills) that can be adapted for use in your communication encounters across a variety of relationships, situations, and cultures. The text will also provide you with opportunities to practice these scripts in a variety of contexts, and suggests when certain scripts may be useful.

Messages also may be carefully constructed to meet the particular situation. Constructed messages are those that we encode at the moment to respond to the situation for which our known scripts are inadequate. These messages help us communicate both effectively and appropriately.

Creatively constructed responses are perhaps the ideal communication vehicle, especially in public-speaking settings. When you find yourself, in a situation, able to both envision what you want to say and construct how you say it, you are likely to form messages whereby your intended meaning can be shared. Another goal of this text is to help you become so familiar with a variety of message-forming skills that you can use them to construct effective and appropriate messages.

Communication Is Relational

Saying that communication is relational means that in any communication setting people not only share content meaning, they are also negotiating their relationship. For instance, in an interpersonal-communication setting when Laura says to Jennie "I've remembered to bring the map," she is not only reporting information. Through the way she says it, she may also be communicating "You can always depend on me" or "I am superior to you. If it weren't for me, we'd be missing an important document for our trip."

Two aspects of relationships can be negotiated during an interaction. One aspect is the affect (love to hate) present in the relationship. For instance, when Jose says "Hal, good to see you," the nonverbal behavior that accompanies the words may show Hal whether Jose is genuinely happy to see him (positive affect) or not. For instance, if Jose smiles, has a sincere sound to his voice, looks Hal in the eye, and perhaps pats him on the back or shakes hands firmly, then Hal will recognize the signs of affection. If, on the other hand, Jose speaks quickly with no vocal inflection with a deadpan facial expression, Hal will perceive the comment as solely meeting some social expectation.

Another aspect of the relational nature of communication seeks to define who's in control.[9] Thus, when Tom says to Sue, "I know you're concerned about the budget, but I'll see to it that we have money to cover everything," he can, through his words and the sound of his voice, be saying that he is "in charge" of finances, that he is in control. How Sue responds to Tom determines the true nature of the relationship. The control aspect of relationships can be viewed as complementary or symmetrical.

In a complementary relationship, one person lets the other define who is to have greater power. Thus, the communication messages of one person may assert dominance while the communication messages of the other person accept the assertion. In some cases the relationship is clarified in part by the context. For instance, in traditional American businesses most boss-employee relationships are complementary, with the boss in the control position. Thus, when the boss assigns Joan a certain job to do, Joan is likely to accept the assignment and do it. Or, in the previous example, if Sue's response to Tom's asserting control of the budget is "OK, Tom, I agree, you should handle our finances," the relationship would be viewed as complementary. Likewise, most public-speaking relationships are complementary, for people in the audience have come to hear what the person has to say and in so doing often consider the speaker's information as authoritative.

In a symmetrical relationship, people do not "agree" about who is in control. As one person shows a need to take control, the other challenges the person's right and asserts his or her own power. For example, Tom may say "I think we need to cut back on credit card expenses for a couple of months," to which Sue may respond, "No way! I need a new suit for work, the car needs new tires, and you promised we could replace the couch." Here both people are asserting control. Or as one person abdicates control, the other refuses to assume it. Tom might ask, "Do you think we need to cut back on credit expenses for a couple of months?" and Sue might respond, "Gee, I'm not sure, what do you think?"—a question that in essence asks Tom to "take control."

Although control is not negotiated in a single exchange, through many message exchanges over time, relational control is determined. The interaction of communication messages, as shown through both language and nonverbal behavior, defines and clarifies the complementary or symmetrical nature of people's relationships. In complementary relationships open conflict is less prevalent than in symmetrical ones, but in symmetrical relationships power is more likely to be evenly shared.

Communication Is Learned

Because communication appears to be a natural, inborn ability, most people pay little attention to the skills that make up their communication styles. Each of us tends to think, "I act naturally." Thus, we often don't really try to improve our behavior. Moreover, some people make no conscious effort to improve their skill levels because they do not appreciate how improving their communication skills can benefit them and because they may not recognize their current inadequacies. Because of our background, each of us has some of the communication skills we need to be effective in our dealings with others. However, we also lack some of the skills we need. As a result, each of us can benefit from continuous learning and skill practice. Throughout this text you will be learning interpersonal, group, and public-speaking skills that can be valuable to you in all walks of life.

Functions of Communication

So far, we have seen how the communication process works and the principles that guide it; now let's consider what communication does for us. The study of communication is important because it serves functions that touch every aspect of our lives.

1. *We communicate to meet needs.* Psychologists tell us that we are by nature social animals; that is, we need other people just as we need food, water, and shelter. Of course, we have all heard of hermits who choose to live and function alone, but they are the exception. Deprived of all contact with others, most people hallucinate, lose their motor coordination, and become generally maladjusted. Often, the content of our interactions is unimportant.[10] Two people may converse happily for hours gossiping and chatting about inconsequential matters that neither remembers afterward. When they part, they may have exchanged little real information, but their communication has met an important need—simply to talk with another human being.

2. *We communicate to enhance and maintain our sense of self.* Through our communication, we seek approval of who and what we are. Indeed, to a great extent it is through communication that we define who we are. How do you know what you are good at? Did you run a good meeting? Did you do the job as expected? Did you give a good speech? Did you show your happiness, anger, or guilt in appropriate ways? You learn the answers to such questions in large part from what others communicate to you verbally and nonverbally. We explore this important function of interpersonal communication in detail in Chapter 2, Perception of Self and Others.

3. *We communicate to develop relationships.* We get to know others through our communication with them. More important, it is through communication that relationships grow and deepen—or stagnate and wither away. Very few relationships—whether social, work, friendly, or intimate—simply stay the same. This is a fact of life and one that is important to the interpersonal communication process. We discuss how relationships begin and develop in Chapter 8, Communication in Relationships.

4. *We communicate to fulfill social obligations.* Why do you say "How are you doing?" to a person you sat next to in class last quarter but haven't seen since? Why do you say such things as "What's happening?" or simply "Hi" when you pass people you know? We use such communications to meet social obligations. By saying "Hi, Josh, how's it going?" you conform to societal norms—you acknowledge a person you recognize with one of the many statements you have learned to use under these circumstances. Not speaking is perceived as a slight—the person may regard you as arrogant or insensitive. Our felt need to recognize others and meet other social obligations serves to demonstrate the ties we have with other people, whether or not we have serious relationships with them.

5. *We communicate to exchange information.* Information is a key ingredient for effective decision making. Some information we get through observation, some through reading, some through television, and a great deal through direct communication with others. Whether we are trying to decide how warmly to dress or whom to vote for in the next presidential election, all of us have countless exchanges that involve sending and receiving information. When such exchanges go awry, we may be deprived of the adequate and accurate information we need to make sound decisions. We discuss communication as information exchange in Chapter 5,

Communication of Ideas and Feelings, in Chapter 9, Participating in Work Groups, and in Chapter 16, Informative Speaking.

6. *We communicate to influence others.* It is doubtful whether a day goes by in which you don't attempt to exert influence over others, or others over you. Examples include convincing your friends to go to a play rather than to a movie, campaigning door to door to gather voter support for a political candidate, persuading your spouse to quit smoking, and (an old favorite) trying to convince an instructor to change your course grade. Some theorists even argue that the primary purpose of all communication efforts is to influence the behavior of others. We discuss the role of influencing others in Chapter 10, Leadership in Groups and Chapter 17, Persuasive Speaking.

Practice in Identifying Communication Functions

By Yourself

Keep a log of the various communication episodes you engage in today. Tonight, categorize each episode by one of the six functions it served. Each episode may serve more than one function. Were you surprised by the variety of communication you engaged in even in such a relatively short period?

Becoming a Competent Communicator

During the past decade, a great deal of emphasis has been placed on the concept of communicator competence. R. B. Rubin and S. A. Henzl suggest that communication competence consists of (1) cognitive aspects, (2) the ability to identify and attain goals, (3) a set of behavioral skills, and (4) an impression formed about the communicator by other individuals.[11]

First, competence as a cognitive or mental phenomenon involves a knowledge of communication and an understanding of the situations facing us. Because every communication situation is different, the competent communicator is able to recognize the differences and select an appropriate approach for each particular situation. This aspect of competence involves both judging the critical elements of the situation and assessing the perspective of others in the communication situation.

Second, competence involves identifying and attaining goals. Competence in this sense is reflected in the ability to define goals and determine the communication styles necessary to achieve them.

Third, competence involves the ability to use the various behavioral skills necessary to achieve goals. In this course, you will both gain knowledge of specific communication skills and have the opportunity to practice them. Your study and practice should improve both your communication behavior and your judgment about which skill or skills are most appropriate in a particular situation.

Fourth, competence involves the perception by others that your communication behavior is appropriate as well as effective. Although competence, like all other aspects of communication, tends to be culturally bound, the truly competent communicator is competent across cultures as well as within a particular culture.[12]

*P*art of learning to communicate well is being able to recognize and use the specific skills called for in different communication settings.

In the remainder of this book we will be discussing the development of communication skills in several communication situations and recommending that you write goal statements for improvement.

Communication Situations

In this book, you will be introduced to skills that you can choose from to help you achieve communication competence. The next part focuses on skills in subject areas that are fundamental to all communication situations: perception, verbal, and nonverbal skills. The following three parts cover the kinds of situations that you are likely to communicate in most frequently: interpersonal communication, problem-solving groups, and public speaking.

Interpersonal Communication.   Interpersonal communication involves interacting with one other person or in a small, informal aggregate of people. Talking to a friend on campus, chatting on the phone with a classmate about an upcoming test, arguing the merits of a movie with friends, soothing an intimate friend who has been jilted, discussing strategies for accomplishing tasks at work, interviewing for a job, and planning the future with a loved one are all forms of interpersonal communication.

Interpersonal communication focuses on developing, maintaining, or improving relationships, shaping messages, listening and responding empathically, and coping with conflict.

Problem-Solving Groups.   Problem-solving groups involve two or more people communicating with one another, in public or in private, to solve a problem or arrive at a decision. For many of us, this kind of communication takes place in meetings.

Problem-solving group communication focuses on group interaction, including task and maintenance roles, problem solving and decision making, and leadership. Group communication is not a separate, unrelated activity, but one that builds on the foundation of interpersonal communication skills.

Public Speaking.   Public speaking involves preparing and delivering relatively formal messages to audiences in a public setting. All the variables of communication are present in this one-to-many situation, but their use in public speaking differs greatly from their use in the other situations.

Public speaking focuses on determining goals, gathering and evaluating material, adapting material to a specific audience, organizing and developing material, selecting appropriate wording, and delivering the speech, as well as variations in procedure for information exchange and persuasion.

If you are like most people, you already make conscious or unconscious use of some of these skills that are necessary to function competently, whereas others are not currently part of your repertoire. Regardless of how accomplished you already are, careful study and practice can enhance your competence and empower you to better achieve your goals.

Developing Written Goal Statements

To get the most from this course, we suggest that you set personal goals to improve specific skills in your own communication repertoire. To do this, we recommend that you commit to specific goals by writing down formal communication goal statements.

Why written goal statements? A familiar saying goes, "The road to hell is paved with good intentions." Regardless of how serious you are about changing some aspect of your communication, bringing about changes in behavior takes time and effort. Writing specific goals makes it more likely that your good intentions to improve don't get lost in the busyness of your life.

Psychologists who study motivation have found that when people set specific, challenging goals they achieve at a higher level than when they simply commit to "do their best." Research also shows that if you write down a description of the change you wish to make, formulate a plan for completing it, and have another person witness your pledge, you are more likely to honor the commitment you have made than you would be if you simply made a mental resolution.

Before you can write a goal statement, you must first analyze your current communication skills repertoire. We recommend that after you read each chapter and practice the skills described you select one or two skills to work on. Then write down your goal statement in four parts:

1. *Describe the problem.* Setting a goal begins by analyzing a problem situation and determining what skills might help you the most. In this first part, then, describe specific circumstances in which you feel the skills of the chapter could help you. For example: "Problem: My boss consistently gives all the interesting tasks to coworkers, but I haven't spoken up because I'm unsure about my ability to describe my feelings." Or "Problem: Usually, when I get up to speak in class or in the student senate, I find myself burying my head in my notes or looking at the ceiling or walls."

2. *Describe the specific goal.* A goal is *specific* if it is measurable and you know when you have achieved it. For example, after Chapter 5, Communication of Ideas and Feelings, you might write, "Goal: To describe my feelings about task assignments to my boss." Or after Chapter 15, Presenting Your Speech, you might write, "Goal: To look at people more directly when I'm giving a speech."

3. *Outline a specific procedure for reaching the goal.* To develop a plan for reaching your goal, first consult the chapter that covers the skill you wish to hone. Then translate the general steps recommended in the chapter to your specific situation. This step is critical because successful behavioral change requires that you state your objective in terms of specific behaviors you can adopt or modify. For example: "Procedure: I will practice the steps of describing feelings. (1) I will identify the specific feeling I am experiencing. (2) I will encode the emotion I am feeling accurately. (3) I will include what has triggered the feeling. (4) I will own the feeling as mine. (5) I will then put that procedure into operation when I am talking with my boss." Or "Procedure: I will take the time to practice oral presentations aloud in my room. (1) I will stand up just as I do in class or in the student senate. (2) I will pretend various objects in the room are people, and I will consciously attempt to look at those objects as I am talking. (3) In giving a speech, I will try to be aware of when I am looking at my audience and when I am not."

4. *Devise a method of determining when the goal has been reached.* Since a good goal is measurable, the fourth part of your goal-setting effort is to determine your minimum requirements for knowing when you have achieved a given goal. For example: "Test of Achieving Goal: This goal will be considered achieved when I have described my feelings to my boss on the next occasion when his behavior excludes me." Or "Test of Achieving Goal: This goal will be considered achieved when I am maintaining eye contact with my audience most of the time."

Once you have completed all four parts of this goal-setting process, you may want to have another person witness your commitment and serve as a consultant, coach, and support person. This gives you someone to talk to about your progress. A good choice would be someone from this class, since he or she is in an excellent position to understand and help. (Also, perhaps you can reciprocate with your support for his or her goal statements.) If one of your goals relates to a particular relationship you have with another person, you should also consider telling that person about your goal. If that person knows you are trying to make changes, he or she may be willing to help. Periodically you can meet with your consultant to assess your progress, troubleshoot problems, and develop additional procedures for reaching your goal.

Goal Statement

Problem:

Usually, when I get up to speak in class or in the student senate, I find myself burying my head in my notes or looking at the ceiling or the walls.

Goal:

To look at people more directly when I'm giving a speech.

Procedure:

I will take time to practice oral presentations aloud in my room. (1) I will stand up just as I do in class or in the student senate. (2) I will pretend various objects in the room are people, and I will consciously attempt to look at those objects as I am talking. (3) In giving a speech, I will try to be aware of when I am looking at my audience and when I'm not.

Test of Achieving Goal:

This goal will be considered achieved when I am maintaining eye contact with my audience most of the time.

Signed:

Dated:

Witnessed by:

Figure 1.2 *Sample goal statement*

At the end of each chapter, you will be challenged to develop a goal statement related to the material presented. A sample goal statement is shown in Figure 1.2.

Summary

We have defined communication as the transactional process of creating meaning. Communication is transactional because the meaning that is created occurs between the two participants based on both the original message and the response to it. The elements of the communication process are context, participants, messages, channels, noise, and feedback.

Based on our understanding of communication, several general principles have been developed. First, communication is purposeful. Second, communication is continuous. Third, communication messages vary in degree of conscious encoding. Messages may be spontaneous, scripted, or constructed. Fourth, communication is relational, defining the power and affection between people. Relational definitions can be complementary or symmetrical. Fifth, and most important, communication is learned.

Communication serves several functions. People communicate to meet needs, to enhance and maintain a sense of self, to develop relationships, to fulfill social obligations, to exchange information, and to influence others.

Effective communication depends on the competence of those communicating. Competence is a result of mental phenomena, the ability to identify and attain goals, a set of behavioral skills, and an impression formed about the communicator by other individuals.

Communication competence comes from learning to use skills effectively in interpersonal, group, and public-speaking situations. Since skills can be learned, developed, and improved, you can help enhance your learning this term by writing goal statements to systematically improve your skill repertoire.

Suggested Readings

Devito, Joseph A. *The Communication Handbook.* New York: Harper & Row, 1986. A dictionary of communication words and concepts and an invaluable addition to the library of any student of communication.

Gudykunst, William B. *Bridging Differences: Effective Intergroup Communication,* 2d ed. Newbury Park, CA: Sage, 1994. An excellent short introduction to elements of intergroup communication.

Littlejohn, Stephen W. *Theories of Human Communication,* 4th ed. Belmont, CA: Wadsworth, 1992. An amazingly comprehensive analysis of major communication theories, focusing on the strengths and weaknesses of each.

Notes

1. Dan B. Curtis, Jerry L. Winsor, and Ronald D. Stephens, "National Preferences in Business and Communication Education," *Communication Education* 38 (January 1989), p. 11.

2. Myron W. Lustig and Jolene Koester, *Intercultural Competence: Interpersonal Communication Across Cultures* (New York: HarperCollins, 1993), p. 41.

3. Larry A. Samovar and Richard E. Porter, *Communication Between Cultures,* 2d ed. (Belmont, CA: Wadsworth, 1995), p. 60.

4. Peter Andersen, "Explaining Intercultural Differences in Nonverbal Communication," in Larry A. Samovar and Richard E. Porter, *Intercultural Communication: A Reader,* 7th ed. (Belmont, CA: Wadsworth, 1994), p. 229.

5. Kay Deaux, Francis C. Dane, and Lawrence S. Wrightsman, *Social Psychology,* 5th ed. (Belmont, CA: Wadsworth, 1994), p. 229.

6. Kathy Kellermann, "Communication: Inherently Strategic and Primarily Automatic," *Communication Monographs* 59 (September 1992): 288.

7. Kathleen K. Reardon, *Interpersonal Communication: Where Minds Meet* (Belmont, CA: Wadsworth, 1987), pp. 11–12.

8. R. P. Abelson, "Script in Attitude Formation and Decision Making," in J. Carroll and T. Payne, eds., *Cognition and Social Behavior* (Hillsdale, NJ: Erlbaum, 1976), p. 33.

9. Paul Watzlawick, Janet H. Beavin, and Don D. Jackson, *Pragmatics of Human Communication* (New York: W. W. Norton, 1967), p. 51.

10. John A. R. Wilson, Mildred C. Robick, and William B. Michael, *Psychological Foundations of Learning and Teaching,* 2d ed. (New York: McGraw-Hill, 1974), p. 26.

11. R. B. Rubin and S. A. Henzl, "Cognitive Complexity, Communication Competence, and Verbal Ability," *Communication Quarterly* 32 (1984): 263–270.

12. See Brian H. Spitzberg, "A Model of Intercultural Communication Competence," in Larry A. Samovar and Richard E. Porter, eds., *Intercultural Communication: A Reader,* 7th ed. (Belmont, CA: Wadsworth, 1994), pp. 347–359.

two

Establishing a Communication Foundation

Although communication occurs in specific settings, certain basic principles are common to communication effectiveness in any of them. The information in this three-chapter unit on perception, language, and nonverbal communication provides a solid foundation on which to develop your skills in interpersonal communication, group communication, and public speaking.

2

Perception of Self and Others

3

Verbal Communication

4

Nonverbal Communication

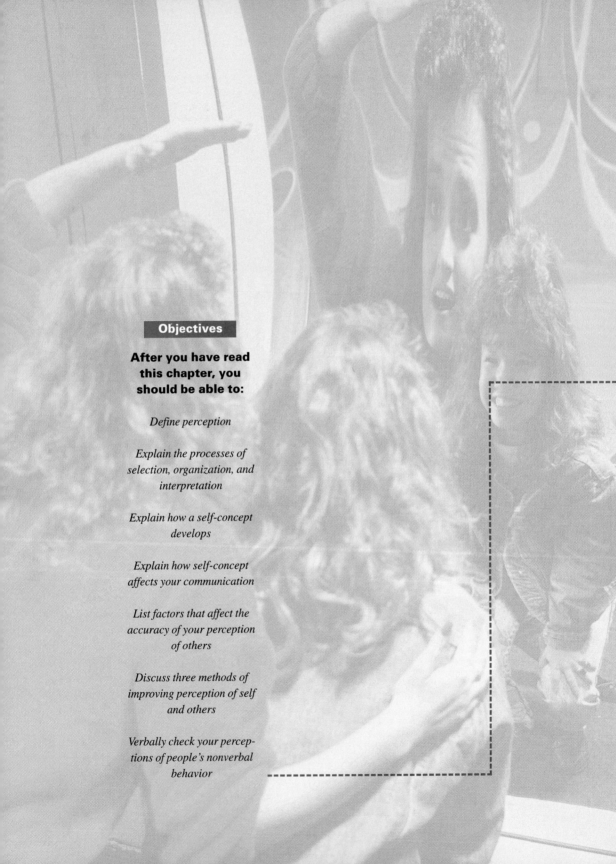

Objectives

After you have read this chapter, you should be able to:

Define perception

Explain the processes of selection, organization, and interpretation

Explain how a self-concept develops

Explain how self-concept affects your communication

List factors that affect the accuracy of your perception of others

Discuss three methods of improving perception of self and others

Verbally check your perceptions of people's nonverbal behavior

2

Perception of Self
and Others

As Justine finishes the beginning of her speech to a group of executives in her company, she sees several of them squinting and frowning as they look at her. As she moves into the body of her speech, her anxiety level builds because she perceives her listeners as being critical of her ideas. Their nonverbal reactions so shake her that she stumbles through her final two, most important, recommendations. After she finishes, she is surprised when several of her listeners tell her that her remarks really stimulated them to think about changes that need to be made. Then when one person comments that the glare from the window behind her made it difficult to look at her, she realizes what really happened. In short, she had misinterpreted the looks on their faces.

As this anecdote suggests, effective communication depends on accurate perception. As we look at the communication model presented in Chapter 1, we see that perception comes into play at every stage. Your perceptions of information affect your message; your perceptions of the environment affect how you send your message; your perceptions of your listeners affect how you shape your message; and your perceptions of how your listeners react to you affect the outcome of your message.

In this chapter, we consider how your perception of yourself and others affects your communication. We begin by examining some basic facts about perception— most significantly, that perception is more subjective than most of us realize. Finally, we'll consider methods of improving both self-perception and perception of others.

Perception

Perception is the process of gathering sensory information and assigning meaning to it. Your eyes, ears, nose, skin, and taste buds gather information; your brain selects from among the items of information gathered, organizes the information, and finally interprets and evaluates it. The result is perception.

Notice that perception involves actively processing sensory data. For this reason, perception does not necessarily provide an accurate representation of the event being perceived. At times our perceptions of the world, other people, and ourselves are highly accurate, but at other times we may distort what comes to us through our senses to such an extent that our perceptions have little to do with reality. Since we base our behavioral responses on what we perceive, when our perceptions are flawed, our communication is likely to be ineffective.

We can think of the perceptual process as occurring in three stages: selection, organization, and interpretation. Although the three stages of perception happen almost simultaneously, let's consider them one at a time.

Selection

You are subject to a barrage of sensory stimuli every second, yet you focus attention on relatively little of it. For instance, right now, as you read this book, you are focusing your attention on making sense out of the written material on this page rather than on the various sights and sounds around you. If your concentration lapses for a moment, the barking of a dog, the hum of an air conditioner, or a song in the background may capture your attention, making it difficult for you to concentrate. As you force yourself to concentrate on the book, the noises that interrupted your concentration seem to disappear. On what bases are these selections made?

Of course, selection is determined in part by the physiological limitations of our senses. Obviously, if you are nearsighted or hard of hearing, you won't perceive some of the stimuli in your environment. But even when the senses are keen, they convey information about only a portion of the physical world. Your eyes do not see light at infrared or ultraviolet wavelengths; you don't perceive the sound of dog whistles. More significant for our purposes, what we perceive is limited even further by three psychological factors: interest, need, and expectation.

Interest. A key factor in determining what we perceive is interest. What do people hear when a person is talking to them about a basketball game? A person who is a rabid fan may hear all the statistics that are presented; a person who is familiar only with the star player may hear only the portion of the explanation that recounts the star player's contribution; a person who is not at all interested in basketball may hear only a jumble of meaningless facts.

Need. A second factor in the selection process is need. If you drive to school, you focus on traffic lights; cars in front of, behind, and next to you; people darting across streets; and potholes in the road. Passengers in the car, however, may be oblivious of these particular sights because they have no need to notice them.

Expectation. A third factor in the selection process is the expectations we form on the basis of experience. To illustrate, take a moment to read the phrases in the triangles in Figure 2.1.

If you are not familiar with this test, you probably read the three triangles as "Paris in the springtime," "Once in a lifetime," and "Bird in the hand." But if you look closely, you will see something different. We tend not to see the repeated words because we don't expect them to be there. We are so familiar with the phrases that our active perception stops once we recognize the phrase.

The combined effect of sensory capability, interest, need, and expectation is to sharply limit our perceptions to a relatively small selection of stimuli that actually impinge on our senses. Now let's consider how the way we process our perceptions adds another layer of subjectivity to perception.

Organization

Information is received from the senses by the brain. Once the brain selects that information, it then organizes its selections. The meaning you get from a perception depends not only on what is selected but on how it is organized.

Apparently, the brain follows certain principles in making sense out of random external elements. Gestalt psychologists suggest that these organizing principles include simplicity (perceiving complex stimuli in simple forms), pattern (perceiving even random stimuli along common lines), proximity (perceiving stimuli that are close together as related), and good form (perceiving complete forms even when parts are missing). To exemplify these principles, suppose that you are instructing a class of students. When you enter the classroom, students may be seated throughout

Figure 2.1 *A sensory test of expectation*

the room, but you are likely to perceive them in simplified terms: your class. In addition, instead of perceiving your audience as individuals, you are likely to seek patterns; you may perceive them as males and females or as young, middle-aged, and elderly. If you notice five people set off from the rest of the people in class, you are likely to perceive them as having something in common. Finally, as you speak, members of the class may perceive the meaning of your sentences correctly even if you leave out an occasional word or use the wrong word.

Interpretation

Interpretation is the process of giving meaning to information that has been selected and organized. People may receive much of the same information, but they are likely to interpret it in their own unique way. Our interpretation of information directly affects the way we communicate about it. For instance, two women pass a clothing store displaying a heavily sequined formal gown. Viewing the same dress, Lorraine describes it as "gorgeous," Doreen as "gaudy."

How we interpret information depends on many factors, including degree of ambiguity, emotional state, preconceived notions, and culture. We have all faced situations in which our interpretation proved to be wrong because of the ambiguity of the stimuli or our emotional state and preconceived notions at the time. Think of the times we have thought we recognized a stranger as someone we knew because we saw what seemed to us a familiar coat or hairstyle or gesture. Likewise, we have all experienced situations in which how we responded was culturally determined. As Samovar and Porter state, "While perception takes place inside each individual, it is culture that primarily determines the meanings we apply to the stimuli that reach us."[1] For instance, how we interpret the act of eating the meat of a pig, fish, dog, cow, or salamander depends upon our cultural background.

Perception and Communication

Although people believe strongly in the accuracy of their senses, their perceptions may well be inaccurate. The degree of inaccuracy varies from insignificant to profound, but communication based on inaccurate perceptions is likely to be misleading. If Lorraine and Doreen recount their experiences later that day, their communication could create very misleading conclusions about apparel. For instance, Lorraine might say, "I wish I had the money to shop at Dawson's—I saw a formal that I'd die for." In contrast, Doreen might say, "I don't know what's with the designers these days. Dawson's devoted their entire front window to an evening gown that was blatantly gaudy—and they wanted a fortune for it."

To this point, we have been discussing the process of perception—how we select, organize, and interpret stimuli. We have illustrated this process at the level of physical perception to show that subjectivity enters into even relatively simple perceptions. In the remainder of this chapter, we examine a special case of perception that is particularly important to communication. *Social perception,* or social cognition, consists of those processes by which people perceive themselves and others. In the study of social perception, particular emphasis is placed on how people interpret their own and others' behavior, how people categorize themselves and others, how people form impressions of themselves and others, and how cultural diversity and gender affect these perceptions. As we will see, both our self-perception and our perception of others significantly affect communication transactions.

By Yourself

Take a minute to look at everything that is around you. Now close your eyes and describe what you "saw." Open your eyes and look again; what did you miss? How can you explain why you selected the items you were able to describe? What caused you to notice these and not other aspects of the scene you were looking at?

Perception of Self

How we communicate depends a great deal on how we define and evaluate ourselves. Yet our definitions and evaluations are a result of our perceptions—and as we have already seen, perceptions are not necessarily accurate. In this section, we consider the self by looking at the related ideas of self-concept, self-image, and self-esteem.

The Self-Concept

The *self-concept* is what a person thinks he or she is. It is the total of a person's generalizations about self—it organizes and guides the processing of information about self. Although the self-concept is well formed by the time we become adults, we continue to present it publicly through various roles we take on. A *role* is a pattern of learned behavior that people adopt to meet the perceived needs of a particular context. Based on how we appraise ourselves and how others respond to us, we may choose or be forced to take on various roles. For instance, during the day you may enact the roles of student, brother or sister, and sales clerk.

Roles that we enact may result from relationships we form, cultural expectations, groups we choose to identify with, and from our own decisions. Cultural expectations are easy to illustrate. Each of us learns that our culture has a prototype for the behaviors expected in such roles as father, mother, lawyer, or doctor.

The expectations of a specific group may also influence our roles. Family, church group, athletic team, theater club—every group expects us to behave in role-appropriate ways. For instance, if you are the oldest child in a large family, your parents may have cast you in a role that included such functions as disciplinarian, brothers' and sisters' keeper, or housekeeper, depending on their view of family relationships. Or if your peers look on you as a "joker," you may go along by enacting your role, laughing and telling funny stories even though you really feel hurt or imposed on.

Other roles are products of our own expectations. You may present yourself as an "organized person," "with-it parent," or "serious student" to fit your perception of self based on your own wishes to reflect a role you have chosen to play.

So, everyone enacts numerous roles. Some roles that we enact in private may be different from those we use in public. For instance, Samantha, who is perceived as a warm, quiet, sensitive person in her family group, may choose to enact the role of boisterous "party animal" in a friendship group. With each new situation, we may choose to enact a familiar role or we may decide to test a new role.

The term *working self-concept* has been used to denote the specific aspects of one's identity that are activated by the role one is enacting at a particular time. The working self-concept changes as we change roles. As Deaux, Dane, and Wrightsman observe in their social psychology book, "To some extent we become different people as we move from situation to situation."[2]

The diversity of the roles we enact help us to withstand stressful situations. For instance, if a person only enacted the role of student, he or she might be devastated by being forced to withdraw from school for a while. When that role of student ends, a large part of the person's self-concept would end as well. In contrast, a person who is the product of many roles is more protected from negative events. Thus the person who also sees himself or herself as parent, sibling, friend, and sales clerk, will have these roles (these parts of the self-concept) to identify with if he or she cannot be a student for a period of time.

Self-Image

Our *self-image* is our perception of our self-concept. It is formed through self-appraisal and is influenced by our reactions to our experiences and the reactions and responses of others.

Self-Appraisal.   We form impressions about ourselves partly from what we see. We look at a recent photograph and make judgments about our physical shape, dress, and facial expression. If we like what we see, we may feel good about ourselves. If we don't like what we see, we may try to change. Perhaps we will go on a diet, buy some new clothes, get our hair styled differently, or begin jogging. If we don't like what we see, and cannot or are unwilling to change, we may begin to develop negative feelings about ourselves.

Our self-appraisal may also result from our reactions to our experiences. Through experience, we learn what we are good at and what we like. If you can strike up conversations with strangers and get them to talk with you without causing yourself undue anxiety, you will probably consider yourself friendly, engaging, or interesting to talk with. The first experience we have tends to have a greater effect in shaping our self-image than later ones.[3] For instance, teenagers who are rejected in their first effort at getting a date may become more reluctant to risk asking people out in the future. Regardless of the outcome of a single experience, if additional experiences produce results similar to the first experience, the initial perception will be strengthened. Interestingly, we are more likely to draw conclusions based on what we choose to do rather than on what we choose not to do. For instance, although people who sketch may see themselves as artistic, people who do not sketch do not necessarily see themselves as unartistic.[4]

In general, then, the more positive our response to the experiences we have—whether as cook, lover, decision maker, student, worker, or parent—the more positive our self-image around that role becomes. Likewise, the greater the number of negative interpretations we make, the more negatively we view our self-image in that role.

Reactions and Responses of Others.   In addition to our self-perceptions, our self-image stems from how others react and respond to us. Suppose that after you've given your opinion on developing alternative means of marketing a product, one of your coworkers tells you, "You're a really creative thinker." Comments like this are likely to positively affect your perception of self, especially if you respect the person making the comment. In fact, research shows that immediate, positive feedback is a powerful modifier of one's self-image.[5] And just as positive comments may have a great impact, so too may negative comments. We tend to use other persons' comments to validate, reinforce, or alter our perception of who and what we are. The more positive comments we get about ourselves, the more positive our total self-image becomes.

Since development of self-image begins early in life, the first and perhaps most important responses from others come from parents and other family members.[6]

What messages about who you are did you learn from your early interactions with your parents and other family members?

One major responsibility that family members have to one another is to "talk" (family talk includes both verbal and nonverbal communication elements) in ways that will contribute to the development of strong self-images of family members and especially of the younger children. Family members' self-images are enhanced by statement of praise ("Roberto, you really did a nice job of cleaning your room" and "Mom, that was really nice of you to let Jasmine stay the night"); statements of acceptance and support ("If you have good reasons to drop out of the Glee Club, we accept your decision" and "Andy doesn't see eye to eye with us, but he's welcome in our home because he's your friend, and we respect that"); and statements of love ("Bart, I know it hurts to play poorly in front of your family, but we love you and we'll be here again next game" and "We both love you very much, Mario"). Of course these verbal statements will only be perceived as positive when they are accompanied by appropriate nonverbal gestures and tones of voice.

Unfortunately, in many families communication is very damaging to self-image and especially to the developing self-images of children. Statements supplemented by nonverbal reinforcing gestures and tones of voice that tease, blame, and evaluate are particularly damaging. All too common are teasing questions ("How are you today, clumsy?" and "Are you still going to be sucking your thumb when you're twenty-one?"); blaming statements ("You know, if I didn't have to raise you, I could be back at college" and "No, you didn't drop the plate, but your constant whining made me so nervous that I dropped it"); and evaluations ("Terry, why are you trying to make breakfast when you know you can't even boil water?" and "Marty, didn't you learn how to add? If what you want to do in life involves numbers, you'd better think of a different profession"). Statements like these are particularly destructive to children and teenagers because they are stored in their minds and may be played back over and over until they come to believe them.

But even adults in the family can be hurt by inappropriate verbal and nonverbal communication. We've seen situations in which a husband or wife is so browbeaten by the spouse that the person loses all confidence in his or her ability. For instance, if one spouse is constantly hounded about his or her "inability to add and subtract accurately," that person will refuse to have anything to do with family finances. An occasional negative statement like the ones quoted here may not have any lasting effect, but if the family's normal communication style is negative—teasing, blaming, and evaluating—damaged self-images and lowered self-esteem are likely to result.

Self-image, in turn, can serve to filter the comments and reactions of others. Even though we may receive all messages accurately—that is, our ears receive the messages and our brain records them—we do not listen equally to all of them. What we choose to listen to will likely be those messages that reinforce our self-image. If someone says something that contradicts our self-perception, we are likely to act as if it had never been said. For example, if you prepare an agenda for your study group and someone comments that you're a good organizer, you may ignore it, not really hear it, or perhaps reply, "Thanks for being kind to me, but it really wasn't that good" or "Anyone could have done that—it was nothing special." On the other hand, if you think you are a good organizer, you will seek out those messages that reinforce this positive view and screen out those that don't.

In summary, certain comments help form a self-image. Then that image begins to work as a filter, screening out selected messages. At times, however, comments will get past the filter and change the self-image. The newly changed self-image then begins to filter other comments. Thus, changes in self-concept do occur.

Self-Fulfilling Prophecies.   Our beliefs about ourselves affect what we think about and what we talk about. Research documents the conclusion that our self-conceptions regulate and direct our behavior.[7] Likewise, the way we think and talk can affect the self-concept and self-image. One way that self-image and communication interact is in creating *self-fulfilling prophecies*—predictions that come true because, consciously or not, we believed and said that they would.

Self-fulfilling prophecies can affect interpersonal performance. Since Stefan thinks of himself as a good public speaker, he predicts that he'll do well on the speech assignment. As a result of his positive self-image, he's likely to remain relaxed, prepare carefully, and give the speech confidently. Just as he predicted, he does well. Austin, who has a poor self-image, predicts that he'll blow the speech. Because of the negative prediction, his preparation is interrupted by negative thoughts, and he goes into his speech tired, irritable, and worried. Just as he predicted, he does poorly. Research suggests a direct relationship between poor self-image and the amount of communication anxiety people experience.[8] In broader terms, positive thoughts and positive language do often produce positive results; unfortunately, negative thoughts and negative language may produce negative results.

Reality and Incongruence.   The reality or accuracy of our self-image depends on the accuracy of our perceptions and how we process them. Everyone experiences some success and failure and hears some praise and blame. If we focus awareness on successful experiences and positive responses only, our self-image will probably be distorted but positive. If, however, we perceive and dwell on negative experiences and remember only the criticism we receive, our self-image may be negatively distorted. In neither case does the self-image we have developed necessarily conform to reality. Yet our perception of self is more likely to affect our behavior than our true abilities. For example, Sean may objectively have the ability to be a good leader, but if he doesn't perceive himself as a good leader, he won't choose to lead.

The gap between our inaccurate self-perceptions and reality is called *incongruence*—"the degree of disparity that exists between one's self-image and one's actual experience."[9] What is ideal, of course, is for a person's self-image to be congruent—that is, reasonably accurate. In reality, everyone experiences some incongruence; problems occur when the disparity is wide.

Self-Esteem

Self-esteem is our evaluation of ourselves in either positive or negative ways. In effect, self-esteem is the evaluative aspect of self-concept.

Effect on Communication.   Because differences in self-esteem affect both achievement behavior and causal attribution, persons with low self-esteem often disapprove of themselves and speak in ways that reflect this disapproval.[10] They may indicate that they expect rejection by others through statements such as, "What I did probably wasn't that important to the company, so I probably won't get a merit raise." Since they have difficulty defending their own views, they may discount them with such statements as, "I have reasons for supporting Hanson, but I guess they're not that good—Parker's probably the better candidate." In contrast, persons with higher self-esteem usually express positive views of themselves and make statements that show an expectation of acceptance. They are likely to state such opinions as, "My suggestions helped the company diversify its sales campaign, so I think I'm likely to get a good raise on that basis alone." Likewise, they are likely to be able to defend their views even in the face of opposing argument. For instance, if someone criticizes Amber for supporting Hanson, she might say, "You might criticize my support, but I think my reasons for supporting Hanson are good ones."

Why does self-esteem affect communication style? It makes sense that if a person has low self-esteem, that person is likely to be unsure of the value of his or her contributions and expect others to view them negatively. When, in contrast, a person has high self-esteem, that person is likely to be more confident of the value of his or her contributions and expect others to see their value. Whether low self-esteem views are realistic or not, people who hold them accept others' real or imagined negative views as additional evidence that they are indeed unworthy.

A particularly interesting function of self-esteem is to moderate internal messages. When we are thinking, we are in fact talking to ourselves. (Some people even go so far as to do much of their thinking aloud.) When we are faced with a decision, we may be especially conscious of the different and often competing voices in our head. Perhaps after returning from a job interview you have had an internal conversation much like Corey's: "I think I made a pretty good impression on the personnel director—I mean, she talked with me for a long time. Well, she talked with me, but maybe she was just trying to be nice. After all, it was her job. No, she didn't have to spend that much time with me. And she really lit up when I talked about the internship I had at Federated. So, she said she was interested in my internship. Talking about that is not exactly telling me that it would make a difference in her view of me as a prospective employee." Notice that several of the messages in this internal conversation are competing. What determines which voice Corey listens to? Self-esteem is a moderator in the choice. If Corey feels good about himself, he will probably conclude that the interviewer was sincere, and he'll feel good about the interview. If, on the other hand, he's down about his life and his behavior, he may well believe that he doesn't have a chance for the job.

Changing Our Self-Perceptions.   Overall, we can improve our self-perceptions. But even though we are constantly growing and developing, we are likely to resist changes in our self-image and self-esteem that may make them more consistent with reality. People with high self-esteem seem to be more resistant to change, perhaps because they are already processing information in a way that is consistent with their sense of self.

People with low self-esteem are more likely to change, because their self-impressions tend to be more malleable. Thus people with low self-esteem may be able to improve their self-perception if they can be shown that the facts support such a change of view. Without help, however, many of us are bent upon maintaining a negative view. For instance, suppose that in high school you just didn't do very well in French. In fact, at some point a parent or teacher may have said, "Face it, foreign language is not your thing." Then you get to college and find that you must take another year of foreign language. As the quarter goes along, you find yourself completing homework in a reasonable time and getting average or better grades. When your professor, advisor, or friend says, "Are you going to continue with French?" you find yourself saying, "No, I've been lucky—I'm not really very good at French." Stubbornly maintaining that "you can't do it" cements artificial limits that may be detrimental to your overall growth.

Change comes only through realistic assessment of strengths and weaknesses. To make any conscious change in self-esteem, we have to be aware of our behavior in order to determine how self-esteem influences it. We have to recognize that some kinds of behavior are more likely to get positive responses. And we need to engage in those kinds of behavior. In this book, we consider many specific communication behaviors that are designed to increase your communication competence. As you begin to perfect the use of these skills, you are likely to begin getting positive responses to your behavior. If your self-esteem tends to be low, if you think that people just don't like you or don't have confidence in you, these positive responses will show you that it was not you that people acted negatively toward but your behavior. For instance, suppose that someone does a favor for you. If, instead of ignoring the behavior, you praise the person and give nonverbal signs of being pleased, that person is likely to begin to treat you as a more pleasant individual, which, in turn, may strengthen your perception of self as a good person.

Cultural Variations

Culture influences perception and affects participants' views of self. Most United States citizens share what is called the Western view of self, which holds that the individual is an autonomous entity that comprises distinct abilities, traits, motives, and values, and that these attributes cause behavior. People with this Western view seek to maintain an independence from others to discover and express their uniqueness. However, people from most of the rest of the world don't share this view. For instance, many Eastern cultures neither assume nor value independence—the goal of many cultures is to maintain *interdependence* among individuals.[11] To make this comparison more vivid, where the United States culture espouses the maxim "It's the squeaky wheel that gets the grease," Eastern cultures, including Japanese and Chinese, as well as Australian, espouse the maxim "The nail that sticks up shall be hammered down."

What are the implications for communication? Interdependent selves will be more attentive and sensitive to others than independent selves. In United States culture it seems important to socialize children away from helplessness and dependence in order to help them be more self-sufficient and independent. In many other cultures the child is seen as needing to be acculturated toward greater dependency.[12]

By Yourself

1.   How you see yourself: On a blank sheet of paper, list characteristics that describe how you see yourself by completing the statement "I am" over and over again. List as many characteristics as you can think of. When you can think of no more, go back through the list. Label the positive statements with a P; label the negative statements with an N. How many statements are positive? How many are negative?

2.   How others see you: On a second sheet of paper, list characteristics that describe how others see you by completing the statement "Other people believe that I am" over and over again. When you can think of no more, go back through the list and label and tally positive and negative statements.

3.   How you wish you were: On a third sheet of paper, list characteristics that describe how you wish you were by completing the statement "I wish I were" over and over again. When you can think of no more, go back through the list and label and tally positive and negative statements.

4.   After you have compared the lists, noting similarities and differences, write a short statement that describes what you have learned about yourself and your self-concept. Can you think of ways your self-image may have influenced your communication with others?

5.   For three days, record the various situations you experience. Describe the images you chose to project in each. At the conclusion of this three-day observation period, write an analysis of your self-monitoring. To what extent does your communication behavior differ and remain the same across situations? What factors in a situation seem to trigger certain behaviors in you? How satisfied are you with the images or "selves" that you displayed in each situation? Where were you most pleased? Least pleased?

Perception of Others

As we encounter strangers, we are faced with a number of questions: Do we have anything in common? Will they accept me? Will be able to get along? We begin with a certain amount of frustration in seeking the information needed to answer these questions. The process of finding answers to such questions is what Charles Berger and his colleagues call *uncertainty reduction.*[13] Their theory states that we seek information about others because if we are uncertain about what they are like, we will have a difficult time predicting their behavior. In this section we focus on our use of perception as a means of coping with uncertainty. In Chapter 8 we'll explore uncertainty-reduction theory in greater detail as we see its relevance to developing relationships.

Our perceptions of others are the result of impressions formed on the basis of sensory data we take in, our organization and processing of that data, and the attributes we select to explain behavior. When two people meet, they form initial impressions to guide their behavior. As they continue to interact, these perceptions will be reinforced, intensified, or changed. Just as with our self-perceptions, our social perceptions aren't always accurate. The factors that are likely to influence our social perceptions are self-image and self-esteem, physical characteristics, social behaviors, stereotyping, and emotional states.

Self-Image and Self-Esteem

Not only do self-image and self-esteem affect our communication, they also affect our perceptions of others. First, there is a direct relationship between how we see ourselves and how we see others. The higher our self-esteem, the more likely we are to see others favorably; the lower our self-esteem, the more likely we are to find fault with others. In addition, there is a relationship between our own personal characteristics and the characteristics we identify in others. For instance, if we are gentle, caring, and giving, we are more likely to perceive others as gentle, caring, and giving. On the other hand, if we are rough, indifferent, and selfish, we are likely to see others as rough, indifferent, and selfish as well.

Physical Characteristics and Social Behaviors

Social perceptions, especially the important first impressions, are often made on the basis of people's physical characteristics and social behaviors. On the basis of a person's physical attractiveness (facial characteristics, height, weight, grooming, dress, and sound of voice), people are likely to categorize people as friendly, courageous, intelligent, cool, or their opposites.[14] In one study, for instance, professional women dressed in jackets were assessed as more powerful than professional women dressed in other clothing.[15] In some cases, a person does not even need a live encounter to attribute a trait to another person. Show a friend a picture of your child, uncle, or grandmother, and your friend may well form impressions of your relative's personality on the basis of that photo alone!

First impressions are also made on the basis of perceptions of a person's social behaviors. Sometimes our impressions are the result of observing a single behavior. For instance, after a company orientation social, Caleb asks Sara what she thinks of Gavin, a fellow who is working with Caleb on the Goodman account. Sara, who observed Gavin interrupt Yolanda once to stress his view as she was recounting the events of last year's social, may say, "Gavin? He's really rude."

Often the behaviors we use in forming these impressions are based on gender. Leslie Zebrowitz states that males are more likely to describe others in terms of their abilities (she writes well), whereas females are more likely to describe others in terms of their self-concepts (she thinks she's a good writer). Likewise, she sees gender differences in categorizing the behaviors. Males' descriptions include more nonsocial activities (he likes to fly model airplanes), whereas females' include more interpersonal interactions (he likes to get together with his friends).[16] Similarly, our cultural heritage strongly influences how we perceive members of other cultures. For instance, see the Perspective about Americans and Japanese on pages 42 and 43, which focuses on some effects of cultural differences, as well as the discussion of cultural differences beginning on page 48.

Why is it important to know about cultural differences? One reason is suggested by this description of encounters between Japanese and Americans. Many misunderstandings come about because of a basic error in social perception: the human tendency to assume that people from another culture are experiencing an interaction in the same way we are.

The assumption that everywhere men and women inhabit the same world and assign essentially the same meanings to events of their lives is perhaps the most pervasive and most intractable barrier to intercultural rapport. . . .

It is not simply that people speak in different tongues but also that they see differently, think differently, feel differently about their experience. "If, by some miracle, Americans and Japanese were to wake up one day and find ourselves talking the same language," observes George Packard, "we would still be faced with the problem of our massive ignorance about each other, we would still have difficulty in knowing what to communicate because we have so much to learn about what motivates the other."

. . . What are some of the probable consequences of encounters between Japanese and Americans? The Japanese are likely to be startled at the ease with which Americans approach and enter into intense conversations with people they scarcely know. Americans' lack of sensitivity to protocol and to status differences, or their deliberate efforts to undermine them, may appear naive or downright insulting. Their constant questions and revealing disclosure may seem intrusive and overbearing, forcing the Japanese to discuss matters they regard as private. . . . Their informality and impulsiveness may deprive social occasions of their congenial predictability. The pace at which Americans move and talk, their verbal and physical flamboyance, may be unnerving. Their eagerness to contra-

Research suggests that people may form highly complex perceptions of someone's personality based on very limited observation. Such judgments are based on what is called "implicit personality theories"—a set of assumptions that people have developed about what physical characteristics and personality traits are associated with one another.[17]

Because your own implicit personality theory says that certain traits go together, you are likely to judge a person's other characteristics based upon observation of a single trait, without further verification. This tendency is known as the *halo effect*. For instance, Heather sees Martina as a warm person. Heather's implicit perdict, even to argue bluntly, disturbs the harmony that should prevail. . . . Their endless analyzing, insistence on verbal precision, and binding agreements reveal an incredible trust in words over people. They are prone to error because they are always in such a hurry. They are an inscrutable people!

The Americans, in turn, confront Japanese who appear reluctant to meet strangers and slow to get to know them. The Japanese seem preoccupied with the relative status of people and are constantly deferring to those above them. They also are constantly apologizing. They seem to view conversation as some sort of formal ceremony rather than a real meeting of the minds. They are reticent about saying much about themselves, preferring to comment on superficial and irrelevant topics. When questions are put directly to them the answers are so vague that one has little idea of where they stand. They all repeat the same things as if fearful of disagreement. They are as physically opaque as they are verbally—except when drinking—and rarely show feelings of any kind, particularly negative ones. They are composed in the way they sit, the way

they stand, the way they talk, as if some accidental and uncalculated act might expose them. There is a reluctance to dig into problems, analyze them step by step, and agree on specific conclusions. And they seem oblivious to deadlines. A highly inscrutable people!

When difficulties arise, as they often do, the American approaches them by calling the misunderstanding to everyone's attention, explaining and justifying his or her behavior and asking others to be equally frank in explaining their position. Once the sources are identified and responsibility for them is admitted, some compromise course of action should be acceptable to everyone. A Japanese, equally sensitive to the fact that things are not going well, decides to postpone further conversation or propose some indirect way of defusing the situation without embarrassing anyone. Thus even the approaches to cross-cultural misunderstandings are culturally distinctive! ■

SOURCE: Dean C. Barnlund, *Communicative Styles of Japanese and Americans* (Belmont, CA: Wadsworth, 1989), pp. 189–191. Reprinted by permission.

sonality theory correlates warmth with goodness and goodness with honesty. As a result, she perceives Martina as being both good and honest as well as warm. In reality, Martina may be warm but dishonest. Thus, if a friend accuses Martina of lying about an important matter, Heather may leap to Martina's defense because the halo effect leads her to assume that Martina is honest.

A halo effect can also work to a person's disadvantage when it is based on a negative perception. In fact, Hollman[18] has found that negative information more strongly influences our impressions of others than does positive information.

How might stereotypes related to age and gender prevent these people from being perceived as they actually are?

Halo effects seem to occur most frequently under one or more of these three conditions: (1) when the perceiver is judging traits with which he or she has limited experience, (2) when the traits have strong moral overtones, and (3) when the perception is of a person that the perceiver knows well.

Given limited amounts of information, then, we fill in details. This tendency to fill in details leads to a second biasing factor in social perception: stereotyping.

Stereotyping

Perhaps the most commonly recognized barrier to accurate judgment of others is our tendency to stereotype. *Stereotyping* is an oversimplified opinion or uncritical judgment of others. It often involves assigning characteristics to individuals solely on the basis of their membership in a certain class or category. Stereotyping is a very common perceptual shortcut. We are likely to develop generalized opinions about any group we come in contact with. Subsequently, any number of perceptual cues—skin color, style of dress, a religious medal, gray hair, gender, and so on—can lead us to automatically project our generalized opinions onto a specific individual.

Stereotypes engender three different types of perceptual inaccuracies: (1) stereotypic inaccuracy—the tendency to view a group as more or less stereotypic than it actually is (saying the Gammas really value/undervalue scholarship when their collective grade point average is only slightly above or below the average for the school); (2) valence inaccuracy—the tendency to view a group as more or less positive than it is (saying the Gammas are the most popular/least popular group on campus when they are not); and (3) dispersion inaccuracy—the tendency to see a group as more or less variable than it actually is (to say that all Gammas are good students when the group represents a variety of grades).[19]

Stereotyping contributes to perceptual inaccuracies by ignoring individual differences. Stereotyping causes us to assume certain characteristics just because a person happens to be a member of the stereotyped group. For instance, Dave holds a stereotype that stockbrokers are unethical. Even if it were true that a majority of stockbrokers are unethical, that would not mean that Denise, a highly principled stockbroker, is unethical. You may be able to think of instances when you have been the victim of a stereotype based on your gender, age, ethnic heritage, social class, physical characteristics, or other qualities. If so, you know how damaging and unfair stereotypes can be.

If stereotypes lead to inaccurate perceptions, why do they persist? There are at least two good reasons. First, we tend to believe that stereotypes are helpful.[20] Although people may learn to go beyond a stereotype in forming opinions of individuals, stereotypes provide a working hypothesis. That is, when encountering a person from a different race or culture, we are likely to attribute characteristics of our stereotype to the person and act as if that stereotype is accurate until we get sufficient information to judge the person as an individual.[21] In short, it is easier to base our perceptions of a person or group of people on a stereotype than to take the time to really learn about each individual we encounter.

In addition, it provides some people with a certain comfort to believe that whites are racist, blacks are lazy, old people are stubborn, Italians are naturally hotheaded, or women are too emotional to be capable of reasoning under stress. Such generalizations enable the person to "know" how to treat new acquaintances.

As these examples suggest, stereotyping and prejudice go hand in hand. *Prejudice* is an unjustified attitude toward a person or group. For instance, when Laura discovers that Wasif, a man she has just met, is a Muslim, she would be stereotyping him if she viewed him solely in terms of her perception of Muslims' beliefs about women rather than in terms of his individual behavior. Moreover, to the extent that Laura permits her stereotype to govern her responses to Wasif, she will be guilty of prejudice. In this case, Wasif may never get the chance to be known for who he really is.

Prejudice, like stereotypes, can be very resistant to change. People who are prejudiced are likely to continue to maintain their prejudices even in the face of evidence that contradicts them. Suppose that Lou, an African-American man, stereotypes all whites as racist. When Lou meets Phil, a white man, Lou will believe that Phil is racist. If someone confronts Lou with evidence showing that Phil treats all people alike regardless of race, Lou may refuse to acknowledge the evidence, find some alternative explanation, or reject its source.

Racism and sexism are two manifestations of prejudice that cause major problems in relationships in our society. *Racism* and *sexism* are defined as any behaviors, however insignificant, that limit people to rigid stereotypic roles based solely on race or gender. Because such attitudes can be both deeply ingrained and often subtle, it is easy to overlook behaviors we engage in that in some way meet this definition of racist or sexist behavior. Remember, the behavior may seem insignificant. For instance, leaving more space between you and another person on a bus, on a plane, in a lounge, or at a counter in a restaurant—a space wider than you would leave if the person next to you were of your race—is racist behavior. Telling jokes, laughing at jokes, or encouraging repetition of jokes that demean people of other races or the opposite sex is racist/sexist behavior. Ignoring the presence or the worth of another person's comments because that person is of another race or the opposite sex is racist/sexist behavior. We may say, "But I didn't mean anything by what I did." Nonetheless, our behavior will be perceived as racist/sexist, and it will seriously harm our attempts to communicate.

More recently, both racism and sexism have been redefined to include the variable of power. From this perspective, racism and sexism occur when members of the dominant culture use their various positions of power and control to explicitly or implicitly deny or inhibit the rights of minority cultures, including women. Notice that women have been defined as a minority even though women outnumber men. Classification of women as a minority is not a function of numbers, but of being subjected to repressive acts by the dominant white/male culture.

This definition does not say that African-Americans, Asian-Americans, Hispanic-Americans, and women can't be prejudiced. What it does say is that, because they lack a significant power base, minorities are unable to manifest their prejudice in ways that explicitly or implicitly deny or inhibit the rights of the majority white/male culture. Thus, under this definition, true racism or sexism is limited to behaviors against those who are in lower power positions.

Although we understand the thinking behind these definitions, from a communication standpoint whether behavior is "truly" racism/sexism or "only" prejudice differs only in degree. Thus, we continue to hold the view that any prejudiced behavior is bad. Because racial and gender stereotypes are deeply ingrained in our culture, very few people manage to completely avoid behaving or thinking in a prejudiced manner. By becoming aware of our own prejudiced attitudes and behaviors, we can guard against inhibiting communication by automatically assuming that other people feel and act the same way we do. We can also guard against saying or doing things that offend other people and perpetuate outdated racial and sex-role stereotypes. If people are confronted with enough information over a long enough period, their attitudes may change.

Of course, prejudiced behavior is not limited to race and sex. For instance, in a recent study by Theodore Grove and Doris Werkman, conversations with visibly disabled strangers produced relatively more negative predicted outcome values than conversations with able-bodied strangers.[22] In short, we must recognize the potential of prejudiced behavior with any group of people who are different from ourselves.

Emotional States

Another barrier to accurate judgments of others is our emotional state. Various research studies completed by Joseph Forgas led him to conclude that "there is a broad and pervasive tendency for people to perceive and interpret others in terms of their feelings at the time."[23] If, for example, you are having a "down" day, your perception of a person you are meeting for the first time will probably be more negative than if you were having a good day. When you receive a low grade on a paper you thought was well written, your perceptions of people around you will surely be colored by your negative feeling. If, however, you receive an A on an important paper that you weren't sure was any good, you're likely to perceive everything and everyone around you positively. So, whether our perceptions of another person are positive or negative, we can ask ourselves before acting on them how our feelings may have affected our perceptions.

Our emotions also cause us to engage in selective perceptions. For instance, we are likely to think highly of someone we would like to be with. If Donna sees Nick as a man with whom she would like to develop a strong relationship, she will tend to see the positive side of Nick's personality and overlook or ignore the negative side that is apparent to others. A person in love is often oblivious of the loved one's faults. Once two people have married, however, they may begin to see each other's negative traits, traits that were perhaps obvious to others all along.

Our emotions also may affect our attributions.[24] *Attributions* are reasons we give for others' behavior. In addition to making judgments about people, we attempt to construct reasons about why people behave as they do. According to attribution theory, what we determine—rightly or wrongly—to be the causes of others' behavior has a direct impact on our perceptions of them.

For instance, suppose that you have made a luncheon appointment with a coworker for noon at a restaurant a few blocks from work. You arrive at noon, but there's no sign of your coworker. At 12:20, he is still a no-show. At this point, you are likely to construct causal attributions. If you like and respect your coworker, you are likely to attribute his lateness to a good reason: an important phone call at the last minute, the need to finish a job before lunch, or some accident that may have occurred. If you are not particularly fond of your coworker, you are likely to attribute his lateness to forgetfulness, inconsiderateness, or malicious intent. In either case, your causal attribution further affects your perception of the person. Like prejudices, causal attributions may be so strong that they resist contrary evidence. If you don't particularly care for the person, when he does arrive and explains that he had an emergency long-distance phone call, you are likely to disbelieve the reason or discount the urgency of the call. Being aware of the human tendency toward such cognitive biases can help you correct your perceptions and thus improve your communication.

Cultural Differences

Since people from different cultures approach the world from different perspectives, they are likely to experience difficulty sharing meaning when they talk with each other. We may think that we don't have to be so concerned with cultural differences because most of our communication will be with people similar to ourselves. But you don't have to cross national borders to encounter different cultures. As we mentioned earlier, the United States contains many different cultures, including African-American, Mexican-American, Hispanic-American, Asian-American, Native American, Appalachian, and others. Differences can also be experienced across generations, regions, social classes, even neighborhoods. The need for awareness and sensitivity in applying our communication skills is not limited to people from another country or otherwise so markedly "different" from ourselves. For instance, in the Los Angeles Unified School District, 108 different languages are spoken; at Hollywood High School alone, students have 85 different first languages.[25]

When confronted with strangers from different cultures, we tend to see differences as barriers to communication because they represent unknown quantities. The more one person differs from another, the less either person is able to predict the behavior of the other. When people are uncertain about how another person will behave, fear often results. Some people express their fear by withdrawing or becoming compliant; others mask their fear with aggressive behavior. Clearly, none of these behaviors improves communication. Cultural differences argue for a greater need for confronting our ignorance about what people are thinking, feeling, and valuing. In the final part of this chapter we focus on procedures that can enable us to improve our social perceptions of people regardless of their culture or gender.

By Yourself

1. Think of a recent encounter you have had with someone of a different race or ethnic background. Describe how you felt. To what extent were you comfortable with this person? How did the person's race or ethnic background influence how you acted or reacted?

2. Describe the last situation in which you found yourself where someone told a racist or sexist joke or made a racist or sexist remark. How did you react? How did others present react? If you are dissatisfied with how you reacted, write a script for how you wish you had reacted.

In Groups

1. Your instructor will ask for three volunteers, who will leave the classroom. One at a time, they will reenter the room and describe to the class a full-page magazine ad that the instructor has given them. On the basis of their descriptions, you are to form a mental picture of the people in the advertisement. As each volunteer describes the ad, write five adjectives about the person or persons in the picture. When all three have finished, your instructor will show you the ad.

a. What were the differences among the three descriptions?

b. Which of the three descriptions helped you form the most accurate picture? How did your image differ from the actual picture? How can you account for the differences?

c. Now that you have seen the picture, again write five adjectives about the person or persons in the picture. Did your five adjectives change after you actually saw the picture? If so, how and why?

2. For the following situation, determine which of the factors discussed in this section contributed to the inaccuracy of the initial perception of the other person. Be able to defend your answers in class.

Amanda was depressed. Her daughter was having problems in school, she had just been informed that her work hours were being cut back, and her mother was facing possible surgery. On her way home from campus, she stopped at the dry cleaner to pick up her laundry. There was a new man working the counter. From looking at him, Amanda could tell he was quite old. She thought to herself that he could be a problem. When she requested her laundry, he asked to see her claim check. Because no one had ever asked her for this before, Amanda responded that she had thrown the receipt away. The man firmly replied, "Well, I'm not able to give you clothes without a claim check. It's store policy." After demanding to see the manager and being informed that she had left for the day, Amanda stormed out of the store. "I'll fix him," she fumed to herself. "It's just like an old man to act so rigidly!"

Improving Social Perception

Because inaccuracies in perception are common and influence how we communicate, improving perceptual accuracy is an important first step in becoming a competent communicator. The following guidelines can aid you in constructing a more realistic impression of others as well as in assessing the validity of your own perceptions.

1. *Look for additional information about people.* Once you have drawn a conclusion about others, you begin to behave in accordance with that conclusion. Yet perceptions are often based on very little information. To counter the tendency to generalize from small amounts of information, try to learn more before you allow yourself to form an impression so that you can increase the accuracy of your perceptions. Remind yourself that initial perceptions should be tentative—that is, subject to change.

The best way to get information about people is to talk with them. If you've perceived someone as inconsiderate on the basis of one experience, hold that perception as tentative until you have a chance to really talk with the person. Only by talking with people can we get to know them; by the same token, a sure way to maintain an inaccurate perception is to use it as a reason for avoiding the person in question.

2. *Actively question the accuracy of your perceptions.* Too often people insist, "I was there—I know what I saw"; that is, they act on their perceptions as though they were reality. Questioning accuracy begins by saying, "I know what I think I saw, heard, tasted, smelled, or felt, but I could be wrong. What else could help me sort this out?" By accepting the possibility of error, you may be motivated to seek further verification. In situations where the accuracy of perception is important, take a few seconds to double-check. It will be worth the effort.

3. *Realize that perceptions of people may need to be changed over time.* Suppose that two years ago you heard a person put down the accomplishments of a friend of yours, so you developed a perception of this person as meanspirited. The chances are that this one incident will lead you to expect meanspirited behavior from this person. As demonstrated earlier in the chapter, we often perceive what we expect to perceive. As a result, you may perceive other behaviors as mean even though they are not. Willingness to change means making an effort to observe this person's behavior at other times without bias and being prepared to modify your perception if the person's behavior warrants it. People often saddle themselves with perceptions that are based on old or incomplete information yet find it easier to stick with a perception, even if it is wrong, than to change it. It takes strength of character to say to yourself or others, "I was wrong." However, your communication based on outdated, inaccurate perceptions can be more costly than revising your perceptions.

4. *When you have formed a perception, check its accuracy verbally.* How can you be sure that the meanings you get from others' nonverbal cues are accurate? Before you act on any conclusion you draw from other people's behavior, you should make a perception check.

A *perception check* is a verbal statement that reflects your own understanding of the meaning of another person's nonverbal cues. Perception checking calls for you to (1) watch the behavior of the other person, (2) ask yourself, "What does that behavior mean to me?" and (3) put your interpretation of the behavior into words to verify whether your perception is accurate.

The following examples illustrate the use of perception checking.

Vera comes walking into the room with a completely blank expression. She neither speaks to Ann nor acknowledges that she is in the room. Vera sits on the edge of the bed and stares into space. Ann says, "Vera, I get the feeling that something has happened that put you in some kind of a shock. Am I right? Is there something I can do?"

Ted, the company messenger, delivers a memo to Erin. As Erin reads the note, her eyes brighten and she breaks into a smile. Ted says, "Hey, Erin, you seem really pleased. Am I right?"

Cesar, speaking in short, precise sentences with a sharp tone of voice, gives Bill his day's assignment. Bill says, "From the sound of your voice, Cesar, I can't help but get the impression that you're upset with me. Are you?"

In each of these examples, the final sentence is a perception check intended to test the receiver's perceptions of the sender's behavior. Notice that body language sometimes provides the clues, whereas at other times the tone of voice does. Also notice that the perception-checking statements do not express approval or disapproval of what is being received—they are purely descriptive statements of the perceptions.

The purpose of checking out any perception of behavior is to bring the meaning that was received through nonverbal cues into the verbal realm, where it can be verified or corrected. Let's carry through with Cesar and Bill's conversation. When Bill says, "I can't help but get the impression that you're upset with me. Are you?" Cesar may say either (1) "No, whatever gave you that impression?" in which case Bill can further describe the cues that he received; (2) "Yes, I am," in which case Bill can get Cesar to specify what has caused the feelings; or (3) "No, it's not you; it's just that three of my team members didn't show up for this shift." If Cesar is not upset with him, Bill can deal with what caused him to misinterpret Cesar's feelings; if Cesar is upset with him, Bill has the opportunity of changing the behavior that caused Cesar to be upset.

To see what might happen when we respond without checking the accuracy of our perceptions, suppose that in place of the descriptive perception check Bill were to say, "Why are you so upset with me?" Bill would not be describing his perception—he would be making a judgment based on his perception. Replying as if his perception is "obviously" accurate amounts to mind reading. Unfortunately, few people can read minds that well, especially given all the subjective factors that influence perception. It could very well be that Bill's response reflects his state of mind far more than it does Cesar's. When mind reading is substituted for perception checking, communication breakdowns are likely to occur.

Perhaps you are thinking, "Well, I know how to read other people's signals. I can tell perfectly well when another person is upset (or happy, angry, and so on) with me." And perhaps you are correct—most of the time. But if you do not check out your perception, you are still guessing what the other person is feeling and whether the person's anger or happiness is centered on you. If you reply judgmentally, the other person may well become defensive about the feelings you appear to be challenging. The response is then likely to be something like "Who said I'm upset?" or, more harshly, "What the hell are you talking about?" Such responses may well trigger an escalating round of emotional outbursts and complete misunderstanding. Very little communication takes place when communicators lose their tempers.

When should you check your perceptions? Whenever the accuracy of your understanding is important (1) to your current communication, (2) to the relationship you have with the other person, or (3) to the conclusions you draw about that person. Most of us use this skill far too little, if at all. We assume that we have a perfectly accurate understanding of the meaning of another's behavioral cues; too often we are wrong. Especially in new relationships, you will find perception checking an important skill to use.

Because a perception check is descriptive rather than judgmental, the other person is much less likely to react defensively. However, a perception check may not always eliminate defensive behavior. There are times when a person's emotional stress is so great that calm, logical communication is nearly impossible. Through the selective use of perception checking, however, you can reduce the likelihood of misinterpreting another's nonverbal cues and thus the likelihood of defensiveness. As with most skills, to become competent, you must practice.

Practice in Perception Checking

By Yourself

1. Write down your responses to the following situations with well-phrased perception checks.

> Franco comes home from the doctor's office with pale face and slumped shoulders. Glancing at you with a forlorn look, he shrugs his shoulders. You say:

> As you return the tennis racket you borrowed from Liam, you smile and say, "Here's your racket." Liam stiffens, grabs the racket, and starts to walk away. You say:

> Natalie comes dancing into her room with a huge grin on her face. You say:

> In the past, your adviser has told you that almost any time would be all right for working out your next term's schedule. When you tell her you'll be in Wednesday at 4 P.M., she pauses, frowns, sighs, and says "Uh" and nods. You say:

2. Compare your written responses to the guidelines for effective perception checking discussed earlier. Edit your responses where necessary in order to improve them. Now say them aloud. Do they sound "natural"? If not, revise them until they do.

In Groups

Working with others in groups of three, A and B should role-play a situation while C observes. During the conversation, A should intentionally give off various non-verbal cues to his or her feelings. B should use perception checking to determine if his or her perception of A's behavior is accurate. When they have finished, C should discuss the behaviors observed and provide an analysis of the effectiveness of B's perception checks. The exercise continues until each person in the group has a chance to be A, B, and C. After completing the exercise, the participants should discuss how the skill of perception checking affected the accuracy of the communication.

Summary

Perception is the process of gathering sensory information and assigning meaning to it. Our perceptions are a result of our selection, organization, and interpretation of sensory information. Inaccurate perceptions cause us to see the world not as it is but as we would like it to be.

The self-concept is the total of a person's generalizations about self; it is presented publicly through the roles we enact. Our self-image—our perception of our self-concept—is formed through self-appraisal and is influenced by our reactions to our experiences and the reactions and responses of others. Our self-image affects communication by creating self-fulfilling prophecies and by filtering messages we receive. Our self-esteem is our evaluation of ourselves in either positive or negative ways. Self-esteem can affect communication style, moderate competing internal messages, and influence our perception of others.

Perception also plays an important role in forming impressions of others. Because research shows that the accuracy of people's perceptions and judgments varies considerably, your communication will be most successful if you do not rely entirely on your impressions to determine how another person feels or what that person is really like. You will improve (or at least better understand) your perceptions of others if you take into account how perceptions are affected by your own self-image and self-esteem, the physical characteristics and social behaviors of the other person, stereotyping, emotional states, and cultural differences.

You can learn to improve perception if you look for additional information about people, actively question the accuracy of your perceptions, realize that perceptions of people may need to be changed over time, and check perceptions verbally before you react.

Suggested Readings

Centi, Paul. *Up With the Positive: Out With the Negative.* Englewood Cliffs, NJ: Prentice Hall, 1981. Emphasizes the positive aspects of dealing with self-concept. Contains many interesting self-tests and exercises.

Covey, Stephen R. *The 7 Habits of Highly Effective People: Restoring the Character Ethic.* New York: Fireside Books, 1989. Premise is that the success of highly effective people comes from within, not without. Includes a great deal of emphasis on adjusting perceptions of reality.

Hattie, John. *Self-Concept.* Hillsdale, NJ: Erlbaum, 1992. An excellent review of past theories of self-concept. Contains two chapters on self-concept and achievement and enhancing self-concept.

Jones, Edward E. *Interpersonal Perception.* New York: W. H. Freeman, 1990. Provides an interpersonal framework for the analysis of perception. Excellent chapters on self-presentation and self-knowledge.

Zebrowitz, Leslie A. *Social Perception.* Pacific Grove, CA: Brooks/Cole, 1990. Provides an excellent research base for theories of social perception.

Notes

1. Larry A. Samovar and Richard E. Porter, *Communication Between Cultures,* 2d ed. (Belmont, CA: Wadsworth, 1995), p. 80.

2. Kay Deaux, Francis C. Dane, and Lawrence S. Wrightsman, *Social Psychology,* 5th ed. (Belmont, CA: Wadsworth, 1993), p. 56.

3. Paul J. Centi, *Up With the Positive: Out With the Negative* (Englewood Cliffs, NJ: Prentice Hall, 1981).

4. Russell H. Fazio, Steven J. Sherman, and Paul M. Herr, "The Feature-Positive Effect in the Self-Perception Process: Does Not Doing Matter as Much as Doing?" *Journal of Personality and Social Psychology* 42 (1982): 411.

5. John Hattie, *Self-Concept* (Hillsdale, NJ: Erlbaum, 1992), p. 251.

6. D. H. Demo, "Family Relations and the Self-Esteem of Adolescents and Their Parents," *Journal of Marriage and the Family* 49 (1987): 705–715.

7. Jonathon D. Brown and S. April Smart, "The Self and Social Conduct: Linking Self-Representations to Prosocial Behavior," *Journal of Personality and Social Psychology* 60 (1991): 368.

8. Lynne Kelly, "A Rose by Any Other Name Is Still a Rose: A Comparative Analysis of Reticence, Communication Apprehension, Unwillingness to Communicate, and Shyness," *Human Communication Research* 8 (1982): 102.

9. Wayne Weiten, *Psychology: Themes and Variations* (Pacific Grove, CA: Brooks/Cole, 1989), p. 449.

10. Jennifer D. Campbell, "Self-Esteem and Clarity of the Self-Concept," *Journal of Personality and Social Psychology* 59 (1990): 538.

11. Hazel R. Markus and Shinobu Kitayama, "Cultural Variation in the Self-Concept," in Jaine Strauss and George R. Goethals, eds., *The Self: Interdisciplinary Approaches* (New York: Springer-Verlag, 1991), p. 19.

12. Judith V. Jordan, "The Relational Self: A New Perspective for Understanding Women's Development," in Jaine Strauss and George R. Goethals, eds., *The Self: Interdisciplinary Approaches* (New York: Springer-Verlag, 1991), p. 137.

13. See Charles R. Berger and James J. Brada, *Language and Social Knowledge: Uncertainty in Interpersonal Relations* (London: Arnold, 1982).

14.   Leslie A. Zebrowitz, *Social Perception* (Pacific Grove, CA: Brooks/Cole, 1990), p. 44ff. In this section, the author cites numerous recent specific studies to support claims of effects of demographic factors and personal characteristics on impression formation.

15.   Linda E. Temple and Karen R. Loewen, "Perceptions of Power: First Impressions of a Woman Wearing a Jacket," *Perceptual and Motor Skills* 76 (February 1993): 345.

16.   Zebrowitz, p. 24.

17.   Deaux, Dane, and Wrightsman, pp. 88–89.

18.   T. D. Hollman, "Employment Interviewer's Errors in Processing Positive and Negative Information," *Journal of Psychology* 56 (1972): 130–134.

19.   Charles M. Judd and Bernadette Park, "Definition and Assessment of Accuracy in Social Stereotypes," *Psychological Review* 100 (January 1993): 111.

20.   Deaux, Dane, and Wrightsman, p. 94.

21.   Edward E. Jones, *Interpersonal Perception* (New York: W. H. Freeman, 1990), p. 110.

22.   Theodore G. Grove and Doris L. Werkman, "Conversations With Able-Bodied and Visibly Disabled Strangers: An Adversarial Test of Predicted Outcome Value and Uncertainty Reduction Theories," *Human Communication Research* 17 (June 1991): 507.

23.   Joseph P. Forgas, "Affect and Person Perception," in Joseph P. Forgas, ed., *Emotion and Social Judgments* (New York: Pergamon Press, 1991), p. 288.

24.   Joseph P. Forgas, Gordon H. Bower, and Stephanie J. Moylan, "Praise or Blame? Affective Influences on Attributions for Achievement," *Journal of Personality and Social Psychology* 59 (1990): 809.

25.   Myron W. Lustig and Jolene Koester, *Intercultural Competence: Interpersonal Communication Across Cultures* (New York: HarperCollins, 1993), p. 10.

**After you have read
this chapter, you
should be able to:**

*Explain the uses of language
in human communication*

*Explain the relationship
between language and
meaning*

*Contrast word denotation and
word connotation*

*Select precise words and
specific and concrete words*

*Date and index
generalizations*

*Explain the nature of
appropriate and
inappropriate language*

Verbal Communication

3

"Kyle, why do you keep obfuscating the plan?"

"Now just a minute, Derek. There's no need for you to get obscene with me. I may not have looked at the job the same way you did but I wouldn't, uh . . . I'm not going to lower myself to repeat your language!"

"Obfuscating" means confusing. What in the world did Derek mean when he accused Kyle of "obfuscating the plan"? And why did Kyle think that Derek was talking obscenely? Many years ago, I. A. Richards observed that communication is "the study of misunderstanding and its remedy."[1] And in this instance, we have a classic example of misunderstanding. The remedy? Clearer and more appropriate language.

Whether you're trying to iron out a problem with a friend or explain your views on reducing domestic violence in a group discussion or a public speech, your effectiveness will depend on verbal and nonverbal communication usage. To communicate your thoughts accurately, you need to be able to select words and nonverbal behavior that will communicate your meanings. And to receive messages accurately, you need to be able to understand the sender's language and nonverbal signals.

We begin this chapter by discussing how people use language. Next, we examine the relationships between language and meaning with emphasis on denotation, connotation, and cultural and gender differences. Finally, we consider skills that focus on speaking clearly and speaking appropriately.

The Nature and Use of Language

Language is the systematic means of communicating ideas or feelings by the use of sounds and symbols that have commonly understood meanings. Some scholars believe that the human capability to think and communicate symbolically best distinguishes us from other species. Language is used in a variety of ways in human communication.

1. *We use language to designate, label, and define.* Language symbols (that is, words) serve to designate, label, and define thoughts, feelings, objects, people, and experiences in order that they may be shared with other people. Certain limitations, however, are built into our use of language symbols. For instance, in referring to a classmate as a "mature adult," you are defining him or her differently from referring to that same classmate as a "student," "singer," or "basketball player." Whichever label you choose, you are calling attention to some particular aspect of that person; in addition, you are suggesting how others should define and thus act toward that person. In short, when we designate and define, we also limit. How might your perceptions and behaviors toward a person labeled a "singer" be different from those toward a person labeled an "athlete"?

When we experience a phenomenon that is unlabeled—that is, for which there is no word or verbal description—we find it difficult to discuss. For instance, over the years women felt uncomfortable when they were subjects of unwanted sexual attention at work. But for a long time discussion of these behaviors was difficult because they were unnamed. It's only been in the past 15 or 20 years that we've designated such behaviors as "sexual harassment." As Julia T. Wood, a leading scholar in gender research, points out, "Because it wasn't named, sexual harassment was not visible or salient, making it difficult to recognize, think about, or stop."[2] Once we began to use the term, we could discuss its nature and determine what kinds of behavior fell within and outside of the term. This labeling was an important first step toward combating both the subtle and more blatant forms of this inappropriate behavior.

2. *We use language to evaluate.* Language scholars emphasize the value-laden characteristics of language: We give the things we talk about a positive or negative slant simply by the words we use to refer to them.[3] Consider the seemingly simple statement, "The chairs in the den are pea green." Even this description may be perceived as a judgment about the chairs, depending on the associations "pea green" has for the listener. Other word choices convey evaluations more explicitly. For instance, if you observe Hal taking his time to make a decision, you could speak of Hal as either "thoughtful and deliberate" or "wishy-washy." Likewise, you can call what your friend is cooking on the grill either "prime steak" or "animal flesh." Clearly, the meaning you transmit varies greatly with your choice of words. The value-laden nature of language requires us to select our words with great care or run the risk of creating reactions we don't intend.

3. *We use language to discuss things outside our immediate experience.* Language enables us to speak hypothetically, to talk about past and future events, and to communicate about people and things that are not present. Through language, we can discuss where we hope to be in five years, analyze a conversation two acquaintances had last week, or learn about the history that shapes the world we live in. Language enables us to learn from others' experiences, to share a common heritage, and to develop a shared vision for the future.

We rely so much on what we learn through language that we sometimes react to the words rather than to the reality. For instance, if Greer says that a certain attorney is a "vulture," your perception of the attorney's behavior is based not on direct experience but on your perception of Greer's assessment. Yet that verbal assessment may influence you as much as a direct experience of the person in question.

4. *We can use language to talk about language.* As a result of the self-reflexive aspect of language, we can discuss how we phrased a question and consider whether better phrasing would have resulted in a more precise question and thus a more informative answer. For instance, another person listening to Greer's analysis might say, "Greer, the term *vulture* doesn't really describe that person accurately."

Collectively, we use language to create, maintain, and alter our environments. Yet, language can be thought of as a two-edged sword: The functions it performs carry a price in the rich possibilities for misunderstanding. To see how misunderstandings arise, we need to consider how language communicates meaning.

Language and Meaning

On the surface, the relationship between language and meaning seems perfectly clear: We select the correct word, and people will interpret our meanings correctly. In fact, the relationship between language and meaning is not nearly so simple. Why? For two reasons: The use of language is creative, and language must be learned.

When we speak, we use language to create new sentences that represent our meaning. Although on occasion we repeat other people's constructions to represent what we are thinking or feeling, most of our speech differs significantly from everyone else's. Language creativity is especially noticeable in children. When children don't know the common designation for a thought, they create one out of the context. For instance, children may refer to restaurants as "meal stores" or sirens as "scary whistles." But all of us create different ways of expressing shared experi-

*O*ne source of verbal misunderstanding is that language is not inborn. Each generation must learn anew how to use a culture's language to communicate meaning.

ences. To illustrate this idea, have three people who witnessed the same event describe what they saw. Although there will be many similarities, each description will reflect unique, creative approaches to the details.

Moreover, each generation within a culture must learn its language anew. But members of each generation may learn only a portion of the meanings of the previous generation. In addition, they are likely to create new words or different meanings for the words they learn. For instance, the third edition of *American Heritage Dictionary* contains 10,000 new words and usages such as *mediagenic* (attractive and appealing to viewers and readers of the news media) and *hip hop* (street subculture language, including rap).[4] And, as examples of our constantly giving new meanings to old words, in some parts of the country *stupid* means "cool," as in "That's a really stupid shirt"; *played* means "no longer relevant or rewarding," as in "This party is played, let's split"; and *dap* means "compliment," as in "We got lots of daps at the office today."[5]

Why do these changes occur? Language is arbitrary. We give meaning to the sounds that represent words and change the uses of words. Of course, meanings don't become a part of our "dictionary" until enough people in a language community accept the meaning. Thus, for every one of the past ten years, some 100,000 new words and changes in meanings have been noted, but the compilers of the *American Heritage Dictionary* believed that only 10,000 of them had gained enough support to become recognized as part of the language.

Changes also occur because of the need to reflect and create perceptions. If we encounter a situation that no word in our vocabulary can describe, we are likely either to form a new word or to use an old word in a new way to describe it.

Likewise, if we see an object that is different from any object we have a word for, we choose a new word to label it. Speakers of English in the 1940s would have no idea what the term *couch potato* means. Only recently has the perception of people who are chronic television viewers been rendered into language with this addition to modern dictionaries.

Denotation and Connotation

What is the meaning of a given word that a person uses in his or her conversation? You may think that's a straightforward question—the meaning is the dictionary definition. In fact, words have at least two kinds of meaning that communicators need to know about. Not only do words have a "naming" function (denotation); they also convey emotional overtones (connotation). Often these overtones play a significant role in communication. Let's consider both the denotation and connotation of words.

Denotation.   Denotation is the direct, explicit meaning people give to a word; in short, denotation is the meaning given in a dictionary. But even denotation is a more complex concept than we may think. Many words are defined differently in various dictionaries, have multiple meanings, and can change meaning; furthermore, the meaning of a word can be influenced by its context.

For example, no two dictionaries are going to give exactly the same meaning for an abstract word like *justice;* moreover, most words, and especially the words we use most often, have more than one distinct meaning. In addition, words change in meaning over time. Take the word *gay.* In the 1950s, gay meant joyous, merry, happy, or bright. Today, of course, "being gay" generally refers to a person's sexual preference. So, if you describe another person as "gay" and you mean happy or joyous, you are likely to be totally misunderstood.

Context has perhaps the most important effect on the denotation of a word. The position of a word in a sentence and the other words around it are likely to change the denotation. Think of the difference communicated between "Bryce plays a really mean drum" and "The way Bryce talked to Heather was downright mean." Or, suppose a man says to a woman, "Let's get together." The context of their relationship will affect what "get together" means. If the context isn't properly understood, the wording may lead to a real misunderstanding.

Connotation.   Whereas denotation refers to the standard dictionary meaning given to a word, connotation refers to the feelings or evaluations associated with a word. And although word denotation affects meaning and may create misunderstanding, sensitivity to word connotation may be even more important.

C. K. Ogden and I. A. Richards were among the first scholars to consider the misunderstandings resulting from the failure of communicators to realize that people's subjective reactions to words are a product of their life experiences.[6] For instance, in a speech to the PTA, Carla comments, "The Board of Education's recommendation for monitoring attendance is a real dog of a plan." The meaning of this comment depends far more on her audience's connotation of a plan that is a "dog" than it does on the dictionary definition of a dog as "a highly variable carnivorous domesticated mammal, probably descended from the common wolf." Similarly, when Melissa whispers to Trisha "Jessica had an abortion last week," Trisha's reaction to the news depends far more on her connotation of the word *abortion* than on its denotation.

What is the value of this kind of knowledge to you in your verbal communication? Suppose you are talking with people about such problems as crime, teenage pregnancies, drugs, AIDS, and welfare. You will need to be very careful how you use such words as *liberal, conservative, police officer, taxes, homeless, gay rights,* and *obscenity,* to name but a few. You may recall that in the 1992 presidential campaign, Bill Clinton had to work very hard to defuse George Bush's accusation that he was a typical "liberal." Now there is nothing inherently wrong with being either liberal or conservative—both words denote credible political positions. But by making an issue of the "L" word, Bush sought to capitalize on such negative connotations as "free spending" and "soft on crime" that had worked so well in his campaign against Michael Dukakis four years earlier.

Practice in Denotation and Connotation

By Yourself

1. Compile a list of current slang or "in" words. Discuss how the meanings you assign to these words differ from the meanings your parents or grandparents assign to them (for example, "He's bad!").

2. Write your own definition of each of the following words; then go to a dictionary and check how closely your definition matches the dictionary's.

building	justice	love	ring	success
band	glass	peace	freedom	honor

In Groups

1. Working with others in groups, select several common nouns such as *college* and *industry.* Each person should list at least five adjectives that he or she associates with the word. When you have finished, compare the results. In what ways are your meanings (the connotations the words have for you) different?

2. Stage an event for the class, such as a person coming into class during the professor's lecture to check whether the shades are working correctly. At the end of the event, send three people into the hall. Then call each in individually to describe the event. Afterward, discuss the creativity in language shown by the three observers.

Speaking Clearly

Clarity is basic to effective communication, whether the setting is interpersonal, group, or public speaking. We want to choose our language with care to improve the chances that the messages we intend to send are the messages that our listeners

"See what I mean? You're never sure just where you stand with them."

receive. Unclear language gives a listener such a range of possible meanings to choose from that shared meaning may be impossible. Furthermore, unclear language runs the risk of frustrating the listener and arousing unintended emotional reactions.

You can clarify your language by selecting precise, specific, and concrete words and by dating and indexing generalizations.

Precision

Selecting the most precise word means selecting the word that most accurately expresses your meaning. Too often we tend to get sloppy. We use a word that isn't quite right, hoping that our listeners will understand the point anyway. Suppose that in a finance committee discussion on budgetary problems in your organization you said, "The problem lies with our inventory." *Inventory* is a very precise word that means "any idle resource that is waiting to be used." If the problem really is a matter of product marketing or sales strategies, "inventory" fails to convey the meaning intended.

Precision is especially important when you are trying to communicate a specific shade of meaning. Suppose that, in speaking about a politician's defense of her principal adviser, who has been accused of mishandling campaign funds, you say "What she's trying to get is a complete acquittal." Notice how the meaning of that sentence changes if, instead of *acquittal,* you use *vindication* or *whitewashing.* Or take the sentence "Quentin said that we need a new approach to the problem." Notice the changes in meaning if instead of *said,* you use *hinted, indicated, suggested, insisted,* or *shouted.* Notice, too, the subtle shifts in meaning if you substitute a more precise word for *new,* such as *revised, fresh,* or *innovative.*

Specificity and Concreteness

Whereas speaking precisely means selecting words that give the most accurate image, speaking specifically and concretely means selecting words that put that image in sharp focus. Specific words indicate a single item within a category; concrete words give a single representation of an abstract concept or value. Often the first words that come to mind when we speak are general and abstract. Using such words forces the listener to choose from many possible images rather than picturing a single, focused image. The more listeners are called on to provide their own images, the more they will see meanings different from what we intend. For instance, if Nevah says that Ruben is a "blue-collar worker," you may picture an unlimited number of occupations that fall within this broad category. If, instead, she says he's a "construction worker," the number of possible images you can picture is reduced. And if she says "a bulldozer operator," your image snaps into focus.

The terms *general* and *specific* refer to categories, whereas *abstract* and *concrete* refer to ideas or values. Concrete language turns an abstract idea or value into one that appeals to our senses; it not only conveys information but also helps us form mental pictures. Sometimes you can make the image more concrete with a better word. Thus, the word *talk* is abstract, but *rant* is concrete: it brings to mind a type of talk that we can visualize. At other times you can make the image more concrete by adding an example. When Linda says "Rashad is very loyal," the meaning of *loyal* (faithful to an idea, person, company, and so on) may still appear fuzzy to the listener. To avoid ambiguity and confusion, Linda might add, "He never criticizes a friend behind her back." By expressing the concept of loyalty through a concrete example, she increases the likelihood that her listeners will understand what she means.

Semanticists speak of levels of abstraction. In many instances, you can take an idea from a general, abstract level and move it to a specific, concrete level through a series of words. For example, in talking about workers, we could write down a sequence that moved from the general term *worker* to *blue-collar worker* to *construction worker* to *construction vehicle operator* to *bulldozer operator* (see also Figure 3.1).

Clarifying language often requires using both more precise and more specific and concrete words. Suppose you were reporting the graduation rate of athletes in a speech to a community group. You might say, "At our school, some athletes are graduating about on time, but a whole lot of them aren't." In this context, "some athletes," "about on time," and "a whole lot" are neither precise nor specific. The range of what people might understand by "some," "about," and "a whole lot" is too wide. See how much clearer the sentence would be if you said, "At State University, roughly 60 percent of athletes on scholarship graduate within five years of the time they started. The problem is that in such 'revenue' sports as football and men's basketball, the number drops to under 30 percent." As this example shows, being precise and specific can involve doing research to nail down exact facts and figures.

Are precision and specificity/concreteness necessary in every communication context? Perhaps not. When you and a friend are engaging in informal, "for the fun of it" interaction, the need for clarity may be less. However, in a conflict situation where

Figure 3.1 *Levels of abstraction*

the other person may be looking for anything to fight about, or in a public speech identifying problems with affirmative action legislation, precise, specific, concrete language is indeed a necessity. Since you probably need to speak more clearly in general, why not try to use language that is as clear as possible in all situations? You will then be more likely to express yourself clearly "when it really matters."

Improving Precision and Specificity/Concreteness

Two ways to learn to speak more precisely and specifically are (1) building your working vocabulary and (2) practicing a structured brainstorming model.

Vocabulary Building. How clearly you speak, and therefore how well you will be understood, depends on your vocabulary. In general, the smaller the vocabulary, the greater will be the potential difficulty in communicating effectively. As a speaker with a meager vocabulary, you have fewer choices from which to select the word you want; as a listener, you are limited in your ability to understand the words that others use. Thus, the richer your vocabulary, the more accurate your communication is likely to be. Although precise, specific wording does not ensure effective communication (the person to whom you are speaking may not have a mastery of a particular word, or other contextual factors may interfere), you are more likely to communicate effectively if your choice is precise and specific.

One way to increase your vocabulary is to use a basic vocabulary book such as *Word Smart,* by Adam Robinson and the staff of the *Princeton Review,* a book designed for SAT and GRE preparation.[7] Or you could complete the "Word Power" feature in *The Reader's Digest* magazine. By completing this monthly quiz and learning the words with which you are not familiar, you can increase your vocabulary by as many as twenty words per month.

A second way to increase your vocabulary is to take a more active role in working with the words you read and hear every day. You can begin by noting words that people use in their conversations with you that you are not able to define precisely. For instance, suppose Jack says, "I was inundated with phone calls today!" If you can't define *inundated,* you could ask Jack what he meant. Or you could make a note of the word, look up its meaning at the first opportunity, and then go back over what Jack said to see whether the dictionary meaning matches his usage. Most dictionaries define *inundated* with synonyms such as *overwhelmed* or *flooded.* If you then say to yourself, "Jack was inundated—overwhelmed or flooded—with phone calls today," you will tend to remember that meaning and apply it the next time you hear the word. You can follow the same procedure in your reading. As you are reading today's assignment in one of your courses, circle or jot down any words whose meanings you are unsure of. After you have finished the assignment, look them up. If you follow this practice faithfully, you will soon increase your vocabulary noticeably.

Although a person with a relatively small vocabulary can communicate most ideas clearly (of the 150,000 words in *Webster's Ninth New Collegiate Dictionary,* some 5,000 of them make up 98 percent of the words in most of the books we read[8]), a person with a 50,000- to 60,000-word vocabulary has many more choices available for expressing complex ideas and shades of meaning as exactly as possible.

Structured Brainstorming.   A second way to develop clarity in speaking is to consciously use structured brainstorming during practice sessions. *Brainstorming* is an uncritical, nonevaluative process of generating ideas, much like the old word-association process. For example, when you are trying to think of more precise or more specific and concrete words for music, you might brainstorm *classical, nostalgic, big band, rock, heavy metal,* and *new age.*

This process of brainstorming can be used to increase your precision, specificity, and concreteness, as follows: (1) As you talk, quickly assess whether a word or phrase you used is less precise or less specific/concrete than it should be. (2) Pause to mentally brainstorm alternative choices. (3) Select a more precise or more specific/concrete word.

For example, in a speech about problems in registration, your first thought might be to say "Preregistration is so bad." At that point stop and ask yourself, What word can I use that would be more precise than "bad"? Brainstorm other words, such as *painful, frustrating,* and *demeaning.* Then restate the sentence: "Preregistration is so frustrating." Or suppose you were describing the action in a recent basketball game. You might consider saying "The game was really sloppy." Stop. Brainstorm some words that would be more specific than "game." *Offense? Dribbling? Passing?* Then restate the sentence: "The passing was really sloppy."

Improving language skills requires hard work, and the brainstorming process should only be done consciously in practice, at least initially. As you gain skill with the process, you may find that you are able to make such adjustments in everyday conversation, group communication, and in public speaking. For instance, in your speaking, you might state ideas in the following ways:

"I think that many of the boss's statements are very [split-second pause while thinking: I want the word that means 'know-it-all'] dogmatic."

"To move these things, we'll need a van—I'm sorry, I don't mean van, I mean one of those extra-large station wagons."

"Mike was just a jerk yesterday—well, I guess I mean he was inconsiderate."

"I agree Pauline is a tough manager, but I think she's a good one because she is fair—she treats everyone exactly alike."

When we are relaxed and confident, our word choice usually flows smoothly and is likely to be most effective. When we are under pressure in group decision making or public speaking, however, our ability to select the best symbols to convey our thoughts is likely to deteriorate. For example, a math professor might say to the class, "We all remember that the numerator is on the bottom and the denominator is on the top of the fraction, so when we divide fractions. . . ." "Professor," a voice from the third row interrupts, "you said the numerator is on the bottom and. . . ." "Is that what I said?" the professor replies. "Well, you know what I meant!" Did everyone in the class know? Maybe not.

You will really know that you have made strides in improving precision, specificity, and concreteness when you find that your language is precise and specific even under pressure.

Dating Generalizations

To *date generalizations* means to specify a time referent that indicates when a given fact was true or known to be true. We draw conclusions based on information. If the information is inaccurate, the conclusions drawn from that information are likely to be inaccurate as well. A common source of inaccuracy is giving the impression that information is current when in fact it may be outdated. For instance, Parker says, "I'm going to be transferred to Henderson City." Laura replies, "Good luck—they've had some real trouble with their schools." On the basis of Laura's statement, Parker may worry about the effect his move will have on his children. What he doesn't know is that Laura's information about this problem in Henderson City is five years old! Henderson City still may have problems, but then, it may not. Had Laura replied, "Five years ago, I know they had some real trouble with their schools. I'm not sure what the situation is now, but you may want to check," Parker would look at the information differently.

Nearly everything changes with time. Some changes are imperceptible; others are so extensive as to make old information inaccurate, obsolete, and even dangerous. To date your generalizations: (1) Consider when you knew the information about an object, a person, or a place to be true. (2) If your statement is not based on current information, be sure to include in your statement a reference to when you knew the information was valid.

Consider each of the following examples. Those on the left contain undated generalizations; those on the right contain dated generalizations.

Palm Springs is really popular with the college crowd.	When we were in Palm Springs *two years ago,* it was really popular with the college crowd.

Professor Powell brings great enthusiasm to her teaching.	Professor Powell brings great enthusiasm to her teaching—at least she did *last quarter* in communication theory.
The Beast is considered the most exciting roller coaster in the country.	*Five years ago,* the Beast was considered the most exciting roller coaster in the country.
You think Mary's depressed? I'm surprised. She seemed her regular high-spirited self when I talked with her.	You think Mary's depressed? I'm surprised. She seemed her regular high-spirited self when I talked with her *the day before yesterday.*

We have no power to prevent change. But we can increase the effectiveness of our messages if we verbally acknowledge the reality of change by dating the statements we make.

Indexing Generalizations

Indexing is a companion skill to dating. By dating generalizations, we acknowledge differences caused by the passage of time; through indexing, we acknowledge the innate differences among groups of people, objects, or places. *Indexing,* then, is the mental or verbal practice of accounting for individual differences that guards against the tendency to make unwarranted generalizations.

Generalizing allows people to use what they have learned from one experience and apply it to another. So, when Glenda learns that tomatoes and squash grow better if the ground is fertilized, she reasons that fertilizing will help all of her vegetables grow better. Likewise, when Miguel notices that his girlfriend seems to enjoy the fragrance of the new after-shave he is wearing, he is likely to wear it again when they are together. Glenda and Miguel have used what they learned from one experience and applied it to another—they have generalized.

You'll recall from the last chapter that misuse of generalization, stereotyping, contributes to perceptual inaccuracies because it ignores individual differences. Thus, just because men have greater strength in general than do women does not mean that Max (one man) is stronger than Barbara (one woman). Likewise, just because Jack, a German, is industrious does not mean either that all Germans are industrious or that Don, who is also German, is industrious.

Now that we've considered the need to account for individual differences, let's see how the skill of indexing is used. Technically, indexing calls for acknowledging differences by mentally assigning numbers to each member of a class. So in the class of men, we have man_1, man_2, man_3, and so forth; in the class of Chevrolets, we have $Chevrolet_1$, $Chevrolet_2$, $Chevrolet_3$, and so forth. Of course, in real life, people don't index by number.

To index generalizations: (1) Consider whether what you want to say is about a specific object, person, or place or whether it is a generalization about a class to which the object, person, or place belongs. (2) If what you want to say is a generalization, qualify it appropriately so that your assertion does not go beyond the evidence that supports it.

Here are several statements that illustrate the process of indexing. Those on the left are generalizations; those on the right are indexed examples.

Because men are stronger than women, Max is stronger than Barbara.	*In general,* men are stronger than women, so Max is probably stronger than Barbara.
State's got to have a good economics department; the university is ranked among the top twenty in the nation.	Because State's among the top twenty schools in the nation, the economics department should be a good one *although it may be an exception.*
Jack is sure to be outgoing; Don is, and they're both Joneses.	Jack is likely to be outgoing because his brother Don is (they're both Joneses), *but Jack could be different.*
Your Chevrolet should go 50,000 miles before you need a brake job; Jerry's did.	Your Chevrolet may well go 50,000 miles before you need a brake job; Jerry's did, *but of course, all Chevrolets aren't the same.*

All people generalize at one time or another, but by indexing statements, we can avoid the problems that hasty generalization sometimes creates.

Cultural Differences

Verbal communication rules and expectations vary from culture to culture. Much of this variation may be attributed to what E. T. Hall describes as low- versus high-context communication.[9] According to Hall, a high-context communication message is one in which "most of the information is either in the physical context or internalized in the person, while very little is in the coded, explicit, transmitted part of the message." In contrast, a low-context communication message is one in which "the mass of information is vested in the explicit code."[10] Various national cultures can be placed on a continuum between the two extremes. The culture of the United States is classified near the lower end with the cultures of Western Europe. Most Asian cultures fall toward the high-context end.[11]

What does this mean to students of communication? On a verbal communication dimension, members of low-context cultures tend to communicate in a direct fashion, whereas members of high-context cultures tend to communicate in an indirect fashion. Thus, people from Western, or low-context, cultures tend to favor precision in language, whereas people from Eastern, or high-context, cultures tend to favor ambiguities.[12] Typically, Asians are comfortable talking for hours without clearly expressing an opinion; they can be suspicious of direct verbal expressions of love and respect. In contrast, people from low-context cultures prize clear and direct communication. Their approach may be characterized by such expressions as "Say what you mean" and "Don't beat around the bush."[13]

Problems with clarity across cultures are at times humorous, for words that have one precise or specific meaning in one language or subculture may have an entirely different precise or specific meaning in another. For instance, Chevrolet created cross-cultural misunderstanding on a large scale when it marketed its Nova model in Latin America. Sales were terrible because Chevrolet didn't realize that Nova (*no va*) means "no go" in Spanish. Likewise, a student reported to his professor that he suffered some embarrassment in South Africa when, in response to his host's asking whether he would like more food, he replied, "I'm stuffed." He didn't know why his host thought the response so humorous until his host told him that in his culture the expression "I'm stuffed" means "I'm pregnant."

People who speak different languages expect to have some problem communicating and thus seem to take extra care to keep that barrier from becoming insurmountable. Surprisingly, language becomes a greater barrier for two people from different cultures who are speaking the same language because they tend to believe they mean the same things when they use the same words. For example, if a person says that the government wants what is "best for the people," it would seem that others should have no difficulty understanding what is meant. Yet "best for the people" can and does mean many different things depending on one's politics, priorities, and so on. When someone from another culture uses a word and you perceive that word as particularly important to understanding, you might ask for concrete examples so that you can be sure of what the person means.

Gender Differences

Although men and women in the United States may appear to be speaking the same language, that language itself is the source of gender variations. Edwin and Shirley Ardener argue that the language of the culture of the United States has an inherent male bias, meaning that men have created the meanings for the group. As a result, the feminine voice has been "muted."[14] This means that women tend to be less expressive in public situations than men and, more important, tend to monitor their own communications more intensely than men.

In *Gender & Communication,* Pearson, Turner, and Todd-Mancillas summarize differences in language usage between men and women that seem consistent with the "muted group" theory.[15] They note that women tend to use both more intensifiers and more hedges and tag questions than men. *Intensifiers* are words that intensify, or give strength to, the words being described. Thus, women are likely to make far greater use of such words as *awfully, quite,* and *so. Hedges* are words, such as *somewhat, perhaps,* or *maybe,* that soften meaning. *Tag questions* are questions relating to the statement just made—for example, "That was a really powerful speech, wasn't it?" or "They all had the same tutor, didn't they?" Even though we all use tag questions at times when we are not certain or when we are trying to get more information, women tend to use them far more than men, perhaps to appear less dogmatic in their communication.

Julia Wood sees these differences in language as representing contrasting views of the role of communication for women and men. For women, she says, "communication is a primary way to establish and maintain relationships with others"; for men, communication is used as a means of "exerting control, preserving independence, and enhancing status."[16] Yet, specific language differences between men and women are not actually as different as the stereotypes of their language. For instance, men are perceived as using more sexual or profane language than women, when in reality few descriptive studies support this conclusion.[17]

Practice with Clarity

By Yourself

1. For each word listed, try to find three words or phrases that are more specific or more concrete.

implements	building	nice	education
clothes	colors	chair	bad
happy	stuff	things	car

2. Make the following statements clearer by editing italicized words that are not precise or not specific and concrete:

"You know I love basketball. Well, I'm practicing *a lot* because I want *to get better.*"

"Paula, I'm really *bummed out. Everything* is *going down the tubes.* You know what I mean?"

"Well, she just does *these things* to tick me off. Like, just *a whole lot of stuff*—and she knows it!"

"I just bought a beautiful *outfit*—I mean, it is really in style. You'll love it."

"I've really got to remember to bring *my things* the next time I visit."

In Groups

Have two members of the group discuss a topic from the ones listed here. The rest of the group should observe when dating and indexing are used, how well they are being used, and when they should have been used. Each person in the group should have an opportunity to practice.

food preferences	cars	minority groups in college
equal opportunity laws	politicians	college course requirements
job interviewers	wedding rituals	political parties

Speaking Appropriately

During the past few years, we have seen a great controversy over "political correctness," especially on college campuses. Although several issues germane to the debate on political correctness go beyond the scope of this chapter, at the heart of this controversy is the question of what language behaviors are appropriate—and what language behaviors are inappropriate.

Speaking *appropriately* means using language that adapts to the needs, interests, knowledge, and attitudes of the listener and avoiding language that alienates. Appropriate language has the positive value of cementing the bond of trust between the parties in a communication transaction. When people like and trust you, they are likely to believe you. The more hostile people are to you and your ideas, the more care you need to take to use language that is sensitive to their needs. Yet, under strain, or in your eagerness to make a point, you can sometimes say things you do not really mean or express feelings that are unlikely to be accepted by strangers. If you do that, you may lose all that you have gained. In this section, we look specifically at appropriate and inappropriate language.

Formal versus Informal Language

Language is appropriate when it is neither too formal nor too informal for the situation. In Chapter 1, we talked about the communication rules that guide our communication behavior. One of those rules is to adapt language to the specific person or group we are addressing. Thus, in an interpersonal setting, we are likely to use more informal language when we are talking with our best friend and more formal language when we are talking with our parents. In a group or public-speaking setting, we are likely to use more informal language when we are talking with our peers and more formal language when we are talking with strangers. In each of these situations, the differences in our language are appropriate.

Freedom from Jargon and Unnecessary Technical Expressions

Language is appropriate when it is free of jargon and unnecessary technical expressions. Many of us become so immersed in our work or hobbies that we forget that people who are not in our same line of work or who do not share the same hobbies are not going to understand language that seems to be such a part of our daily communication. For instance, when a computer whiz gives a speech to a general audience about computer hardware, the whiz is going to want to carry on about bits, bytes, RAM, and other technical jargon. But unless the whiz can learn to express ideas in language that the audience understands, little communication will take place. In short, anytime you are talking with people outside your specific work or hobby area, you need to carefully explain, if not abandon, the technical jargon and speak in language that is recognized by the person to whom you are talking.

Shoe, by Jeff MacNelly, reprinted by permission: Tribune Media Services.

Sensitivity

Language is appropriate when it is sensitive to usages that others perceive as offensive. Some of the mistakes in language that we make result from using expressions that are perceived as sexist, racist, or otherwise biased—that is, any language that is perceived as belittling any person or group of people by virtue of their sex, race, age, handicap, or other identifying characteristic. Two of the most prevalent linguistic uses that communicate insensitivity are generic language and nonparallel language (see "I Now Pronounce You Man and Wife" on pages 74 and 75).

Generic Language.   Generic language is a problem because it excludes a group of people, grammatically or connotatively, on the basis of sex. English-language examples include the generic use of *he* and *man*.

Generic He.   Traditionally, English grammar called for the use of the masculine pronoun *he* to stand for the entire class of humans regardless of sex. So, in the past, standard English called for such usage as "When a person shops, he should have a clear idea of what he wants to buy." Even though such statements are grammatically correct, they are now considered sexist because they inherently exclude females. Despite traditional usage, it would be hard to maintain that we picture people of both sexes when we hear the word he.

   Guideline: Do not construct sentences that use only male pronouns when no gender-specific reference is intended. You can generally avoid this usage in one of two ways. One is by using plurals. For instance, instead of saying, "Since a doctor has high status, his views may be believed regardless of topic," you could say, "Since doctors have high status, their views may be believed regardless of topic." The second method is to use both the male and female pronoun: "Since a doctor has high status, his or her views may be believed regardless of topic." These changes may seem small, but they can make the difference between alienating or not alienating the people with whom you are speaking.

Generic Man.   A second problem results from the traditional reliance on the use of generic *man*. Many words have become a common part of our language that are inherently sexist because they seem to apply to only one gender. Consider the term

"I Now Pronounce You Man and Wife"

Language not only expresses cultural views of gender, it can reinforce those biases.

- "I now pronounce you man and wife."
- Bob babysat his son while his wife attended a meeting.
- Looking sharp with an updated wardrobe and a chic hairstyle, Geraldine Ferraro is on the campaign trail again.
- Freshmen find it difficult to adjust to college life.
- We reached a gentlemen's agreement on how to proceed.

These five sentences are commonplace ones we might hear or read at any time. Each one reflects cultural assumptions about gender. Did any of the sentences bother you? In the first one, did you notice that "man" is portrayed as an individual, while "wife" is defined only by her relationship to the man? In the second sentence, the use of the word *babysat* implies that the father was performing a special service, one we usually pay for; have you ever heard of a mother's time with her children called babysitting? The third sentence defines Ferraro in terms of appearance and deflects attention from her qualifications as a political candidate. Unless the fourth sentence refers to first-year students at an all-male school, the word *freshmen* includes only those students who are male. Finally, the term *gentlemen's agreement* expresses the cultural association between men and professional activities.

Male generic language is language that purports to include both women and men, yet specifically refers only to men. Examples are nouns such as *businessmen, chairmen, mailmen,* and *mankind,* and pronouns such as *he* to refer to both women and men. Some people think it is understood that women are included in terms such as *mankind* and *chairman.* However, research demonstrates conclusively that masculine generics are perceived as referring predominantly or exclusively to men.

Responding to the incontestable evidence that male generics distort perceptions, the newest *Webster's Dictionary* follows a policy of avoiding male generics and other sexist language. In addition to avoiding man-linked words, the new dictionary cautions against other ways of defin-

man-made. What this really means is that a product was produced by human beings, but its underlying connotation is that a male human being made the item. Using such terms when speaking about all human beings is troubling, but using them to describe the behavior or accomplishments of women (as in "Sally creates and arranges man-made flowers") is ludicrous.

ing men as the standard and women as the exception. For instance, it discourages spotlight, which is the practice of highlighting a person's sex. Terms such as *lady doctor* and *woman lawyer* define women as the exception in professions and thereby reinforce the idea that men are the standard.

A second way that language expresses cultural views of gender is by defining men and women in different ways. Women tend to be defined by appearance and/or relationships with others, while men are more typically defined by activities, accomplishments, and/or positions. Differences in how women and men are defined reflect society's views of women as decorative, emotional, and sexual and men as independent, active, and serious.

Media offer countless examples of defining women by their physical qualities. Headlines announce "Blonde wins election." Stories on female athletes often emphasize wardrobes ("Chris is changing her style with a snappy new outfit"), slimmed-down bodies ("She's gotten back in shape and is looking good on the field"), and changed hairstyles ("When she stepped on the court, fans noticed her lightened hair"), while stories about male athletes focus on their athletic abilities ("He sunk two dream shots").

Our language also reflects society's view of women as defined by their relationships. For example, the titles *Miss* and *Mrs.* designate a woman's marital status. There are no parallel titles for men. The alternative term *Ms.* to designate a woman without identifying her marital status is a relatively new addition to the language and not yet fully accepted. It was not until 1987 that *The New York Times* would print "Ms." if a woman preferred that title. The extent to which our society defines women by marriage and family is further evidenced in the still-prevalent tradition of a wife adopting her husband's name on marrying. Symbolically, she exchanges her individual identity for one based on her relationship to a man: Mrs. John Smith.

Some women choose to retain their own names when they marry. A number of men and women adopt hyphenated names such as Johnson-Smith to symbolize the family heritage of both partners. In coming years, we will doubtless see other alternatives to traditional naming practices. Their existence reminds us of the importance we attach to naming and of our power to use language creatively. ■

SOURCE: Julia T. Wood, *Gendered Lives* (Belmont, CA: Wadsworth, 1994), pp. 123–129.

Guideline: Avoid using words that have built-in sexism, such as *policeman, postman, chairman, man-made,* and *mankind.* For most expressions of this kind, you can use or create suitable alternatives. For instance, for the first three examples, you can use *police officer, mail carrier,* and *chairperson.* For man-made, you might substitute *synthetic.* For *mankind,* you may need to change the construction—for example, from "All of mankind benefits" to "All the people in the world benefit."

Nonparallel Language.　Because it treats groups of people differently, nonparallel language is also belittling. Two common forms of nonparallelism are marking and unnecessary association.

Marking.　Marking means adding sex, race, age, or other designations unnecessarily to a general word. For instance, *doctor* is a word representing any person with a medical degree. To describe Jones as a doctor is to treat Jones linguistically as a member of the class of doctors. For example, you might say, "Jones, a doctor, contributed a great deal to the campaign." If, however, you identified Jones as "a woman doctor" (or a black doctor, or an old doctor, or a handicapped doctor), you would be marking. By marking, you may be perceived to be trivializing the person's role by laying emphasis on an irrelevant characteristic. For instance, if you say "Jones is a really good female doctor" (or black doctor, or old doctor, or handicapped doctor), you may be intending to praise Jones. But your listeners can interpret the sentence as saying that Jones is a good doctor, for a woman (or a black, or an old person, or a handicapped person), but not necessarily as good as a male doctor (or a white, young, or nonhandicapped doctor).

Guideline: Avoid markers. If it is relevant to identify a person by sex, race, age, and so on, do so, but leave such markers out of your labeling when they are irrelevant. One test of whether a characteristic is relevant and appropriate is whether you would mention the person's sex, race, or age (and so on) regardless of what sex, race, or age the person happens to be. It is relevant to specify "female doctor," for example, only if in that context it would be equally relevant to specify "male doctor." In general, leave sex, race, age, and other markers out of your labeling.

Unnecessary Association.　Another form of nonparallelism is to emphasize one person's association with another when you are not talking about the other person. Very often you will hear a speaker say something like "Gladys Thompson, whose husband is CEO of Acme Inc., is the chairperson for this year's United Way campaign." In response to this sentence, you might say that the association of Gladys Thompson with her husband gives further credentials to Gladys Thompson. But using the association may be seen to imply that Gladys Thompson is important not because of her own accomplishment but because of her husband's. The following illustrates a more flagrant example of unnecessary association: "Dorothy Davis, the award-winning principal at Central High School, and wife of Bill Davis, a local contractor, is chairperson for this year's Minority Scholarship campaign." Here Bill Davis's occupation and relationship to Dorothy Davis are clearly irrelevant. In either case, the pairing takes away from the person who is supposed to be the focus.

Guideline: Avoid associating a person irrelevantly with others. If the person has done or said something noteworthy, you should recognize it without making unnecessary associations.

Avoiding Insensitive Language

You've heard children shout, "Sticks and stones may break my bones, but words will never hurt me." This rhyme is popular among children perhaps because they know it is a lie but it gives them a defense against cruel name-calling. Whether we admit it or not, words do hurt—sometimes permanently. Think of the great personal damage done to individuals throughout history as a result of being called "hillbilly," "nigger," "fag," or "yid." Think of the fights started by one person calling another's sister or girlfriend a "whore." Of course, we all know that it is not the words alone that are so powerful; it is the context of the words—the situation, the feelings of the participants, the time, the place, or the tone of voice. You may recall circumstances in which a friend called you a name or used a four-letter word to describe you and you did not even flinch; you may also recall other circumstances in which someone else made you furious by calling you something far less offensive.

Very few people can escape all unfair language. By monitoring your usage, however, you can guard against frustrating your attempts to communicate by assuming that others will react to your language the same way you do, and you can guard against saying or doing things that offend others and perpetuate outdated sex roles, racial stereotypes, and other biased language. Here again, you can make use of structured brainstorming: (1) Assess whether the word or phrase used is inappropriate. (2) Pause to mentally brainstorm alternatives. (3) Select a more appropriate word.

We should always be aware that our language has repercussions. When we do not understand or are not sensitive to our listeners' frame of reference, we may state our ideas in language that distorts the intended communication. Many times a single inappropriate sentence may be enough to ruin an entire interaction. For instance, if you say "And we all know the problem originates downtown," you may be alluding to the city government. However, if your listeners associate downtown not with the seat of government but with the residential area of a particular ethnic or social group, the sentence will have an entirely different meaning to them. Being specific will help you avoid such problems; recognizing that some words communicate far more than their dictionary meanings will help even more.

Practice with Appropriateness

By Yourself

1. Develop nonsexist alternatives to the following:

fireman	foreman	serviceman	brakeman
airman	stewardess	craftsman	repairman
councilman	doorman	night watchman	hostess
coed	waitress	bellman	anchorman

2. Tape-record at least ten minutes of a conversation that you have with a friend or a family member. Talk about a subject that you hold strong views about: affirmative action, welfare, college fees, taxes, immigration, candidates for office. Be sure to get the permission of the other person before you tape. At first you may feel self-conscious about having a recorder going, but as you get into the discussion it's quite likely that you'll be able to converse normally.

Play back the tape and take notes of sections where your language might have been clearer. Using these notes, write better expressions of your ideas for each section you noted by using more precise and specific/concrete language and by dating and indexing generalizations.

Replay the tape. This time take notes on any racist, sexist, or other biased expressions that you used. Using these notes, write more appropriate expressions for the ones you used.

Write a paragraph or two that describes what you have learned about your use of language from this experience.

In Groups

Have group members share incidents in which the bias in another person's language was offensive. How might that language have been amended to prevent the offense?

Summary

Language is a system of symbols used for communicating. Through language, we designate, label, and define; evaluate; talk about things outside our immediate experience; and talk about language itself.

You will be a more effective communicator if you recognize that language symbols are arbitrary, that language is learned and is creative, and that language and perception are interrelated.

The denotation of a word is its dictionary meaning. Despite the ease with which we can check a dictionary meaning, word denotation can still present problems because most words have more than one dictionary meaning, changes in meanings occur faster than dictionaries are revised, words take on different meanings as they are used in different contexts, and meanings can become obscured as words become more abstract.

The connotation of a word is the emotional and value significance the word has for the listener. Regardless of how a dictionary defines a word, we carry with us meanings that stem from our experience with the object, thought, or action the word represents.

You can improve your clarity of language by selecting the most precise and the most specific and concrete word possible and by dating and indexing generalizations. Relevant skills include vocabulary building and structured brainstorming. Clarity of communication can also be affected by cultural and gender differences.

Speaking appropriately means using language adapted to the needs, interests, knowledge, and attitudes of the listener and avoiding language that alienates. Inappropriate language can be minimized by avoiding such exclusionary usages as generic male references and such nonparallel usages as marking and unnecessary association.

Suggested Readings

Bates, Jefferson D. *Writing With Precision,* 6th ed. Washington, DC: Acropolis Books, 1993. Although this is primarily a writing book, much of the advice is equally important for verbal skills and effective oral communication.

Gudykunst, William B. *Bridging Differences: Effective Intergroup Communication,* 2d ed. Newbury Park, CA: Sage, 1994. Generally good overall advice on communicating with strangers, with several sections that speak specifically to differences in approaches to verbal communication.

Hopper, Joan N., and Carter-Wells, Jo Ann. *The Language of Learning.* Belmont, CA: Wadsworth, 1994. In addition to chapters on language and general vocabulary building, the book focuses on fields of study, presenting key words that provide a firm foundation for intelligent conversation in those fields.

Morehead, Philip D. *The New American Roget's College Thesaurus in Dictionary Form.* New York: New American Library, 1985. A book of synonyms that can be very useful in vocabulary building.

Wood, Julia T. *Gendered Lives: Communication, Gender, and Culture.* Belmont, CA: Wadsworth, 1994. A refreshing and readable account of the complexities of communication between men and women.

Notes

1. I. A. Richards, *The Philosophy of Rhetoric* (New York: Oxford University Press, 1965), p. 3.
2. Wood, Julia T. *Gendered Lives: Communication, Gender, & Culture* (Belmont, CA: Wadsworth, 1994), p. 129.
3. Richards, p. 3.
4. *The American Heritage Dictionary,* 3d ed. (Boston: Houghton Mifflin, 1992).
5. "Buzzwords," *Newsweek,* August 26, 1991, p. 6.
6. C. K. Ogden and I. A. Richards, *The Meaning of Meaning* (London: Kegan, Paul, Trench, Trubner, 1923).
7. Adam Robinson and the staff of the *Princeton Review, Word Smart* (New York: Villard Books, 1993).
8. I. S. P. Nation, *Teaching and Learning Vocabulary* (New York: Newbury House, 1990), p. 16.
9. E. T. Hall, *Beyond Culture* (New York: Doubleday, 1976).
10. Ibid., p. 91.
11. William B. Gudykunst and Young Yun Kim, *Communicating with Strangers: An Approach to Intercultural Communication,* 2d ed. (New York: McGraw-Hill, 1992), pp. 44–45.
12. Ibid., p. 158.
13. D. Levine, *The Flight from Ambiguity* (Chicago: University of Chicago Press, 1985), p. 28.
14. For a more complete explanation of muted group theory, see Stephen Littlejohn, *Theories of Human Communication,* 4th ed. (Belmont, CA: Wadsworth, 1992), pp. 241–243.
15. Judy Cornelia Pearson, Lynn H. Turner, and William Todd-Mancillas, *Gender and Communication,* 2d ed. (Dubuque, IA: Wm. C. Brown, 1991), pp. 106–121.
16. Wood, pp. 141, 143.
17. Pearson, Turner, and Todd-Mancillas, p. 108.

After you have read this chapter, you should be able to:

Contrast verbal and nonverbal communication

Discuss five ways in which body motions are used in communication

Describe the use of emblems, illustrators, affect displays, regulators, and adaptors

Define paralanguage and its major elements

Explain how clothing, touching behavior, and use of time affect self-presentation

Explain how the use of space affects communication

Discuss the ways in which temperature, lighting, and color affect communication

Nonverbal Communication

Marsha Collins steps into Houston's office and says, "I'm not going to be able to meet with you to talk about the report you wrote because I'm swamped with work."

In a speech to her constituents, Stephanie Morris, a candidate for Congress, says, "I want you to know I am committed to the needs of the people of this district."

How will Houston take Marsha Collins's excuse? The answer will be determined by how Houston interprets her vocal inflection and facial expression as much as by her words. Likewise, how will her constituents respond to Stephanie Morris's statement of commitment? Whether her audience believes her will depend on the look on her face, the gestures she makes, and the sound of her voice. In communication, as in so many matters, actions speak louder than words. Actions, in the form of nonverbal communication elements, are critical to the communication process. In fact, researchers have statistical support to show that as much as 65 percent of the social meaning in face-to-face communication may be carried in the nonverbal message.[1] Moreover, how we are perceived as communicators is based in part on our ability to use nonverbal skills appropriately.

In this chapter, we provide a framework for analyzing and improving nonverbal communication. We begin by studying the nature of nonverbal communication and the way verbal and nonverbal communication interrelate. We then look at the major elements of nonverbal communication: body motions, paralanguage, self-presentation, and management of the environment. Along the way, we consider cultural differences and suggest ways of using these elements more effectively in your own communication.

The Nature of Nonverbal Communication

Nonverbal communication includes both body motions and vocal sounds that are used regularly and intentionally by members of a social community.[2] It also includes the use of clothing, furniture, lighting, temperature, and color, all of which can affect the communication that takes place. Before considering these elements, however, let's see how nonverbal communication differs from verbal communication.

1. *Nonverbal communication is more ambiguous.* Nonverbal communication is ambiguous in part because nonverbal cues may be sent either intentionally or unintentionally and in part because the same behaviors can represent many different messages. For example, a person who smiles may intend to communicate a sense of friendliness. When a receiver interprets the smile as friendly, communication has taken place. But a smile can mean many other things, such as a cover-up for being ill at ease. At other times, a smile may have no communication intent—it may be a response to a random thought about something pleasant that happened earlier in the day. Nevertheless, other people will try to decode the smile and assign meaning to it.

2. *Nonverbal communication is continuous.* Verbal symbols begin when sound comes from the mouth and end when that sound stops. In contrast, nonverbal communication continues for as long as people are in one another's presence. For instance, suppose Parker is giving a speech to a local service organization to get them to vote for him for city council. From the moment he rises to speak, Parker is communicating. He may rush or stroll casually to the speaker's stand; he may have a soft or a cutting tone to his voice; he may have a smile or a frown on his face. All of these nonverbal behaviors affect how the audience will react to his candidacy.

© 1993 by Sidney Harris.

3. *Nonverbal communication is multichanneled.* Words come to us one at a time, in a single channel: we hear spoken words; we see printed or written words. Nonverbal cues, however, may be seen, heard, felt, smelled, or tasted, and several of these cues may occur simultaneously. For instance, if you tell a friend, "I'll go to bat for you," the meaning your friend receives depends not only on the words, but also on your tone of voice, your facial expressions, and your gestures.

4. *Nonverbal communication gives more insight into emotional states.* Whereas words do not necessarily communicate the depth of a person's feelings, nonverbal reactions do. For instance, when you hear that a close friend has disclosed damaging personal information about you that you discussed in confidence, your body will show some nonverbal sign of pain even if you say, "It's nothing." When something strikes you as funny, you may smile slightly or laugh loudly, depending on how amused you feel. When you are sad, the corner of your mouth may twitch or your eyes might fill with tears even though your words do not convey sadness. As a

Communicating without words: What is each of these people "saying"? How many specific nonverbal cues can you find that contribute to the message?

result, when verbal and nonverbal reactions seem to be in conflict, people are likely to place more stock in nonverbal cues.

   5. *The meanings of nonverbal communication are culturally determined.* Although people from around the world use many of the same nonverbal cues, they use them differently. For instance, a smile may mean positive experience, it may mean enjoyment with contact, it may mean saving of face. At the same time, even though languages differ so much that people are unable to understand the words of a person speaking a foreign language, they may well be able to understand some of what the person is thinking or feeling through nonverbal cues. Although all nonverbal signs don't carry the same meanings in every culture, there are many commonalities. For instance, people from different cultures often share the same facial expressions for expressing such emotions as happiness, anger, fear, and surprise. In fact, in their review of research, Ekman and Oster found "remarkable cross-cultural similarity in facial expressions and their interpretations."[3]

Now let us consider the various elements that comprise nonverbal communication.

Body Motions

Of all nonverbal behavior, you are probably most familiar with *kinesics,* the technical name for body motions. The major types of body motions are eye contact, facial expression, gesture, posture, and poise.

Eye Contact

Eye contact, also referred to as *gaze,* involves looking directly at the person or people with whom we are communicating. In addition to meeting psychological needs, eye contact enables us to monitor the effect of our communication. By maintaining eye contact, you can tell when a person is paying attention to your words, when a person is involved in what you are saying, whether what you are saying is causing anxiety, and whether the person you are talking with has something to hide.

The amount of eye contact differs from person to person and from setting to setting. Studies show that people are likely to look at each other 50 to 60 percent of the time as they converse interpersonally. For the talker, the average amount of eye contact is about 40 percent; for the listener, the average is nearer 70 percent.[4] Whether in interpersonal, group, or public-speaking situations, we generally maintain better eye contact when we are discussing topics with which we are comfortable, when we are genuinely interested in a person's comments or reactions, or when we are trying to influence the other person. Conversely, we tend to avoid eye contact when we are discussing topics that make us uncomfortable; when we lack interest in the topic or person; or when we are embarrassed, ashamed, or trying to hide something. Of course, these are only tendencies; some individuals are skilled in using eye contact and other cues deceptively.

Because people often judge others by the degree of eye contact, you want to ensure that your eye-contact behavior is perceived as appropriate. You may need to alter your behavior if you find that you maintain a less-than-normal amount of eye contact when you are interested in the person or topic of conversation, when you feel confident, or when you have no cause to feel shame or embarrassment. We will consider eye contact in more detail in Chapter 15, Presenting Your Speech.

Facial Expression

Facial expression involves the arrangement of facial muscles to communicate emotional states or reactions to messages. The three sets of muscles that we manipulate to form facial expressions are the brow and forehead; the eyes, eyelids, and root of the nose; and the cheeks, mouth, remainder of the nose, and chin.[5] Normally, our facial expressions mirror our thoughts or feelings. Paul Ekman and W. V. Friesen have discovered that across cultures people recognize those expressions conveying six basic emotions: happiness, sadness, surprise, fear, anger, and disgust.

Gesture

Gestures are the movements of hands, arms, and fingers that we use to describe or to emphasize. When a person says "about this high" or "nearly this round," we expect to see a gesture accompany the verbal description. Likewise, whether the setting is interpersonal, group, or public-speaking, when a person says "It's up to you to decide" or "We can't let this happen," pointing a finger, pounding the fist, or some other gesture often reinforces the point. People do vary, however, in the amount of gesturing that accompanies their speech—some people "talk with their hands" far more than others.

Posture

Posture involves the positioning and movement of the body. Changes in posture can also communicate. For instance, suddenly sitting upright and leaning forward show intensity of attention, standing up may signal "I'm done now," and turning one's back shows a cutting off of attention.

Poise

Poise refers to an overall control of the body that suggests an assurance of manner. As much as 20 percent of the population experiences a high degree of nervousness in encountering strangers, speaking in a group, and in public-speaking settings.[6] Others may be quite comfortable encountering strangers, but tense up in another setting such as speaking in a group or in public. For most people, nervousness decreases as they gain confidence in their ability to function well in the particular setting. Mastery of the skills discussed in this text should help you cope with the nervousness you may experience in differing communication situations. Because poise is so important to public speaking, we will discuss an aspect of poise called *communication anxiety* in Chapter 15, Presenting Your Speech.

Cultural and Gender Variations

While a majority of people in the United States and other Western cultures expect those with whom they are communicating to "look them in the eye," Samovar and Porter report in their review of research that direct eye contact is not a custom throughout the world.[7] For instance, in Japan, people are taught not to look at another's eyes, but at a position around the Adam's apple. Chinese, Indonesians, and rural Mexicans also lower their eyes as a sign of deference; to them, too much eye contact is a sign of bad manners. Arabs, in contrast, look directly into the eyes of the person with whom they are talking for long periods; to them, direct eye contact shows interest. There are also differences in use of eye contact in the various subcultures within the United States. For instance, African-Americans use more continuous eye contact than European-Americans when they are speaking, but less when they are listening.[8]

People of different cultures also show considerable variations in their use of gestures, movements, and facial expressions. Gestures in particular can assume completely different meanings. For instance, the forming of a circle with the thumb and forefinger, the OK sign in the United States, means zero or worthless in France, is a symbol for money in Japan, a curse in some Arab countries, and an obscene gesture in Germany, Brazil, and Australia.[9] In addition, displays of emotion also vary. For instance, in some Eastern cultures, people have been socialized to deintensify emotional behavior cues, whereas members of other cultures have been socialized to amplify their displays of emotions. These cultural differences in emotional displays are often reflected in the interpretation that can be given to facial expressions.[10]

Although researchers have tried to identify specific problems that result from gender differences in nonverbal communication, these differences may be more apparent than real. Few real differences have been documented, but people tend to believe that such differences do exist.

One definite difference appears to be in eye contact or gaze. Women tend to have more frequent eye contact during conversations than men do.[11] Women tend to hold eye contact more than men regardless of the sex of the person they are interacting with.[12]

Some differences also appear in the use of facial expression and gesture. Women tend to smile more than men, but their smiles are harder to interpret. Men's smiles generally mean positive feelings, whereas women's smiles may be a response to affiliation and friendliness.[13] Concerning gesture, Pearson, Turner, and Todd-Mancillas assert that the gesturing style of women and men is so different that people can distinguish masculinity and femininity on the basis of gesture alone.[14] For instance, women are more likely to keep their arms close to their body, are less likely to lean forward with their body, play more often with their hair or clothing, and tap their hands more often than men.

The major difference between men and women appears to be more in the interpretation than in the use of nonverbals. Major male–female relationship difficulties are often characterized by the failure to encode and decode nonverbal messages accurately. Patricia Noller recommends that men particularly need to be involved in communication skills training, because they generally seem less sensitive to the meaning of women's nonverbal behaviors than women are to men's.[15] This interpretive ability seems to have long-range implications. For instance, Noller found that couples with a high degree of marital satisfaction were likely to be accurate in decoding each other's nonverbal messages and in predicting whether or not their spouse would correctly decode their messages.

How Body Motions Are Used

An awareness of *how* we use body motions is crucial to understanding nonverbal communication. To the unobservant, all body motion may appear to be random movement; however, body movements serve important communication functions.[16]

1. *Body motions may be used to take the place of a word or phrase.* Just as we learn what words mean, so we learn what various signs and gestures mean. As coded by Ekman and Friesen,[17] when nonverbal symbols take the place of a word or phrase, they are called *emblems.* A contemporary North American dictionary of nonverbal emblems would include such definitions as "everything is go" for thumbs up; "peace" for the extension of the first and second fingers in a V shape; "no" for shaking the head from side to side and "yes" for nodding; and "maybe," "I don't care," or "I don't know" for shrugging the shoulders.

In many contexts, emblems are used as a complete language. *Sign language* refers to systems of gestures that include sign languages of the deaf and alternate sign languages used by Trappist monks in Europe and the women of Australia.[18]

2. *Body motions may be used to complement what a speaker is saying.* These complementary uses of nonverbal communication are called *illustrators.* We use gestures to illustrate in at least five ways: (1) to *emphasize* speech: A man may pound the table in front of him as he says, "Don't bug me"; (2) to show the *path* or *direction* of thought: A professor may move her hands on an imaginary continuum when she says, "The papers ranged from very good to very bad"; (3) to show *position:* A waiter may point when he says, "Take that table"; (4) to *describe:* People may use their hands to indicate size as they say, "The ball is about three inches in diameter"; and (5) to *mimic:* People may nod their heads as they say, "Did you see the way he nodded?"

Conversely, body motions can detract from a speaker's message if inappropriately used or if their use calls attention to the movements themselves rather than adding to the speaker's meaning (think of a speaker who fidgets or paces unnecessarily while giving a speech).

3. *Body motions can augment the verbal expression of feelings.* Nonverbal behaviors that augment the verbal expression of feelings are called *affect displays.* If you drag yourself out of bed in the morning and stub your toe as you stumble to the bathroom, a grimace expressing pain is likely to accompany your verbal comment. (Do you have a favorite word for these occasions?) More often than not, these spur-of-the-moment displays are not intended as conscious communication. One reason for labeling such reactions as "displays" is that the reaction will take place automatically, whether you are alone or someone else is present, and it will probably be quite noticeable.

People generally react through their body motions in one of four ways:
(1) Sometimes people show less emotion with their body than they are really feeling. Dan, a baseball player, may refuse to rub the spot where he has been struck by a pitch, and Natasha may deliberately control her facial expression to play down the pain she feels when she learns that her niece is chemically dependent. (2) Sometimes people show more emotion with their bodies than they are really feeling. Thus, nine-year-old Ken may howl and jump up and down when his brother happens to bump into him in the hall. (3) Sometimes people act as if nothing has happened regardless of how they are feeling. Wayne may go about his business even though he just received news that his mother is in the hospital. (4) Sometimes people react in a

manner totally different from what we'd expect in the situation. For instance, Maria may smile when someone makes a cutting remark about her appearance. Because people differ in the way they display feelings, we need to be very careful about the conclusions we draw from nonverbal cues. It is very easy to be fooled.

4. *Body motions may be used to control or regulate the flow of a conversation or other communication transaction.* Nonverbal cues such as shifting eye contact, slight head movements, shifts in posture, raising of the eyebrows, and nodding of the head tell a person when to continue, to repeat, to elaborate, to hurry up, or to finish. Good public speakers learn to adjust what they are saying and how they are saying it on the basis of such audience cues, or *regulators.*

5. *Body motions may be used to relieve tension.* As we listen to people and watch them while they speak, we may see them scratch their head, tap their foot, or wring their hands. These nonplanned releases of energy, called *adaptors,* serve to reduce the stress a speaker may be feeling.

Improving Your Skills

You can improve your use of body motions if you are willing to practice. Let's consider eye contact as an example. If you would like to improve your eye contact, write a communication improvement goal statement, following the guidelines given in Chapter 1.

To begin your program of improvement, create a situation in which you are the speaker. As you talk, concentrate on looking at the source of your attention. You can even practice by holding "conversations" with objects in your room. For a minute, talk to your book, then shift your attention to your lamp, and finally, talk to the window. Once you become conscious of maintaining eye contact with objects, you can continue to practice by having a close friend help you monitor the amount of your eye contact. For example, you might say to your friend, "As I'm telling you about the movie I saw, I'd like you to keep track of how much I look at you while I talk. When I'm done, tell me if you thought I looked at you 25 percent, 50 percent, 75 percent, or nearly all the time." The friend can also raise a hand when you are (or are not) maintaining eye contact—that will make you aware of your gazing behavior. If you need to practice eye contact in the role of listener or receiver, have your friend tell you about something that happened; then ask how much you maintained eye contact while you were listening. Whether you are practicing improvement in eye contact, facial expression, gesture, or posture, you can follow the same procedure.

Practice in Analyzing Body Motions

By Yourself

1. How do you use gestures when you converse with friends or give a speech? List examples of times when you use body motions as emblems, illustrators, affect displays, regulators, or adaptors.

2. Observe others' use of nonverbal behavior when they are giving instructions, criticizing, apologizing, or supporting a statement. Do their body motions help or hurt the effectiveness of their communication? How?

With Another

1. Working with a partner, try to communicate for a full minute or two entirely through nonverbal communication on a subject such as how to clean a piece of machinery, knit a sweater, or play a card game. At the end of the minute or two, analyze your efforts. What kinds of information did you find easiest to communicate nonverbally? What kinds of information did you feel the greatest frustration in communicating?

2. Prepare a short personal experience to communicate to another person. Before you begin, give the person clear directions about what he or she should be looking for in your use of eye contact, facial expression, gesture, or posture. When you have finished, have the person share his or her findings with you. Use what you learn from one practice session as a foundation for the next session.

Paralanguage

In contrast to kinesic behavior, which refers to the bodily movements we see, *paralanguage,* or *vocalics,* refers to the nonverbal sounds we hear. Paralanguage concerns how something is said rather than what is said. We have all developed some sensitivity to the cues people give through their voices. Let's consider two major categories of paralanguage: vocal characteristics and vocal interferences.

Vocal Characteristics

The four major *vocal characteristics* are pitch (highness or lowness of tone), volume (loudness), rate (speed), and quality (the sound of the voice).

Pitch. The highness or lowness of a voice is its *pitch.* Your voice is produced in the larynx by the vibration of your vocal folds. To feel this vibration, put your hand on your throat at the top of the Adam's apple and say "ah." Just as the pitch of a violin string is changed by making it tighter or looser, so the pitch of your voice is changed by the tightening and loosening of the vocal folds.

Fortunately, most people speak at a pitch that is about right for them. A few persons do have pitch problems—that is, they talk using tones that are too high or too low for their voice. If you have questions about your pitch level, ask your professor about it. If you are one of the few people with a pitch problem, your professor can refer you to a speech therapist for corrective work. Because our normal pitch is usually satisfactory, the question for most of us is whether we are making the best use of our pitch range.

Volume. The loudness of the tone you make is its *volume.* You increase volume by contracting your abdominal muscles, thus giving greater force to the air you expel when you breathe.

To feel how these muscles work, place your hands on your sides with your fingers extended over the stomach. Say "ah" in a normal voice. Now say "ah" as loudly as you can. If you are making proper use of your muscles, you should feel an increase in stomach contractions as you increase volume. If you feel little or no muscle contraction, you are probably trying to gain volume from the wrong source; such a practice can result in tiredness, harshness, and insufficient volume to make yourself heard in a large room.

Each person, regardless of size, can make his or her voice louder. If you have trouble talking loudly enough to be heard in a large classroom, work on increasing pressure from the abdominal area on exhalation.

Rate.   The speed at which we talk is our *rate* of speech. Although most of us utter between 140 and 180 words per minute, the optimal rate is a highly individual matter. The test of rate is whether listeners can understand what you are saying. Usually, even very fast talking is acceptable if words are well articulated and if there is sufficient vocal variety and emphasis. If your instructor believes you talk too rapidly or too slowly, he or she will suggest ways you can improve.

Quality.   The tone, timbre, or sound of your voice is its *quality*. The best vocal quality is clear and pleasant to listen to. Problems of quality include nasality (too much resonance in the nose on vowel sounds), breathiness (too much escaping of air during voice production), harshness (too much tension in throat and chest), and hoarseness (a raspy sound to the voice). If your voice tends to one of these qualities, consult your professor. Although you can make some improvement on your own, improvement can require a great deal of work and rather extensive knowledge of vocal anatomy and physiology. Severe problems of vocal quality should be referred to a speech therapist.

Each of these vocal characteristics, by itself or in concert with others, complements, supplements, or contradicts the words we use. People talk loudly when they wish to be heard over greater distances, but they may also talk more loudly when they are angry, and some may talk more softly when they are being loving. People tend to raise and lower their pitch to accompany changes in volume. They may also raise pitch when they are nervous or lower pitch when they are trying to be forceful. People may talk more rapidly when they are happy, frightened, or nervous; they may talk more slowly when they are unsure or trying to emphasize a point.

In addition to combined changes in volume, pitch, and rate, each of us uses a slightly different quality of voice to communicate a particular state of mind. We may associate complaints with a whiny, nasal quality; seductive invitation with a soft, breathy quality; and anger with a strident, harsh quality.

As listeners, we assign to each of these different qualities a value judgment about how people are feeling or what they are thinking . However, none of these specific voice qualities necessarily has the meaning we assign to it. Some people have high-pitched or breathy or nasal or strident voices all the time, and some may use these different qualities for reasons other than those we assign to them. Nevertheless, how people say what they say does convey meaning, whether intended or not. The primary purpose here is not so much to suggest changing your own paralanguage as it is to make you more aware of the meanings that may be received through paralanguage. If you do have concerns about your vocal characteristics, talk them over with your professor.

Vocal Interferences

Sounds that interrupt or intrude into fluent speech are termed *vocal interferences.* Some interferences cause distraction and, occasionally, total communication breakdown. Excessive vocal interferences are bad speech habits that we develop over time. The most common interferences that creep into our speech include "uh," "er," "well," and "OK," and those nearly universal interrupters of Americans' conversation, "you know" and "like." Vocal interferences that may be minor distractions in interpersonal or group settings can be totally disruptive in public speaking.

Vocal interferences are difficult to eliminate from our speech, but they can be reduced through a program of awareness and practice. Vocal interferences are often caused by a fear of momentary silence. We have been taught that it is impolite to interrupt another person until the flow of sound stops. A problem occurs for people when they pause for the right word or idea because they fear that the second or two it takes for them to come up with the word may be perceived by listeners as "dead air time." Therefore, they fill the dead air time with sound that, more often than not, has no meaning. For some speakers the customary filler sounds are "uh" or "er"; for others, they are "well" or "um." Although the chance of being interrupted may be real (some people will seek to interrupt at any pause), the intrusion of an excessive number of fillers is a high price to pay to prevent an occasional interruption.

Equally prevalent, and perhaps even more disruptive than "uh" and "um," is the incessant use of "you know" and "like." The "you know" habit may begin as a way to find out whether what the person is saying is already known by others. For some, "you know" may be a source of identification—a way of showing that they and those to whom they are talking have common knowledge as a binding element. For most people, however, the flooding of sentences with "you know" is simply a bad habit, resulting in such incoherent statements as "You know, Maxwell is, you know, a good, you know, lecturer."

Similarly, the use of "like" may start from making comparisons, as in "He's hot, he looks like Tom Cruise." Soon the comparisons become shortcuts, as in "He's like really hot!" Finally, the use of "like" becomes pure filler: "Like, he's really cool, like I can't really explain it, but I'll tell you he's like wow!"

Curiously, no matter how irritating the use of "you know" or "like" may be to listeners, they are unlikely to acknowledge their irritation. Although you may feel uncomfortable pointing out this irritant in others' speech, you should request others to tell you whether you are an offender. Keep in mind that even if such interferences are accepted between peers in everyday speech, they can be quite inappropriate to more formal settings such as a job interview or a problem-solving group. But the habits tend to persist across settings.

In the normal give-and-take of conversation, even the most fluent speakers may use an occasional "uh," "like," or "you know." Interferences become a problem when they are perceived by others as excessive and when they begin to call attention to themselves and so prevent listeners from concentrating on meaning. These interferences become especially detrimental in public-speaking effectiveness. With some practice, you can limit the occurrence of vocal interferences in your speech. Here are some steps you can take.

1. *Train yourself to hear your interferences.* Even people with a major problem seem to be unaware of the interferences they use. You can train your ear in at least two ways:

a. Tape-record yourself talking for several minutes about any subject—the game you saw yesterday, the course you plan to take next term, or anything else that comes to mind. Before you play it back, estimate the number of times you think you peppered your speech with "uh's," "you know's," and the like. Then compare the actual number with your estimate. As your ear becomes trained, your estimates will be closer to the actual number.

b. Have a close friend listen to you and raise a hand every time you use a filler such as "uh" or "you know." You may find the experience traumatic or nerve-racking, but your ear will soon start to pick up the vocal interferences as fast as the listener.

2. *Practice to see how long you can go without using a vocal interference.* Start out by trying to talk for fifteen seconds. Continue to increase the time until you can talk for two minutes without a single interference. Meaning may suffer; you may spend a disproportionate amount of time avoiding interferences. Still, it is good practice.

3. *Mentally note your usage of interferences in conversation.* You will be making real headway when you can recognize your own interferences in normal conversation without affecting the flow. When you reach this stage, you will find yourself beginning to avoid or limit the use of interferences.

Ridding yourself of these habits is hard work—you will have to train your ear to catch your usages. But the work is worth it.

Practice in Paralanguage

By Yourself

1. What happens to your voice in stressful situations? When does your pitch go up? Down? When do you talk loudly? Softly? When are you likely to talk fast? Slowly? Are you aware of these changes, or do you need feedback on how you use paralanguage?

2. Are there any vocal interferences that you use frequently? Are you always aware of their use? How might you try to reduce or eliminate their use?

In Groups

1. Have two members of the group role-play various situations. For instance, a student has received a low grade on a theme that she worked on for hours and she wants to confront her instructor, a person who does not have much patience when talking with students. The rest of the group should listen for paralanguage and discuss it.

2. Each person in the group should try to talk continuously for two minutes. When it is your turn, you can select your own topic—for example, a movie you saw recently, the success of your school team, or a problem you are having at work. Whenever the speaker uses an interference, one of the members of the group should raise a hand. At the end of two minutes, count the number of times hands were raised. Give everyone two chances. See who can use the fewest interferences.

Self-Presentation

People learn a great deal about us from the way we choose to present ourselves nonverbally. Elements over which we have some control include choice of clothing, amount of touch, and the way we treat time.

Clothing

Although our reactions to other people's appearance vary in intensity, we do draw conclusions about others based on the way they dress. Since choice of clothing communicates a message, you need to determine what you are trying to say and then dress accordingly.

Clothes are perceived as clues to a person's attitudes and behaviors.

Defense attorneys understand this principle very well. They know that a defendant charged with assault and battery would be foolish to show up in the courtroom wearing a black leather jacket, jeans, and boots. Similarly, business managers generally have a clear idea of the images they want their businesses to project. To succeed in those businesses, you must dress in a way that is in line with those images.[19] Thus, the woman who goes into an interview with a major oil company wearing sweatpants and a tanktop had better have a lot going for her if she expects even to be heard, let alone considered for the job.

People have a right to their individuality. Nevertheless, clothes are perceived by others as clues to a person's attitudes and behaviors. Part of being a skilled communicator is realizing that clothes do communicate, and the message they send depends as much on the receiver's perceptions as it does on the sender's intentions.

Touch

Touch, known as *haptics*, is often considered to be the most basic form of communication; as such it is a fundamental aspect of nonverbal communication in general and of self-presentation in particular. We use our hands to pat, slap, pinch, stroke, hold, embrace, and tickle. We employ such touching behaviors for a variety of reasons, ranging from random and impersonal to purposeful and intimate. We shake hands to be sociable and polite, we pat a person on the back for encouragement, we hug a person to show love.

But whether people touch and like to be touched is a matter of individual preference and cultural background. Although the North American culture is relatively noncontact-oriented, the kinds and amounts of touching behavior within our society vary widely. Behavior that seems impersonal to one person may seem very intimate or threatening to another. Moreover, the perceived appropriateness of touch differs with the context, so that a normally touch-oriented person may act differently in public or with a large group of people. Research shows that women tend to initiate and respond to touch more than men. The conclusion drawn is that touch may be perceived as "feminine-appropriate behavior" and "masculine-inappropriate behavior."[20] What you communicate by touching (or by not touching) depends not only on your intentions but on the expectations of those with whom you interact.

The complexities of touch lead Judee Burgoon, a major researcher in nonverbal behavior, and her associates to conclude that touch is one of the most provocative but least understood nonverbal behaviors. And although touching can often be perceived positively, they conclude that many more investigations will have to be done before we can prescribe when and what kinds of touch are advisable in communication contexts.[21]

Chronemics

Chronemics is the study of how we use and structure time. Its significance for nonverbal behavior is that people perceive actions and reactions in the context of when they occur.[22] Thus, how we manage time and how we react to others' use and management of time are important aspects of self-presentation.

Probably the aspect of time that is most important to self-presentation is what Edward T. Hall calls *informal time*,[23] time usages that are learned through observation and imitation. We focus here on three aspects of informal time: duration, activity, and punctuality.

Duration refers to the amount of time that we regard as appropriate for certain events. For instance, people expect a sermon to last twenty to thirty minutes, a typical class to run fifty minutes, and a movie to be roughly two hours long. When the length of an event differs significantly from our expectations, the time involved becomes an obstacle to communication. We get impatient with the professor who holds us beyond normal class time; we become frustrated if someone seems to cut short an interview or an intimate exchange. Our sensitivity to duration is thus an important aspect of our self-presentation.

Activity refers to what people perceive should be done in a given period, including the time of day that is considered appropriate for certain activities to take place. Most of us work during the day, sleep at night, eat lunch around midday, and so on. When someone engages in behavior at a time that we deem inappropriate, we are likely to react negatively. For instance, Kirsten, who is normally quite willing to discuss interpersonal problems with her employees, is likely to show irritation if an employee calls during her dinner hour to discuss a problem she had with a client.

Punctuality, which refers to meeting a time expectation, may be the most important of these three aspects because so many of us draw conclusions about people based on it. If your professor asks you to stop by her office at 10 A.M., her opinion of you may be affected if you knock on her door at 9:45, at 10:00, at 10:10, or at 10:30. Likewise, your perceptions of your professor might alter depending on whether or not she is in her office when you get there. Keep in mind, however, that time expectations, as well as touching, are culturally based.

Cultural Variations

Differences in touching behavior are, according to Gudykunst and Kim, highly correlated with culture. "People in high contact cultures evaluate 'close' as positive and good, and evaluate 'far' as negative and bad. People in low contact cultures evaluate 'close' as negative and bad, and 'far' as positive and good."[24] Specifically, Latin America and the Mediterranean countries are high contact, the United States is moderate contact, and the Far East is low contact.

A particularly important area of cultural differences concerns perceptions of time. In general, North Americans are likely to view time monochronically, compartmentalizing time and scheduling one event at a time. Thus, Americans tend to emphasize schedules and value promptness. Being even a few minutes late may require a person to acknowledge lateness; being ten to fifteen minutes late usually requires an apology; and being more than thirty minutes late is likely to be perceived as an insult requiring a great deal of explanation to earn the person's forgiveness.[25]

People from other cultural backgrounds, such as those from the Middle East, tend to view time polychronically, a view that resists compartmentalization and involves engaging in several activities at the same time. To those with a polychronic view of time, being late is common and is not considered unusual, and the concept of a schedule that is supposed to be adhered to may be meaningless. In Latin American or in Arab cultures, for instance, it is not unusual for a person to be more than thirty minutes late, and this behavior is likely to occasion only a few words of apology.[26]

Although we have been focusing on differences among people from various countries, these differences can also be seen in subcultures within the United States. For instance, people from Latin American or African-American cultures may also show a more polychronic view of time in their behavior.

The point is that there is no universally held "right" way of viewing time designations. There are, however, different ways of doing so. For instance, an Anglo-American with a business appointment in Latin America might be very frustrated with what he or she sees as a "cavalier" attitude toward time; likewise, a Latin American who has a business appointment with an Anglo-American may be frustrated by the perceived "rigidness" of time schedules.

Practice in Analyzing Self-Presentation

By Yourself

1. Take a clothing inventory. Divide your clothes into three groups: those you wear for special occasions, those you wear for everyday activities, and those you wear for "grubbing around." Over the next week, note how your interactions with others are affected by your clothing. Do you act differently when wearing one type of clothing rather than another? Do others treat you differently?

2. Next time you go to class, dress completely differently from the way you normally do. Notice what effect, if any, this has on your communication with those around you.

3. Analyze your reactions to people's time behavior. Describe an incident in which someone's violation of your time expectations caused communication problems.

4. Observe the conversations of men and women and people of different cultures. Based on these observations, what conclusions can you draw about their touching behavior?

Communication Through Management of Your Environment

In addition to the way we use body motions, paralanguage, and self-presentation, we communicate nonverbally through management of the physical environment. The principal elements of the environment over which we can exercise control are space, temperature, lighting, and color.

Space

How much control we have over space depends on whether we are dealing with permanent structures, movable objects within space, or informal space.

Management of Permanent Structures.   The buildings in which we live and work and the parts of those buildings that cannot be moved fall in the category of permanent structures. Although we may not have much control over the creation of such structures, we do exercise control in our selection of them. For instance, when you rent an apartment or buy a condominium or a house, you consider whether or not the structure is in tune with your lifestyle. People who select a fourth-floor loft may view themselves differently from those who select a one-room efficiency. Businesspeople, doctors, and lawyers usually search with care to find surroundings that fit the image they want to communicate. In addition, specific features of that choice affect our communication within that environment. For instance, people who live in apartment buildings are likely to become better acquainted with neighbors who live across the hall and next door than with those who live on other floors.

Management of Movable Objects within Space.   We have the opportunity to manage objects in space by arranging and rearranging them to create the desired atmosphere. Whether the space is a dormitory room, a living room, a seminar room, or a classroom, you can move the furnishings around until you achieve the effect you want. For example, in a living room, you can arrange furniture in a way that contributes to conversation or that focuses attention on a television set. A room with

We can arrange objects in space to create a desired atmosphere.

Victorian furniture and hard-backed chairs arranged formally will produce an entirely different kind of conversation from a room with a thick carpet, pillows, beanbag chairs, and a low sectional sofa. In general, the more formal the arrangement, the more formal the communication setting.

A supervisor's office will give you clues about the kind of climate that he or she is trying to establish just by the arrangement of the office and where visitors are expected to sit. A supervisor who shows you to a chair across the desk may be saying, "Let's talk business—I'm the boss and you're the employee." Such an arrangement, with the desk between you and the supervisor, lends itself to formal conversation. On the other hand, the supervisor who shows you to a chair at the side of her desk may be saying, "Don't be nervous—let's just chat." In this case, the lack of any formal barrier between you and the supervisor, as well as the relatively small space, is designed to lead to much more informal conversation. Although such conclusions about the management of objects within space should not be regarded as absolute, the use of space nevertheless is one index of how people are going to treat you and how they expect you to treat them.

The effect on communication of the arrangement of objects can be illustrated by examining your various classrooms. The communication atmosphere of a classroom in which several rows of chairs face the lectern differs from that of a classroom in which chairs are grouped into one large circle or one in which there are four or five smaller circles. In the first environment, most students anticipate a lecture format. In the second setting, they might expect a give-and-take discussion between the instructor and members of the class. In the third one, they might expect the class to work on group projects.

Management of Informal Space.   The space around the place we are occupying at the moment is known as *informal space.* The study of informal space is called *proxemics.* Managing informal space requires some understanding of attitudes toward both space around us and our territory.

You are probably aware that communication is influenced by the distances between people. Edward T. Hall, a leading researcher in nonverbal communication, has studied the four distinct, generally accepted distances for different types of conversations in our dominant culture.[27] *Intimate distance,* up to eighteen inches, is appropriate for private conversations between close friends. *Personal distance,* from eighteen inches to four feet, is the space in which casual conversation occurs. *Social distance,* from four to twelve feet, is where impersonal business such as job interviews is conducted. *Public distance* is anything more than twelve feet. Note that these four distances were not determined arbitrarily; they represent descriptions of what many people consider appropriate in various situations. Individuals do, of course, vary.

Of greatest concern to us is the intimate distance, that which we regard as appropriate for intimate conversation with close friends, parents, and younger children. People usually become uncomfortable when "outsiders" violate this intimate distance. For instance, in a movie theater that is less than one-quarter full, couples will tend to leave a seat or more between them and another couple. If in such a setting, a stranger sits right next to you, you are likely to feel uncomfortable and may even move away.

Intrusions into our intimate space are acceptable only when all involved follow the unwritten rules. For instance, when people are packed into a crowded elevator and possibly touching others, they often try to stand rigidly, look at the floor or the indicator above the door, and pretend they are not touching. Sometimes they exchange sheepish smiles or otherwise acknowledge the mutual invasion of intimate distance.

Interpersonal problems occur when one person violates the behavioral expectations of another. For instance, Jaron may come from a family that conducts informal conversations with others at a range closer than the eighteen-inch limit that most Americans place on intimate space. When he talks to a colleague at work and moves in closer than eighteen inches, the coworker may back away from him during the conversation. Another example of violation of expectations occurs when people engage in nonverbal behaviors that may be defined as sexual harassment. Dominic, in an apparently "playful" mood, may use posture, movements, or gestures that Daniela interprets as somewhat threatening to her. In keeping with current sentiments toward harassment, people need to be especially sensitive to others' definition of intimate space.

Normally, our intimate or personal space moves when we move because we tend to define these spaces in terms of our current location. Yet in many situations, we seek to claim a given space whether we are occupying it currently or not. That is, we are likely to look at certain space as our *territory,* as space over which we may claim ownership. If Marcia decides to eat lunch at the company commissary, the space at the table she selects becomes her territory. Suppose that during lunch Marcia leaves her territory to get butter for her roll. The chair she left, the food on the table, and the space around that food are "hers," and she will expect others to stay away. If, when she returns, Marcia finds that someone at the table has moved a glass or a dish into the area that she regards as her territory, she is likely to feel resentful.

Many people stake out their territory with markers. For example, Ramon, who is planning to eat in the commissary, finds an empty table and puts his newspaper on the table and his coat on a chair before he gets his food. If someone comes along while Ramon is gone, moves his newspaper and coat to the floor, and occupies his space, that person is violating what Ramon perceives as his territory.

As a student of nonverbal communication, you must understand, however, that other people may not look at either the space around you or your territory in quite the same way as you do. That the majority of Americans have learned the same basic rules governing the management of space does not mean that everyone shares the same respect for the rules or treats the consequences of breaking the rules in the same way. Thus, it is important to be observant so that you can be sensitive to how others react to your behaviors.

Temperature, Lighting, and Color

Three other elements of the environment that people seem sensitive to and over which they generally have considerable control are temperature, lighting, and color.

Temperature acts as a stimulant or deterrent to communication. To illustrate the negative effect of temperature on communication, recall when the June or September

Differing concepts of informal space: While you might find it rude for non-intimates to get this close to you in conversation, these men would find it rude if you backed away.

heat made listening to the teacher in a stuffy classroom especially difficult. Or, if you live in a northern climate, think of how a sudden cold snap that caused buildings to be much colder than normal made concentration that much more difficult.

Lighting can also act as a stimulant or deterrent to communication. In lecture halls and reading rooms, bright light is expected—it encourages good listening and comfortable reading. By contrast, in a chic restaurant, a music listening room, or a television lounge, you expect the lighting to be soft and rather dim, which makes for a cozy atmosphere and leads to intimate conversation.[28]

Differences in *color* seem to have a particularly significant effect on how people behave. We react to color both emotionally and physically. For instance, many people see red as exciting and stimulating, blue as comfortable and soothing, yellow as cheerful and jovial. Interior designers thus will decorate in blues when they are trying to create a peaceful, serene atmosphere for a living room, whereas they will decorate in reds and yellows when they are trying to create a stimulating atmosphere for a playroom.

Color has other associations as well. We describe a cowardly person as yellow, a jealous person as green with envy, an angry person as seeing red; Mondays, of course, are often seen as blue. The effect of color is most noticeable when the color violates our expectations. Mashed potatoes tinted green in honor of Saint Patrick's Day may nauseate diners even before they attempt to eat.

Cultural Variations

Finally, people around the world have different attitudes about what constitutes appropriate distances for various interactions. Recall that North Americans typically consider the space of up to a foot or eighteen inches from their bodies as personal or intimate space, and they do not expect people to violate that space. In the Middle East, however, men seek to move much closer to other men when they are talking. Thus, when an Arab man talks with a North American, one of the two is likely to be uncomfortable. Either the North American will experience a sense of territorial invasion or the Arab will feel himself too far removed for serious conversation.

Problems in communicating with strangers occur at times because we are uncertain and anxious about the meanings of nonverbal cues. And when strangers violate our expectations of nonverbal usage, we tend to react negatively.[29]

Practice in Analyzing the Effects of Environment

By Yourself

1. How territorial are you? Make a list of territories that you "own." What do you do when those territories are invaded?
2. Analyze your use of personal space. What are your expectations about space when you are talking with an instructor? When you are talking with a good friend? When you are talking with a stranger? How do they differ?
3. Change the arrangement of furniture in your dorm room or a room of your home. Observe people's reactions. Comment on whether these changes seem to affect the conversations of the people who are usually in these spaces.
4. Think of where you live (dorm, apartment, house). How well do you know your neighbors? Which of your neighbors do you know best? Can you account for your interactions with neighbors by where you live in relation to them?
5. For the next few days, record instances of your communication with people from different cultures in which their nonverbal behavior is different from what you expected in that situation. Indicate the results of the times you used perception checking (see Chapter 2) to clarify the meaning.

With Another

1. Visit six different restaurants in your city. Choose some that specialize in fast food and some that specialize in more leisurely dining. Make notes on the management of objects within space, as well as on the color and lighting. What conclusions can you draw?
2. Enlist the aid of a friend. Start on the opposite sides of a room (at least twenty feet apart) and begin to walk toward each other. (1) Stop when you are twelve feet apart and hold a conversation. (2) Stop when you are seven feet apart and hold a conversation. (3) Stop when you are one or two feet apart and hold a conversation. (4) Continue moving closer and conversing until you feel uncomfortable. Step back until the distance seems comfortable. Notice how far apart you are. Compare your reactions to your friend's.

Summary

Nonverbal communication refers to how people communicate by nonverbal means—that is, through the use of body motions, paralanguage, self-presentation, and environment. The nature of nonverbal communication is revealed through its contrasts with verbal communication. Nonverbal communication is more ambiguous, is continuous, is multichanneled, and gives more insight into emotional states. In addition, meanings of nonverbal communication are culturally determined.

Perhaps the most obvious aspect of nonverbal communication is what and how a person communicates through body motions and paralanguage. Eye contact, facial expression, gesture, posture, and poise are major types of body motions. Eye contact is especially important because people will form judgments about you and your message based on the amount of eye contact you make. Body motions act as emblems, illustrators, affect displays, regulators, and adaptors. Likewise, a person's vocal characteristics and vocal interferences affect the meaning communicated.

Although verbal and nonverbal communication work together best when they are complementary, nonverbal cues may replace or even contradict verbal symbols. Generally, nonverbal communication is more to be trusted when verbal and nonverbal cues are in conflict.

Self-presentation, manifested in such factors as clothing, touching behavior, and use of time, further affects communication. The environment is an often overlooked aspect of nonverbal communication. Yet the way people arrange and react to space and the way they control or react to temperature, lighting, and color contribute to the nature of the communication that will occur.

Cultural differences in the use of nonverbals occur with eye contact or gaze, gesture, touching behavior, and perceptions of time and space. These differences are real, and effective communicators must be sensitive to them. Some gender differences are found in gaze, facial expression, gesture, and touch. The major difference between men and women is not so much their use of nonverbals as it is their interpretation of them.

Suggested Readings

Axtell, Roger E., ed. *Do's and Taboos Around the World,* 2d ed. New York: Wiley, 1990. A highly informative guide that takes a lighthearted approach to examples of appropriate and inappropriate international behavior. Must reading for anyone attempting to avoid the pitfalls of international misunderstanding.

Knapp, Mark L., and Hall, Judith A. *Nonverbal Communication in Human Interaction,* 3d ed. New York: Holt, Rinehart & Winston, 1992 (paperback). A collection of research data. Mark L. Knapp, the lead author, is a pioneer in analysis of nonverbal communication.

Samovar, Larry A., and Porter, Richard E. *Communication Between Cultures,* 2d ed. Belmont, CA: Wadsworth, 1995 (paperback). A highly readable book that gives excellent insight into nonverbal communication differences between cultures.

Tannen, Deborah. *You Just Don't Understand: Women and Men in Conversation.* New York: Ballantine Books, 1990. Provides insights into gender differences in both verbal and nonverbal communication.

Notes

1.   Judee K. Burgoon, David B. Buller, and W. Gill Woodall, *Nonverbal Communication: The Unspoken Dialogue* (New York: Harper & Row, 1989), p. 155.

2.   Ibid., p. 33.

3.   Paul Ekman and H. Oster, "Facial Expression of Emotion," *Annual Review of Psychology* 30 (1979): 527–554.

4.   Mark L. Knapp and Judith A. Hall, *Nonverbal Communication in Human Interaction,* 3d ed. (New York: Holt, Rinehart & Winston, 1992), p. 298.

5.   Paul Ekman and W. V. Friesen, *Unmasking the Face* (Englewood Cliffs, NJ: Prentice-Hall, 1975), pp. 137–138.

6.   Virginia P. Richmond and James C. McCroskey, *Communication: Apprehension, Avoidance, and Effectiveness,* 2d ed. (Scottsdale, AZ: Gorsuch Scarisbrick, 1989), pp. 94–101.

7.   Larry A. Samovar and Richard E. Porter, *Communication Between Cultures* (Belmont, CA: Wadsworth, 1991), p. 198.

8.   Ibid., p. 199.

9.   Roger E. Axtell, *Gestures: The Do's and Taboos of Body Language Around the World* (New York: Wiley, 1991), p. 47.

10.   J. R. Davitz, *The Communication of Emotional Meaning* (New York: McGraw-Hill, 1964), p. 14.

11.   Donald J. Cegala and Alan L. Sillars, "Further Examination of Nonverbal Manifestations of Interaction Involvement," *Communication Reports* 2 (1989): 45.

12.   Julia T. Wood, *Gendered Lives: Communication, Gender, and Culture* (Belmont, CA: Wadsworth, 1994), p. 164.

13.   Judy Cornelia Pearson, Lynn H. Turner, and William Todd-Mancillas, *Gender and Communication,* 2d ed. (Dubuque, IA: Wm. C. Brown, 1991), p. 137.

14.   Ibid., p. 139.

15.   Patricia Noller, "Nonverbal Communication in Marriage," in Daniel Perlman and Steve Duck, eds., *Intimate Relationships: Development, Dynamics, and Deterioration* (Newbury Park, CA: Sage, 1987), p. 173.

16.   Paul Ekman and W. V. Friesen, "The Repertoire of Nonverbal Behavior: Categories, Origins, Usage, and Coding," *Semiotica* I (1969): 49–98.

17.   Ibid.

18.   Dale Leathers, *Successful Nonverbal Communication: Principles and Applications* (New York: Macmillan, 1992), p. 75.

19.   Two influential books that report on the power of clothing are John T. Molloy's *New Dress for Success* (New York: Warner Books, 1988) and Pamela Satran's *Dress Smart: The Thinking Women's Guide to Style* (New York: Doubleday, 1989).

20.   Pearson, Turner, and Todd-Mancillas, p. 142.

21.   Judee K. Burgoon, Joseph B. Walther, and E. James Baesler, "Interpretations, Evaluations, and Consequences of Interpersonal Touch," *Human Communication Research* 19 (December 1992): 259.

22.   Knapp and Hall, p. 59.

23.   Edward T. Hall, *The Silent Language* (Greenwich, CT: Fawcett, 1959), p. 135.

24.   William B. Gudykunst and Young Yun Kim, *Communicating with Strangers: An Approach to Intercultural Communication,* 2d ed. (New York: McGraw-Hill, 1992), p. 178.

25.   Samovar and Porter, p. 220.

26.   Gudykunst and Kim, p. 129.

27.   Edward T. Hall, *The Hidden Dimension* (Garden City, NY: Doubleday, 1969), pp. 116–125.

28.   Knapp and Hall, p. 72.

29.   Ibid., p. 186.

Establishing a Communication Foundation
Chapters 2–4

What kind of a communicator are you? The following analysis looks at ten specifics that are basic to effective communicators. On the line provided for each statement, indicate the response that best captures your behavior: 1, never; 2, rarely; 3, occasionally; 4, often; 5, almost always.

_____ When I speak, I tend to present a positive image of myself. (Ch. 2)

_____ In my behavior toward others, I look for more information to confirm or negate my first impressions. (Ch. 2)

_____ Before I act on perceptions drawn from people's nonverbal cues, I seek verbal verification of their accuracy. (Ch. 2)

_____ My conversation is helped by a large vocabulary. (Ch. 3)

_____ I speak clearly using words that people readily understand. (Ch. 3)

_____ When I am speaking with people of different cultures or of the opposite sex, I am careful to monitor my word choices. (Ch. 3)

_____ I tend to look at people when I talk with them. (Ch. 4)

_____ Most of my sentences are free from such expressions as "uh," "well," "like," and "you know." (Ch. 4)

_____ I consider the effect of my dress on others. (Ch. 4)

_____ I try to control my environment in ways that help my communication. (Ch. 4)

Based on your responses, select the communication behavior that you would most like to change. Write a communication improvement goal statement, following the guidelines provided in Chapter 1, and similar to the sample goal statement on page 24. If you would like verification of your self-analysis before you write a goal, have a friend or coworker complete this same analysis for you.

three

Interpersonal Communication

Interpersonal communication is your informal interaction with yourself and others. The effectiveness of your interpersonal communication is fundamental both to your understanding of self and to the development and maintenance of your relationships with others. Most of us are excited about discovering people with whom we have a lot in common, yet sometimes our interpersonal communication fails at key places. This four-chapter unit begins with the development of important skills: disclosing ideas and feelings, listening, and responding. It concludes with what is often considered to be the primary goal of interpersonal communication: developing and maintaining relationships.

Objectives

Objectives

After you have read this chapter, you should be able to:

Describe the characteristics of effective conversationalists

Define conversational coherence

Explain the cooperative principle and turn taking

Define self-disclosure

Explain guidelines for disclosing

Distinguish between displaying feelings and describing feelings

Describe your feelings

Take responsibility for your own feelings and opinions

Assert yourself appropriately

5

Communication of Ideas and Feelings

Y vonne has just read an account of the reforms that the new superintendent is putting into practice in the public schools. She's pleased with the overall aims of the reforms but skeptical about several of the specifics. During lunch with several colleagues, she begins a conversation on the subject.

Kareem has been going through difficult times with his wife. He's concerned that if something doesn't change, his marriage might be in jeopardy. That evening he gets together with his friend Travis, a marriage counselor, to talk about his feelings about recent events.

Yvonne and Kareem are about to converse. But the nature of their messages will be qualitatively different. Why? Yvonne will be sharing her ideas on the program of school reforms; the effectiveness of her communication will depend on the quality of the information she presents. Kareem will be sharing his feelings about recent events that have affected his marriage; the effectiveness of his communication will depend on his ability to discribing sensitive information about himself and his feelings.

Although your roles of sender and receiver of information are likely to overlap in your daily communication, at times you will initiate topics by disclosing your ideas and feelings. Because the extent and nature of your disclosures will affect how others relate to you, your self-disclosure style lays the foundation for the development of relationships with others. In this chapter, we consider the sender skills of sharing ideas, self-disclosure, describing feelings, assertiveness, and crediting.

Communicating Ideas: Conversation and Information Sharing

We tend to look up to people who are effective conversationalists. Yet, we may not fully understand what we need to do to improve our competence as conversationalists. In this section, we consider some broad characteristics of effective conversationalists and then turn to specific guidelines for maintaining conversational coherence.

Characteristics of Effective Conversationalists

Although some people have what appears to be a natural gift for effective conversation, almost all of us can learn to be more effective. Effective conversationalists are likely to share at least the following six characteristics:

1. *Effective conversationalists have quality information.* Although a portion of your conversation time involves small talk, you need to be able to participate when the conversation becomes more substantive. The key to solid, stimulating conversation is to have information that others value. Have you ever noticed how conversations come to life when one or more people have knowledge or expertise to share? Recently, a group of people were talking about the plight of the homeless and those who were stuck in almost uninhabitable housing owned by slumlords. The conversation picked up considerably when one of the participants shared the specific information she had learned firsthand from volunteering at agencies that deal with the homeless. As a result of that one person's knowledge, the entire conversation was significantly more meaningful than it would otherwise have been.

Although you don't have to be an expert on a subject, the more you know about a range of subjects, the greater the chances are that you will be an interesting conversationalist. Do you read a newspaper every day (not just the comics or the sports)? Do you read at least one news or special-interest magazine regularly? Do you sometimes watch television documentaries and news specials as well as entertainment and sports programs? (Of course, sports and entertainment are favorite topics of conversation, too—but not with everyone.) Do you make a point of going to the theater, to concerts, to museums or historical sites? If you answered no to most of these questions, you may find yourself at a loss when trying to join in on social conversations. Exposing yourself to a broad array of information and experiences allows you to develop ideas that others will find interesting and provides grist for the conversation mill.

2. *Effective conversationalists have a plan of operation.* Although many topics of conversation just "come up," more of our conversation than we may realize has a definable purpose that was known beforehand. For instance, you may be talking with your family to determine travel plans for the holidays, with your professor about how to study for his tests, or with a friend to get her support for a plan you want to bring to a church committee. Such purposeful conversations benefit from a *conversational plan,* a "consciously constructed conceptualization of one or more sequences of action aimed at achieving a goal."[1] Because conversation is a dynamic process, you cannot plan for every possible response; instead, the plan usually involves an opening approach and some idea of how to proceed, given the most likely listener reactions. So, if your goal is to get a friend's support for a proposal you want to bring to a church committee, you should anticipate possible reactions and be prepared to offer clear reasons and supporting data for your plan.

3. *Effective conversationalists enjoy the give-and-take of informal discussion.* Do you enjoy listening to others present ideas? Do you like to comment on, discuss, and even disagree with what they say? If you do, you probably enjoy the conversations you have. People you converse with are likely to sense your enjoyment through the nonverbal messages you send.

4. *Effective conversationalists ask good questions.* Many times the quality of your conversation depends on how well you can draw out the other person. Even when you are the major source of information in a conversation, the interaction will be satisfying to all only if the other people react to the issue being discussed. To encourage this kind of exchange, you need to develop your skill as a questioner. In both Chapter 7 and Module A, we discuss asking questions in some detail.

5. *Effective conversationalists listen to others' ideas.* Although some people regard a conversation as successful when they do all the talking, the other participants are likely to feel frustrated. A true conversation is not a one-way broadcast but an interaction that develops a shared meaning. In an effective conversation, you can expect to be the listener at least half the time. Listening and responding also involve specific skills, which we consider in Chapters 6 and 7.

6. *Effective conversationalists are willing to try.* No one becomes interesting, witty, provocative, and stimulating overnight. Becoming a good conversationalist requires practice and a bit of risk taking. Don't overlook opportunities to develop your conversational skills—scores of them occur every day.

Guidelines for Maintaining Conversational Coherence

Conversational coherence is the extent to which conversational contributions of the people involved show relatedness,[2] or as Littlejohn puts it, the "connectedness and meaningfulness in conversation" that keeps a conversation well organized.[3] In this section, we consider following the cooperative principle, crediting others, and taking turns.

Following the Cooperative Principle.   To achieve conversational coherence, H. Paul Grice identifies four conversational maxims that contribute to what he calls the *cooperative principle*—the need for contributions to be in line with the purpose of the conversation.[4]

1.   *Try to provide an amount of information that is sufficient or necessary but not too much.* We can err by being either too brief or too wordy. Thus, if a person asks you why you think the advertisement is ineffective, you would neither mumble some off-hand comment nor give a seven-minute lecture. Grice calls this the *quantity maxim*.

2.   *Try to provide information that is truthful.* Being truthful means not only avoiding deliberate lies or distortions but also taking care to avoid any kind of mis-representation. Thus, if a person asks whether you know why the company is in a financial crisis, you wouldn't make up an explanation just to have something to say. This is called the *quality maxim*.

3.   *Try to provide information that is relevant to what is being discussed.* Including unrelated information disrupts conversational coherence. Thus, if you are asked about your boss's plans for the department, you wouldn't go into a recital of your problems getting along with the boss. This is the *relation maxim*.

4.   *Try to be specific and organized in your contributions.* Coherence suffers when we give information that listeners find obscure, ambiguous, or disorganized. Thus, if a person asked you to explain how to use the new photocopier, you would "walk the person through" the steps of using it rather than rambling on about the machine's features in a haphazard and confusing order. Grice calls this the *manner maxim*.

Good conversation: a bridge between strangers.

When we get the sense that people are not conversing in the spirit of these maxims, we enact a set of interpretive procedures designed to help us figure out what is going on. For instance, suppose that Rob and Julia are standing by the water cooler chatting about how employees are being treated when Rob says, "You know, we've all been a bit peeved at having to kick in twenty-five dollars to brighten up our conference room." If Julia then says, "The water just doesn't seem as cold as it should be," Rob will infer something about her response such as, "She must not want to talk about it, and what she is doing is telling me in a nice way that it's none of my business." Such an inference would be based on a conscious or unconscious analysis of her response going something like this: "Julia's comment isn't relevant, but there must be some point to it. I'm sure that she heard me, but rather than say what she thinks, she has chosen to say something irrelevant so I'll drop the topic."

Bach and Harnish have proposed two additional maxims they call the *politeness maxim* and the *morality maxim*.[5] To be in compliance with the politeness maxim, a speaker must not be obnoxious or rude; to be in compliance with the morality maxim, a speaker avoids repeating information that is confidential, asking for privileged information, requiring the hearer to say or do something that the hearer ought not to, or doing things for the hearer that the hearer has no interest in having done.

Crediting Others.   A second aspect of conversational coherence is crediting others, a communication skill that is in keeping with this set of maxims. *Crediting others* means verbally footnoting the source from which you have drawn your ideas. In a term paper, you give credit to authors you have quoted or paraphrased by footnoting the sources. Similarly, when you use other people's words or ideas in your oral communication, you can credit the source. Crediting is important because people expect others to recognize it when ideas are theirs. When we fail to credit, whether through neglect or thoughtlessness, we hurt people and our relationships with them.

Consider the following situation: Jorge suggests to Tina that their organization might make money by selling raffle tickets on a product they have bought at discount. Tina tells him that she thinks the idea is a good one. The next day at a meeting of the group's fund-raising committee, Tina says, "What about buying a television at discount and selling raffle tickets? We could probably make a couple of hundred dollars!" The group responds immediately with such comments as "Great idea, Tina!" and "Tina, you always come up with good ideas." At this point, Jorge, the originator of the idea, will probably feel hurt or resentful that Tina is accepting credit for his idea, yet he realized that if he says, "That was my idea," the group may think less of him for quibbling over whose idea it was.

In this instance, it was Tina's responsibility to give credit to Jorge for originating the idea. Had Tina said, "Jorge had a great idea—what about buying a television at discount and selling raffle tickets?" the group probably would have reacted with the same enthusiasm, and Jorge would have felt gratified because he received credit for his idea. You can understand the importance of crediting if you think of the times you were hurt because an idea of yours was not credited.

Taking Turns.   A third aspect of conversational coherence involves mastering the skill of *turn taking*—engaging in appropriate conversational sequencing. Robert Nofsinger defines turn taking as "the various practices that participants use to change from one speaker to another."[6] Let's consider several guidelines that will help you with the turn-taking process.

1.   *Avoid speaking too often.* If there are four people in a conversation, the ideal is for all four to have approximately the same number of turns. In reality, one or two people are likely to speak more times than the others; yet, it is usually inappropriate for any one person to dominate the conversation. If you tend to speak two or three times for every other person's one time, try to mentally check whether everyone else has had a chance to talk once before you talk a second time. If you find others violating this rule, you can help those who haven't been able to talk by saying something like, "Donna, I get the sense that you've been wanting to comment on this point."

2.   *Avoid turns that are too long.* Just as we expect all participants to have a relatively equal number of turns, we also expect them to talk about the same length of time. People are apt to react negatively to those whose total speaking time per turn is out of proportion to the maximum length of statements by others in the conversation.

3.   *Listen and watch for turn-taking and turn-exchanging cues.* Duncan and Fiske have identified several cues that tell people that it may be time to talk. People are likely to perceive that a person is about finished speaking when that person decreases loudness, lowers pitch, and/or uses gestures that seem to show obvious completion of a point.[7] As you try to enter a conversation, look for such cues that "give you permission" to speak and sometimes even to interrupt.

4.   *Be careful of giving inadvertent turn-taking cues.* Sometimes people who are not finished still give off such turn-exchange cues as lowering volume or taking long pauses, and are surprised when they are interrupted. If you find people breaking in on your sentences before you have finished, you might ask people whether you tend to give false turn-taking cues.

5.   *Listen for conversation-directing behavior.* One prerogative of a person holding the floor is to define who may speak next. For instance, Paul may conclude his turn by saying, "Susan, did you understand what he meant?" In light of such a statement, Susan will expect to have the right to speak. Of course, if a person does not direct speaking behavior, the turn goes to the first person to speak.

6.   *Restrict interruptions to appropriate situations.* Interruptions occur rather frequently in conversation. You may wonder why some people can interrupt without causing difficulty, whereas others cannot. The reason is often associated with the method of interruption. In general, interrupting for "clarification" and "agreement" (confirming) are interpersonally acceptable.[8] For instance, people are likely to accept being interrupted when the interrupter asks relevant questions or paraphrases. Thus, such interruptions as asking "What do you mean by 'presumptuous'?" or paraphrasing by saying "I get the sense that you think presumptuous behavior is especially bad" or reinforcing statements with such comments as "Good point, Max" or "I see what you mean, Suzie," are likely to be accepted. Interruptions that change the subject or that seem to minimize the contribution of the interrupted person are likely to be viewed as disruptive or impolite.

7. *Be sensitive to people's nonverbal reactions to your conversational method.* If you notice people glaring or groaning when you interrupt, you need to apologize for the offense.

For a review of conversational skills in checklist form, see Figure 5.1.

Conversational Skills Checklist

For each of the following questions, rate yourself on a scale of 1 to 5:
1 = high, 2 = good, 3 = average, 4 = fair, 5 = poor.

Conversational Characteristics
In my conversation, I

	1	2	3	4	5
had quality information	☐	☐	☐	☐	☐
had a plan of operation	☐	☐	☐	☐	☐
asked good questions	☐	☐	☐	☐	☐
listened to others' ideas	☐	☐	☐	☐	☐
was willing to try to be a good conversationalist	☐	☐	☐	☐	☐

Conversational Maxims
In my responses, I

	1	2	3	4	5
provided sufficient information but not too much	☐	☐	☐	☐	☐
provided information that was truthful	☐	☐	☐	☐	☐
provided information that was relevant to what was being discussed	☐	☐	☐	☐	☐
was specific and organized with my contributions	☐	☐	☐	☐	☐
was polite	☐	☐	☐	☐	☐
avoided repeating information that was confidential or privileged	☐	☐	☐	☐	☐

Crediting and Turn Taking
When I spoke, I

	1	2	3	4	5
credited others' ideas	☐	☐	☐	☐	☐
avoided speaking too often	☐	☐	☐	☐	☐
avoided turns that were too long	☐	☐	☐	☐	☐
listened and watched for turn-taking and turn-exchanging cues	☐	☐	☐	☐	☐
was careful of giving inadvertent turn-taking cues	☐	☐	☐	☐	☐
listened for conversation-directing behavior	☐	☐	☐	☐	☐
restricted interruptions to appropriate situations	☐	☐	☐	☐	☐
was sensitive to people's nonverbal reactions to my comments	☐	☐	☐	☐	☐

Figure 5.1 *Conversational skills checklist*

By Yourself

1. List the five subject areas you believe you know the most about. Is there some variety in your repertoire of knowledge? To what extent does your repertoire help or hinder you in conversations?

2. Try to deliberately introduce greater variety in conversations with others. How well are you able to develop and maintain such conversations? Are they more or less satisfying than conversations on weather, sports, and daily happenings? Why?

3. For a recent conversation, complete the checklist in Figure 5.1. Analyze your strengths and weaknesses in the three categories of conversational characteristics, conversational maxims, and crediting and turn-taking behavior. Consider what you might do to improve behaviors that were least effective.

Self-Disclosure

Effective interpersonal communication requires some degree of self-disclosure. In the broadest sense, *self-disclosure* means sharing biographical data, personal ideas, and feelings. Statements such as "I was 5′6″ in seventh grade" reveal biographical information—facts about you as an individual. Biographical disclosures are the easiest to make, for they are, in a manner of speaking, a matter of public record. By contrast, statements such as "I don't think prisons ever really rehabilitate criminals" disclose personal ideas and reveal what and how you think. And statements such as "I get scared whenever I have to make a speech" disclose feelings. In terms of accurate understanding of self and others, it is this last sense in which most people think of self-disclosure—that is, revealing personal, unknown information about self.

Self-disclosure is at the heart of what is called *social penetration theory.* According to this theory, the more people know each other as persons, the more *interpersonal* their communication becomes; conversely, the less they know, the more impersonal the communication becomes. G. R. Miller, a leading researcher in interpersonal relations, believes that through communication people move their knowledge of others from a cultural information level (information revealed in general social conversation), through a sociological level (communicating in relation to a person's group roles), to a psychological information level (knowing a person's individual traits, feelings, attitudes, and so on).[9] Thus, the role of communication is to move people from nonintimate levels to deeper, more personal ones.[10]

Usually, the more people know about a person, the better the chances that they will like that person. Yet self-disclosure does carry a degree of risk. Just as knowing a person better is likely to result in closer interpersonal relations, learning too much about a person may result in alienation. The saying "Familiarity breeds contempt" means that over time people may learn something that detracts from the relationship. Because some people fear that their disclosures could have negative rather than positive consequences, they prefer not to disclose.

Although appropriate self-disclosure helps people become more comfortable with each other, unlimited self-disclosure may have negative effects. As Arthur Bochner puts it, "There is no firm empirical basis for endorsing unconditional openness."[11] By far the most consistent finding is that self-disclosure has the greatest positive effect on relationships when it is reciprocated.[12]

Cultural and Gender Differences in Disclosing Behavior

As we might expect, levels of self-disclosure and appropriateness of disclosure differ from culture to culture. For instance, people from the United States tend to engage in higher rates of disclosure than people from Western Europe or the Far East.

Particularly in the beginning stages of a friendship, such cultural differences can easily lead to misperceptions and discomfort if the people involved are unaware of them. For instance, a person from the United States may perceive an acquaintance from an Eastern culture as reserved or less interested in pursuing a "genuine" friendship, whereas the acquaintance may see the person from the United States as discourteously assertive or excessively open about personal feelings and other private matters. Being aware of cultural differences can help us recognize when we need to check out our perceptions instead of assuming that everyone shares the same standards of appropriateness and the verbal and nonverbal cues that we are used to in our own culture.

Allowing for such differences, the question becomes whether advice about disclosure—that when appropriate it helps strengthen a relationship—holds true across cultures. Gudykunst and Kim have discovered that, across cultures, when relationships become more intimate, self-disclosure increases. In addition, they found that the more partners self-disclosed to each other, the more they were attracted to each other, and the more uncertainty about each other was reduced.[13]

Moreover, consistent with conventional wisdom, women tend to disclose more than men, are disclosed to more than men, and are more aware than men of cues that affect their self-disclosure.[14] Of course, this generalization is not true in all cases.[15] In their discussion of differences in disclosure, Pearson, Turner, and Todd-Mancillas suggest several reasons why women tend to disclose more than men, including social expectations (a kind of self-fulfilling prophecy), the greater importance of self-disclosure to women, and developmental differences.[16]

Differences in learned patterns of self-disclosure can create misunderstandings between men and women, especially in intimate relationships. In *You Just Don't Understand,* Deborah Tannen argues that one way to capture the differences between men's and women's verbal styles is to use the terms *report-talk* and *rapport-talk.* Her point is that men in our society are more likely to view conversation as "report-talk"—a way to share information, display knowledge, negotiate, and preserve independence. In contrast, women are more likely to use "rapport-talk"—a way to share experiences and establish bonds with others. When men and women fail to recognize these differences in the way they have learned to use conversation, the stage is set for misunderstandings about whether or not they are being truly open and intimate with each other. "Learning about style differences won't make them go away," Tannen remarks, "but it can banish mutual mystification and blame."[17]

Guidelines for Appropriate Self-Disclosure

Although a risk-free life (probably impossible to attain) might be safe, some risk is vital to achieving satisfying interpersonal relationships. At the same time, too much risk can be more costly than we wish. The following are guidelines for determining an appropriate amount of self-disclosure in interpersonal encounters.

1. *Self-disclose the kind of information you want others to disclose to you.* When people are getting to know others, they look for information that is generally shared freely among people, such as hobbies, sports, school, and views of current events.

2. *Self-disclose more intimate information only when you believe the disclosure represents an acceptable risk.* Personal disclosures are usually withheld until people believe they have reason to trust the other person not to share the disclosures with others. As trust builds, the disclosure of more revealing information is less likely to have negative consequences. Ironically, some people find it safer to self-disclose to bartenders or with strangers they meet in travel. They perceive such disclosures as safe (representing reasonable risk) because these people do not know them or are in no position to use the information against them. It's unfortunate that some people don't feel safe in sharing personal information with family and friends.

3. *Move self-disclosure to deeper levels gradually.* Because receiving self-disclosure can be as threatening as giving it, most people become uncomfortable when the level of disclosure exceeds their expectations. As a relationship develops, the depth of disclosure increases as well.

4. *Reserve intimate or very personal self-disclosure for ongoing relationships.* Disclosures about fears, loves, and other deep or intimate matters are most appropriate in close, well-established relationships. When people disclose deep secrets to acquaintances, they are engaging in potentially threatening behavior. Making such disclosures before a bond of trust is established risks alienating the other person. Moreover, people are often embarrassed by and hostile toward others who try to saddle them with personal information in an effort to establish a relationship where none exists.

5. *Continue intimate self-disclosure only if it is reciprocated.* People expect a kind of equity in self-disclosure. When it is apparent that self-disclosure will not be returned, you should limit the amount of disclosure you make. Lack of reciprocation generally suggests that the person does not feel the relationship is one in which extensive self-disclosure is truly appropriate. When the response to your self-disclosure tells you that the disclosure was inappropriate, ask yourself what led to this effect. You can learn from a mistake and avoid making the same kind of mistake in the future.

Practice in Determining Self-Disclosure Guidelines

By Yourself

The following exercise will help you recognize the variations in what people see as appropriate self-disclosure and provide you with a useful base of information from which to work. Label each of the following statements L (low risk), meaning you believe it is appropriate to disclose this information to almost any person; M (moderate risk), meaning you believe it is appropriate to disclose this information to persons you know fairly well and with whom you have already established a friendship; H (high risk), meaning you would disclose such information only to the few friends you have great trust in or to your most intimate friends; or X (unacceptable risk), meaning you would disclose it to no one.

_____   **a.** Your hobbies, how you like best to spend your spare time
_____   **b.** Your preferences and dislikes in music
_____   **c.** Your educational background and your feelings about it
_____   **d.** Your personal views on politics, current leaders, and foreign and domestic policy
_____   **e.** Your personal religious views and the nature of your religious participation
_____   **f.** Habits and reactions of yours that bother you at the moment
_____   **g.** Characteristics of yours that give you pride and satisfaction
_____   **h.** The unhappiest moments in your life—in detail
_____   **i.** The occasions in your life when you were happiest—in detail
_____   **j.** The actions you have most regretted taking in your life and why
_____   **k.** The main unfulfilled wishes and dreams in your life
_____   **l.** Your guiltiest secrets
_____   **m.** Your views on the way a husband and wife should live their marriage
_____   **n.** What to do, if anything, to stay fit
_____   **o.** The aspects of your body you are most pleased with
_____   **p.** The features of your appearance you are most displeased with and wish to change
_____   **q.** The person in your life whom you most resent and the reasons why
_____   **r.** Your use or abuse of alcohol or illegal drugs
_____   **s.** The people with whom you have been sexually intimate and the circumstances of your relationship with each

In Groups (Optional)

Working in a group, discuss your labeling of the statements. The goal of the discussion is not to make any of the disclosures, only to discuss why you would or would not make them and under what circumstances. The purpose of the discussion is to see how people differ in what they view as acceptable disclosure.

Disclosing Feelings

An extremely important aspect of self-disclosure is the sharing of feelings. We all experience feelings such as happiness at receiving an unexpected gift, sadness about the breakup of a relationship, or anger when we believe we have been taken advantage of. The question is whether to disclose such feelings, and if so, how. Generally, the most effective way of dealing with feelings is neither to withhold them nor to display them indiscriminately but to describe them. Let's consider each of these forms of dealing with feelings.

Withholding or Masking Feelings

In our culture, *withholding feelings*—that is, keeping them inside and not giving any verbal or nonverbal cues to their existence—is generally regarded as an inappropriate means of dealing with feelings. Withholding feelings is best exemplified by the good poker player who develops a "poker face," a neutral look that is impossible to decipher. The look is the same whether the player's cards are good or bad. Unfortunately, many people use poker faces in their relationships so that no one knows whether they are hurt, excited, or saddened. For instance, Doris feels very nervous when Anitra stands over her while Doris is working on her report. When Anitra says, "That first paragraph isn't very well written," Doris begins to seethe, yet she says nothing—she withholds her feelings.

Psychologists believe that habitually withholding feelings can lead to physical problems such as ulcers, high blood pressure, and heart disease, as well as psychological problems such as depression and low self-esteem. Moreover, people who withhold feelings are often perceived as cold, undemonstrative, and not much fun to be around.

Is withholding ever appropriate? When a situation is inconsequential, you may well choose to withhold your feelings. For instance, a stranger's inconsiderate behavior at a party may bother you, but there is often little to be gained by disclosing your feelings about it. You don't have an ongoing relationship with the person, and you can deal with the situation simply by moving to another part of the room. In the example of Doris seething at Anitra's behavior, however, withholding could be costly to both parties; Doris's feelings of irritation and tension are likely to affect their working relationship as well as Doris's well-being.

Displaying Feelings

Displaying feelings means expressing those feelings through facial reactions, body responses, or paralinguistic and linguistic reactions. Cheering over a great play at a sporting event, howling when you bang your head against the car doorjamb, and patting a coworker on the back for doing something well are all displays of feelings.

Displays are usually appropriate when the feelings you are experiencing are positive. For instance, when your friend Gloria does something nice for you, and you experience a feeling of joy, giving her a big hug is appropriate; when your supervisor gives you an assignment you've wanted, a big smile and an "Oh, thank you, Don" is an appropriate display of your feeling of appreciation. In fact, many people need to be more demonstrative of good feelings than they typically are. The bumper sticker "Have you hugged your kid today?" reinforces the point that people we care about need open displays of love and affection.

Displays become detrimental to communication when the feelings you are experiencing are negative—especially when the display of a negative feeling appears to be an overreaction. For instance, when Anitra says to Doris, "That first paragraph isn't very well written," Doris might display her feelings of resentment by shouting, "Who the hell asked you for your opinion?" Such a display would doubtless embarrass and offend Anitra and short-circuit their communication. Although displays of negative feelings may make you feel better temporarily, they are likely to be bad for you interpersonally.

If neither withholding nor displaying negative feelings is effective, what is the most appropriate way to handle them? Describe them.

Describing Feelings

Describing feelings—putting your feelings into words in a calm, nonjudgmental way—tends to be the most productive method of disclosing feelings. Describing feelings increases the chances of positive interaction and decreases the chances of short-circuiting lines of communication. Moreover, describing feelings teaches others how to treat us. When you describe your feelings, people are made aware of the effect of their behavior. This knowledge gives them the information they need to determine whether they should continue or repeat that behavior. If you tell Paul that you feel flattered when he visits you, your description of how you feel should encourage him to visit you again. Likewise, when you tell Tony that you feel very angry when he borrows your jacket without asking, he is more likely to ask the next time. Describing your feelings allows you to exercise a measure of control over others' behavior simply by making them aware of the effects their actions have on you.

Describing and displaying feelings are not the same. Many times, people think they are describing when in fact they are displaying feelings or evaluating the other person's behavior. For instance, when questioned, Doris may believe her outburst, "Who the hell asked you for your opinion?" is a description of feelings. The first part of the communication practice at the end of this section focuses on the difference between describing feelings and either displaying feelings or expressing evaluations.

If describing feelings is so important to effective communication, why don't more people do it regularly? There seem to be at least five reasons why many people don't describe feelings.

The skills of assertiveness lead to more satisfying communication by allowing us to stand up for ourselves in a way that respects the rights and feelings of others.

1. *Many people don't have a very good vocabulary of words for describing the various feelings they experience.* People can sense that they are angry; however, they may not be able to distinguish between feeling annoyed, betrayed, cheated, crushed, disturbed, envious, furious, infuriated, outraged, or shocked. Each of these terms describes a slightly different aspect of what many people lump together as anger. A surprising number of shades of meaning can be used to describe feelings, as shown in Figure 5.2. In the communication practice at the end of this section, we use this list to focus on developing your vocabulary so that you can describe your feelings more precisely.

2. *Many people believe that describing their true feelings reveals too much about them.* If you tell people what hurts you, you risk their using the information against you when they want to hurt you on purpose. Nevertheless, the potential benefits of revealing your true feelings far outweigh the risks. For instance, if Pete has a nickname for you that you don't like, and you tell Pete that calling you by that nickname upsets you, Pete does have the option of calling you by that name when he wants to hurt you, but he is more likely to stop calling you by that name. If, on the other hand, you don't describe your feelings to Pete, he's probably going to continue calling you by that name simply because he doesn't know any better. By saying nothing, you reinforce his behavior. The level of risk varies with each situation, but you will more often improve a relationship by describing feelings than be hurt by doing so.

3. *Many people believe that if they describe feelings, others will make them feel guilty about having such feelings.* At a tender age, we all learned about "tactful" behavior. Under the premise that "the truth sometimes hurts," we learn to avoid the truth by not saying anything or by telling "little" lies. Perhaps when you were young, your mother said, "Don't forget to give grandma a great big kiss." At that time, you may have blurted out, "Ugh—it makes me feel yucky to kiss grandma. She's got a mustache." If your mother then responded, "That's terrible—your grandma loves you. Now you give her a kiss and never let me hear you talk like that again!" you probably felt guilty for having this "wrong" feeling. Yet the thought of kissing your grandmother did make you feel "yucky" whether it should have or not. In this case, the issue was not your having the feelings but the way you talked about them. Chapter 7 introduces skills for responding appropriately to others' feelings.

4. *Many people believe that describing feelings causes harm to others or to a relationship.* If it really bothers Fyodor when his girlfriend, Heather, bites her fingernails, Fyodor may believe that describing his feelings may hurt her feelings so much that it will drive a wedge into their relationship. So it's better if Fyodor says nothing, right? Wrong! If Fyodor says nothing, he's still going to be irritated by Heather's behavior. In fact, as time goes on, Fyodor's irritation will probably cause him to lash out at Heather for other things. But if Fyodor describes his feelings to Heather in a nonjudgmental way, she might try to quit biting her nails, or Fyodor might come to see that it really is a small thing and it may not bother him as much. In short, describing feelings yields a better chance of a successful outcome than does not describing them.

Words Related to *Angry*

agitated	annoyed	bitter	cranky
enraged	exasperated	furious	hostile
incensed	indignant	infuriated	irked
irritated	mad	offended	outraged
peeved	resentful	riled	steamed

Words Related to *Helpful*

agreeable	amiable	beneficial	caring
collegial	compassionate	constructive	cooperative
cordial	gentle	kindly	neighborly
obliging	supportive	useful	warm

Words Related to *Loving*

adoring	affectionate	amorous	aroused
caring	charming	fervent	gentle
heavenly	passionate	sensitive	tender

Words Related to *Embarrassed*

abashed	anxious	chagrined	confused
conspicuous	disconcerted	disgraced	distressed
flustered	humbled	humiliated	jittery
overwhelmed	rattled	ridiculous	shamefaced
sheepish	silly	troubled	uncomfortable

Words Related to *Surprised*

astonished	astounded	baffled	bewildered
confused	distracted	flustered	jarred
jolted	mystified	perplexed	puzzled
rattled	shocked	startled	stunned

Words Related to *Fearful*

afraid	agitated	alarmed	anxious
apprehensive	bullied	cornered	frightened
horrified	jittery	jumpy	nervous
petrified	scared	shaken	terrified
threatened	troubled	uneasy	worried

Words Related to *Disgusted*

afflicted	annoyed	nauseated	outraged
repelled	repulsed	revolted	sickened

Figure 5.2 *A list of more than 200 words that can be used to describe feelings*

Words Related to *Hurt*

abused	awful	cheated	deprived
deserted	desperate	dismal	dreadful
forsaken	hassled	ignored	isolated
mistreated	offended	oppressed	pained
piqued	rejected	resentful	rotten
scorned	slighted	snubbed	wounded

Words Related to *Belittled*

betrayed	defeated	deflated	demeaned
diminished	disparaged	downgraded	foolish
helpless	inadequate	incapable	inferior
insulted	persecuted	powerless	underestimated
undervalued	unfit	unworthy	useless

Words Related to *Happy*

blissful	charmed	cheerful	contented
delighted	ecstatic	elated	exultant
fantastic	giddy	glad	gratified
high	joyous	jubilant	merry
pleased	satisfied	thrilled	tickled

Words Related to *Lonely*

abandoned	alone	bored	deserted
desolate	discarded	empty	excluded
forlorn	forsaken	ignored	isolated
jilted	lonesome	lost	rejected
renounced	scorned	slighted	snubbed

Words Related to *Sad*

blue	crestfallen	dejected	depressed
dismal	dour	downcast	gloomy
heavyhearted	joyless	low	melancholy
mirthless	miserable	moody	morose
pained	sorrowful	troubled	weary

Words Related to *Energetic*

animated	bold	brisk	dynamic
eager	forceful	frisky	hardy
inspired	kinetic	lively	peppy
potent	robust	spirited	sprightly
spry	vibrant	vigorous	vivacious

Figure 5.2   *(Continued)*

5. *Many people come from cultures that teach them to hide their feelings and emotions from others.* In some cultures, for example, harmony among the group or in the relationship is felt to be more important than individuals' personal feelings. People from such cultures may not describe their feelings out of concern for the health of the group.

To describe your feelings: (1) Clearly identify your feeling. (2) Put the feeling into words specifically. (3) Indicate what has triggered the feeling. (4) Make sure you acknowledge that the feeling is yours.

Here are two examples of describing feelings: (1) "Thank you for your compliment [trigger]; I [the person having the feeling] feel gratified [the specific feeling] that you noticed the effort I made." (2) "When you criticize my cooking on days that I've worked as many hours as you have [trigger], I [the person having the feeling] feel very resentful [the specific feeling]."

To begin with, you may find it easier to describe positive feelings: "You know, your taking me to that movie cheered me up" or "I feel delighted when you offer to help me with the housework." As you gain success with positive descriptions, you can try describing negative feelings attributable to environmental factors: "It's so cloudy; I feel gloomy" or "When the wind howls outside, I get jumpy." Finally, you can move to negative descriptions resulting from what people have said or done: "When you step in front of me like that, I'm annoyed" or "I feel confused because of the tone of your voice."

Practice in Describing Feelings

By Yourself

1. In each of the following sets of statements, place a D next to the statement or statements that describe feelings:

1. _____ **a.** That was a great movie!
   _____ **b.** I was really cheered up by the story.
   _____ **c.** I feel this is worth an Oscar.
   _____ **d.** Terrific!

2. _____ **a.** I feel you're a good writer.
   _____ **b.** Your writing brings me to tears.
   _____ **c.** [You pat the writer on the back] Good job.
   _____ **d.** Everyone likes your work.

3. _____ **a.** Yuck!
   _____ **b.** If things don't get better, I'm going to move.
   _____ **c.** Did you ever see such a hole!
   _____ **d.** I feel depressed by the dark halls.

4. _____ **a.** I'm not adequate as a leader of this group.
   _____ **b.** Damn—I goofed!
   _____ **c.** I feel inadequate in my efforts to lead the group.
   _____ **d.** I'm depressed by the effects of my leadership.

5. _____ **a.** I'm a winner.

_____ **b.** I feel I won because I'm most qualified.

_____ **c.** I did it! I won!

_____ **d.** I'm ecstatic about winning that award.

5.d. (a) is evaluative; (b) is evaluative; (c) is expressive.

except that here the feeling is described, not stated as an evaluation.

4.c and d. (a) is expressive/evaluative; (b) is expressive; (c) is similar to (a)

ings; (c) is an evaluation in question form.

3.d. (a) is expressive; (b) is the result of feelings but not a description of feel-

(d) is expressive/evaluative.

2.b. (a) is expressive/evaluative (there's that word *feel* again); (c) is expressive;

(d) is expressive.

clothing—despite the word *feel*, the person is evaluating, not describing feelings;

1.b. (a) is expressive/evaluative; (c) is an evaluation dressed in descriptive

2. Look at each word in Figure 5.2 (pp. 123–124) and say "I feel . . ." Try to identify the feeling this word would describe. Which words are meaningful enough to you that you could use them to help make your communication of feelings more precise?

3. Think back over the events of the day. At any time during the day did you feel particularly happy, angry, disappointed, excited, sad? How did you communicate your feelings to others? Under what circumstances, if any, did you describe your feelings? What appear to be your most common ways of displaying (expressing) your feelings? Consider what you might do to make your sharing of feelings more interpersonally effective.

In Groups

Working with at least one other person, role-play typical situations (for example, Tom's roommate borrows Tom's car without asking permission; the roommate comes into the room later and, giving Tom the keys, says, "Thanks for the car"), and then describe your feelings. After you have finished, have the other person or people describe their feelings in response to the same situation. Continue the exercise until each member of the group has had two or three chances to practice describing feelings.

Owning Feelings and Opinions

A related self-disclosure skill is owning your feelings. Instead of owning their feelings and opinions, people often tend to wrap them in impersonal or generalized language or attribute them to unknown or universal sources. *Owning feelings or opinions* (or crediting yourself) means making "I" statements to identify yourself as the source of a particular idea or feeling.

An "I" statement can be any statement that uses a first-person pronoun such as *I, my, me,* or *mine.* "I" statements help the listener understand fully and accurately the nature of the message. Consider the following paired statements:

"Advertising is the weakest department in the corporation."	"I believe advertising is the weakest department in the corporation."
"Everybody thinks Collins is unfair in his criticism."	"It seems to me that Collins is unfair in his criticism."
"It's common knowledge that the boss favors anything that Kelly does."	"In my opinion, the boss favors anything that Kelly does."
"Nobody likes to be laughed at."	"Being laughed at embarrasses me."

Each of these examples contrasts a generalized or impersonal account with an "I" statement. Why do people use vague referents to others rather than owning their ideas and feelings? There are two basic reasons.

1. *To strengthen the power of their statements.* Saying "Everybody thinks Collins is unfair in his criticism" means that if listeners doubt the statement, they are bucking the collective evaluation of countless people. Of course, not everybody knows that Collins is unfair. In this instance, the statement really means that one person holds the belief. Yet because people may think that their feelings or beliefs will not carry much weight, they may feel the need to cite unknown or universal sources for those feelings or beliefs.

2. *To escape responsibility.* Similarly, people use collective statements such as "everybody agrees" and "anyone with any sense" to escape responsibility for their own feelings and thoughts. It seems far more difficult for a person to say "I don't like Herb" than it is to say "No one likes Herb."

The problem with such generalized statements is that at best they are exaggerations and at worst they are deceitful. Being both accurate and honest with others requires taking responsibility for our own feelings and opinions. We all have a right to our reactions. If what you are saying is truly your opinion or an expression of how you really feel, let others know, and be willing to take responsibility for it. Otherwise, you may alienate people who would have respected your opinions or feelings even if they didn't agree with them.

Practice in Owning Feelings and Opinions

By Yourself

1. Are you likely to take responsibility for statements of your own? Under what circumstances?

2. Write down five opinions, beliefs, or feelings you have. Check to make sure each is phrased as an "I" statement. If not, correct each one. For example, "Nobody likes a sore loser" becomes "I don't like a sore loser."

Assertiveness

Assertiveness means standing up for ourselves in interpersonally effective ways that exercise our personal rights while respecting the rights of others. It entails describing our feelings honestly and/or verbalizing our position on an issue for the purpose of achieving a specific goal. Assertiveness may focus on describing feelings, giving good reasons for a belief, or suggesting a behavior or attitude we think is fair, without exaggerating for dramatic effect or attacking the other individual. We can understand the specific qualities of assertive behavior best if we contrast it with other ways of responding to adversity.

Coping with Adversity

When we believe we have been wronged, we are likely to behave in one of three ways: passively, aggressively, or assertively.

Passive Behavior.   People behave passively when they are reluctant to state their opinions, share feelings, or assume responsibility for their actions. Thus, instead of attempting to influence others' behavior, they often submit to other people's demands, even when doing so is inconvenient or against their best interests. For example, when Bill uncrates the new color television set he purchased at a local department store, he notices a large, deep scratch on the left side of the cabinet. If Bill is angry about the scratch but nevertheless keeps the set without trying to influence the store clerk to replace it, he is behaving passively.

Aggressive Behavior.   People who behave aggressively lash out at the source of their discontent with little regard for the situation or for the feelings of those they are attacking. Unfortunately, too many people confuse aggressiveness with assertiveness. Unlike assertive behavior, aggressive behavior is judgmental, dogmatic, faultfinding, and coercive.

Suppose, for example, that after discovering the scratch on the cabinet of his new television set, Bill storms back to the store, loudly demands his money back, and accuses the clerk of intentionally or carelessly selling him damaged merchandise. During his tirade, he may threaten the store with a lawsuit. Such aggressive

behavior may or may not get Bill a new television set; it will certainly damage his interpersonal relationships with the store personnel.

Assertive Behavior.   Behaving assertively means standing up for ourselves in an interpersonally constructive way. The difference between assertive behavior and passive or aggressive behavior is not the original feeling behind the response but the way in which we choose to react as a result of the feeling. If Bill behaved assertively, he would still be angry about bringing home a damaged set. But instead of either doing nothing or verbally assaulting the clerk, Bill might call the store and ask to speak to the clerk from whom he had purchased the set. When the clerk answered, Bill would describe his feelings on discovering a large scratch on the cabinet when he uncrated the set. He would then go on to say that he was calling to find out what to do to return the damaged set and get a new one. Whereas aggressive behavior might also achieve Bill's purpose of getting a new television set, the assertive behavior would achieve the same result at lower emotional costs to everyone involved.

Passive, Aggressive, and Assertive Responses

It is inevitable that our interpersonal exchanges will often involve the need to assert ourselves. For this reason, and because so much difficulty in relationships stems from ineffective responses to adversity, learning to distinguish between passive, aggressive, and assertive responses is a key interpersonal skill. To highlight the contrast among these three response styles, let's examine situations in which the issue is the quality of interpersonal relations.

At Work.   Tanisha works in an office that employs both men and women. Whenever the boss has an especially interesting and challenging job to be done, he assigns it to a male coworker whose desk is next to Tanisha's. The boss has never said anything to Tanisha or to the male employee that would indicate he thinks less of Tanisha or her ability. Nevertheless, Tanisha is hurt by the boss's behavior.

> *Passive:* Tanisha says nothing to the boss. She's very hurt by what she feels is a slight but swallows her pride.
> *Aggressive:* Tanisha marches into her boss's office and says, "Why the hell do you always give Tom the plums and leave me the garbage? I'm every bit as good a worker, and I'd like a little recognition!"
> *Assertive:* Tanisha arranges a meeting with her boss. At the meeting, she says, "I don't know whether you are aware of it, but during the last three weeks, every time you had a really interesting job to be done, you gave the job to Tom. To the best of my knowledge, you believe that Tom and I are equally competent—you've never given me any evidence to suggest that you thought less of my work. But when you 'reward' Tom with jobs that I perceive as plums and continue to offer me routine jobs, it hurts my feelings. Do you understand my feelings about this?" In this statement, she has both described her perception of the boss's behavior and her feelings about that behavior.

If you were Tanisha's boss, which of her responses would be most likely to achieve her goal of getting better assignments? Probably the assertive behavior. Which of her responses would be most likely to get her fired? Probably the aggressive behavior. Which of her responses would be least likely to "rock the boat"? Undoubtedly the passive behavior—but then she would continue to get the boring job assignments.

With a Friend.   Dan is a doctor doing his residency at City Hospital. He lives with two other residents in an apartment they have rented. Carl, one of the other residents, is the social butterfly of the group. It seems whenever he has time off, he has a date. But like the others, he's a bit short of cash. He doesn't feel a bit bashful about borrowing clothes, money, or jewelry from his roommates. One evening, Carl asks Dan if he can borrow his watch—a new, expensive watch that Dan received as a present from his father only a few days before. Dan is aware that Carl does not always take the best care of what he borrows, and he is very concerned about the possibility of Carl's damaging or losing the watch.

> *Passive:* "Sure."
> *Aggressive:* "Forget it! You've got a lot of nerve asking to borrow a brand-new watch. You know I'd be damned lucky to get it back in one piece."
> *Assertive:* "Carl, I know I've lent you several items without much ado, but this watch is special. I've had it only a few days, and I just don't feel comfortable lending it. I hope you can understand how I feel."

What are likely to be the consequences of each of these behaviors? If he behaves passively, Dan is likely to worry the entire evening and harbor some resentment of Carl even if he gets the watch back undamaged. Moreover, Carl will continue to think that his roommates feel comfortable in lending him anything he wants. If Dan behaves aggressively, Carl is likely to be completely taken aback by his explosive behavior. Dan has never said anything to Carl before, so he has no reason to believe that he can't borrow whatever he likes. Moreover, the relationship between Dan and Carl might become strained. But if Dan behaves assertively, he puts the focus on his own feelings and on this particular object—the watch. His response isn't a denial of Carl's right to borrow items, nor is it an attack on Carl. It is an explanation of why Dan does not want to lend this item at this time.

In a Social Situation.   Kim has invited two of her girlfriends and their dates to drop by her dormitory room before the dance. Shortly after the group arrives, Nick, who has come with Ramona, Kim's best friend, reaches into his pocket for a flask of whiskey, takes a large sip, and passes it to Kim. Kim knows that alcohol is strictly off-limits in the dorm and, moreover, is concerned about anyone in the group drinking before driving.

> *Passive:* Muttering, "Uh, well," Kim pretends to take a sip and passes the flask on.
> *Aggressive:* "Nick, that's really stupid, bringing whiskey into my dorm room. Can't anybody here have a good time without drinking, or are you all lushes? Now get out of here before somebody notices, and take the bottle with you."
> *Assertive:* "Nick, Ramona probably didn't tell you that drinking isn't allowed in the dorm. Besides, I'd feel a lot more at ease if we all stayed

sober in order to drive to the dance. So I'd appreciate it if you would take the whiskey out to the car. We can have a great time without getting into trouble or risking an accident."

Again, let's contrast the three behaviors. In this case, the passive behavior is not at all in Kim's interests. Kim knows the dormitory rules, and even if no one finds out, she'll feel uncomfortable because she did nothing to protect her friends from taking a needless risk with their safety. But the aggressive behavior is hardly better. She knows nothing about Nick, but her outburst assumes bad intentions not only from Nick but also from her friends. If Nick is at all inclined to be belligerent, her method is only going to incite him and damage her relationship with Ramona besides. The assertive behavior presents the issue firmly—the dorm rules must not be violated, especially since it is her room—and her feelings about the group's safety are described firmly but pleasantly. She also follows up with her original intent in getting together—to have a good time.

Behaving Assertively

Now let's consider some of the characteristics of behaving assertively that are illustrated or implied in the previous examples.

1. *Owning feelings.* In all cases, the assertive statement acknowledged that the thoughts and feelings were those of the person making the statement.

2. *Avoiding confrontational language.* In none of the assertive responses did the speaker act aggressively by using threats, evaluations, or dogmatic language.

3. *Using specific statements directed to the behaviors at hand.* In each case, potential issues could have been raised. For instance, Dan could have brought up Carl's untrustworthiness, but he chose instead to focus on the issue that was most relevant—his feelings about a special possession.

4. *Maintaining eye contact and firm body position.* People will not be perceived as being firm if they shift gaze, look at the floor, sway back and forth, hunch over, and use other signs that may be perceived as indecision or lack of conviction.

5. *Maintaining a firm but pleasant tone of voice.* Whereas aggressiveness is signaled with yelling or harsh tones, assertiveness is shown through steady, firm speech at a normal pitch, volume, and rate.

6. *Avoiding hemming and hawing.* Recall the passive example in which Kim says, "Uh, well." Vocalized pauses and other nonfluencies are other signs of indecisiveness.

7. *Speaking clearly.* Sometimes when people have something uncomfortable to say, they mutter so that what they have to say is almost unintelligible. Again, lack of clarity will be seen as indecision.

It's important to recognize that being assertive will not always achieve your goals. The skills discussed here in Part Three are designed to increase the probability of achieving interpersonal effectiveness. Just as with self-disclosure and describing feelings, there are risks involved in being assertive. People who have difficulty asserting themselves often do not appreciate the fact that the potential benefits far outweigh the risks. Remember, our behavior teaches people how to treat us. When we are passive—when we have taught people that they can ignore our feelings—they will. When we are aggressive, we teach people to respond in kind. By contrast, when we are assertive, we can influence others to treat us as we would prefer to be treated.

Reasons for Nonassertiveness

If assertiveness is the best way to achieve our goals, why are some people less likely to assert themselves? Probably for one or more of the following reasons:

1. *They fear reprisal.* People sometimes do not assert themselves because they are afraid that the person they are dealing with will punish them or withhold some reward. Is this fear justified? Certainly, there will be times when you are penalized for being assertive. Some people with power are very defensive and will react accordingly if they think you are threatening their security. For instance, if Adolfo's boss is giving him more to do than Adolfo thinks is fair, Adolfo may be reluctant to assert his position because his boss may decide not to reward him in the future. Often people let others run over them because they think that giving in will help them secure some other reward they seek.

2. *They are insecure about their knowledge or expertise.* Sometimes people are unassertive because they downplay their own knowledge or expertise in whatever subject is being considered. For instance, when buying cars, clothing, or other goods, people are often intimidated by the salesperson because they assume the person is more knowledgeable about the product. Of course, salespeople are not always masters of information; their primary skill is often persuasiveness rather than knowledge. More important, you are the expert when it comes to your own needs, wants, and tastes. No one needs to feel intimidated by the possibility of being shown up by another person's knowledge. Whether buying a coat, having the car repaired, or consulting a physician, a customer has a perfect right to ask questions about what is happening and why, and to look out for his or her own best interests.

3. *They question their self-worth.* Some people do not assert themselves because they question their self-worth. Perhaps because of their socialization in childhood or because of perceived failures as adults, they lack confidence in their own thoughts and feelings. Suppose Marcus receives a C on a term paper. As he reads his paper over, he's sure that what he said was worth more than a C. He thinks about going in to talk to his professor but says to himself, "He's not going to listen to me—I'm just a student." Is this a realistic appraisal? Maybe. It is also possible that Marcus generally doubts his ability to argue on his own behalf when his judgment differs from those of other people.

4. *They believe it is not worth the time or effort.* Sometimes people are not assertive because they believe that it takes too much work to be assertive. Occasionally, it does. If, however, you habitually find yourself thinking or saying it's not worth the time or effort to assert your thoughts and feelings, you may be offering an excuse that reflects anxiety or lack of self-confidence. Being assertive does take both work and practice, especially at first—but you will find that the rewards are worth it. Occasionally, you may find a champion who will look out for your interests. Usually, however, you are the only one who can or will represent your position.

5. *They accept others' expectations.* For example, some American women exhibit passive behavior because they accept the social stereotype that women should be accepting, warm, loving, and deferential. Regrettably, too many people see any signs of assertiveness as "unfeminine." Fortunately, the stereotype that perpetuates such passive behavior is no longer as influential as it once was, and many women who have spent much of their lives being passive now recognize the value of being assertive. Of course, socially conditioned passive behavior is not restricted to women. We may be socialized to be unassertive for many reasons, whether we are male or female.

Cultural Differences

Although assertiveness can be thought of as a basic human need, assertive behavior is primarily practiced in Western cultures. In Asian cultures, how one is seen is often felt to be more important than asserting one's beliefs or rights, and a premium is often placed on maintaining a formally correct standard of social interaction. For people from such cultures, maintaining "face" and politeness may be more important than achieving personal satisfaction. On the other hand, in Latin and Hispanic societies, men, especially, are often taught to exercise a form of self-expression that goes far beyond the guidelines presented here for assertive behavior. In these societies, the concept of "machismo" guides male behavior. Thus, the standard of assertiveness appropriate in our dominant culture can seem inappropriate to people whose cultural frame of reference leads them to perceive it as either aggressive or weak.

For this reason, with assertiveness—just as with any other skill—you need to be aware that there is no single standard of behavior that ensures you will achieve your goals. When talking with people whose culture, background, or lifestyle differs from your own, you may need to observe their behavior and their responses to your statements before you can be sure of the kinds of behavior that are likely to communicate your intentions effectively (see The Cultural Communication Gap on pages 134 and 135).

Practice in Being Assertive

By Yourself

1. For the next day or two, observe people and their behavior. Make notes of situations in which you believe people behaved in passive, aggressive, or assertive ways. Which of the ways seemed to help people achieve what they wanted? Which seemed to maintain or even improve their relationship with the other person or persons?

2. Identify five situations in the past in which you were nonassertive or aggressive. Try to write the dialogue for each situation. Then substitute an assertive response for the nonassertive or aggressive reactions you expressed in each case.

3. For each of the following situations, write a passive or aggressive response, and then contrast it with a more appropriate assertive response:

You come back to your dorm, apartment, or house to type a paper that is due tomorrow, only to find someone else is using your typewriter.

Passive or aggressive response:
Assertive response:

The Cultural Communication Gap

Basic cultural differences in perception can cause an "assertive" speaker to appear barbaric to someone whose tradition calls for harmony and accord.

American culture is known for its assertive and aggressive communication style. We are a culture that recently turned a self-help book with the title *Confessions of an S.O.B.* into a best-seller. We are a culture in which assertiveness-training courses are offered to teach people a communication style that stresses confrontation and aggressive verbal and nonverbal techniques. We are a culture that has more lawyers per 10,000 people (19.6) than any other culture in the world and that exposes its members to countless hours of television talk shows glorifying verbal combat.

As is the case with all the values of a culture, Americans receive rewards for an assertive communication style. Summarizing research on assertive people, Judy Pearson, Lynn Turner, and William Todd-Mancillas tells us that they tend to be more "self-accepting," "enthusiastic about communication and interactional opportunities," "have better interpersonal relationships," and "fare better at their workplace." When we combine these results with the countless other ways in which we reward assertiveness, it is no wonder assertive communication is the American standard rather than the exception.

Many Middle Eastern and Mediterranean cultures also value a communication style that is bellicose, aggressive, dynamic, assertive, and argumentative. A Yiddish proverb says, "Where there are two Jews, there are three arguments."

As you can imagine, communication problems arise when cultures that value assertiveness come in contact with cultures that value accord and harmony. One of us authors recalls that at a recent international conference, members of the Israeli delegation, who were arguing their position in a dynamic manner, complained that the representatives from Thailand showed no interest in or enthusiasm for the meeting because they "were just sitting there." The Thai delegates, on the other hand, thought the professors from Israel were angry because they were "using loud voices."

You're working at a store part-time. You want to rush home after work because you have a nice dinner planned with someone special. Just as you are ready to leave, your boss says, "I'd like you to work overtime if you would—Martin's supposed to replace you, but he just called and can't get here for at least an hour."

Passive or aggressive response:
Assertive response:

Filipinos also value a communication style that stresses calmness, equanimity, and interpersonal harmony. One term, *amor propio,* translates into English as "harmony" and refers to a very fragile sense of personal worth and self-respect. In interactions with others, it denotes being treated as a persona rather than an object. This value makes the Filipino especially vulnerable to negative remarks that may affect his or her standing in society. Consequently, Filipinos seldom criticize others; and if they do, it is in the most polite manner. They see bluntness and frankness as uncivilized, and will speak vaguely and ambiguously in a meeting to avoid a stressful confrontation. They have such high respect for others' feelings that they will always agree and keep their reservations to themselves.

The Japanese also place a high value on interpersonal harmony, which has a history in Japan that dates back thousands of years. The cultural thinking that stresses harmony can clearly be seen in the method the Japanese employ when doing business. Japanese business has evolved an elaborate process called *nemawashii:* "binding the roots of a plant before pulling it out." In this process, any subject that might cause disorder at a meeting is discussed in advance. Anticipating and obviating interpersonal antagonism allow the Japanese to avoid impudent and discourteous behavior.

Harmony is a guiding principle for the Chinese, as well. They will not tolerate outright displays of anger. A Chinese proverb observes, "The first man to raise his voice loses the argument."

Co-cultures in the United States hold contrary views of assertive and aggressive communication. For example, North American Native Indians, say Moghaddam, Taylor, and Wright, "have developed a distaste for Western assertiveness and tend to avoid those who interact in assertive ways." Cheyenne children are even removed from the tribe for short periods if they act aggressively toward other members.

We can also observe in the United States varying assertive patterns as they apply to gender. Summarizing research on the topic, Pearson, Turner, and Todd-Mancillas conclude that "women tend to fall in the range from nonassertive to assertive, while men tend to fall in the range from assertive to aggressive."

Cultivating your awareness about these different patterns is an essential first step to understanding and communicating with people whose cultural roots and/or speaking styles may be different from your own. ■

SOURCE: Larry A. Samovar and Richard E. Porter, *Communication Between Cultures* (Belmont, CA: Wadsworth, 1995), pp. 106–108.

During a phone call to your parents, who live in another state, your mother says, "We're expecting you to go with us when we visit your uncle on Saturday." You were planning to spend Saturday working on your résumé for an interview next week.

Passive or aggressive response:
Assertive response:

You and your friend made a date to go dancing, an activity you really enjoy. You've even bought a new outfit for the occasion. When you meet, your friend says, "I've changed my mind. If it's all the same to you, I thought we'd stay home and watch a movie instead."

Passive or aggressive response:
Assertive response:

Summary

Communicating ideas and feelings begins with initiating a conversation. People gravitate toward individuals who are knowledgeable, who enjoy interaction, and who are willing to converse. Good conversationalists know how to keep a conversation well organized and coherent. Conversational coherence is achieved by following the cooperative principle, including the quantity maxim, the quality maxim, the relation maxim, the manner maxim, the politeness maxim, and the morality maxim. In addition, conversation is enhanced by crediting others and taking turns appropriately.

Self-disclosure means sharing biographical data, ideas, and feelings that are unknown to another person. Appropriate self-disclosure deepens relationships, whereas inappropriate self-disclosure is likely to short-circuit communication.

The skill of describing feelings helps teach people how to treat you. Describing feelings is a sounder way of handling feelings, especially negative ones, than either withholding or displaying them. Owning your own feelings and opinions means taking responsibility for them.

Assertiveness is the skill of stating our ideas and feelings openly in interpersonally effective ways. Passive people are often unhappy as a result of not stating what they think and feel; aggressive people get their ideas and feelings heard but may create more problems for themselves because of their aggressiveness. When people do not assert themselves, it is likely to be because they fear reprisal, they are insecure about their knowledge or expertise, they question their self-worth, they believe it is not worth the time or effort, or they accept others' expectations. And as we might expect, appropriateness of assertiveness varies across cultures.

Some of the characteristics of behaving assertively are owning feelings, avoiding confrontational language, using specific statements directed to the behaviors at hand, maintaining eye contact and firm body position, maintaining a firm but pleasant tone of voice, avoiding hemming and hawing, and speaking clearly.

Suggested Readings

Alberti, Robert E., and Emmons, Michael L. *Your Perfect Right: A Guide to Assertive Living,* 6th ed. San Luis Obispo, CA: Impact, 1990. Gives excellent contrasts among assertive, nonassertive, and aggressive behavior, with emphasis on showing people how to assert themselves in various situations.

Derlega, Valerian J., and Berg, John H., eds. *Self-Disclosure: Theory, Research, and Therapy.* New York: Plenum, 1987. An excellent collection of writings on various self-disclosure issues emphasizing current research.

Nofsinger, Robert E. *Everyday Conversation.* Newbury Park, CA: Sage, 1991. Focuses on pragmatics—the study of actual language use in specific situations—and suggests that everyday conversation is a collection of language games involving a defined set of behaviors, often called moves, which are designed to contribute to the attainment of goals.

Tavris, Carol. *Anger: The Misunderstood Emotion.* New York: Touchstone, 1984. Draws on a great deal of research to show that most information about anger and dealing with anger is inaccurate. Points out that, as a mature person, you can determine the way to handle anger that is best for both you and those around you. Provides a detailed rationale for much of the analysis of dealing with feelings in this chapter.

Notes

1. J. R. Hobbs and D. A. Evans, "Conversation as Planned Behavior," *Cognitive Science* 4 (1980): 349–377.

2. Mary L. McLaughlin, *Conversation: How Talk Is Organized* (Newbury Park, CA: Sage, 1984), pp. 88–89.

3. Stephen W. Littlejohn, *Theories of Human Communication,* 4th ed. (Belmont, CA: Wadsworth, 1992), p. 91.

4. H. Paul Grice, "Logic and Conversation," in Peter Cole and Jerry L. Morgan, eds., *Syntax and Semantics,* Vol. 3: *Speech Acts* (New York: Academic Press, 1975), pp. 44–46.

5. K. Bach and R. M. Harnish, *Linguistic Communication and Speech Acts* (Cambridge, MA: MIT Press, 1979), p. 64.

6. Robert E. Nofsinger, *Everyday Conversation* (Newbury Park, CA: Sage, 1991), p. 81.

7. S. Duncan, Jr., and D. W. Fiske, *Face-to-Face Interaction: Research, Methods, and Theory* (Hillsdale, NJ: Erlbaum, 1977), pp. 184–196.

8. C. W. Kennedy and C. T. Camden, "A New Look at Interruptions," *Western Journal of Speech Communication* 47 (1983): 55.

9. Littlejohn, pp. 274–275.

10. See Irwin Altman and Donald Taylor, *Social Penetration: The Development of Interpersonal Relationships* (New York: Holt, Rinehart & Winston, 1973). Altman and Taylor coined the phrase *social penetration.*

11. Arthur P. Bochner, "The Functions of Human Communicating in Interpersonal Bonding," in Carroll C. Arnold and John Waite Bowers, eds., *Handbook of Rhetorical and Communication Theory* (Needham Heights, MA: Allyn & Bacon, 1984), p. 608.

12. John H. Berg and Valerian J. Derlega, "Themes in the Study of Self-Disclosure," in John H. Berg and Valerian J. Derlega, eds., *Self-Disclosure: Theory, Research, and Therapy* (New York: Plenum, 1987), p. 4.

13. William B. Gudykunst and Young Yun Kim, *Communicating with Strangers: An Approach to Intercultural Communication,* 2d ed. (New York: McGraw-Hill, 1992), p. 202.

14. Judy Cornelia Pearson, Lynn H. Turner, and William Todd-Mancillas, *Gender and Communication,* 2d ed. (Dubuque, IA: Wm. C. Brown, 1991), p. 177.

15. Charles T. Hill and Donald E. Stull, "Gender and Self-Disclosure: Strategies for Exploring the Issues," in John H. Berg and Valerian J. Derlega, eds., *Self-Disclosure: Theory, Research, and Therapy* (New York: Plenum, 1987), p. 95.

16. Pearson, Turner, and Todd-Mancillas, p. 177.

17. Deborah Tannen, *You Just Don't Understand* (New York: Morrow, 1990), p. 48.

Objectives

After you have read this chapter, you should be able to:

Focus your attention

Listen actively

Use four different techniques to remember information

Listen critically and evaluate inferences

Listening Skills

Sue says to Dan, "I'm going to be with the film crew on location and won't be able to pick up Marsha at 3:30, so you will have to pick her up." Catching a reference to the film crew, Dan nods and says, "OK." At 4:15 he casually answers the phone, only to hear Marsha say, "Dad, aren't you picking me up?"

Margot tells Jack, "I need you to run 25 forms on regular-size paper with a blue cover page and 75 on legal-size paper with a yellow cover page." Later in the day when Jack brings the forms, Margot notices that the 25 with a blue cover are on legal-size and the rest with a yellow cover are on regular-size paper. When Margot says, "Jack, I said 25 on regular-size and 75 on legal-size," Jack replies, "Oh, I'm sorry, I mixed it up."

Have you had experiences like these? Most of us have. But these listening mistakes strain family and work relationships and can raise questions about a person's priorities. They can cost time, money, and energy, and they can hurt feelings.

Perhaps these problems wouldn't be so significant if listening played a smaller role in communication. But the fact is that in your daily communication you may spend more of your time listening than you do speaking, reading, and writing combined. One study found that college students spend 16 percent of their time speaking, 17 percent reading, 14 percent writing, and 53 percent listening.[1] Yet, after 48 hours, most listeners can remember only about 25 percent of what they heard.[2] Considering its importance and how little attention most of us pay to it, listening may be the most underrated of all communication skills.

What is listening? When Wolvin and Coakley studied various definitions, they found that more than 25 overlapping words and phrases were used.[3] In this book, we define *listening* as an active, five-step process that includes attending, understanding, remembering, evaluating, and responding. Because each of the phases of listening requires distinct, specific skills, we discuss each separately—the first four in this chapter and the fifth, responding, in the next chapter.

Attending: Focusing Attention

The first phase of the listening process is to attend to—to focus our attention in such a way that we hear what people are saying and disregard extraneous sounds. *Attending* is the perceptual process of selecting specific stimuli from the countless stimuli reaching the senses.

Although we hear any sounds emitted within our hearing range, we exercise a certain amount of psychological control over the sounds we attend to. For instance, as you and a friend are chatting while you walk to class, you both receive and attend to each other's words. At the same time, you may physically "hear" footsteps behind you, the chiming of school bells, and birds singing, but you are able to block them out. In fact, you may be so unconscious of background noise that you would deny that certain sounds occurred.

One Big Happy by Rick Detorie. By permission of Rick Detorie and Creators Syndicate.

Poor listeners are likely to exercise insufficient control over which sounds they attend to. Improving your listening skills begins with learning to bring some sounds to the foreground while keeping others in the background. People who have developed this skill are able to focus their attention so well that only such sounds as a fire alarm, a car crashing into a post, or the cry of their child can intrude on their attention.

Let's consider five techniques for consciously focusing attention.

1. *Try to eliminate physical impediments to listening.* First, we need to be assertive about seeing to it that conditions for listening are well maintained. If, for instance, the radio is playing so loudly that you are having difficulty hearing your roommate, you can turn down the radio while she's talking.

Second, we need to be aware of our own physical limitations. Nearly 15 million Americans suffer from some hearing impairment that may be significant enough to affect their ability to listen.[4] If you are among this number, you may wear a hearing aid or you may have learned to adapt to the problem. If you often miss spoken words and have to ask that they be repeated, however, you may have a hearing impairment that you are unaware of that limits your listening effectiveness. If you suspect you may have a hearing problem, have a complete hearing test. Most colleges have facilities for testing hearing acuity. The test is painless and is usually provided at small, if any, cost to the student.

2. *Get physically and mentally ready to listen.* Oftentimes poor listening results from our failure to get ready to listen. Many of us have developed a set of behaviors we associate with attentive listening. Suppose that a few minutes after class begins your professor says, "In the next two minutes, I'm going to cover some material that is especially important—in fact, I can guarantee that it will be on the test." How would you behave? Although we do not all behave the same way, we are likely to sit upright in our chairs, lean slightly forward, and cease any extraneous physical movement. All of these are physical signs of being ready to listen. We may also look directly at the professor. When eye contact is not maintained, at least some information is lost.[5]

Mentally, we are likely to direct all of our attention to what the professor is saying. This includes attempting to block out the miscellaneous thoughts constantly passing through our minds. Recall that when people are talking with you, their ideas and feelings compete with the internal noise created by whatever's on your mind at the moment—a basketball game, a calculus test, a date you're excited about, a movie you've just seen. And what you're thinking about may be more pleasant to attend to than what someone is saying to you. Attending to these competing thoughts and feelings is one of the leading causes of poor listening.

3. *Make the shift from speaker to listener a complete one.* In a public-speaking setting, where you listen continuously for long stretches, it is relatively easy to develop a "listening attitude." In conversation, however, you are called on to switch back and forth from speaker to listener so frequently that you may find it difficult at times to make these shifts completely. If, instead of listening, you spend your time rehearsing what you're going to say as soon as you have a chance, your listening effectiveness will take a nosedive. We have all experienced situations in which two persons talked right past each other—both broadcasting and neither receiving! Especially when you are in a heated conversation, take a second to check yourself. Are you preparing speeches instead of listening? Shifting from the role of speaker to that of listener requires constant and continuous effort.

Can you think of times when you wished someone had simply listened to you quietly and attentively? According to Robert Bolton, attentive silence is one of the most underused listening skills in our culture. Like most skills, it takes practice—and the willingness to experience the discomfort of trying something new.

The beginning listener needs to learn the value of silence in freeing the speaker to think, feel, and express himself. "The beginning of wisdom is silence," said a Hebrew sage. "The second stage is listening."

Most listeners talk too much. They may speak as much or even more than the person trying to talk. Learning the art of silent responsiveness is essential to good listening. After all, another person cannot describe a problem if you are doing all the talking.

Silence on the part of the listener gives the speaker time to think about what he is going to say and thus enables him to go deeper into himself. It gives a person space to experience the feelings churning within. Silence also allows the speaker to proceed at his own pace. It provides time to deal with his ambivalence about sharing. In the frequent silences, he can choose whether or not to continue talking and at what depth. Silence often serves as a gentle nudge to go further into a conversation. When an interaction is studded with significant silences and backed by good attending, the results can be very impressive. . . .

More than half the people who take communication skills training with us are initially uncomfortable with silence. Even a few seconds' pause in a conversation causes many of them to squirm. These people feel so ill at ease with silences that they have a strong inner compulsion to shatter the quiet with questions, advice, or any other sound that will end their discomfort by ending the silence. For these people, the focus of attention is not on the speaker but rather on their own inner disquiet. . . .

Fortunately, most people can increase their comfort with silence in a

4. *Hear a person out before you react.* Far too often, we stop listening before the person has finished speaking because we "know what a person is going to say." Yet until the person has finished, we don't have all the data necessary to form an appropriate response; our "knowing" what a person is going to say is really only a guess. Moreover, even if we guess right, the person may still feel that we weren't really listening, and the communication will suffer as a result. Accordingly, cultivate the habit of always letting a person complete his or her thought before you stop listening or try to respond. At times your attentive listening may be the best response you can make. Most of us need to learn the value of silence in freeing the speaker to think, feel, and express himself. As the old Hebrew adage goes, "The beginning of wisdom is silence" (see When Silence Is Golden, above).

relatively short period of time. When people find out what to do in silence, they become far less uptight in the verbal lulls that are so important to vital communication. During the pauses in an interaction, a good listener does the following:

Attends to the other. His body posture demonstrates that he is really there for the other person.

Observes the other. He sees that the speaker's eyes, facial expressions, posture, and gestures are all communicating. When you are not distracted by the other's words, you may "hear" his body language more clearly.

Thinks about what the other is communicating. He ponders what the other has said. He wonders what the speaker is feeling. He considers the variety of responses he might make. Then he selects the one that he thinks will be most facilitative.

When he is busy doing these things, the listener does not have time to become anxious about the silence. . . .

Before the birth of Jesus, the author of the book Ecclesiastes said there is a "time to keep silent and a time to speak." The effective listener can do both. Some people sit quietly during a whole conversation, pushing the other into a monologue. Excessive silence can be as undesirable as no silence. To sit mute like a "bump on a log" does not constitute effective listening. It is rarely possible to listen effectively for a long time without making some kind of verbal response. . . . Silence, when overdone, is not golden—it is then merely a lack of response to the person with needs.

The effective listener learns to speak when that is appropriate, can be silent when that is a fitting response, and feels comfortable with either activity. The good listener becomes adept at verbal responses while at the same time recognizing the immense importance of silence in creative conversation. He frequently emulates Robert Benchley, who once said, "Drawing on my fine command of language, I said nothing." ■

SOURCE: Robert Bolton, *People Skills* (New York: Simon & Schuster, 1979), pp. 30–48. Copyright © 1979 by Simon & Schuster, Inc. Reprinted by permission of Simon & Schuster, Inc.

In addition to prematurely ceasing to listen, we often let certain mannerisms and words interfere with hearing a person out, perhaps to the extent of "tuning out." For instance, we may become annoyed when a speaker mutters, stammers, or talks in a monotone. But in these situations, we should work even harder at concentrating on what the person is saying.

Likewise, we may tune out when the speaker uses language or presents ideas that are irritating to us. Are there any words or ideas that create bursts of semantic noise for you, causing you to stop listening attentively? For instance, do you have a tendency to react negatively or tune out when people speak of *gay rights, skinheads, welfare frauds, political correctness,* or *rednecks*? To counteract this effect, try to let a warning light go on when a speaker trips the switch to your emotional reaction.

Instead of tuning out or getting ready to fight, be aware of this "noise" and work that much harder to listen objectively. If you can do it, you will be more likely to receive the whole message accurately before you respond.

5. *Adjust to the listening goals of the situation.* Listening is similar to reading in that you need to adjust *how* you listen to the particular goal you wish to achieve and to the degree of difficulty of the material you will be receiving. The intensity with which you attend to a message should depend on whether your purpose or goal is primarily enjoyment, learning/understanding, evaluating/critiquing, or responding helpfully to the needs of another.

When your goal is primarily "pleasure listening," you can afford to listen without much intensity. People often speak of "vegging out in front of the tube." In most cases, they mean "listening" to comedy or light drama as a means of passing time pleasurably. Unfortunately, many people approach all situations as if they were listening to pass time. Yet how we listen should change qualitatively with the level of difficulty of the information.

Suppose that instead of watching a situation comedy, you attend a professor's lecture on cultural diversity. Now instead of just passing time, your goal is learning or understanding. In listening situations such as attending to directions (how to get to a restaurant), instructions (how to shift into reverse in a foreign car), or explanations (a recounting of the new office procedures), the intensity of your "listening" is likely to increase, for the goal of understanding requires more careful attending. Moreover, you are likely to switch to a more active listening mode. In the next two sections of this chapter, we consider several skills for adjusting our listening when the goals are understanding and remembering.

At other times, your goal may be to listen critically. Every day we are flooded with countless messages—from friends and family members, coworkers, advertisers, political candidates—designed to influence our behavior. To choose wisely in these situations, we must not only listen more actively, but also be able to recognize the facts, weigh them, separate emotional appeals, and determine the soundness of the conclusions presented. In the final section of this chapter, we consider several skills for adjusting to critical listening.

A special challenge is listening to enable us to give helpful responses. Often, people come to us to share their problems and concerns. Sometimes, they simply want someone to talk with; other times they come to us for help. Many of the skills we cover in the next chapter are response skills that will work in helping situations.

Practice in Attending

By Yourself

Select an information-oriented program on your public television station (such as "Nova," "The McNeil-Lehrer News Hour," or "Wall Street Week"). Watch at least twenty minutes of the show while lounging in a comfortable chair or while stretched out on the floor with music playing on a radio in the background. After about twenty minutes, quickly outline what you have learned.

Now, make a conscious decision to be attentive to the next twenty minutes of the show. Turn off the music and sit in a straight-back chair as you watch the program. Your goal is to increase your listening intensity in order to learn, so block out other distractions. After this twenty-minute segment, you should again outline what you remember.

Compare your notes. Is there any difference between the amount or quality of the information you retained? Discuss your results with your classmates. Are their results similar or different? Why?

Understanding: Listening Actively

The second phase of the listening process is understanding what we have heard. *Understanding* refers to the ability to decode a message by correctly assigning a meaning to it. Sometimes failure to understand is a result of people using words that are not in our vocabulary. Suppose someone asks "Quelle heure est-il?" and you do not know French. You hear the sounds, but you are unable to understand that the person is asking "What time is it?" But even when people are speaking in your native language, they may use words that are not in your vocabulary; moreover, they may talk quickly, run together sounds, and mispronounce words so that you have trouble decoding the message.

Understanding requires active listening. *Active listening* means using specific techniques to ensure your understanding. Since we can think faster than a speaker can talk, we can learn to process information while it is being given. Active-listening

Have you ever been consoled by talking to a good listener, like this school counselor? Such listeners are usually made, not born: through study and practice they have learned specific skills such as attending closely, watching for nonverbal clues, and checking their understanding before they respond.

techniques include determining the organization of the message, paying attention to nonverbal cues, asking questions to get necessary information, and silently paraphrasing the meanings we have understood. Let's consider these four procedures.

1. *Determine the organization.* Effective speakers are likely to have some basic organization for the information they are presenting. This underlying structure includes a purpose or goal, key ideas (or main points) to develop the purpose, and details to explain or support the main points. Active listeners pay attention to and seek out organizational patterns. Suppose that during a parents' meeting, Gloria brings up the subject of teenage crime. As Gloria talks, she may focus on the effects of poverty and broken homes. For each topic she may provide information she has read or heard. When Gloria finishes speaking, her listeners will understand the message if they distinguish Gloria's view of the causes of teenage crime (her purpose), the two specific factors she sees as causes (her key points), and the evidence she has provided to support each factor (details).

Sometimes people organize their messages in such a way that it is relatively easy to understand the purpose, key points, and details. At other times, however, we must supply the structure for ourselves. You can sort out the purpose, key points, and details of a complex message, and thus increase your understanding of the message, by mentally outlining the message. Asking "What am I supposed to know/do because I listened to this?" will allow you to determine purpose. Asking "What are the categories of information?" and "Why should I do/think this?" will enable you to identify key points. Asking "What's the support?" will enable you to identify the details.

2. *Attend to nonverbal cues.* Active listeners interpret messages more accurately when they observe the nonverbal behaviors that accompany the words, for meaning may be shown as much by the nonverbals as by the words that are spoken. In the chapter on nonverbal communication, we noted that up to 65 percent of the meaning of a social message may be carried nonverbally. Thus, when Franco says "You really got through to Professor Grant on that one," whether you take his statement as a compliment or a jibe will depend on your perception of the sound of Franco's voice. Likewise, when Deborah says "Go on, I can walk home from here," we have to interpret cues such as tone of voice, body actions, and facial expression to tell whether she is sincerely interested in walking or whether she'd really like a ride.

So, whether you are listening to a coworker explaining her stance on an issue, a friend explaining the process for hanging wallpaper, or a loved one explaining why he or she is upset with you, you must listen to how something is said as well as to what is said. We return to the interpretation of nonverbal cues when we discuss the important concept of empathy at the beginning of Chapter 7.

3. *Ask questions.* Active listeners are willing to ask questions to help them get the information they need to understand. Yet, many of us seem unwilling to question: we don't understand, but we say nothing. Sometimes people are too shy or too hesitant to admit that they do not know what the speaker means. But isn't it equally foolish to respond as if we understand when we really do not? If your professor tells you your term paper reached the "nadir," and you smile and say "Thank you" even though you don't know what she is talking about, that behavior would be foolish. *Nadir* means the low point—the "pits." Although we may feel embarrassed that the word is not a part of our vocabulary, we are likely to behave foolishly if we do not ask what the word means. Politely saying, "I'm not sure I understand the word *nadir;* could you define it for me?" does not brand you as deficient. On the contrary, it indicates that you are serious about trying to understand the message.

At other times, our failure to understand goes beyond vocabulary. When a person's explanation is too vague or incomplete, slurred, disorganized, or unintelligible, you need to ask for clarification. Suppose the department secretary says, "Just take the papers you want to run and put them in the tray, and the machine will run them, collate them, and staple them," you may have the general idea, but you still may not know how to set the papers up so that they will be stapled in the right place. The only way you're going to understand is to ask. You might say, "I can see that the papers need to be in order and face down, but should the top of the page be toward me or away from me?"

In Chapter 7, we consider in detail how to ask for information in interpersonally appropriate ways.

4. *Silently paraphrase.* Active listeners are adept at paraphrasing. A *paraphrase* is a statement of your understanding of what a person said in your own words. A paraphrase can be silent or verbal. For example, after a friend has spent a few minutes explaining how to prepare a certain dish, you might say silently to yourself, "In other words, how the mixture is put together may be more important than the ingredients used." Keep in mind that the accuracy of your paraphrase—especially with messages involving feelings—is likely to depend on how well you have attended to the nonverbal cues as well as to the words. If you cannot paraphrase a message, the message may not have been well encoded, there may have been contradictions between the verbal and nonverbal messages, or you may not have been listening carefully enough. In Chapter 7, you will have an opportunity to study and practice verbal paraphrases as a means of ensuring shared meaning and for purposes of making appropriate responses.

Practice in Understanding

In Groups

Have group members take turns talking for one to two minutes on a topic with which they are familiar and on which they have an opinion. The other members try to listen actively. When each speaker is finished, have the listeners quickly outline what they have understood to be the purpose and the key points. Afterward, share, compare, and discuss your outlines to determine both similarities and differences between the intended meaning and the received meaning.

Remembering: Retaining Information

The third phase of the listening process, and a natural follow-up to understanding, is *remembering*—retaining information in memory. All of our skill in understanding may go to waste if we cannot remember what we have learned.

As we observe our own behavior, we sometimes have difficulty determining any pattern to what we remember and what we forget. On the one hand, we may

What sources of noise—physical and psychological— might this man have to "tune out" in order to actively process and remember what his supervisor is telling him?

find ourselves forgetting items that we want to remember almost immediately. How many times have you been unable to recall the name of a person to whom you were introduced just thirty seconds earlier? On the other hand, some ideas and feelings seem to imprint themselves so deeply on our memories that a lifetime of trying to forget will not erase them. For instance, a song lyric may rattle around in your mind for days, or a cutting remark made by a loved one may haunt you for years. Nevertheless, we can have a great deal of control over what we remember. Effective listeners learn to apply four well-documented techniques: rehearsal, constructing mnemonics, regrouping material, and when possible, note taking. We consider each of these techniques in turn.

Rehearsal

The act of remembering involves moving information from short-term, or working, memory to long-term memory.[6] And the simplest procedure for accomplishing this goal is rehearsal. *Rehearsal* is the act of mentally repeating material immediately after receiving it. Rehearsing information two, three, or even four times makes it far more likely that we will remember the material at a later date. Rehearsal provides necessary reinforcement for the information. If the information is not reinforced, it will be held in short-term memory for as little as twenty seconds and then forgotten. So, when you are introduced to a stranger named Jack McNeil, if you mentally say "Jack McNeil, Jack McNeil, Jack McNeil, Jack McNeil," you increase the chances that you will remember his name. Likewise, when a person gives you the directions "Go two blocks east, turn left, turn right at the next light, and it's in the next block," you should immediately repeat to yourself, "two blocks east, turn left, turn right at light, next block—that's two blocks east, turn left, turn right at light, next block.'"

Constructing Mnemonics

We are far more likely to remember material if we can find or create some organizational pattern for it. Constructing mnemonics helps listeners put information in forms that are more easily recalled. A *mnemonic device* is any artificial technique used as a memory aid. One of the most common ways of forming a mnemonic is to take the first letters of a list of items you are trying to remember and forming a word. For example, suppose you are listening to a lecturer explaining speech goals. The lecturer mentions that people are likely to give speeches to entertain, to inform, and to persuade. By rearranging the order to *p*ersuade, *i*nform, and *e*ntertain, you can create the word *pie* as a mnemonic.

When you want to remember items in a sequence, try to form a sentence using those items in order, or assign words that begin with the first letter of each item in sequence to form an easy-to-remember phrase or sentence. For instance, many of us who took music lessons in our youth will recall the mnemonic for the lines of the treble clef (E, G, B, D, F) by reciting "*E*very *g*ood *b*oy *d*oes *f*ine."

Regrouping Material

Another way of organizing information is to see whether a chronological, spatial, or topical relationship exists among the ideas and then group them accordingly. Directions are best remembered chronologically, descriptions can be remembered spatially, and other kinds of material can be grouped topically.

We are far more likely to remember long lists of items if we can regroup them under two or three headings.[7] Many times, people express their thoughts as a series of items of equal weight. For instance, a person who is explaining what you need to do to complete a woodworking project might tell you to gather the materials, draw a pattern, trace the pattern on wood, cut out the pattern so that the tracing line can still be seen, file to the pattern line, sandpaper edges and surfaces, paint the object, sand lightly, apply a second coat of paint, and varnish. This list includes ten steps of apparently equal weight, and the chances of your remembering all ten steps in order are not very good. But if you analyze the ten steps, you will see that you can regroup them under three headings: (1) Plan the job (gather materials, draw a pattern, trace the pattern on wood). (2) Cut out the pattern (saw so the tracing line can be seen, file to the pattern line, sand edges and surfaces). (3) Finish the object (paint, sand lightly, apply a second coat of paint, varnish). The regrouping appears to add three more steps, but in reality, by turning ten separate steps of apparently equal weight into three steps with three, three, and four subdivisions, respectively, you are much more likely to remember the entire process.

This technique is effective because it takes into consideration the limitations of most people's abilities to process information. Psychologists who study human memory processes have discovered that seven bits of information is about the limit of what most of us can hold in our active consciousness at one time.[8] Thus, the list of ten steps is too long for us to remember. Instead, we "store" three main points and their three to four subpoints, amounts of information we can easily retain.

Note Taking

Although note taking would be inappropriate in most casual interpersonal encounters, it represents a powerful tool for increasing our recall of information from telephone conversations, briefing sessions, interviews, business meetings, and speeches. Note taking provides a written record that we can go back to. Moreover, the literature suggests that the act of note taking may be more important than the notes themselves. That is, by engaging in taking notes, we take a more active role in the listening process.[9] Thus, when you are studying for an exam, taking the time to write out ideas you are trying to remember serves as a reinforcing agent.

What constitutes good notes will vary with the situation. Useful notes may consist of a brief list of main points or key ideas plus a few of the most significant details. Or they may be a short summary of the entire concept (a type of paraphrase) after the message is completed. For lengthy and rather detailed information, however, good notes likely will consist of a brief outline of what the speaker has said, including the overall idea, the main points of the message, and key supporting material. Good notes are not necessarily very long; in fact, many classroom lectures can be reduced to a brief outline.

Suppose you are listening to a supervisor instruct her staff about the importance of clear writing in their reports. In her instructions, the supervisor discusses the need to test the readability of a report by computing its "fog index." Anticipating the likelihood of receiving detailed information, the active listener will take notes. The supervisor might say:

> The boss is really concerned with the quality of the report writing that is coming from the major divisions. The word is that reports just aren't as readable as they should be. In the future, every report will be required to include a Fog Index, including a summary of the figures used to calculate it.
>
> A Fog Index is one of the most common tests of readability. It's an easy one to use and generally reliable. Like most readability tests, it is based on computations of sentence length and word length. The theory is that the shorter the sentences and the words, the easier the reading.
>
> Computing a Fog Index for a report involves six easy steps.
>
> First, select five random sections of at least 100 words each. In a five-page report, this would be one passage per page. Begin at the start of a paragraph, count off 100 words, and continue to count until the end of that sentence. Each passage will thus have 100 words or more.
>
> Second, compute the average sentence length of each passage. If a 116-word passage has five sentences, the average sentence length of that passage would be 23.2 words.
>
> Third, compute the number of difficult words per hundred. The beauty of this test is that "difficult" words are easily identified as any word of more than two syllables except proper names and verbs that become three syllables by adding -es, -ed, or -ing. So, if that 116-word passage has 12 difficult words, you would divide 12 by 116, then multiply by 100, giving you 10.3 difficult words per hundred. For both steps two and three, round off the figures to the nearest whole number.

Fourth, add the average sentence length to the number of difficult words per hundred. In our example, you would add 23 and 10.

Fifth, multiply the answer by .4. The result is the Fog Index. The resulting figure stands for the number of years of schooling required to read the passage easily.

Sixth, because you will have done five passages, you will then compute the average index for the five passages. Write that figure at the end of the report, and include your computations.

We have been instructed to rewrite reports until we achieve a Fog Index of between 10 and 13 for each.

This short passage includes a great deal of specific detail, much more than you will find in most oral instructions. Yet the 393 words of explanation can be outlined in just 125 words (see Figure 6.1). In good note taking, the number of words used may range from 10 percent of the original material to as high as 30 percent (the amount in our example). The point is not the number of words, however, but the accuracy of the notes in reflecting the sense of what the speaker said.

Practice in Remembering

With Another

Have a friend assume the role of a fellow worker on your first day in an office job and read the following information to you once, at a normal rate of speech. As the friend reads the instructions, take notes. Then give yourself the test that follows *without* referring to your notes. Then repeat the quiz, but this time use your notes. How much does your score improve? Although the temptation is great to read this item to yourself, try not to. You will miss both the enjoyment and the value of the exercise if you do.

Since you are new to the job, I'd like to fill you in on a few details. The boss probably told you that typing and distribution of mail were your most important duties. Well, they may be, but let me tell you, answering the phone is going to take most of your time. Now about the typing. Goodwin will give the most, but much of what he gives you may have nothing to do with the department—I'd be careful about spending all my time doing his private work. Mason doesn't give much, but you'd better get it right—she's really a stickler. I've always asked to have tests at least two days in advance. Bernstein is always dropping stuff on the desk at the last minute.

The mail situation sounds tricky, but you'll get used to it. Mail comes twice a day—at 10 A.M. and at 2 P.M. You've got to take the mail that's been left on the desk to Charles Hall for pickup. If you really have some rush stuff, take it right to the campus post office in Harper Hall. It's a little longer walk, but for really rush stuff, it's better. When you pick up at McDaniel Hall, sort it. You'll have to make sure that only mail for the people up here gets delivered here. If there is any that doesn't belong here, bundle it back up and mark it for return to the campus post office.

Computing a Fog Index

I. Include a Fog Index on future reports.
 Fog Index, a readability test based on sentence and word length.
 Short sentences and words, easier reading.
II. Computing involves six steps.
 1. Select five random sections, at least 100 words each.
 2. Compute the average sentence length of each.
 3. Compute number of difficult words per hundred
  Count words three syllables or more.
  Don't count proper names, verbs that become three syllables by adding -es, -ed, or -ing.
  Round off.
 4. Add two figures.
 5. Multiply answer by .4 to get FI.
  Number of years of schooling required to read the passage easily.
 6. Compute the average for the five passages.
  Write figure at the end of the report with computations.
III. Rewrite reports until FI is between 10 and 13.

Figure 6.1 *Example of effective note taking*

Now, about your breaks. You get ten minutes in the morning, forty minutes at noon, and fifteen minutes in the afternoon. If you're smart, you'll leave before the 10:30 classes let out. That's usually a pretty crush time. Three of the teachers are supposed to have office hours then, and if they don't keep them, the students will be on your back. If you take your lunch at 11:45, you'll be back before the main crew goes.

Oh, one more thing. You are supposed to call Jeno at 8:15 every morning to wake him. If you forget, he gets very upset. Well, good luck.

1. Where are you to take the mail that does not belong here?
2. How often does mail come?

3. When should you be back from lunch?

4. What is Bernstein's problem with work?

5. Who gives the most work?

6. What's the problem with Goodwin's typing requests?

7. What are your main jobs, according to the boss?

8. Where are you to take outgoing mail?

9. Where is the campus post office?

10. How many minutes do you get for your morning break?

11. What is the preferred time to take your lunch?

12. Who are you supposed to give a wake-up call?

1. Campus post office   2. Twice a day   3. 12:30   4. Last minute   5. Goodwin
6. Not work related   7. Typing, distributing mail   8. Charles Hall   9. Harper Hall
10. ten   11. 11:45   12. Jeno

In Groups

Have each person in a group select a newspaper or magazine article and prepare a two-minute reading of it. As each person reads, everyone else should take notes. At the end of each reading, group members should compare notes and discuss why they chose to write what they did.

Evaluating: Listening Critically

The fourth phase of the listening process is evaluating. In addition to using the active listening and remembering skills discussed in the previous two sections, *evaluating* or *critical listening* consists of critically analyzing the message we have understood in order to determine how truthful, authentic, or believable we judge it to be. For instance, when a person tries to convince you to vote for a particular candidate for office or to support efforts to legalize RU 486 (the so-called "abortion pill"), you will want to listen critically to these messages so as to determine how much you agree with the speaker and how you wish to respond. If you fail to listen critically to the messages you receive, you risk inadvertently concurring in ideas or plans that may violate your own values, be counterproductive to achieving your goals, or be misleading to others (including the speaker) who value your judgment.

Critical listening includes (1) separating facts from inferences and (2) evaluating the inferences that have been made. Let's consider each of these in turn.

Separating Facts from Inferences

Critical listeners are able to separate facts from inferences. *Facts* are items of information whose accuracy can be verified or proven, often by direct observation. By contrast, *inferences* are conclusions or generalizations based on what has been observed. Separating fact from inference thus means being able to tell the difference between a verifiable observation and an interpretation related to that observation.

Let's clarify this distinction with an example. Ellen tells a friend that she saw a Bob's TV Repair truck in her neighbor's driveway for the fifth time in the last two weeks. Ellen is reporting only what she saw; she is relating a fact. If, however, Ellen adds, "That new TV they bought is really a lemon," she would be making an inference. Ellen would be concluding—without actually knowing—that the truck was at her neighbor's house because someone was trying to repair the new television set. But think of how many other interpretations, or inferences, could be drawn from that fact. The driver of the truck may be a friend of Ellen's neighbor, or perhaps a special video system is being installed, or an old TV may have broken. The presence of the truck is fact; the explanation for the presence of the truck is inference.

The reason for distinguishing between facts and inferences is that an inference may be false, even if it is based on verifiable facts. Making sound judgments entails basing our opinions and responses to messages on facts or on inferences whose correctness we have evaluated. So, when we encounter such statements as "Better watch it; Carl is really in a bad mood today—did you see the way he was scowling?" or "I know you're hiding something from me; I can tell it in your voice," or "Olga and Kurt are having an affair—I've seen them leave the office together nearly every night," we know that each of them is an inference. Each of them may be true, but none is necessarily true.

Evaluating Inferences

Critical listeners not only recognize inferences, but they also know how to evaluate them to determine their validity. As we have said, inferences are conclusions or assertions drawn from or based on factual information. An inference is usually presented as part of an argument; that is, a person makes a claim (an inference) and then presents other statements in support of the claim. Here is an example of a simple argument. Joyce says, "Next year is going to be a lot easier than the past year. I got a $200-a-month raise, and my husband's been relieved of some of the extra work he's had to do while they were looking for a replacement for Ed." Her claim "Next year is going to be a lot easier than the past year" is an inference—a statement that requires support to validate it. The statement "I got a $200-a-month raise, and my husband's been relieved of some of the extra work he's had to do while they were looking for a replacement for Ed" contains facts that can be verified. Notice that Joyce's argument suggests that she infers a relationship between her claim and the facts she presents. Her argument is based on the assumption that more money per month and less work for her husband will make the year easier because it will relieve stress.

The critical listener asks at least three questions when evaluating any inference: (1) Is there factual information to support the inference? Perhaps there is no supporting information, perhaps there is not enough, or perhaps the supporting information is inaccurate. (2) Is the factual support relevant to the inference? Perhaps the actual or implied statement of relevance is logically weak. (3) Is there known information that would prevent the inference from logically following the factual statements? Perhaps there is information that is not accounted for that affects the likelihood of the inference. In the previous example, Joyce does have factual statements for support: She received a raise, and her husband has less work to do. Moreover, increased income and less work are both relevant to "having an easier time." At this stage it would appear that Joyce does have the makings of a sound argument. However, if we learn that the $200-a-month raise involves substantial extra duties for Joyce, then we still might question whether this year is likely to be "easier" than the last one.

Let us consider one more example. Dan says, "This is a great time to buy a car—interest rates are at the lowest point they've been in three years." The inference is that this is a great time to buy a car. First, does Dan give any support for the inference? Yes. Second, is the support relevant to the inference? Yes—interest rates are a factor in determining whether the time is right for car buying. Third, is there known information that would prevent the conclusion following from the data? If other indicators showed that we were entering a period of recession, that information might be more important to the decision than the stability of interest rates.

For many of us, the most difficult of the three questions to answer is the second one: Is the factual support relevant to the inference? This question is difficult to answer primarily because the listener must be able to verbalize a statement that shows the relevance. The listener must create the statement because in most informal reasoning the link is only implied by the person presenting the argument. Recall that in the first example, Joyce never said anything like "A raise in income and a reduction in work are two criteria for predicting that next year will be a lot easier." Because the relevance is more often implied than stated, we must learn to phrase it.

The key to phrasing the relationship between inference and support in order to judge its relevance is to ask yourself, "What can I say that would make sense for this inference to follow from this material?" For instance, suppose Hal says, "I see frost on the grass—I think our flowers are goners." What can we say that establishes the relevance of the supporting fact, "frost on the grass," to the claim "our flowers are goners"? If I were Hal, I would likely be thinking, "The presence of frost means that the temperature is low enough to freeze the moisture on the grass. If it's cold enough to freeze the moisture on the grass, it's cold enough to kill my flowers." This seems to make sense, because we can demonstrate a relationship between frost and the death of unprotected flowers.

Let's try another one. Gina says, "I studied all night and only got a D on the first test—I'm not going to do any better on this one." This statement suggests that Gina sees a direct connection between the amount of study time before a test and the grade. We could phrase this implied relationship as follows: "Since the time of study before the test, which determines the grade, can be no greater, Gina can't improve her grade." In this case, the stated relationship seems questionable. Her reasoning suggests that the only factor in determining a grade is the amount of study time before the test. However, experience suggests that many other factors, such as previous time studying and frame of mind, are of equal if not greater importance.

In short, you are listening critically when (1) you question whether the inference is supported with meaningful factual statements, (2) you question whether the

	Good Listeners	Bad Listeners
Attending	Attend to important information	May not hear what a person is saying
	Ready themselves physically and mentally	Fidget in their chairs, look out the window, and let their minds wander
	Listen objectively regardless of emotional involvement	Visibly react to emotional language
	Listen differently depending on situations	Listen the same way regardless of type of material
Understanding	Assign appropriate meaning to what is said	Hear what is said, but are unable to understand, or assign different meaning to the words
	Seek out apparent purpose, main points, and supporting information	Ignore the way information is organized
	Ask mental questions to anticipate information	Fail to anticipate coming information
	Silently paraphrase to solidify understanding	Seldom or never mentally review information
	Seek out subtle meanings based on nonverbal cues	Ignore nonverbal cues
Remembering	Retain information	Interpret message accurately but forget it
	Rehearse key information	Assume they will remember
	Mentally create mnemonics for lists of words and ideas	Seldom single out any information as especially important
	Take notes	Rely on memory alone
Evaluating	Listen critically	Hear and understand information, but are unable to weigh and consider it
	Separate facts from inferences	Don't differentiate between facts and inferences
	Evaluate inferences	Accept information at face value

Figure 6.2 *A summary of the four aspects of listening*

stated or implied connection between the support and the inference makes sense, and (3) you question whether there is any other known information that lessens the quality of the inference.

Figure 6.2 summarizes how good listeners and poor listeners deal with the four aspects of listening: attending, understanding, remembering, and evaluating.

Figure 6.3 is a checklist that you can use to test your listening effectiveness.

Will you listen better now that you have read this chapter ? Answer *yes* or *no* for each of the following items:

_____ 1. I will listen differently depending on whether I am listening for enjoyment, understanding, or evaluating.

_____ 2. I will stop listening when what the person is saying isn't interesting to me.

_____ 3. I will consciously recognize the speaker's goal.

_____ 4. I will pretend to listen to people when I am really thinking about other things.

_____ 5. When people talk, I will differentiate between their main points and their supporting details.

_____ 6. When a person's manner of speaking annoys me (such as muttering, stammering, or talking in a monotone), I will stop listening carefully.

_____ 7. At various places in a conversation, I will paraphrase what the speaker said in order to check my understanding.

_____ 8. When I perceive the subject matter as very difficult, I will stop listening carefully.

_____ 9. When the person presents complex information, I will take good notes of major points and supporting details.

_____ 10. When people use words I find offensive, I will stop listening and start preparing responses.

If you answered yes to the odd-numbered items, and you really follow these behaviors, then your listening will likely be more effective. If you answered yes to the even-numbered items, and you actually follow these behaviors, then you may want to review the relevant chapter material to help you understand why such behaviors are likely to be harmful to your listening.

Figure 6.3 *Listening checklist*

Practice in Evaluating

By Yourself

1. Read the following story, and evaluate each witness's statement as either F (fact) or I (inference).

Two people came hurrying out of a bank with several large bundles, hopped into a long black car, and sped away. Seconds later, a man rushed out of the bank, waving his arms and looking quite upset. You listen to two people discuss what they saw.

_____ **a.** "The bank's been robbed!"

_____ **b.** "Yes, indeed—I saw the robbers hurry out of the bank, hop into a car, and speed away."

_____ **c.** "It was a long black car."

_____ **d.** "The men were carrying several large bundles."

_____ **e.** "Seconds after they left, a man came out of the bank after them—but he was too late, they'd already escaped."

a. I b. I c. F d. I (men?) e. I

2. For each item, a–h, ask and answer the following three questions: (1) Is the inference supported with meaningful factual statements? (2) Does the stated or implied connection between the support and the inference make sense? (3) Is any other information known that lessens the quality of the inference? Remember that you need to phrase a reasoning link that ties the supporting information logically to the inference.

    a. "The chess club held a raffle, and they made a lot of money. I think we should hold a raffle, too."

    b. "Chad is aggressive, personable, and highly motivated—he ought to make a good salesman."

    c. "Three of my students last year got A's on this test, five the year before, and three the year before that. There certainly will be some A's this year."

    d. "I saw Kali in a maternity outfit—she must be pregnant."

    e. "Listen, I like the way Darren thinks, Solomon is an excellent mathematician, and Marco and Ethan are two of my best students. All four are Alpha Alphas. As far as I'm concerned, the Alphas are the group on campus with academic strength."

    f. "If Greg hadn't come barging in, I never would have spilled my iced tea."

    g. "Maybe that's the way you see it, but to me when high city officials are caught with their hands in the till and when police close their eyes to the actions of people with money, that's corruption."

    h. "Krista wears her hair that way and guys fall all over her—I'm getting myself a hairdo like that."

Summary

Listening is an active process that involves attending, understanding, remembering, evaluating, and responding. Effective listening is essential to competent communication.

    Attending is the process of selecting the sound waves we consciously process. We can increase the effectiveness of our attention by (1) trying to eliminate physical impediments to listening, (2) getting ready to listen, (3) making the shift from speaker to listener a complete one, (4) hearing a person out before we react, and (5) adjusting our attention to the listening goals of the situation.

    Understanding is the process of decoding a message by assigning meaning to it. A key to understanding is to practice active listening. Look for or create an organization for the information, pay attention to nonverbal cues, ask questions, and silently paraphrase.

    Remembering is the process of storing the meanings that have been received so that they can be recalled later. Remembering is increased by rehearsing information, constructing mnemonics, grouping information to make it easier to remember, and when feasible, taking notes.

    Evaluating, or critical listening, is the process of separating fact from inference and judging the validity of the inferences made. A fact is a verifiable statement; an inference is a conclusion drawn from facts. You are listening critically when you question (1) whether the inference is supported with meaningful factual statements, (2) whether the reasoning statement that shows the relationship between the support and the inference makes sense, and (3) whether there is any other known information that lessens the quality of the inference.

Suggested Readings

Brownell, Judi. *Building Active Listening Skills.* Englewood Cliffs, NJ: Prentice-Hall, 1986. Not only covers the major components of listening, but also has an excellent section on such communication contexts as listening to superiors and listening in the family.

Buzan, Tony. *Use Your Perfect Memory,* 3d ed. New York: Plume, 1991. Presents numerous means and systems for remembering names, dates, numbers, faces, objects, and other factual information. Focuses on both classic memory systems and Buzan's own mind mapping technique.

Steil, Lyman K.; Barker, Larry L.; and Watson, Kittie W. *Effective Listening: Key to Your Success.* Reading, MA: Addison-Wesley, 1983. Provides specific procedures for different kinds of listening situations.

Wolvin, Andrew D., and Coakley, Carolyn Gwynn. *Listening,* 4th ed. Dubuque, IA: Wm. C. Brown, 1992. Includes chapters on appreciative listening, discriminative listening, comprehensive listening, therapeutic listening, and critical listening, and provides a list of skills involved in each type.

Notes

1. L. Barker, R. Edwards, C. Gains, K. Gladnes, and F. Holley, "An Investigation of Proportional Time Spent in Various Communication Activities by College Students," *Journal of Applied Communication Research* 8 (1980): 101–109.

2. Lyman K. Steil, Larry L. Barker, and Kittie W. Watson, *Effective Listening* (Reading, MA: Addison-Wesley, 1983). See also C. Day, "How Do You Rate as a Listener?" *Industry Week,* 28 April 1980, p. 30–35; and R. W. Rasberry, "Are Your Students Listening? A Method for Putting Listening Instruction into the Business Communication Course," *Proceedings of the Southwest American Business Communication Association Spring Conference,* 1980, p. 215.

3. Andrew Wolvin and Carolyn Gwynn Coakley, *Listening,* 4th ed. (Dubuque, IA: Wm. C. Brown, 1992), pp. 70–71.

4. National Institutes of Health, *Hearing Loss* (Washington, DC: National Institutes of Health, 1982), p. 1.

5. Joan Gorham, "The Relationship Between Verbal Teacher Immediacy Behaviors and Student Learning," *Communication Education* 37 (1988): 51.

6. W. K. Estes, "Learning Theory," in Alan Lesgold and Robert Glaser, eds., *Foundations for a Psychology of Education* (Hillsdale, NJ: Erlbaum, 1989), pp. 6–8.

7. David Baine, *Memory and Instruction* (Englewood Cliffs, NJ: Educational Technology Publications, 1986), pp. 45–53.

8. George A. Miller, "The Magical Number Seven, Plus or Minus Two: Some Limits on Our Capacity for Processing Information," *Psychological Review* 63 (1956): 81–97.

9. Wolvin and Coakley, p. 251.

**After you have read
this chapter, you
should be able to:**

*Explain ways of determining
emotional states of others*

Question for information

Paraphrase information

*Support positive and negative
feelings*

*Give alternative
interpretations*

Praise

*Give and receive constructive
criticism*

*Eliminate inappropriate
responses*

7

Response Skills

"We need to take a phenomenological approach to this issue. Once we understand that knowledge is not inferred from experience but is expressed in conscious experience itself, I think we can start to gain a necessary insight."

"For crying out loud—talk English."

"I'm not doing as well in his classes this quarter as I expected to. You know, I'm studying longer hours than I ever have, but something just isn't right."

"You can say that again—you're really screwing up."

"The last time we went out Beth seemed really cool to any show of intimacy. In fact I've had the feeling that something's been troubling her, and I'm afraid it has to do with our relationship."

"Hm, I can see why you're concerned. Her behavior does seem a little different from what you've described in the past. Is there any chance that something else might be troubling her?"

Each of the preceding examples is a *response*—a reflection of how the receiver hears the message. But there are major differences in the examples. In neither of the first two does the receiver show sensitivity to the speaker's ideas or the speaker's feelings. The third example is different. In this one, we get the sense that the speaker is sensitive to the situation. The first two are largely inappropriate; the third is helpful. As we go through this chapter, you will learn both what makes the difference and how to phrase appropriate responses.

As we discussed in Chapter 6, the final phase of listening is responding appropriately. Response is qualitatively different from the other phases of listening, for when we respond, we shift roles from receiver to sender. Nevertheless, responding is an integral part of listening because it is the response, or lack of it, that shows whether communication has really taken place, whether meaning is shared.

We begin the chapter with a discussion of empathy, a quality that lays the groundwork for effective response skills; then we continue with types of empathic responses. We conclude the chapter with a brief discussion of inappropriate responses that effective communicators should try to avoid.

Empathizing

Responding appropriately goes beyond using the skills of attending, understanding, remembering, and evaluating—it requires a degree of empathy with the speaker. Empathy involves detecting and identifying another person's emotional state and responding appropriately.[1]

Detecting and Identifying Feelings

The first aspect of this definition—detecting and identifying how a person is feeling—emphasizes that part of the skill of empathy is perceptual: noticing the person's verbal and nonverbal cues and then, based on these observations, identifying the person's emotional state. In Chapter 4, we noted that up to 65 percent of the meaning of a social message may be carried nonverbally. When Rico says "Great catch, Paulo" after Paulo drops a lazy fly ball hit right to him, the sound of Rico's voice will signal that his message is just the opposite of what he said. Likewise, when Tanya says "Go on, I'll just finish my homework," we have to interpret cues such as tone of voice, body motions, and facial expression to tell whether Tanya really wants to be left alone or whether she actually plans to do her homework. Thus, being sensitive to the nonverbal behaviors that accompany the words is prerequisite to understanding the feeling that underlies a verbal message.

The ability to detect and identify feelings may be a result of (1) our own experience in a similar situation, (2) our fantasized reaction to that situation, or (3) our experiences in observing this person in similar situations. The key point is that in perceiving someone's emotional state, we see a situation through the other person's eyes. Our understanding is based not on what we think someone "should" feel in that situation but on what it is really like to be that person, having the feeling he or she is actually experiencing. Thus, empathizing is "other" oriented rather than "I" oriented.

Let's look at an example of empathy. Troy says to Evonne, "I worked a lot harder on this ad campaign and I really thought it was on the money, but the client said she wanted to see another plan." As Troy talks, Evonne reads the look on his face and notes the cues provided by his gestures, movements, and posture. As Evonne hears the words Troy speaks, she perceives the changes in vocal quality and pitch as well as the presence or absence of vocal interferences. Then, based on both verbal and nonverbal cues, she can interpret Troy's feelings as expressed in the message. If, from her observation of Troy's words and nonverbal cues, Evonne is able to identify with the disappointment he experienced, or if she can imagine the disappointment, she is empathizing.

Responding Appropriately

The second aspect of the definition of empathy focuses on responding appropriately. When Troy says, "but the client said she wanted to see another plan," Evonne could respond by saying, "That must have really jolted you," spoken in a way that suggests an understanding of Troy's pain and surprise. Such a response would show Troy that (1) Evonne understands what happened, (2) she shares in Troy's emotions in that she knows what it is like to suffer pain or surprise, and (3) she is willing to allow Troy to talk about his feelings and to offer what comfort she can.

People sometimes confuse empathy with sympathy. Although empathy and sympathy have similar meanings, sympathy usually denotes (1) a duplication of the feeling or (2) a feeling of pity or compassion for another person's trouble. For instance, Troy's description could cause Evonne to feel so disappointed herself, or so sorry for Troy, that she begins to cry. But if she shares in his emotion to that extent, she is less likely to be able to help him through his feelings. Moreover, it is unnecessary for her to join in Troy's response in order to understand and empathize with it. Even if she thought his response was excessive, she could accept and understand his feelings. In general, empathy requires a more cognitive approach than merely participating in the other person's feelings.

In summary, empathy has two clearly definable elements: the recognition of another's feeling, which is a perception skill, and the response to it, which is a communication skill. Since both skills imply a genuine understanding of what the other person is experiencing, let's talk further about how to achieve an empathic state of mind.

Increasing Empathy

Increasing our level of empathy involves caring and concentrating. How much we empathize is directly related to how much we really care about a person. This does not mean that we need to have a deep, personal relationship with others in order to empathize with them. Caring can mean simply the ability to put ourselves in the other person's shoes. You are likely to feel better when the people you like or respect identify with your feelings of pain, fear, anger, joy, and amazement. Similarly, other people want and need the same expression of empathy from you that you want and need from them. By asking yourself how you would feel under the circumstances and acting accordingly, you are more likely to achieve an empathic state.

Empathy is a skill—but one that rests on a foundation of genuine caring.

Sometimes we are reluctant to show that we care about others for fear of showing weakness or being vulnerable. For example, you may have learned that emotions should not be shared or acknowledged. Yet everybody has feelings, whether they display them or not, and the willingness to share feelings empathically is not unmanly or unwomanly or "un" anything. When you empathize with another person's joy or pain, your willingness to show it will usually be rewarding for both of you.

How much you can empathize is also related to how well you concentrate on observing behavior. When another person begins a conversation with you, develop the habit of silently posing at least two questions to yourself: "What state of mind do I believe the person is in right now?" and "What are the cues the person is giving that I am using to draw this conclusion?" Consciously raising these questions will help you focus your attention on the nonverbal aspects of messages. Is this a realistic expectation? When people concentrate, they have been shown to be good at recognizing such primary emotions as happiness, sadness, surprise, anger, and fear (above 90 percent), and rather good at recognizing contempt, disgust, interest, determination, and bewilderment (80 to 90 percent).[2] And as researchers in the field have discovered, recognizing facial expressions is the key to perceiving emotion.[3] As you develop the habit of making these assessments, you will become more adept at sensing the moods, feelings, and attitudes of those with whom you are communicating.

To empathize effectively, (1) concentrate on both the verbal and nonverbal messages, (2) adopt an attitude of caring for the person, (3) try to recall or imagine how you would feel in similar circumstances, (4) use the person's behavioral cues to speculate on his or her emotional state, and (5) respond in a way that indicates your sensitivity to the feelings you have perceived.

Practice in Empathizing

By Yourself

1. Consider the following three comments you might hear from a friend:
   a. Tyrell sent me flowers for no apparent reason.
   b. I got a C on the test.
   c. I banged my head on the doorframe.

In each of these cases, the speaker could have any of at least three states of mind: The speaker could look at the event as positive or humorous, as negative or troublesome, or as neither. List the nonverbal cues that you would expect to see associated with each of these possible frames of mind; then phrase statements that would show your recognition of each perceived state.

2. Recall the last time you effectively empathized with another person. Write a short analysis of the episode. Be sure to cover the following: What type of relationship do you have with this person? How long have you known the person? What was the person's emotional state? How did you recognize it? What were the nonverbal cues? Verbal cues? Did you identify with the person through remembering a similar situation you had experienced, or did you fantasize how you would feel? What did you do that showed you were empathizing? What was the outcome of this communication episode?

In Groups

Have each person in the group relate a recent experience to which they had an emotional response, without labeling the response. The response need not be a dramatic one. After the speaker has related an episode, have the group discuss what emotional states they perceive the speaker to have experienced and describe the verbal and nonverbal cues that led them to their conclusions. Then group members should indicate whether they were able to empathize based on experiences or based on fantasy. Finally, the group should solicit comments from the speaker concerning the accuracy of their perceptions.

Clarifying Meaning

Perhaps the greatest barrier to effective communication is misunderstanding. *Misunderstanding* commonly results from erroneously assuming understanding of the meaning, from inattention to what is being communicated, and from hurrying. We misunderstand far more often than we realize. In Chapter 6, we focused on building internal listening skills; now we consider how you can test or increase your degree of understanding through appropriate responses. Two skills we can use to clarify meaning are questioning and paraphrasing.

Questioning

When we don't have enough information to fully understand a person's message, we are likely to ask questions. Effective questioning is not always easy. When your questions don't get the information you want or irritate or fluster the other person, it may well be that they were poorly phrased. Here are guidelines for phrasing questions in a sensitive way that lessens the likelihood of arousing defensiveness.

1. *Be specific about the goal of the question.* Suppose Shana says to you, "I am really frustrated. Would you stop at the store on the way home and buy me some more paper?" At this point, you may need more information to understand what Shana is telling you. However, a response like "I don't get what you mean" is unlikely to elicit a helpful reply. The question you ask depends on the kind of information you need to make the communication complete.

- *You can ask questions to get important details.* "What kind of paper would you like me to get, and how much will you need?"
- *You can ask questions to clarify the use of a term.* "Could you tell me what you mean by 'frustrated'?"
- *You can ask questions to bring out a person's feelings.* "What is it that seems to be frustrating you?"

Whether it is more details, how a word is used, or how the person feels, a well-phrased, specific question will help you get the information you want.

2. *Avoid one- or two-word questions that may be perceived as too curt or abrupt.* A person may often misinterpret the motivation behind a curt or abrupt question. For instance, when Miles says "Molly just told me that I always behave in ways that are totally insensitive to her needs," instead of asking "What?" you might ask "Did she give you specific behaviors she was concerned with?" Now instead of having to puzzle out the meaning of "What," Miles understands the kind of information you are seeking. Curt, abrupt questions often seem to challenge the speaker instead of focusing on the kind of information the respondent needs to understand the statement.

3. *Use positive nonverbal cues.* Ask questions with a tone of voice that is sincere—not a tone that could be interpreted as sarcastic, cutting, superior, dogmatic, or evaluative. We need to constantly remind ourselves that the way we speak can be even more important than the words we use.

4. *Put the burden of ignorance on your own shoulders.* If people are under tension, they may interpret any question as being critical of their ability to speak clearly. A useful strategy for avoiding defensive reactions is to put the burden of ignorance on your own shoulders. Try to preface your question with a short statement that suggests that any problem of misunderstanding is likely to be yours. For instance, when Drew says, "I've really had it with Malone jumping all over me all the time," you might say, "Drew, I'm sorry, I may have missed something you said—what kinds of things has Malone been doing?"

The following two examples contrast appropriate empathic questions with unhelpful or inappropriately phrased questions.

Tamara comes out of the committee room and says, "They turned down my proposal again!" How might Art respond?

Inappropriate: "Well, did you explain it the way you should have?" (This question is a veiled attack on Tamara in question form.)

Appropriate: "Did they tell you why?" (This question is a sincere request for additional information.)

As Javier and Renee are driving home from a party, Renee says, "With all those executives there, I really felt strange." How might Javier respond?

Inappropriate: "When you're with our bosses, why do you always act so stupid?" (With this question, Javier is intentionally hurting Renee. He is making no effort to be sensitive to her feelings or to understand them.)

Appropriate: "What is it about the bosses' presence that makes you feel strange?" (Here the question is designed to elicit information that may help Renee.)

Note how the empathic questions get the necessary information but with less probability of a defensive reply. The inappropriate questions, on the other hand, seem deliberately designed to undermine or attack the person being questioned. Questioning represents a useful response when the information sought is relevant to the conversation and when the questions derive from a spirit of inquiry and support and not from a conscious or unconscious need to make the person look bad.

To question effectively, (1) listen carefully to the message, (2) determine the kind of information you need to increase your understanding of the message, (3) phrase your questions so that they focus on getting that information, and (4) deliver them in a sincere tone of voice.

Paraphrasing

Although it seems like common sense to ask a question to obtain additional information, most of us don't feel a need to say anything when we think we understand what a person means. Yet, serious communication problems can occur even when we believe we are certain we understand the person. Why? Because what we think a person means may be far different from what the person really means.

Paraphrasing means putting *your* understanding of the message into words. Paraphrasing is not mere repetition. Suppose Charley, who blew the first test, says, "I'm really going to study this time." Replying "This time you're really going to study" is mere repetition. The reply shows that you have *heard* the response but not that you have *understood* it. An effective paraphrase states the meaning received in the listener's own words. If you think Charley is talking about specific study skills, your paraphrase might be "I take it this time you're going to read and outline every chapter carefully." This statement is a paraphrase because it tells Charley the meaning you have for the words "really going to study." If your interpretation is on the mark, Charley might say "Right!" But if you have received a meaning different from what Charley intended, Charley has an opportunity to clarify the meaning with a statement such as "Well, I'm going to spend a lot more time reading chapters carefully, but I wasn't planning on outlining them." At this point, you have the chance to advance the communication by encouraging Charley to use additional study skills.

Types of Paraphrases.   The meaning you get from any statement may focus on its content, the feelings represented, or both, depending on the situation. A *content paraphrase* summarizes the substantive, or denotative, meaning of the message; a *feelings paraphrase* expresses what you understand to be the emotions the person is experiencing as shown by his or her nonverbal cues.

To illustrate the difference, let's go back to Charley's statement, "I'm really going to study this time." The paraphrase "I take it this time you're going to read and outline every chapter carefully" is a content paraphrase—it focuses on the denotative meaning of the message. Depending on how Charley sounded as he spoke, an appropriate feelings paraphrase might be "So you were pretty upset with your grade on the last test." Which response is more appropriate for the situation depends on whether you perceive the emphasis of Charley's statement to be on *how* to study for a test or on his *feelings* about not doing as well as he should. Let's look at another example that contains a longer message.

"Five weeks ago, I gave the revised manuscript of my independent study to my project adviser. I felt really good about it because I felt the changes I had made really improved my explanations. You can imagine how I felt when I got the manuscript back yesterday and my adviser said she couldn't see that this draft was much different from the first."

> *Content paraphrase:* "If I have this correct, you're saying that your adviser saw little difference, yet you think your draft was both different and much improved."

> *Feelings paraphrase:* "You seem really frustrated that your adviser didn't recognize the changes you had made."

Of course, in real-life settings, we often don't distinguish clearly between content and feelings paraphrases; rather, we tend to use both together to give a more complete picture of the meanings we received. For instance, a combination content/feelings paraphrase of the manuscript message might well be, "If I have this right, you're saying that your adviser could see no real differences, yet you think your draft was not only different but much improved. I also get the feeling that your adviser's comments really irk you."

You may be thinking that if people stated their ideas and feelings accurately in the first place, we would not have to paraphrase. Accurate wording might help us understand better, but as our study of the communication process has shown, we can seldom be sure we accurately understand what others say. Both verbal and nonverbal messages can be misunderstood; internal or external noise can interfere with our understanding; and our beliefs, assumptions, and feelings may differ from those of the speaker. Perfecting our paraphrasing ability is a significant way of improving the effectiveness of our communication.

When to Paraphrase.   Common sense suggests that we wouldn't paraphrase every message we receive; nor would we paraphrase after every few sentences. Still there are times when it is important to clarify meaning before stating your own ideas or feelings. Try paraphrasing the ideas or feelings of the other person

- when you need a better understanding of a message—in terms of content, feelings, or both—before you can respond appropriately.
- when you think you understand what a person has said or how the person feels, but you're not absolutely sure.
- when you perceive that what the person has said is controversial or was said under emotional strain and, therefore, may not really be what the person meant to say.
- when you have some strong reaction to what the person has said or how the person has said it that may have interfered with your interpretation of the message.
- when you are speaking in a language that is not your native language or talking with people in a language that is not their first.

To paraphrase effectively, (1) listen carefully to the message, (2) determine what the message means to you, and (3) if you believe a paraphrase is necessary, restate the message using your own words to indicate the meaning you have received.

Practice in Clarifying Meaning

By Yourself

Try to clarify the following statements by providing an appropriate question or paraphrase. To get you started, the first example has been completed for you.

"It's Dionne's birthday, and I've planned a big evening. Sometimes, I think Dionne wonders whether I take her for granted—well, I think after tonight she'll know I think she's something special!"

Question: "What are you planning to do?"

Content paraphrase: "I get the idea you've planned a night that's totally different from what Dionne expects on her birthday."

Feelings paraphrase: "From the way you're talking, I get the feeling you're really excited about your plans for the evening."

"Brother! Another nothing class. I keep thinking one of these days he'll get excited about something. Professor Romero is a real bore!"

Question:

Content paraphrase:

Feelings paraphrase:

"Everyone seems to be talking about that movie on Channel 5 last night, but I didn't see it. You know, I don't watch much that's on the 'idiot box.' "

Question:

Content paraphrase:

Feelings paraphrase:

"I don't know if it's something to do with me or with Mom, but lately she and I just aren't getting along."

Question:

Content paraphrase:

Feelings paraphrase:

"I've got a report due at work and a paper due in management class. On top of that, it's my sister's birthday, and so far I haven't even had time to get her anything. Tomorrow's going to be a disaster."

Question:

Content paraphrase:

Feelings paraphrase:

In Groups

In this exercise for three people, A and B will hold a conversation on a topic such as "Why I like the type of work I'm doing," "The pros and cons of abortion," or "Dealing with drug or alcohol abuse," while C will observe the conversation. Speakers are not allowed to state their ideas until they paraphrase what the other person has just said. At the end of three to four minutes, C (the observer) discusses the paraphrasing of the two participants. Then B and C converse for three to four minutes while A observes; for the final three to four minutes, C and A converse while B observes. After completing the exercise, the participants should discuss how they felt about paraphrasing and how the paraphrasing affected the conversations.

Helping Responses

Helping responses are statements that show approval of a person's feelings or acknowledgment of the person's right to have those feelings; at times, they may reinforce people's behavior or show them how to do something better. Within this group of responses, we consider supporting, interpreting, praise, and constructive criticism.[4]

Supporting

People who express their feelings often look for or need some kind of supporting response. In fact, Albrecht, Burleson, and Goldsmith, leading researchers in supportive communication, state that supportive communication has a major effect on emotional and physical well-being.[5] *Supporting responses* soothe, approve, reduce tension, or pacify. They show that the listener empathizes with a person's feelings, whether positive (joy, elation, pride, satisfaction) or negative (sadness, anger, sorrow, disappointment). Whatever the direction or intensity of the feeling, the supporting statement indicates that we care about the person and what happens to him or her.

Supporting Positive Feelings. We all like to treasure our good feelings; when we share them, we don't want them dashed by inappropriate or insensitive responses. When a person's feelings are positive, an effective supporting statement helps the person sustain those feelings.

> KENDRA (hangs up the telephone and turns to Selena): "That was my boss. He said that he'd put my name in for promotion. I didn't realize he had ever really considered me promotable."
> SELENA: "Kendra, that's great. I'm so happy for you. You really seem excited."

Supporting positive feelings is generally easy; however, it does require a degree of empathy. Notice that, to begin with, Selena must perceive that Kendra is happy with the news. For Selena to then make an appropriate response, she need not share in Kendra's joy, but she must appreciate the feeling people get when they receive

Supporting responses show approval of behavior.

good news. Thus, when Selena says, "I'm so happy for you. You really seem excited," she is supporting Kendra's right to get excited.

Statements like these are much needed. Think of times when you have experienced an event that made you feel happy, proud, pleased, soothed, or amused and needed to express those feelings. Didn't it further your good feelings when others recognized and supported them?

Supporting Negative Feelings.　When a person's feelings are negative, an effective supporting statement acknowledges the person's right to those feelings and helps the person work through the feelings without intensifying them or further upsetting the person.

Appropriate responses to negative feelings seem to be much more difficult for most of us to make. When something bad happens to someone, we may feel embarrassed by the other person's pain and, as a result, want to be somewhere else. But in these situations, people need supportive statements even more than they do when their feelings are positive.

> KENDRA (slams down the phone): "That was my boss—he called to tell me that they're letting me go at work, but he wouldn't even tell me why!"
> SELENA: "Oh, Kendra—that must hurt. Anything I can do to help?"

Effective supporting statements of negative feelings require the ability to empathize. Even those of us with the hardest of hearts know the pain that comes with being rejected, disappointed, disillusioned, or hurt. To support, we do not have to share in the feelings, but we do need to respond in a way that recognizes the person's right to them. Thus, in our example, Selena, empathizing with Kendra, perceives her shock and anger. The statement "Oh, Kendra—that must hurt" verbalizes her recognition of the feeling; the statement "Anything I can do to help?" indicates that she cares about what is happening to Kendra and is ready to help her through this moment of pain and disbelief.

Because negative feelings and negative situations are the most difficult to handle, let's look at two more examples that deal with negative situations.

> JIM (comes out of his boss's office clutching the report he had been so sure he would receive praise for): "Jacobs rejected my report. I worked my tail off, did everything she asked, and she rejected it."
> AARON: "She rejected it? As hard as you worked, I can see why you're so upset. That's a real blow."

Aaron's response is primarily an empathizing statement that shows an understanding of why Jim is so upset. By saying "That's a real blow," Aaron also demonstrates that he is in tune with Jim's feelings. Perhaps you think Aaron should say, "Jim, I can see why you feel so bad. You deserved praise for what you did!" Although such a statement would have supporting qualities, Aaron is in no position to judge whether the report did in fact deserve praise. The support comes with Aaron's showing an understanding of how hard Jim worked and, therefore, why Jim feels especially bad. Giving empathic support is not the same as making statements that aren't true or that only tell people what they want to hear. When supportive statements are out of touch with the facts, they can encourage behavior that is actually destructive.

Making an appropriate response may be most difficult in situations of high emotion and stress. A person whose feelings are highly negative may need a few seconds, a few minutes, or even a few hours to calm down and think rationally. Sometimes, there's virtually nothing anyone can say that will be perceived as helpful. At these times, perhaps the best way of showing support is with a purely nonverbal response. Consider this situation:

> With a few seconds left in the basketball game and her team trailing by one point, Nancy steals the ball from her opponent, dribbles down the court for an uncontested layup—and misses. The gun sounds ending the game. Nancy runs to her coach with tears in her eyes and cries, "I blew it! I lost us the game!"

A first reaction might be to say, "Don't feel bad, Nancy." But Nancy obviously does feel bad, and she has a right to those feelings. Another response might be, "It's OK, Nancy, you didn't lose us the game." But in fact Nancy's miss did affect the outcome, and she is unlikely to be helped by a response that she knows is inaccurate. Perhaps the best thing the coach can do at that moment is to put her arm around Nancy to show that she understands. At that time, or later, she could say, "Nancy, I know you feel bad—but without your steal, we wouldn't even have had a chance to win." Still, for the moment, Nancy is going to be difficult to console.

Making supporting statements is not always easy, and a frequent temptation is to give advice instead. But since your goal is to soothe or to reduce tension, giving advice may well be counterproductive and result in further irritation or increased tension.

To support effectively, (1) listen closely to what the person is saying, (2) try to empathize with the dominant feelings, (3) phrase a reply that is in harmony with the feeling you have identified, (4) supplement your verbal response with appropriate nonverbal responses, and (5) if it seems appropriate, indicate your willingness to help.

Interpreting

When a person sees only one possible explanation for a given event, the most helpful response may be to provide an interpretation. *Interpreting* consists of attempting to point out an alternative or hidden view of an event to help a person see things from a different perspective.

Many times, especially when people are depressed, they say things that show a very limited view. Consider the following situation:

> After returning from his first date with Angie, a woman he believes he might become very fond of, Luis is upset. He had an excellent time, yet the end of the evening was very disappointing.
>
> LUIS: "I take her to dinner and a great show, and when I get to her door, she gives me a quick little kiss, says 'Thanks a lot,' and rushes into

the house. We didn't even have much time to talk about the play. I guess she really didn't like me."

Luis is interpreting Angie's behavior negatively—he sees her action as a rejection of him as a person. Martin does not know what Angie thinks, but since he perceives that Luis is taking a very limited view of the events, he might respond as follows: "I wonder whether she might not have been afraid that if she said or did any more, she'd be leading you on?"

Whose interpretation is correct? We don't know. What we do know is that behavior can frequently be interpreted in more than one way. Too often, especially when people feel slighted, angry, or hurt, they interpret events negatively.

The following are two additional examples of appropriate interpreting.

> KARLA: "I just don't understand Deon. I say we've got to start saving money, and he just gets angry with me."
>
> SHELLEY: "I can understand why his behavior would concern you [a supportive statement prefacing an interpretation]. Perhaps he feels guilty about not being able to save money or feels resentful that you seem to be putting all the blame on him."

> MICAH: "I just don't seem to understand Bradford. He says my work is top-notch, but I haven't gotten a pay raise in over a year."
>
> KHALIF: "I can see why you'd be frustrated, but maybe the company just doesn't have the money."

Since you are not a mind reader—you cannot know for sure why something was done or said—your purpose in interpreting is simply to help a person look at an event from a different point of view. As with supporting statements, offer interpretations only when they seem plausible and worth considering.

To interpret effectively, (1) listen carefully to what a person is saying, (2) if there are other reasonable ways to look at the event, phrase an alternative to the person's own interpretation—one that is intended to help the person see that other interpretations are available, and (3) when appropriate, preface the interpretive statement with a supportive one.

Praise

Too often the positive things people say and do are passed over with little comment. Yet, from our earlier discussion of self-concept, you'll remember that our view of who we are, as well as our behavior, is often shaped by how others respond to us. Praise reinforces positive behavior as well as recognizing accomplishments. When people have done something you appreciate, take the time to tell them.

For praise to achieve its goal and not be perceived merely as flattery, we need to focus the praise on the specific action and make sure that the wording is in keeping with the value of the accomplishment or behavior. If a child who tends to be forgetful remembers to return the scissors he borrowed, that's an event that needs to be praised. In this case, saying "Thanks for returning the scissors—I really appreciate that" praises the behavior and describes the specific feeling the behavior has caused in a credible way. In contrast, saying "You remembered to return the scissors—that's wonderful—I want to tell everyone about this" is likely to be perceived as overkill or even sarcasm. Likewise, saying "You're so wonderful, you're on top of everything" is general flattery—it doesn't reinforce a particular behavior.

Consider the following examples of appropriate praise:

When Sonya helps you select a gift for a coworker, you might say, "Sonya, thank you for helping me with this one—your idea was just right for the occasion."

When Cole offers to share his lunch with a student who forgot his lunch money that day, you might say, "Cole, that was nice of you to share your lunch with Rico. You're a very considerate person."

When your mother prepares an excellent dessert, you might say, "Mom, after working all day you still had energy to make a pie. Thanks."

Praising effectively doesn't take much time, and it is almost always appreciated.

To praise effectively, (1) make sure the context allows for praise, (2) describe the behavior you are praising, (3) focus on that specific behavior, and (4) if possible, identify the positive feeling you experience as a result of the praiseworthy behavior.

Constructive Criticism

At times we seek information from others in order to identify and correct our mistakes. At other times, we feel a need to identify and correct the mistakes of others. However, both receiving and giving criticism can make us uncomfortable and even harm the relationship, especially if we haven't used the appropriate skills. In this section, we first look at guidelines for asking for criticism; then we consider guidelines for giving criticism.

Asking for Criticism.   Although asking for constructive criticism is the most direct way of finding out whether our behavior is effective, we are often reluctant to do so because we feel threatened by criticism. Instead, we rely entirely on others' nonverbal cues. Yet even when we interpret nonverbal cues accurately, they fail to help us understand why our behavior missed the mark. Nor will such cues help us decide what changes are needed in order for us to improve. By employing the verbal skill of asking for criticism, we accomplish these two objectives.

The following guidelines can help you ask for constructive criticism.

1. *Ask for criticism so that you will avoid surprises.* Taking the initiative in asking for criticism prepares you psychologically to deal with the criticism.

2. *Think of criticism as being in your best interest.* No one likes to be criticized, but through valid criticism we often learn and grow. When you receive a negative appraisal—even when you expected a positive one—try to look on it not as critical of you personally but as a statement that reveals something about your behavior that you did not know. Whether you will do anything about the criticism is up to you, but you cannot make such a decision if you do not know that the behavior exists or how it affects others.

3. *Specify the kind of criticism you are seeking.* Rather than asking very general questions about ideas, feelings, or behavior, ask specific questions. If you say, "Colleen, is there anything you don't like about my ideas?" Colleen is likely to consider this a loaded question. But if you say, "Colleen, do you think I've given enough emphasis to the marketing possibilities?" you will encourage Colleen to speak openly to the specific issue.

4. *Ask for criticism only when you really want an honest response.* If you ask a friend "How do you like this coat?" but actually want the friend to agree that the coat is attractive on you, you are not being honest. Once others realize that when you request an appraisal you are actually fishing for a compliment, valuable appraisals will not be forthcoming.

5. *Try to avoid contradiction between your verbal and nonverbal cues.* If you say, "How do you like my paper?" but your tone of voice indicates that you do not really want to know, the other person may be reluctant to be honest with you.

6. *Give reinforcement to those who take your requests for criticism as honest requests.* Suppose you ask your colleagues how they like your ideas for the ad campaign, and you get the response "The ideas seem a little understated." If you then get annoyed and say, "Well, if you can do any better, you can take over," your colleagues will learn not to give you criticism even when you ask for it. Instead, reward people for their constructive criticism. Perhaps you could say, "Thanks for the opinion—I'd like to hear what led you to that conclusion." In this way, you encourage honest appraisal.

7. *Be sure you understand the criticism.* Before you react to what you've heard, paraphrase your understanding to make sure it is what the person meant.

Asking for criticism does not require that you always act on every comment. You may decide against making a change in what you've said or done for other good reasons. But asking for criticism does enable you to make a conscious, rational choice about whether or not you will change your behavior.

Giving Constructive Criticism. Even though some people learn faster and better through praise, there are still times when criticism is useful—especially when a person requests it. Even when people don't ask, we are sometimes in the best position to offer critical comments to help others perform better. Unfortunately, most of us are far too free in giving criticism; we often feel a need to help others "become better persons" even if they aren't interested in hearing from us at the moment. Moreover, even when the time is right for criticism, we may not do the best job of giving it. The following guidelines should help you compose criticism that is both constructive and beneficial.

1. *Make sure that the person is interested in hearing criticism.* The safest rule to follow is to withhold any criticism until it is asked for. Criticism will seldom help if a person is not interested in hearing it. If you believe that criticism is called for, ask whether the person is interested in hearing it. For instance, you might ask a group chairperson, "Are you interested in hearing my comments about the way you handled the meeting?" If the person answers "Not really," then go on to a different subject. Even if the answer is yes, proceed carefully.

2. *Describe the person's behavior carefully and accurately. Describing behavior* means accurately recounting behavior without labeling the behavior good or bad, right or wrong. By describing behavior, you lay an informative base for the criticism and increase the chances that the person will listen receptively. Criticism that is preceded with a description of behavior is less likely to be met defensively. Your description shows that you are criticizing the behavior rather than attacking the person, and it points the way to a solution. For example, if DeShawn asks "What do you think of the delivery of my report?" instead of saying "It wasn't very effective," it would be better to say something like "You tended to look down at the report as if you were reading it verbatim—this detracted from your really relating with your clients." This criticism does not attack DeShawn's self-concept, and it tells him what he needs to do to be more effective.

3. *Preface a negative statement with a positive one whenever possible.* When you are planning to criticize, it is a good idea to start with some praise. Of course, common sense suggests that superficial praise followed by crushing criticism will be seen for what it is. Thus, saying "Leah, that's a pretty blouse you have on, but you did a perfectly miserable job of running the meeting" will be rightly perceived as patronizing. A better approach would be "Leah, you did a good job of drawing Jarrell into the discussion. He usually sits through an entire meeting without saying a word. But you seem hesitant to use the same power to keep the meeting on track. By not taking charge more, you let people talk about things that were unrelated to the agenda." Here the praise is relevant and significant. If you cannot preface a criticism with significant praise, don't try. Prefacing criticism with empty praise will not help the person accept your criticism.

4. *Be as specific as possible.* The more specific the criticism, the more effectively a person will be able to deal with the information. In the situation just discussed, it would not have been helpful to say, "You had some leadership problems." This comment is so general that Leah would have little idea of what she did wrong. Moreover, she may infer that she is, in your eyes, incapable of leadership. If the point was that Leah wasn't in control, say so; if Leah failed to get agreement on one item before moving on to another, say so.

5. *Restrict criticism to recent behavior.* People are not generally helped by hearing about something they did last week or last month. With the passage of time, memories fade and even change, and it may be difficult to get agreement about the behavior being criticized. If you have to spend time recreating a situation and refreshing someone's memory, the criticism will probably be ineffective.

6. *Direct criticism at behavior the person can do something about.* It is pointless to remind someone of a shortcoming over which the person has no control. It may be true that Jack would find it easier to prepare arguments if he had taken a course in logic, but pointing this out to him will not improve his reasoning. Telling him he needs to work on stating main points clearly and backing them up with good evidence is helpful because he can change these behaviors.

7. *If possible, include a statement that shows how the person could correct the problem.* Don't limit your comments to what a person has done wrong. Tell the person how what was done could have been done better. If Gail, the chairperson of a committee, cannot get her members to agree on anything, you might suggest that she try phrasing her remarks to the committee differently; for example, "Gail, when you think discussion is ended, say something like 'It sounds as if we agree that our donation should be made to a single agency. Is that correct?'" By including a positive suggestion, you not only help the person improve—which is the purpose of constructive criticism—you also show that your intentions are positive.

Practice in Helping Responses

By Yourself

1. For each of the following situations, supply two responses, one supportive and one interpretive.

"The pie is all gone! I know there were at least two pieces left just a while ago. Kids! They can be so inconsiderate."

Supportive response:
Interpretive response:

"My boss was really on me today. I worked hard all day, but things just didn't jell for me. I don't know—maybe I've been spending too much time on some of the accounts."

Supportive response:
Interpretive response:

"I just got a call from my folks. My sister was in a car accident. They say she's OK, but the car was totaled. Apparently she had her seat belt fastened when it happened. But I don't know whether she's really all right or whether they just don't want me to worry."

Supportive response:
Interpretive response:

2. Write down one to three specific communication-related behaviors that you would like to have criticized. For instance: "Does the way I dress make me look younger than I am?" "Do you think I talk too much at meetings?" "Did the way I presented my analysis of Paul's plan help the discussion?"

3. Ask a close friend for criticism on one or more of the communication behaviors you have listed. Note how you react to the criticism.

4. Write out exactly what you said the last time you criticized someone's behavior. Which, if any, of the guidelines for constructive criticism did you follow or violate? If you were to do it again, what would you say differently?

In Groups

Consider the following two situations. Work out an appropriate phrasing of constructive criticism for each. Then, with others in your group, share your phrasings of the criticism. Which of the wordings best meets the guidelines for constructive criticism?

You have been driving to school with a fellow student whose name you got from the transportation office at school. You have known him for only three weeks. Everything about the situation is great except that he drives too fast for you.

A good friend says "you know" more than once every sentence. You like her very much, but you see that others are beginning to avoid her. She is very sensitive and does not usually take criticism well.

Problem Responses

Sometimes even the best communicators respond in ways that create problems. Good communicators are aware of when they have made mistakes and try to repair them immediately and avoid them in the future. Responses create problems when they cause people to feel defensive or question their self-worth, and when they fail to achieve their goal.

We have already considered evaluation as a problem response. Four other problem responses are irrelevant, tangential, incongruous, and interrupting responses. You will see that most of these also violate the rules of conversational coherence and turn taking discussed in Chapter 5.

Irrelevant Responses

An *irrelevant response* is one that bears no relation to what has been said. In effect, it ignores the speaker's message entirely.

> JOSH: "I'm concerned with the way Paul is handling arrangements for the benefit."
> TOM: "Umm. Hey, Pearl Jam is coming to town—I've got to get tickets for that."

When people's statements are ignored, they not only question whether they were heard but also wonder about the worth of what they were thinking or saying. In this example, Tom's irrelevant response causes Josh to wonder about the importance to Tom of what he was saying.

Tangential Responses

A *tangential response* is really an irrelevant response phrased in tactful language. Although the tangential response at least suggests acknowledgment of what a person was saying, the net result—changing the subject—is the same as with an irrelevant response.

> JOSH: "I'm concerned with the way Paul is handling arrangements for the benefit."
> TOM: "Well, you know Paul. I remember once when I was in charge of arrangements and forgot who I was supposed to contact."

Even though Tom has acknowledged Josh's statement, by shifting emphasis to his own experience, Tom appears to be saying that the issue bothering Josh is not important enough to discuss. Again, such responses chip away at a person's feelings of self-worth. Josh thought that he was raising a significant issue. Either Tom fails to see the importance of Josh's statement or Josh places too much emphasis on Paul's behavior. The real problem is that Tom's response addresses neither possibility, and the subject of Paul's behavior is left unresolved. Tom's apparent withdrawal from discussing Paul's behavior thus creates a problem between Josh and Tom.

Incongruous Responses

In our discussion of nonverbal communication, we indicated that problems occur when nonverbal messages appear to conflict with verbal messages. An *incongruous response* is an example of this problem.

> JOSH: "Well, we got some things done today."
> TOM (in a sarcastic tone): "Yeah, that was a great meeting."

On the surface, Tom seems to be acknowledging and verifying Josh's statement, but his sarcastic tone causes Josh to wonder whether he is confirming Josh's ideas or making fun of them. Because nonverbal reactions are likely to override verbal meaning with most people, Josh will probably take Tom's words as sarcasm. If they are in fact sarcastic, Tom's insensitivity to Josh's honest statement of feelings will contribute to the creation of a barrier between them. And if Tom's words are sincere, Josh's confusion about Tom's meaning likewise will lead to a barrier between them.

Interrupting Responses

An *interrupting response* (violating turn-taking rules) occurs when a person breaks in before the other person has finished a statement.

> JOSH: "I'm concerned with the way Paul . . ."
> TOM: "I know—that Paul is something else, but I don't think there's any real problem."

People interrupt inappropriately when they believe what they have to say is more important than what the other person is saying, when they believe they know what the other person is going to say and they want that person to know that they already know, or when they are not paying close attention. The resulting interrupting response communicates either a lack of sensitivity, a superior attitude, or both. People need to be able to verbalize their ideas and feelings fully; inappropriate interruptions are bound to damage their self-concepts or make them hostile—and possibly both. Simply stated, whatever you have to say is seldom so important that it requires you to interrupt a person. When you do interrupt, you should realize that you may be perceived as putting a person down and are increasing the chances of a defensive reaction. The more frequent the interruptions, the greater is the potential harm.

Are you an interrupter? This behavior is so common that many of us don't even realize how often we do it. To check on your own interrupting behavior, for the rest of the day try to be conscious of any time you interrupt—whatever the reason. Then ask whether the interruption was necessary or whether you could have waited for the other person to finish. Although interrupting behavior has been attributed to men more than women, in their recent study of sex-related behavior Tammy March and Carole Peterson report that total acceptance of sex differences in interruption behavior is not warranted.[6] They go on to say that interruption is most likely influenced by personality and social variables that are likely to change with the context and situation.

Practice in Problem Responses

By Yourself

Think back over conversations with your friends and acquaintances in the past day or two. Which kinds of problem responses (irrelevant, tangential, incongruous, interrupting) did you use most frequently? Under what circumstances did they occur? What do you need to do to limit your use of these responses?

Summary

The final phase of listening is responding appropriately. Responding well involves a complete set of skills.

Appropriate responses show a person's empathy. Empathy involves determining the emotional state of another person and responding in an appropriate manner. Empathic responses recognize the person's right to his or her feelings and show that we can share in those feelings.

Clarifying responses help ensure that people are sharing the same meanings. Questioning and paraphrasing are two skills that you can use to ensure understanding. Well-phrased questions are specific and sensitive. Paraphrases can check understanding of message content, feelings, or both.

Helping responses give people information about themselves or their behavior. These responses include supporting, interpreting, praising, and giving constructive criticism. Both praise and criticism should be specific and timely. In addition, several guidelines can ensure that criticism is beneficial: Make sure the person is interested in hearing criticism, describe the behavior on which the criticism is based, precede negative statements with positive ones if possible, be specific, criticize only recent behavior, direct criticism at behavior the person can do something about, and show what a person can do to correct a problem.

Problem responses hinder communication by planting the seeds of discontent within people about themselves or about the relationship. Furthermore, inappropriate responses can scuttle efforts at understanding meaning. Irrelevant, tangential, incongruous, and interrupting responses are among the most common types of problem responses.

Suggested Readings

Brammer, Lawrence M. *The Helping Relationship: Process and Skills.* Englewood Cliffs, NJ: Prentice-Hall, 1988. A short, well-written book that gives additional insight into helping skills.

Buckman, Robert. *"I Don't Know What to Say . . ." : How to Help and Support Someone Who Is Dying.* Boston: Little, Brown, 1989. Focuses on the process of dying, especially on how to communicate and empathize with those who are dying; also covers empathic listening and, particularly, response skills.

Burley-Allen, Madelyn. *Listening: The Forgotten Skill.* New York: Wiley, 1987. Discusses all aspects of listening but focuses on the skills of describing behavior, paraphrasing, and perception checking. A short, easy-to-read paperback and an excellent reinforcement for skills we discuss in Chapters 6 and 7.

Gazda, George, et al. *Human Relations Development: A Manual for Educators,* 3d ed. Needham Heights, MA: Allyn & Bacon, 1984 (paperback). Focuses on developing "helpful response" skills. Provides a good supplement to material in this chapter.

Gilbert, David G., and Connolly, James J., eds. *Personality, Social Skills, and Psychopathology: An Individual Differences Approach.* New York: Plenum, 1991. Contains an excellent rationale for the importance of developing social skills.

Notes

1. Robert J. Campbell, Norman Kagan, and David R. Krathwohl, "The Development and Validation of a Scale to Measure Affective Sensitivity (Empathy)," *Journal of Counseling Psychology* 18 (1971): 407.
2. See Dale G. Leathers, *Successful Nonverbal Communication: Principles and Applications,* 2d ed. (New York: Macmillan, 1992), p. 42.
3. Ibid., p. 26.
4. George Gazda et al., *Human Relations Development: A Manual for Educators,* 3d ed. (Needham Heights, MA: Allyn & Bacon, 1984).
5. Terrance L. Albrecht, Brant R. Burleson, and Daena Goldsmith, "Supportive Communication," in Mark L. Knapp and Gerald R. Miller, eds., *Handbook of Interpersonal Communication,* 2d ed. (Thousand Oaks, CA: Sage, 1994), p. 419.
6. Tammy A. March and Carole Peterson, "The Development and Sex-Related Use of Interruption Behavior," *Human Communication Research* 19 (March 1993): 405.

After you have read this chapter, you should be able to:

Define levels of relationships

Explain and contrast interpersonal needs and exchange theory

Describe the life cycle of a relationship

Use four different methods of starting conversations

Explain the kinds of climates in which sound relationships thrive

Use skills that create a positive climate for communication

Explain the negative characteristics of withdrawal, surrender, and aggression

Explain the positive characteristics of persuasion and discussion

Outline guidelines for managing conflict

8

Communication
in Relationships

"Janeen, you're spending a lot of time with Angie. What is Liam going to think about that?"

"Come on, Mom, I know you're just teasing me. Yeah, Liam's my boyfriend, and we get along really well, but there are things I just can't talk about with him."

"And you can with Angie?"

"Right. I can tell her what's going on with my writing, for example, and she really understands. And I do the same for her. We enjoy a lot of the same activities, so Angie is good company for me."

Janeen is lucky because she has two good relationships. Because so many of the interpersonal skills we use are for the purpose of starting, building, and maintaining relationships, we conclude this part with an analysis of relationships. A *good relationship* is any mutually satisfying interaction with another person, whether at the level of acquaintanceship, friendship, or intimacy. But because relationships on all levels are dynamic—that is, they begin, grow, stabilize, and at times, deteriorate—developing and maintaining good relationships requires skillfulness and a great deal of work.

In this chapter we examine the nature of relationships, consider two theories of why relationships develop, explain the stages that typically comprise the life cycle of a relationship, and explore means of managing conflict, one of the main factors that determine whether relationships will grow or deteriorate.

The Nature of Relationships

Relationships vary in their intensity as a function of the amount of information that each person shares with the other and the kinds of interactions between them. We generally classify the people with whom we have relationships as acquaintances, friends, and close friends or intimates.

Acquaintances

Acquaintances are people we know by name and talk with when the opportunity arises, but with whom our interactions are limited in quality and quantity. We become acquainted with those who live in our apartment building or dorm or in the house next door, who sit next to us in class, who go to our church or belong to our club. Many acquaintance relationships grow out of a particular context. Thus Melinda and Paige, who meet in biology class, may strike up an acquaintanceship, but they may make no effort to see each other outside of class; if they do meet in some other context, it is by chance.

Friends

Over time, we make friends with many of our acquaintances. *Friends* are people with whom we have negotiated more personal relationships voluntarily.[1] For instance, Melinda and Paige, who are acquaintances in biology class may, as a result of in-class conversation, voluntarily decide to get together after school one afternoon just to talk. As they continue such voluntary meetings, they begin to speak of each other as friends. People move toward friendships because they like being with each other; they actively seek each other out because they enjoy each other's company.

Good friendships are marked by warmth and affection, trust, high level of commitment, and enduring nature.[2]

Friends often express warmth and affection by spending time with each other. Friends look forward to being with each other because they experience a joy in each other's company, they enjoy talking with each other, and they enjoy sharing experiences and feelings.

Although friendships may seem "natural," communication skills can help them to deeper levels of disclosure and intimacy.

Although trust almost always involves some risk, friends willingly place trust in each other believing that the result with be to their advantage. Friends earn trust by delivering on promises, keeping secrets, and providing emotional support when needed.

Friends show a high level of commitment by sacrificing their time and energy to help each other in times of need. Good friends will go out of their way to help each other when necessary. It may be taking a friend to work when his or her car breaks down, or taking care of a child when a friend is sick or away on business, or helping with house repairs in times of emergencies.

Finally, good friendships endure over time. Circumstances such as a change of job or a move to another city may keep friends from seeing each other frequently, yet when they get together they continue to share ideas and feelings freely and rely on each other's counsel.

Close Friends or Intimates

Close friends or *intimates* are those with whom we share our deepest feelings. People may have countless acquaintances and many friends, but they are likely to have only a few truly intimate friends.

Close friends or intimates differ from "regular" friends mostly in degree of intimacy. For instance, although friends engage in levels of self-disclosure, they are not likely to share every aspect of their lives; intimate friends, on the other hand, often gain knowledge of the innermost being of their partner. Some people feel more comfortable sharing their deepest secrets with a close friend than with their lover or spouse. As a result of this increasing amount of disclosure, close friends or intimates increase their investment in the relationship and develop a sense of "we-ness."

Likewise, the degree of intimacy between friends is often characterized by the extent to which one person gives up other relationships in order to devote more time and energy to the primary relationship. Especially when two people are testing the suitability of an enduring relationship—going together, engagement, or marriage—they spend long periods of time together.

Practice in Defining Relationships

By Yourself

Make a list of the people you have spoken with in the last day or two. Now categorize each. Which are strangers? Acquaintances? Friends? Intimates?

In Groups

1. Discuss how you determine whether a person is an acquaintance, a friend, or an intimate. What characteristics seem to signal that an acquaintance has become a friend? That a friend has become an intimate?

2. Contrast the nature of your communication with acquaintances and friends. What kinds of differences do you notice in sharing information and sharing feelings in each context?

Theoretical Perspectives on Relationships

What determines whether or not we will try to build a relationship with another person? Why do some relationships never move beyond a certain level, or begin to deteriorate? Two helpful theories—interpersonal needs theory and exchange theory—offer insights into these questions.

Interpersonal Needs Theory

Relationships are started, built, and maintained on the basis of how well each person meets the interpersonal needs of the other. William Schutz, a psychologist, has identified three primary interpersonal needs: affection, inclusion, and control.[3]

The need for *affection* reflects a desire to express and to receive love. The people you know probably run the gamut of showing and expressing affection both verbally and nonverbally. At one end of the spectrum are "underpersonal" individuals who avoid close ties, seldom show strong feelings toward others, and shy away from people who show or want to show affection. At the other end are "overpersonal" individuals who thrive on establishing "close" relationships with everyone. Somewhere in between these two extremes are "personal" people who can express and receive affection easily and who derive pleasure from many kinds of relationships with others.

The need for *inclusion* reflects a desire to be in the company of other people. Although everyone has a need to be social, people differ in the amount of interaction with others that will satisfy this need. At one extreme are "undersocial" persons who usually want to be left alone. They may seek company or enjoy being included with others if specifically invited, but they do not require a great deal of social interaction to feel satisfied. At the other extreme are "oversocial" persons who need constant companionship and feel tense when they must be alone. Their doors are always open—everyone is welcome, and they expect others to welcome them. Of course, most of us do not belong to either of these extreme types. Rather, we are sometimes comfortable being alone and at other times need and enjoy interacting with others.

The need for *control* reflects a desire to successfully influence the events and people around us. At one extreme are persons who need no control, who seem to shun responsibility and do not want to be in charge of anything. "Abdicrats," as they are called by Schutz, are extremely submissive and are unlikely to make decisions or accept responsibility. At the other extreme are persons who feel a need to be in charge. Such "autocrats" need to dominate others at all times and become anxious if they cannot. Again, most people fall somewhere between these two extremes. These "democrats" need to lead at certain times, but at other times they are content to follow the lead of others. Democrats can stand behind their ideas, but they also can be comfortable submitting to others, at least some of the time.

How can this analysis help us understand communication in relationships? Relationships develop and deteriorate in part because of the compatibility or incompatibility of individuals' interpersonal needs. Through verbal and nonverbal communication behavior, we display cues that reveal the level of our immediate interpersonal needs. As you interact with others, you can detect whether their needs for affection, inclusion, and control seem compatible with yours. Suppose that Emily and Dan have been seeing each other regularly and both see their relationship as close. If in response to Dan's attempt to put his arm around Emily while they are watching television, Emily slightly stiffens, it might suggest that Emily doesn't have quite the same need for affection as Dan. It should be emphasized that people's needs do differ; moreover, people's needs change over time. When other people's needs at any given time differ significantly from ours and we fail to understand that, we can misunderstand what's going wrong in our communication.

Schutz's theory of interpersonal needs is useful because it helps explain a great deal of interpersonal behavior.[4] In addition, research on this model has been generally supportive of its major themes.[5] Interpersonal needs theory does not, however, explain *how* people adjust to one another in their ongoing relationships. The next theory we discuss will help us develop this understanding.

Exchange Theory

Another way of analyzing relationships is on the basis of exchange ratios. John W. Thibaut and Harold H. Kelley, who originated exchange theory, believe that relationships can be understood in terms of the exchange of rewards and costs that takes place during the individuals' interaction.[6] *Rewards* are outcomes that are valued by the receiver, such as good feelings, prestige, economic gain, and fulfillment of emotional needs. *Costs* are outcomes that the receiver does not wish to incur, such as time, money, energy, and negative feelings. For instance, Sharon may be eager to spend time talking with Jan if she anticipates feeling good as a result; she may be reluctant to spend that time if she expects to be depressed at the end of the conversation.

According to Thibaut and Kelley, people seek interaction situations in which their behaviors will yield an outcome of high reward and low cost. For example, if Jill runs into Sarah on campus, she could ignore Sarah, smile, say "Hi" in passing, or try to start a conversation. What Jill does will depend in part on her *cost–reward analysis* of the outcome of the interaction. For instance, if Jill had been thinking about calling Sarah to arrange a tennis match, she may take the time now to seek that outcome; she will be willing to pay the cost of taking time and using energy in hopes of receiving a suitable reward, a tennis match. If Jill and Sarah do talk, the interchange will continue until one or both realize that the cost–reward ratio is falling below the satisfactory level. For Jill, this point might be reached once a match is set. For Sarah, it might be reached when she perceives Jill's lack of interest at that moment in other topics of conversation.

This analysis can be extended from single interactions to relationships. If, over an extended period, a person's cost–reward ratio in a relationship falls below a certain level, that person will come to view the relationship itself as unsatisfactory or unpleasant. But if the cost–reward ratio is higher than the level viewed as satisfactory, the person will regard the relationship or interaction as pleasant and satisfying.

Thibaut and Kelley suggest that the requisite ratio between cost and reward varies from person to person and within one person from time to time. One reason people differ in their assessments of costs and rewards is that they have different definitions of what is satisfying. If people have a number of relationships they perceive as giving them a good cost–reward ratio, they will set a high satisfaction level and will probably not be satisfied with low-outcome relationships. By contrast, people who have few positive interactions will be satisfied with relationships and interactions that people who enjoy high-outcome relationships would find unattractive. For instance, Calvin may continue to go with Erica even if she treats him very poorly because based on experiences he has in his other relationships, the rewards he gets from the relationship are on par.

The ratio of costs and rewards determines how attractive or unattractive a relationship or an interaction is to the individuals involved, but it does not indicate how long the relationship or interaction will last. Although it seems logical that people would terminate a relationship or an interaction in which costs exceed rewards, circumstances sometimes dictate that people will stay in a relationship that is plainly unsatisfactory.

Thibaut and Kelley's explanation for such a situation involves what they call the *comparison-level of alternatives*. They suggest that the decision to continue in a relationship may depend on what alternatives or other choices a person perceives as being available. A person who feels dissatisfied will tend to leave a relationship or interaction if there is a realistic alternative that seems to promise a higher level of satisfaction. But if there are no such alternatives, the person may choose to stay in the situation because, unsatisfactory though it is, it is the best the person believes can be attained at that time. Thus, if Joan has four or five men she gets along well with, she is less likely to put up with Jeremy, who irritates her. If, however, Joan believes that Jeremy is the only man who can provide the companionship she is seeking, she will be more inclined to tolerate his irritating habits.

Like Schutz's interpersonal needs theory, Thibaut and Kelley's exchange theory helps illuminate important aspects of relationship development. Yet critics of this theory point out an important limitation. Exchange theory suggests that people consciously and deliberately weigh the costs and rewards associated with any relationship or interaction. That is, people rationally choose to continue or terminate relationships. Thus, the theory assumes that people behave rationally from an economic standpoint: they seek out relationships that benefit them and avoid those that are costly.[7] In fact, although people may behave rationally in most situations, rational models such as Thibaut and Kelley's cannot always explain complex human behavior. Nevertheless, it can be useful to examine your relationships from a cost–reward perspective. Especially if the relationship is stagnating, you may recognize areas in which costs are greater than rewards, either for you or for the other person. If so, you may be able to change some aspects of the relationship before it deteriorates completely.

You may discover that it is fruitful to use both of these theories. What you (or your partner) count as "costs" and "rewards" may depend significantly on what your particular *needs* are. If your needs differ, you may misunderstand the other person's perceptions of rewards and costs. Looking at relationships in this way might help resolve misunderstandings and reduce defensiveness. That is, if you understand the other person's needs and can take his or her perceived costs and rewards into account, you may understand the situation better and in a way that is less destructive to your own self-esteem. How helpful this kind of analysis is in your relationships is likely to depend on your use of listening, sharing feelings, and empathic understanding skills.

Practice in Analyzing Relationships

By Yourself

Think of one specific intimate relationship you have. Explain the development and maintenance of this relationship in terms of needs theory. Choose and use one specific interactional episode as evidence to support your explanation. Then explain the development and maintenance of this relationship using exchange theory. Again, focus on a single interactional episode. What insights into the relationship have you gained from these analyses? How might these insights affect your future interactions?

Communication in the Life Cycle of Relationships

Even though no two relationships develop in exactly the same manner, they tend to move through stages following a "life cycle" that includes starting or building, stabilizing, and deterioration.[8]

Starting or Building Relationships

Fundamental to starting or building a relationship is the need for information about the other person. We give information about ourselves to others so that they will have more accurate perceptions of who we are, and we seek information about others so that we can determine whether we wish to develop a relationship with them. Charles Berger and his colleagues call this theory of the need for sharing information *uncertainty reduction.*[9]

We get information about others *passively* by observing their behavior, *actively* by seeking information from third parties, and *interactively* by conversing with them directly. Gathering information to reduce uncertainty seems to be important in all cultures in the early stages of relationship development. People from some cultures may rely on passive methods of getting the information; people from other cultures may rely on more active or interactive strategies.[10]

The three communication activities we engage in to start and build relationships are striking up a conversation, keeping a conversation going, and moving toward intimacy.

Striking Up a Conversation. What happens in the first few minutes of a conversation will have a profound effect on the nature of the relationship that develops. As the old saying goes, you seldom get a second chance to create a first impression. Although thinking up "getting to know you" lines is easy for some, many people become nearly tongue-tied when they want to meet someone and, as a result, make a bad first impression. For those of us who find starting conversations with strangers difficult, the following four strategies may be useful. Notice that each of these is developed in question form, inviting the other person to respond. A cheerful answer to your question suggests interest in continuing. Refusal to answer or a curt reply may mean that the person isn't really interested in talking at this time.

1. *Introduce yourself.* The simplest way to start a conversation with a person is to introduce yourself and to ask for similar information. For example, "Hi, my name is Gordon. What's yours?" may sound trite, but it works.

2. *Refer to the physical context.* Referring to some aspect of the physical context is a more indirect way to get started. One of the oldest and most effective strategies is a comment on the weather such as, "This is awful weather for a game, isn't it?" Other contextual references include comments related to place such as "They've really decorated this place beautifully," "I wonder how they are able to keep such a beautiful garden in this climate?" and "Darlene and Verne have sure done a lovely job of remodeling this home—did you ever see it before the renovation?"

3. *Refer to your thoughts or feelings.* "I really like parties, don't you?" "I live on this floor too—do these steps bother you as much as they do me?" and "Doesn't it seem stuffy in here?" all share thoughts and feelings and ask for responses.

4. *Refer to others.* "Marge seems to be an excellent hostess—have you known her long?" and "I don't believe I've had the pleasure of seeing you before—do you work in Marketing?" seek direct information from the other person.

Keeping a Conversation Going. People keep conversations going through such "small talk" as gossip and idea exchange.

Gossip is relating information whose accuracy may be unknown about people you both know. Statements such as "I hear Bill has a really great job," "I hear Mary and Tom are back together," and "Eileen is really working hard at losing weight" are all examples of gossip. You can gossip for a long time with another person without really saying anything about yourself or without learning anything about the other person. Gossip may be a pleasant way to pass time with people you know but with whom you have no desire or need for a deeper relationship. It also provides a safe way to explore the potential for the relationship to grow since it allows each person to see whether the other reacts similarly to the views expressed about the object of the gossip.

Gossip can, of course, be malicious. If the information exchanged is found to be inaccurate, the gossip may damage both the relationship in which it was exchanged and other relationships as well. More often than not, however, gossip represents a means of interacting amicably with others without becoming personally involved. This is why conversations at parties are comprised largely of gossip.

In *idea-exchange communication* people share factual information, opinions, and beliefs. At the office Dan may ask Walt about last night's sports scores, Maria may talk with Louise about new cars, and Pete may discuss the upcoming elections with Teresa. Or, on a more serious level, Jan may talk with Gloria about the U.S. role in the Middle East or Dave may seek Bill's views on the rising rate of teenage pregnancy. Although the discussions of foreign policy and teen pregnancies are "deeper" than those about sports or cars, both sets of conversations represent idea exchanges. This type of communication is important to early stages of relationships because it help you learn the kinds of things about the other person that helps you decide whether or not you want the relationship to grow.

Moving to More Intimate Levels.   People who are thinking of moving to more intimate levels begin to talk about more serious ideas and to share their feelings about important matters. Through the sharing of feelings and talks about serious topics people tell each other that they are comfortable with each other and seek an intimate relationship. When people find that they get satisfaction out of being together and talking, their friendship grows.

As you may have noticed, the different kinds of communication that occur during the development of a relationship follow a continuum from impersonal/superficial to personal/deep. Because intimate relationships are time-consuming and require a level of mutual trust that is difficult to attain, people generally have only one or two truly intimate friends at any one time.

Stabilizing Relationships

When two people have a satisfactory relationship, whether as acquaintances, as friends, or as intimates, they look for *stability*—a means of maintaining the relationship at that level for some time. Relationships are stable when two people agree on what they want from each other and are satisfied that they are achieving it.

An essential aspect of a stable relationship is maintaining a *positive climate for communication,* one that encourages the mutually satisfying discussion of ideas.

Laura Stafford and Daniel Canary's research supports the idea that maintenance strategies seem to operate in conjunction with equity.[11] A positive climate is facilitated by communication that is perceived as descriptive, equal, open, and provisional.

Speaking Descriptively.   Relationships thrive in a climate in which communication is descriptive rather than evaluative or judgmental.[12] Speaking *descriptively* simply means stating what you see or hear in objective, nonevaluative language. For instance, Maria walks out of a marketing strategy meeting with Juan and says, "Juan, the reason why Doreen and Ivan treated your idea so summarily is that when we talked about it at the last meeting, everyone agreed that it didn't take into account the reality of the economy." Compare that descriptive statement with "Juan, that was a stupid idea, and everyone knew it." Evaluating Juan's statement as "stupid" does not describe the problem.

Why is evaluation harmful to climate? First, evaluation does not inform; it places a judgment on what has been said or done. Misunderstandings often result from a shortage of information. Before an evaluation can be understood, a person must have the data on which it was based. In conversation, however, people are inclined to skip over the information (the description). For instance, in a heated moment, the coach may pull Arnold from the game and say, "Keep up show-off play like that and you'll be on the bench permanently." Arnold may recognize that he made some offensive or defensive mistakes, but the phrase "show-off play" gives him no clear picture of the specific behaviors the coach resented. But Arnold would have been able to understand the coach's evaluation of his behavior had the coach said, "Arnold, you're not following the plans. The last two times you had the ball you had a chance to pass to an open man, and in both cases you took off-balance shots. Selfish, show-off play is going to put you on the bench permanently."

Second, evaluations are likely to make other people defensive, especially if those evaluations are perceived to be personal, negative, or contrary to the other person's perception. *Defensiveness* is a negative feeling or behavior that results when a person feels threatened. For instance, as Henry and Susan leave a musical comedy, Henry says, "That was a really enjoyable show." In a cutting tone, Susan replies, "Enjoyable? That shows your level of taste. That was the most miserable excuse for a professional production I've seen in a long time." Since Henry enjoyed the songs, her hostile evaluative statement is almost sure to draw a defensive reaction from him because it is both negative and an attack on his taste. Henry may sharply contradict Susan, or he may withdraw in anger from further communication with her. In either case, the climate for effective communication between them is likely to be spoiled—at least for the moment.

You'll recall that we discussed descriptions of behavior ("Did you know your eyes sparkle when you're happy?" or "Are you aware how much you increase the volume of your voice when you show me the mistakes that I made?") in Chapter 7 (page 177).

Speaking to Others as Equals.   Relationships grow in climates where people treat each other as equals rather than in climates where one person is perceived as superior to another.

*W*hat allows relationships to endure? There is no single answer, but one important ingredient is a climate of mutual respect and equality.

Equality in communication requires careful wording that avoids a perception of superiority. Department heads or older family members may think that their authority gives them a right to treat others as inferiors. But acting in a superior way often results in a negative rather than a positive communication climate, particularly when others involved are not convinced that the claim of superiority is justified. In contrast, choosing language that conveys an attitude of equality respects the humanity of the other person.

For instance, in a work setting, a boss has authority over his or her secretary. But line authority does not mean that the boss is superior to the secretary. So, instead of saying "Bethany, get on this letter right away—I want it on my desk in twenty minutes," the boss could say, "Bethany, I got behind on framing this letter, and it really should be in the 3:00 mail. I'd appreciate it if you could get it typed by 2:30 for me. I'm sorry for having to put you in such a bind." Even though the person is "the boss," and Bethany is required to comply, the second phrasing provides a reason for the request and shows sensitivity to the fact that the boss is responsible for the lateness.

In addition to choosing language carefully, our nonverbal behaviors (tone of voice and facial expressions) are just as important in demonstrating equality. Tone of voice, facial expression, and willingness to pitch in and work with another person all contribute to a climate of equality.

Speaking Openly.   Speaking *openly* means sharing true thoughts and feelings without resorting to manipulation and hidden agendas. Relationships grow best in a climate where the subject or the purpose of the communication is readily apparent.

When Shelby thanks Brent for the information he gave her that helped her write her report, Brent will assume that thanking him is Shelby's reason for talking with him. A person's purpose—or *agenda*—may be determined before the conversation or may emerge as the conversation develop.

Occasionally, however, people have a secret underlying motive, known as a *hidden agenda*. For instance, if Shelby has been looking for Brent to find out what, if anything, he has done to schedule a band for the company's holiday party, Shelby may start the conversation by thanking him, but her real reason, or hidden agenda, is different. In some cases, people use hidden agendas as a matter of tact, propriety, or lack of nerve. For instance, Shelby may be too embarrassed to come right out and ask Brent whether he's done any calling yet, so she hopes that by thanking him for helping her, she can manipulate him into revealing whether he is meeting his responsibility for the party.

But when people aren't open about their reasons for talking, they risk erecting communication barriers. In Shelby's case, the hidden agenda may appear to be beneficial to her. But when the real subject is revealed, her deviousness in trying to find out about his progress without his really knowing it may do harm to their relationship. Not only will he be angry over her failure to be direct, but also he's likely to be angry about her lack of trust.

Since not being open can hurt relationships, approaching a difficult problem directly is usually the best tactic. If Shelby really needs to know whether Brent has done anything about music for the party, she can have two agendas, but both should be open. For instance, after thanking him for helping her, Shelby could say, "Brent, I haven't heard from you yet about how you were coming in getting music for the party. Are you making any progress?" Dealing with the issue may prove difficult, but at least the difficulty will be the issue itself and not something else.

Hidden agendas that attempt to manipulate another person's behavior until the manipulator gets some payoff can be very destructive. Notice the destructive nature of hidden agendas in the following two examples:

> Glen knows that Judy gets angry when he smokes in the bedroom. He lights up in the bedroom and acts amazed when Judy loses her temper.

> Urie knows that Ming is likely to become very uncomfortable when his former girlfriend, Kyoka, is mentioned. In Ming's presence, Urie "innocently" asks, "Say, has anyone seen Kyoka lately?"

In both cases, the person's hidden agenda is to create a painful experience for the other person. If the behavior elicits the desired response, that person "wins." It is this win–lose element that makes such statements so destructive.

Speaking Provisionally.   Relationships grow best in a climate where people state their beliefs provisionally rather than dogmatically. Speaking *provisionally* means that the ideas expressed are thought to be correct but may not be; dogmatic wordings leave no room for discussion. Whereas provisional language helps create or maintain a good climate for communication, dogmatic statements stop discussion and tend to create defensiveness.

Consider the differences between the two sentences in each of the following pairs:

"If I remember correctly, Dalton was the sales leader last month."
"I'm telling you, Dalton had the most sales last month."

"I think you should consider talking with Glenna before doing anything on your own."
"You'd be an idiot not to talk with Glenna before doing anything on this."

What differences did you notice? The first sentence of each pair is stated provisionally; the second is stated dogmatically. Why are the first sentences more likely to result in better interpersonal communication? First, the tentativeness of the phrasings is likely to be less antagonizing. Second, they acknowledge that the words come from the speaker—who may have it wrong. "I'm telling you" leaves no room for possible error; "If I remember correctly" not only leaves room for error but also shows that it is the speaker's recollection and not a statement of universal certainty.

Speaking provisionally may seem unassertive and wishy-washy, and if carried to extremes, it can be. But there is a world of difference between stating what you think to be true and phrasing your views in a way that is likely to arouse hostility. Speaking provisionally allows for conflicting opinions and the possibility that even a strongly held opinion may not be correct.

Many times the things we say that hurt the climate come because we are just not thinking. It's a good idea to follow the old advice of "engaging your brain before putting your mouth in action." Take a second to remind yourself that a single thoughtless sentence can take minutes, hours, or days to repair—if it is repairable.

To assure yourself that your statements are descriptive, open, provisional, and treat others as equals: (1) Consider what you are about to say. (2) Determine whether it contains a wording that shows an attitude of evaluation, deviousness, certainty, or superiority. (3) If it does, recast the sentence to change the tone.

Relationship Disintegration

Regardless of how much we would like all of our relationships to remain stable, some of them come to an end.

The first sign that a relationship is weakening sometimes appears in subtle indications of dissatisfaction. One person begins to lose interest in the opinions and feelings of the other, and the orientation changes from *we* to *I*. Subjects that once were easy to discuss become sources of conflict, many of which remain unresolved.

As deterioration progresses, people begin to drift apart. Their communication changes from deep sharing of ideas and feelings to small talk and other "safe" communication to no significant communication at all. It may seem strange that people who had so much to share can find themselves with nothing to talk about. But, in this stage, people don't see the need for an effort to build or maintain the relationship. Not only are they no longer interested in exchanging significant ideas, they may begin to avoid each other altogether, seeking out other people with whom to share interests and activities.

The final stage of a deteriorating relationship is ending it. As Cupach and Metts show, people give many reasons for ending relationships, including poor communication, lack of fulfillment, differing lifestyles/interests, rejection, outside interference, absence of rewards, and boredom.[13] At the heart of many of these reasons is the failure to deal with conflict effectively. Because resolving conflict is so important to relationship maintenance, the remainder of this chapter deals with this important topic.

Practice in Analyzing Stages of Relationships

By Yourself

1. Label the following statements as E (evaluative), D (dogmatic), S (superior), or M (manipulative, involving a hidden agenda). In each case, rephrase the statement so that it is descriptive, provisional, equal, or open. The first one has been completed for you. When you are done, share your revisions with other members of the class.

  __D__   a. "Shana, turn that off! No one can study with the radio on!"
Suggested rephrasing: "Shana, I'd suggest turning the radio down or off. You may find that you can study better without the distraction."

  _____   b. "Did you ever hear of such a tacky idea as having a formal wedding and using paper plates?"

  _____   c. "That advertising program will never sell."

  _____   d. "Oh Jack, you're so funny wearing plaids with stripes. Well, I guess that's a man for you!"

  _____   e. "Paul, you're acting like a baby. You've got to learn to use your head."

  _____   f. Noticing that she has only a short time before she intends to meet Gavin, Tori says, "Yvonne, I don't see anything that looks right for you here—let's plan to try Northgate Mall sometime next week."

  _____   g. "You may think you know how to handle the situation, but you are just not mature enough. I know when something's right for you."

Answers b. E c. D d. S e. E f. M g. S

2. Think of the last time you had a long discussion with another person. Which aspects of climate helped or hindered the effectiveness of that discussion?

3. Think of two recent interactions you have had. Choose one that was characterized by a positive communication climate and one that was characterized by a negative climate. Recall as best you can some of the specific conversation from each interaction. Write this down like a script. Now, analyze each script. Count specific instances of being descriptive and giving evaluation. Recall whether hidden agendas were evidenced. Count instances of provisional wordings and of dogmatic wordings. Look for instances where equality was present and instances where one

person spoke in a way that conveyed an attitude of superiority. Discuss your results. How much did using or failing to use the four skills presented in this section contribute to the climate you experienced? For a sample analysis, see the Appendix: Interpersonal Conversation and Analysis (pp. 468–470).

Managing Conflict in Relationships

This final section confronts one of the primary causes leading to the deterioration of relationships: failure to manage conflict successfully. In his research review, Dudley Cahn defines *interpersonal conflict* as "interaction between persons expressing opposing interests, views, or opinions."[14]

Conflicts include clashes over facts and definitions ("Charley was the first one to talk." "No, it was Mark." or "Your mother is a battle-ax." "What do you mean, a 'battle-ax'?"); over values ("Bringing home pencils and pens from work is not stealing." "Of course it is." or "The idea that you have to be married to have sex is completely outdated." "No, it isn't."); and, perhaps the most difficult to deal with, over ego involvement ("Listen, I've been a football fan for thirty years; I ought to know what good defense is." "Well, you may be a fan, but that doesn't make you an expert.").

Although many people view conflict as bad (and, to be sure, conflict situations are likely to make us anxious and uneasy), it is inevitable in any significant relationship. Moreover, conflict is sometimes useful in that it forces us to make choices; to resolve honest differences; and to test the relative merits of our attitudes, behaviors, needs, and goals. Now let's consider methods of dealing with conflict and guidelines for managing conflict.

Methods of Dealing with Conflict

Left to their own devices, people engage in many behaviors, both negative and positive, to cope with or manage their conflicts. The various methods of dealing with conflict can be grouped into five major patterns: withdrawal, surrender, aggression, persuasion, and problem-solving discussion. Let's consider each of these methods in turn.

Withdrawal. One of the most common, and certainly one of the easiest, ways to deal with conflict is to withdraw. When people withdraw, they physically or psychologically remove themselves from the situation. Withdrawal is a form of the passive behavior discussed in Chapter 5.

Physical withdrawal is, of course, easiest to identify. Suppose Eduardo and Justina get into a conversation about Eduardo's smoking. Justina says, "Eduardo, I thought you told me that whether you stopped smoking completely or not, you weren't going to smoke around the house. Now here you are lighting up!" Eduardo may withdraw physically by saying "I don't want to talk about it" and going to the basement to finish a project he was working on.

Because withdrawal leaves conflicts unresolved, habitually resorting to this way of managing disagreement only postpones—and probably worsens—the inevitable confrontations.

Psychological withdrawal may be less noticeable but is every bit as common. Using the same example, when Justina begins to talk about Eduardo's smoking in the house, Eduardo may sit quietly in his chair looking at Justina, but all the time she speaks he is thinking about the poker game he will be going to the next evening.

Besides being quite common, both kinds of withdrawal are basically negative. Why? Because they neither eliminate nor attempt to manage the conflict. As Roloff and Cloven note, "Relational partners who avoid conflicts have more difficulty resolving their disputes."[15] In the case of the physical withdrawal, Justina may follow Eduardo to the basement, where the conflict will be resumed; if not, the conflict will undoubtedly surface later—and will probably be intensified—when Justina and Eduardo try to resolve another, unrelated issue. In the case of the psychological withdrawal, Justina may force Eduardo to address the smoking issue, or she may go along with Eduardo's ignoring it but harbor a resentment that may negatively affect their relationship.

Another reason why withdrawal is negative is that it results in what Cloven and Roloff call "mulling behavior." By *mulling* they mean thinking about or stewing over an actual or perceived problem until the participants perceive the conflict as more severe and begin engaging in blaming behavior.[16] Thus, in many cases, not confronting the problem when it occurs only makes it more difficult to deal with in the long run.

Nevertheless, conflicts do occasionally go away if left alone.[17] There appear to be two sets of circumstances in which withdrawal may work. First, when the withdrawal represents temporary disengagement for the purpose of letting the heat of the conflict subside, it can be an effective technique for managing conflict. Consider this example: Bill and Margaret begin to argue over having Bill's mother for Thanksgiving dinner. During the conversation, Margaret begins to get angry about what her mother-in-law said to her recently about the way she and Bill are raising their daughter. Margaret says, "Hold it a minute; let me make a pot of coffee. We can both relax a bit, and then we'll talk about this some more." A few minutes later, having calmed down, she returns, ready to approach the conflict more objectively. Margaret's action is not true withdrawal; it's not meant as a means of avoiding confrontation. Rather, it provides a cooling-off period that will probably benefit them both.

The second set of circumstances in which withdrawal may work is when a conflict occurs between people who communicate infrequently. Consider Josh and Mario, who work in the same office. At two office gatherings, they have gotten into arguments about whether the company really cares about its employees. At the next office gathering, Mario avoids sitting near Josh. Again, this form of withdrawal serves as a means of avoiding conflict rather than contributing to it. In this case, Mario judges that it simply isn't that important to resolve the disagreement. It is fair to say that not every conflict needs to be resolved. Withdrawal is a negative pattern only when it is a person's major way of managing conflict.

Surrender. A second method of managing conflict is to surrender. As you might suspect, *surrender* means giving in immediately to avoid conflict. Although altering a personal position in order to accommodate another can be positive when it's done in the spirit of cooperation, using surrender as a primary coping strategy is unhealthy.

Some people are so upset by the prospect of conflict that they will do anything to avoid it. For instance, Juan and Mariana are discussing their vacation plans. Juan would like for just the two of them to go, but Mariana has talked with two of their friends who will be vacationing the same week about going together. After Juan mentions that he'd like the two of them to go alone, Mariana says, "But I think it would be fun to go with another couple, don't you?" Juan replies, "OK, whatever you want." Even though Juan really wants the two of them to go alone, rather than describe his feelings or give reasons for his position, he gives in to avoid conflict.

Habitual surrender is a negative way of dealing with conflict for at least two reasons. First, decisions should be made on their merits, not to avoid conflict. If one person gives in, there is no testing of the decision—no one knows what would really be best. Second, surrender can be infuriating to the other person. When Mariana tells Juan what she thinks, she probably wants Juan to see her way as the best. But if Juan simply surrenders, Mariana might believe that Juan still dislikes her plan but is playing the martyr. And his unwillingness to present his reasons could lead to even more conflict.

The contention that surrender is a negative way of dealing with conflict should be qualified to the extent that it reflects a Western cultural perspective. In some cultures, surrendering is a perfectly legitimate way of dealing with conflict. In Japanese culture, for instance, it is thought to be more humble and face-saving to surrender than to risk losing respect through conflict.[18]

Aggression. A third method of dealing with conflict is through aggression. *Aggression* entails the use of physical or psychological coercion to get one's way. Through aggression, people attempt to force others to accept their ideas or wishes, thereby emerging as "victors" in conflicts.

Aggression seldom improves a relationship, however. Rather, aggression is an emotional reaction to conflict. Thought is short-circuited, and the person lashes out physically or verbally. People who use aggression are not concerned with the merits of an issue but only with who is bigger, who can talk louder, who can act nastier, or who can force the other to give in. With either physical or verbal aggression, conflict is escalated or obscured but not managed.

Persuasion.   A fourth method of managing conflict is by persuasion. *Persuasion* is the attempt to change either the attitude or the behavior of another person in order to seek accommodation. At times during the discussion of an issue, one party might try to persuade the other that a particular action is the right one. Suppose that at one point in their discussion about buying a car, Sheila says, "Don't we need a lot of room?" Kevin might reply, "Enough to get us into the car together, but I don't see why we need more than that." Sheila and Kevin are now approaching a conflict situation. At this point, Sheila might say, "Kevin, we are constantly complaining about the lack of room in our present car. Remember last month when you were upset because we couldn't even get our two suitcases in the trunk and we had to put one of them in the back seat? And how many times have we been embarrassed when we couldn't drive our car with friends because the back seat is too small for even two normal-sized people?" Statements like these represent an attempt at resolving the conflict through persuasion.

When persuasion is open and reasonable, it can be a positive means of resolving conflict. However, persuasion can also degenerate into manipulation, as when a person says, "You know, if you back me on this, I could see to it that you get a few more of the good accounts, and if you don't, well. . . ." Although persuasive efforts may fuel a conflict, if that persuasion has a solid logical base, it is at least possible that the persuasion will resolve the conflict.

Discussion.   A fifth method of dealing with conflict is through *problem-solving discussion*—the verbal weighing and considering of the pros and cons of the issues in conflict. Discussion is the most desirable means of dealing with conflict in a relationship because it provides for open consideration of issues and because it preserves equality. Resolving conflict through discussion is often difficult to accomplish, however, because it requires all parties involved to cooperate: the participants must be objective in their presentation of issues, honest in stating their feelings and beliefs, and open to the solution that proves to be most satisfactory and in the best interests of those involved.

Problem-solving discussion includes defining and analyzing the problem, suggesting possible solutions, selecting the solution that best fits the analysis, and working to implement the decision. We discuss these stages of problem solving in Chapter 9, in the context of work groups. In everyday situations, all five steps are not always considered completely, nor are they necessarily considered in the order given. But when two people perceive a conflict emerging, they need to be willing to step back from the conflict and proceed systematically toward a solution.

Does this process sound too idealized? Or impracticable? Discussion is difficult, but when two people commit themselves to trying, chances are they will discover that through discussion they arrive at solutions that meet both their needs and do so in a way that maintains their relationship. (For an example of how not to conduct a "discussion," see Seven Magic Rules for Ruining Any Discussion on pages 204 and 205.)

two are needed to neutralize the best of intentions. Follow these guidelines, even a little sloppily, and you are guaranteed a miserable time.

1. *Bring the matter up when at least one of you is angry.*

Variations: Bring it up when nothing can be done about it (in the middle of the night; right before guests are due; when one of you is in the shower). Bring it up when concentration is impossible (while driving to a meeting with the IRS; while watching the one TV program you both agree on while your spouse is balancing the checkbook).

2. *Be as personal as possible when setting forth the problem.*

Variations: Know the answer before you ask the question. While describing the issue, use an accusatory tone. Begin by implying who, as usual, is to blame.

3. *Concentrate on getting what you want.*

Variations: Overwhelm your partner's position before he or she can muster a defense (be very emotional; call in past favors; be impeccably reasonable). Impress on your partner what you need and what he or she must do without.

If you begin losing ground, jockey for position.

4. *Instead of listening, think only of what you will say next.*

Variations: Do other things while your partner is talking. Forget where your partner left off. In other words, listen with all the interest you would give a bathroom exhaust fan.

5. *Correct anything your partner says about you.*

Variations: Each time your partner gives an example of your behavior, cite a worse example of his or hers. Repeat "That's not what I said" often. Do not accept anything your partner says at face value (point out exceptions; point out inaccuracies in facts and in grammar).

6. *Mention anything from the past that has a chance of making your partner defensive.*

Variations: Make allusions to your partner's sexual performance. Remind your husband of his mother's faults. Compare what your wife does to what other women do, and after she complains, say, "I didn't mean it that way."

7. *End by saying something that will never be forgotten.*

Variations: Do something that proves you are a madman. Let your parting display proclaim that no exposure of your partner could be amply revealing, no characterization too profane, no consequence sufficiently wretched. At least leave the impression you are a little put out. ■

SOURCE: Hugh Prather and Gayle Prather, *A Book for Couples* (New York: Doubleday, 1988) Copyright © 1988 by Hugh and Gayle Prather. Used by permission of Doubleday.

"I know you feel very strongly about what you believe is right. Before we consider whether your plan is the best one, perhaps we could consider what we want to accomplish."

"I know I sometimes get a little hotheaded in conflict situations, and I'm going to try to look at this problem as objectively as I can, but I may need all your help."

"You have good reasons for your belief, and I believe I have, too. Perhaps if we share our reasons and then consider the consequences of each of them, we can make a decision that we'll both find satisfying."

If we approach others openly and respectfully, we should at least get a hearing; however, if we demean people's ideas or the people themselves by our words or actions, we will probably create defensiveness, cause hard feelings, and escalate the conflict.

Working to maintain a cooperative atmosphere takes practice. If you feel yourself becoming ego-involved, mentally step back, take a deep breath, and reapply yourself to seeking a workable solution. When you see the other person becoming competitive, paraphrase your perception, perhaps with a statement such as "From the way you're making your point, I get the feeling that this particular approach is very important to you personally." The skills of describing feelings, listening, paraphrasing, and maintaining a climate of positive communication are especially relevant to creating a cooperative atmosphere.

3. *Read the nonverbal signs.* As C. R. Berger puts it, failure to read nonverbal signs is to "doom oneself to study the tip of a very large iceberg."[21] What can you learn from a person's nonverbal signs? Deborah Newton and Judee Burgoon argue that by analyzing nonverbal behaviors you can tell how the person is feeling, his or her degree of intimacy, whether the person is intentionally sending mixed messages, and when the person is attempting to exert control.[22]

For instance, suppose Jan asks, "Where did you put my dress that you got from the cleaners?" and Lonnie replies, "Oh no, I forgot all about it." If Jan then says, "Sure, I could have predicted that," what Jan really means by her comment is likely to be revealed more by her nonverbal communication than by her words. If she has a gleam in her eye and a chuckle in her voice, Lonnie might infer that he is really forgiven for being a forgetful lout. If, on the other hand, the statement is made in a deep brooding tone, Jan may well be commenting on how she perceives their relationship—that she is very unimportant in the scheme of things. In this case, Lonnie might want to check out his perceptions, apologize for his forgetfulness, and clear up the misunderstanding.

Successful use and reading of nonverbal cues, then, can defuse or fuel a conflict. To put it another way, nothing you say verbally will help manage conflict if the nonverbal signs contradict the words; on the other hand, even clumsy verbal efforts to manage conflict can be successful if both parties read the others' nonverbal cues as positive signs that they really are trying to manage the conflict.

4. *Use humor.* As suggested by the Jan and Lonnie example, humor can be an important part of your conflict-management repertoire. Janet Alberts reminds us that humor "can serve to promote solidarity, establish intimacy, and excuse a slight."[23] Yet, she also tells us that the success of humor depends a great deal on the perceived success of the relationship.[24] That is, if two people believe that they have a good relationship, they are likely to perceive ribbing, teasing, and joking in a positive way rather than taking offense. For instance, Tom goes to the refrigerator for an egg for breakfast only to find that all the eggs are gone. He looks at Greg, his roommate, and says, "Damn it, Greg, can't you remember to replace something when you've used the last one? For crying out loud!" Greg replies, "Oh woe is me! What a colossal blunder! Oh, I have sinned—stone me, take me to the stocks." At this point, Tim may be disarmed and reply, "OK, it's not a big deal, but I do wish you'd be a little more considerate." Notice, though, that Greg's histrionics will work only if Greg and Tom really get along. If their relationship has been severely strained, Greg's attempt at humor in a conflict setting may be taken as sarcastic or as a sign that he really doesn't care about Tom's feelings. In that case, using humor is likely to exacerbate rather than defuse the conflict. To be helpful in a conflict, humor must be both well intended and likely to be well received.

5. *Negotiate the conflict. Negotiation* means managing conflicts through trade-offs. Conflict often results when two actions are proposed but only one can be taken. You cannot go to a baseball game and a concert at the same time; you cannot eat at a Chinese and an Italian restaurant at the same time; if you can afford only one house payment, you can't buy a house and rent a house at the same time. After people have considered every aspect of a conflict rationally and still believe that their own way is the best, then they may need to negotiate.

Negotiating solutions to simple conflicts is relatively easy. For example, in trying to resolve whether to go to the ball game or the concert, negotiating by saying "I'll tell you what, Tammy, I'll go to the concert with you tonight if you'll go to the ball game with me this weekend" will probably work. Since the activities can both be undertaken at different times, the conflict does not represent an either–or situation, unless both parties insist on making it so.

For negotiation to work, the activities, goals, or ideas must be of fairly equal importance. Thus, in a dispute over whether to eat Chinese or Italian, the conflict may be resolved if one of the participants says, "Joe, if you'll let me make the decision on where to eat tonight, I'll go along with you on whatever movie you want to see." On the other hand, saying "Alice, if you'll let me decide on the kind of car to buy, I'll let you decide where to go on our next weekend trip" is not likely to work, because car purchases and weekend outings are not of equal weight. Trying to negotiate unequal choices is not acting in good faith.

In negotiation, as in all kinds of conflict management, a climate of equality is essential. Finding trade-offs that are indeed parallel in importance may be difficult, but when they can be found, they make an excellent base for negotiation.

6. *Seek outside help.* If a conflict is truly not negotiable—such as a conflict about whether to rent a house or buy one—and you and the other person cannot work out a decision cooperatively by yourselves, you are not necessarily defeated. When negotiation fails, you may wish to seek the help of a facilitator or an arbitrator.

A *facilitator* is an impartial third person who can help you discuss the conflict cooperatively. This person will not make the decision for you but will help the two of you apply the problem-solving method to your conflict. Psychologists, psychiatrists, marriage counselors, and other clinicians are skilled in facilitating decision making. A good facilitator not only sees to it that you are following the steps of problem solving but also helps you weigh and evaluate the variables.

An *arbitrator* is an impartial third person who, after hearing both sides, weighs and evaluates the alternatives and makes a binding decision for you. Labor unions and management sometimes use arbitration. It may work for you.

For interpersonal conflicts, arbitration will work only if you can agree on an arbitrator who, in turn, will agree to make the decision for you. The arbitrator must be a person whose judgment you both trust. The arbitrator also should be competent in some way to make a decision on the issue. Your lawyer may act as arbitrator for you over whether or not to sue after a car accident, but he or she is not qualified to help you resolve a conflict over whether to send your child to public or private school. Likewise, your financial counselor may arbitrate a conflict over whether to invest in a high-risk stock or a high-dividend stock but not in a conflict over whether to live in the city or the country.

Too often people seek to pull in a close friend or a relative to arbitrate. Not only may these bystanders not have the expertise needed for the particular issue, but more important, they are not independent, impartial agents. They may well be close to both parties or may have a vested interest in the outcome. Calling on such people puts them in a no-win situation or, at best, makes them feel very uncomfortable in the role.

If you do agree to arbitration, the verbal contract between you and the other person should include a clause stating that whatever decision is made, you will both willingly and happily comply. Remember, you will have gone to a third person because the two of you were unable to come to an agreement; if you are unwilling to abide by the decision, whichever way it goes, you should not agree to arbitration in the first place.

7. *Learn from conflict-management failures.* Ideally, you want to resolve every conflict as it comes up. As the saying goes, never let the sun set on your anger. There will be times, however, when no matter how hard both persons try, they will not be able to resolve the conflict. As Sillars and Weisberg point out, conflict can be an extremely complex process, and some conflicts may not be resolvable even through improved communication.[25]

Especially when the relationship is important to you, take time to analyze the failure to resolve a conflict. Ask yourself such questions as "Where did things go wrong?" "Did one or more of us become competitive? Or defensive?" "Did we fail to implement the problem-solving method adequately?" "Were the vested interests in the outcome too great?" You may find that attempts failed because you need more work on basic communication skills such as paraphrasing, describing feelings, and perception checking. By seeing why conflict resolution failed, you put yourself in a better position to manage the next conflict more successfully.

Practice in Identifying Methods of Dealing with Conflict

By Yourself

1. Describe a conflict situation that arose between you and a friend. Did you and your friend cope with the conflict through withdrawal, surrender, aggression, persuasion, or discussion? What was the outcome of the conflict? If the outcome was negative, sketch a method of coping with the conflict that would have been more productive for you.

2. Recount a recent conflict situation in which you believe you "won" or "lost." What contributed to the outcome? Did you have any control? What skills mentioned in this chapter might have improved the means of resolving the conflict? Reflect on a time when you won a battle but lost the war; that is, you appeared to come out ahead at the moment, but the long-term quality of the relationship was damaged. What behaviors were responsible for the damage? What might you have done to prevent harm to the relationship?

Summary

One of the main purposes of interpersonal communication is developing and maintaining relationships. A good relationship is any mutually satisfying interaction, on any level, with another person.

People have three types of relationships. Acquaintances are people we know by name and talk with, but with whom our interactions are limited in quality and quantity. Friends are people we spend time with voluntarily. Friendships are marked by degrees of warmth and affection, trust, self-disclosure, commitment, and expectation that the relationship will endure. Close or intimate friends are those with whom we share our deepest feelings, spend great amounts of time, and mark the relationship in some special way.

Two theories about how relationships work are especially useful for explaining the dynamics of relationships. Schutz sees relationships in terms of the ability to meet the interpersonal needs of affection, inclusion, and control. Thibaut and Kelley see relationships as exchanges: People evaluate relationships through a cost–reward analysis, weighing the energy, time, and money invested against the satisfaction gained.

Relationships go through a life cycle that includes starting or building, stabilizing, and ending. In the starting or building stage, people strike up a conversation, keep conversations going, and move to more intimate levels. People nurture good relationships through the skills of describing, openness, provisionalism, and equality. Relationships that are no longer mutually satisfying are likely to end.

One of the primary factors leading to the deterioration of relationships is failure to manage conflict successfully. Conflict can be defined as interaction between persons expressing opposing interests, views, or opinions. Some conflict is inevitable in most relationships, and managing conflict successfully can help relationships grow. Withdrawal, surrender, and aggression are methods of managing conflict that generally have negative consequences for relationships. Persuasion and discussion are positive methods. Specific skills for managing conflict include developing a desire for successful management, cooperating rather than competing, accurately reading nonverbal reactions, using humor, negotiating when appropriate, seeking facilitation or arbitration when negotiation fails, and learning from conflict-management failures.

Suggested Readings

Huseman, Richard C., and Hatfield, John D. *Managing the Equity Factor: Or "After All I've Done for You. . . ."* Boston: Houghton Mifflin, 1989. Discusses how to apply the cost–reward theory presented in this chapter. Includes numerous insightfully written examples and illustrations to help readers visualize the points they make.

Knapp, Mark L., and Vangelisti, Anita L. *Interpersonal Communication and Human Relationships,* 2d ed. Needham Heights, MA: Allyn & Bacon, 1992. Provides an analytical approach to communication in relationships with discussions of such topics as attraction, love, commitment, and conflict.

Ogley, Roderick C. *Conflict Under the Microscope.* Brookfield, VT: Gower, 1991. Contains chapters on games, aggressiveness, and the management of conflict.

Ury, William. *Getting Past No: Negotiating with Difficult People.* New York: Bantam Books, 1991. Ury, coauthor of the best-seller *Getting to Yes: Negotiating Agreement Without Giving In,* puts emphasis on coping with unruly teenagers, office bullies, and recalcitrant opponents. He focuses on a five-step strategy designed to bring adversaries to their senses rather than to their knees.

Wood, Julia T. *Relational Communication: Continuity and Change in Personal Relationships.* Belmont, CA: Wadsworth, 1995. Relationship development is the focus of the entire book.

Notes

1. Brian R. Patterson, Lorraine Bettini, and Jon F. Nussbaum, "The Meaning of Friendship across the Life-Span: Two Studies," *Communication Quarterly* 41 (Spring 1993): 145.

2. See M. Prisbell and J. F. Andersen, "The Importance of Perceived Homophily, Level of Uncertainty, Feeling Good, Safety, and Self-Disclosure in Interpersonal

Relationships," *Communication Quarterly* 28 (Summer 1980): 22–33. They reinforce the importance of many of the characteristics we have listed.

3. William Schutz, *The Interpersonal Underworld* (Palo Alto, CA: Science and Behavior Books, 1966), pp. 18–20.

4. Sarah Trenholm, *Human Communication Theory,* 2d ed. (Englewood Cliffs, NJ: Prentice-Hall, 1991), p. 191.

5. Marvin Shaw, *Group Dynamics: The Psychology of Small Group Behavior,* 3d ed. (New York: McGraw-Hill, 1981), pp. 228–231.

6. John W. Thibaut and Harold H. Kelley, *The Social Psychology of Groups,* 2d ed. (New Brunswick, NJ: Transaction Books, 1986), pp. 9–30.

7. Trenholm, p. 72.

8. See Mark L. Knapp, *Interpersonal Communication and Human Relationships* (Boston: Allyn & Bacon, 1984); Dalman A. Taylor and Irwin Altman, "Communication in Interpersonal Relationships," in Michael E. Roloff and Gerald R. Miller, eds., *Interpersonal Processes: New Directions in Communication Research* (Beverly Hills, CA: Sage, 1987), p. 259; and Steve Duck, "How to Lose Friends Without Influencing People," in Roloff and Miller, pp. 290–291.

9. See Charles R. Berger and James J. Brada, *Language and Social Knowledge: Uncertainty in Interpersonal Relations* (London: Arnold, 1982).

10. William B. Gudykunst and Young Yun Kim. *Communicating with Strangers: An Approach to Intercultural Communication,* 2d ed. (New York: McGraw-Hill, 1992), p. 194.

11. Daniel J. Canary and Laura Stafford, "Relational Maintenance Strategies and Equity in Marriage," *Communication Monographs* 59 (September 1992): 259.

12. A good background of descriptive versus evaluative, provisional versus dogmatic, and equal versus superior is provided in Jack R. Gibb, "Defensive Communication," *Journal of Communication* 11 (September 1961): 141–148.

13. C. R. Cupach and S. Metts, "Accounts of Relational Dissolution: A Comparison of Marital and Nonmarital Relationships," *Communication Monographs* 53 (1986): 319–321.

14. Dudley D. Cahn, "Intimates in Conflict: A Research Review," in Dudley D. Cahn, ed., *Intimates in Conflict: A Communication Perspective* (Hillsdale, NJ: Erlbaum, 1990), p. 1.

15. Michael E. Roloff and Denise H. Cloven, "The Chilling Effect in Interpersonal Relationships: The Reluctance to Speak One's Mind," in Dudley D. Cahn, ed., *Intimates in Conflict: A Communication Perspective* (Hillsdale, NJ: Erlbaum, 1990), p. 49.

16. Denise H. Cloven and Michael E. Roloff, "Sense-Making Activities and Interpersonal Conflict: Communicative Cures for the Mulling Blues," *Western Journal of Speech Communication* 55 (Spring 1991): 136.

17. Alan L. Sillars and Judith Weisberg, "Conflict as a Social Skill," in Michael E. Roloff and Gerald R. Miller, eds., *Interpersonal Processes: New Directions in Communication Research* (Beverly Hills, CA: Sage, 1987), p. 146.

18. Michael Argyle, "Intercultural Communication," in Larry A. Samovar and Richard E. Porter, *Intercultural Communication: A Reader,* 6th ed. (Belmont, CA: Wadsworth, 1991), p. 40.

19. James P. Folger, Marshall Scott Poole, and Randall K. Stutman, *Working Through Conflict: Strategies for Relationships, Groups, and Organizations,* 2d ed. (New York: Harper Collins, 1993), p. 184.

20. See Johnathan G. Healey and Robert A. Bell, "Assessing Alternative Responses to Conflicts in Friendship," in Dudley D. Cahn, ed., *Intimates in Conflict: A Communication Perspective* (Hillsdale, NJ: Erlbaum, 1990), p. 29. In their article, Healey and Bell discuss findings from C. E. Rusbult, "A Longitudinal Test of the Investment Model: The Development (and Deterioration) of Satisfaction and Commitment in Heterosexual Involvements," *Journal of Personality and Social Psychology* 45 (1983): 101–117.

21. C. R. Berger, "Social Power in Interpersonal Communication," in M. L. Knapp and G. R. Miller, eds., *Handbook of Interpersonal Communication* (Beverly Hills, CA: Sage, 1985), p. 483.

22. Deborah A. Newton and Judee K. Burgoon, "Nonverbal Conflict Behaviors: Functions, Strategies, and Tactics," in Dudley D. Cahn, ed., *Intimates in Conflict: A Communication Perspective* (Hillsdale, NJ: Lawrence Erlbaum, 1990), p. 77.

23. Janet K. Alberts, "The Use of Humor in Managing Couples' Conflict Interactions," in Dudley D. Cahn, ed., *Intimates in Conflict: A Communication Perspective* (Hillsdale, NJ: Erlbaum, 1990), p. 109.

24. Ibid., p. 117.

25. Sillars and Weisberg, p. 143.

Interpersonal Communication
Chapters 5–8

What kind of an interpersonal communicator are you? The following analysis looks at specific behaviors that are characteristic of effective interpersonal communicators. On the line provided for each statement, indicate the response that best captures your behavior: 1, never; 2, rarely; 3, occasionally; 4, often; 5, almost always.

_____ In conversation, I am able to make relevant contributions without interrupting others. (Ch. 5)

_____ I describe objectively to others my negative feelings about their behavior toward me without withholding or blowing up. (Ch. 5)

_____ I change the way I listen depending on the purpose of my listening. (Ch. 6)

_____ I listen attentively, regardless of my interest in the person or the ideas. (Ch. 6)

_____ I am able to remember names, telephone numbers, and other specific information that I have heard only once. (Ch. 6)

_____ When I'm not sure whether I understand, I seek clarification. (Ch. 7)

_____ I am quick to praise people for doing things well. (Ch. 7)

_____ I criticize people for their mistakes only when they ask for criticism. (Ch. 7)

_____ I am able to maintain a positive communication climate by speaking in ways that others perceive as descriptive, provisional, and nonmanipulative. (Ch. 8)

_____ When I find myself in conflict with another person, I am able to discuss the issue openly without withdrawing or appearing competitive or aggressive. (Ch. 8)

Based on your responses, select the interpersonal communication behavior that you would most like to change. Write a communication improvement goal statement similar to the sample goal statement in Chapter 1 (page 24). If you would like verification of your self-analysis before you write a goal statement, have a friend or coworker complete this same analysis for you.

four

Group
Communication

O urs is a government by committee—small groups of people working together to reach decisions. Indeed, reliance on the group process as
an instrument of decision making extends into nearly every facet of our
lives. But as informal conversation moves to the structure of small-
group communication, the group itself presents a new set of variables
we need to consider.

This two-chapter unit begins with an analysis of the nature of an
effective work group, focusing on the necessary roles of participants. It
concludes with discussion of the most important role in effective group
communication, leadership.

**After you have read
this chapter, you
should be able to:**

*Identify key characteristics of
effective group
communication*

*Contrast task roles with
maintenance roles*

Identify negative roles

*Write questions of fact, value,
and policy*

*Follow the problem-solving
procedure*

9

Participating
in Work Groups

Members of the advertising division of Meyer Foods were gathered
to review their hiring policies. At the beginning of the first meeting,
Kareem, head of the division, began, "You know why I called you
together. Each department has to review its hiring practices. So, let's get
started." After a few seconds of silence, Kareem said, "Drew, what have
you been thinking?"

"Well, I don't know," Drew replied. "I haven't really given it much
thought."

"I'd like to contribute," Dawn said. "I just don't have much information."

"But I sent around a preliminary analysis of our practices with
some questions for discussion," Kareem said.

"Oh, is that what that was," Byron said. "I read the part about the
meeting, but I guess I didn't pay much attention to the material."

"Why don't we just say that we've given our guidelines careful
thought and wish to keep them the way they are?" Dawn asked.

"But," replied Kareem, "I think the CEO is looking for some specific recommendations. They'd like us to comment on how we process
minority and female applicants."

"Anything you think would be important would be OK with me," Byron replied.

"Well, how about if we each try to come up with some ideas for next time," Kareem suggested. "Meeting's adjourned."

As the group dispersed, Kareem overheard Drew say, "These meetings sure are a waste of time, aren't they?"

Perhaps you belong to a fraternal, business, governmental, or religious group. Or perhaps you have worked on a committee. Does this opening dialogue reflect the way your group meetings have gone? When group work is ineffective, it is easy to point the finger at the leader, but often, as is the case with this group, the responsibility for the "waste of time" lies squarely on the shoulders of the individuals involved. Because most of us spend some of our communication time in groups, we need to know how to participate in ways that maximize group effectiveness.

In this chapter, we consider characteristics of effective *work groups*—groups of two or more people using logical means, in public or in private, to solve a problem or arrive at a decision. Then we consider the specific roles group members play and a method for group problem solving. In the next chapter, we consider one of the most important group roles, leadership.

Characteristics of Effective Work Groups

Since work groups seek to achieve specific goals, it is relevant to ask what makes work groups effective. Research shows that effective groups generally have a good working environment, have an optimum number of members, show cohesiveness, are committed to the task, respect group rules, find ways to achieve consensus, are well prepared, and meet key role requirements.[1]

Good Working Environment

A good working environment is one that promotes group interaction. An important aspect of a good working environment is a seating arrangement that will encourage full participation. Seating can be formal or too informal for optimum interaction. Too formal would be a board of directors seating style, in which seating location is an indication of status. Imagine the long polished oak table with the chairperson at the head, the leading lieutenants at right and left, and the rest of the people down the line, as illustrated in Figure 9.1a. In this style, a boss-and-subordinate pattern emerges, which can inhibit group interaction. People are unlikely to speak until they are asked to do so. Moreover, no one has a good view of all the people present.

On the other hand, an excessively informal setting can also inhibit interaction. In an informal arrangement, people just sit where they feel comfortable. In Figure 9.1b, the three people sitting on the couch form their own little group; the two people seated next to each other form another group; and two members have placed themselves out of the main flow. People sitting in the two clusters may feel free to interact with one another, but it is unlikely that all the people in such an informal arrangement will interact as one group.

The ideal arrangement is the circle, depicted in Figure 9.1c. Being seated in a circle increases participant motivation to speak. Contrast the perceived equality of participants seated in a circle with those seated at an oblong table where those at the ends will be perceived as having higher status—and thus be encouraged to lead. Or with those sitting on the corners who will tend to speak less than those on the ends or in the middle. In the circle arrangement, sight lines are better: Everyone can see everyone else. And, at least in terms of seating position, everyone has equal status. If the meeting place does not have a round table, the group may be better off without a table or with an arrangement of tables that makes a square, as in Figure 9.1d, which approximates the circle arrangement.

From the beginning, it is important for the group to establish a climate that allows each person to participate. Anything suggesting that only one person is to be listened to or that some persons have ideas that are generally unworthy will hurt the group's efforts to achieve a balance of participation. People will not participate if they fear personal attack; if they believe that their ideas will be belittled, ridiculed, or discounted; or if they feel that no one will intervene to allow their ideas to be heard.

As a group deliberates, certain individuals will earn higher status than others. In a particular subject area, for instance, one person may be acknowledged as having better information, greater insight, or a more logical perspective. As a result, that person's comments will carry more weight in that area. But an effective group provides a climate in which everyone has an equal opportunity to earn higher status.

Optimum Number of Members

Effective groups contain enough members to ensure good interaction but not so many members that discussion is stifled. Because conventional wisdom dictates that "bigger is better," task forces created to examine major problems are almost always too large to work effectively. Having too many members causes several problems: Many people cannot or will not contribute, cohesiveness is nearly impossible to develop, and the decision is seldom a product of the group's collective thought.

Although optimum size depends on the nature of the task, groups consisting of five members are most desirable.[2] Why five? Groups with fewer than five members almost universally complain that they are too small and that there are not enough people for specialization. To be effective, a group needs certain skills. When the group contains only three or four members, chances are not all these skills will be present. Moreover, if one member of a group of three does not feel like contributing, you no longer have much of a group. Nevertheless, for small tasks the three-person group often works well. It's easier to get three people together than five or more. And if the task is relatively simple or within the expertise of the individuals, the three-person group may be a good choice.

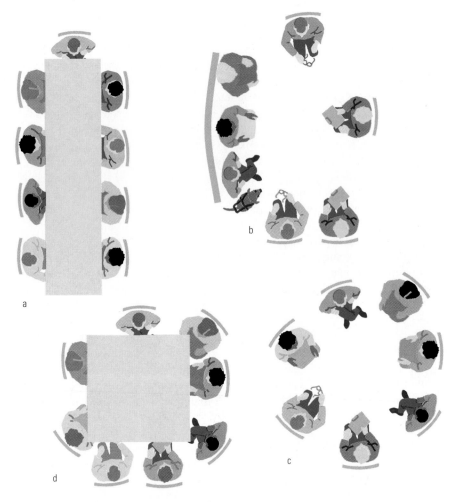

Figure 9.1 *Which group members do you think will be able to arrive at a decision easily? Why or why not?*

When a group numbers more than seven or eight people, reticent members are even less likely to contribute. As the group grows larger, two, three, or four people may become the central spokespersons, with others playing more passive roles.[3]

In a group of any size, an odd number is better than an even number. Why? Although voting is not the best way of reaching a decision, if a group finds it necessary to resolve an issue on which it cannot achieve consensus, the odd number will prevent tie votes.

Cohesiveness

Cohesiveness means sticking together, pulling for one another, and being caught up in the task. Remember the Three Musketeers, who were all for one and one for all? They are the prototype of a cohesive group.

What determines the potential for group cohesiveness? At least three qualities seem particularly important. One is the attractiveness of the group's purpose. Members identify with one another when the group's goals are particularly appealing. Social or fraternal groups, for example, build cohesiveness out of devotion to service or brotherhood. In a decision-making group, attractiveness is likely to be related to how important the task is to members. Suppose a church congregation forms a committee to consider how its outreach program can be made more responsive to community needs. The cohesiveness of the members of that committee will depend, at least in part, on the importance they attribute to this issue.

A second important quality necessary for cohesiveness is similarity of the needs and interests of members. Groups can be characterized as homogeneous or heterogeneous. A *homogeneous group* is one in which members have a great deal in common. For example, a group of five women of the same age who are all strong feminists would be homogeneous. By contrast, a *heterogeneous group* is one in which various ages, levels of knowledge, attitudes, and interests are represented. A homogeneous group generally will achieve cohesiveness more quickly than a heterogeneous group because the members are more likely to identify with one another's needs and interests from the start.

A third important quality is reinforcement of interpersonal needs. As we noted in Chapter 8, William Schutz has identified three major interpersonal needs: affection (showing affection to others and receiving affection from others), inclusion (including others in activities and being included by others in their activities), and control (having a role in determining what will happen). Group cohesiveness seems directly related to the belief of individual members that they are liked, included, and respected. As people decide that they like one another, that they want to be around one another, and that their opinions will be respected, they begin to work more effectively as a unit.

Cohesiveness is difficult to develop in a one-meeting group, but it is and should be characteristic of ongoing groups. Cohesiveness is usually generated after initial meetings and should be well established during or before the group reaches its most productive stages.

Commitment to the Task

Whether the group is assigned a task or the group determines its task, members must be sufficiently committed to the group for it to succeed. When the task is deemed important and when the group believes that what it is doing will matter, members are much more inclined to devote their full energies to the task.

When someone appoints you to a committee or asks you to serve on one, you have to decide whether you really want to be a part of that work group. If you aren't fully committed to the task described, you are better off declining. When people aren't committed, they miss meetings, avoid work, and fail to do what is expected of them.

Development of and Adherence to Group Rules

Rules, as we noted in Chapter 1, are the guidelines for behavior that are established or are perceived to be established for conducting group business. They are the most powerful determiners of behavior in groups. Rules begin to be established at the onset of a group's deliberations, and they grow, change, and solidify as people get to know one another better.

Rules for a group may be formally spelled out in a group's operating guidelines (as in parliamentary procedures for organizational meetings), they may be adapted from proven social guidelines (such as "Don't talk about yourself in a decision-making group meeting"), or they may simply develop within a particular context. For instance, without any conscious decision, group members may avoid using common four-letter words during the meeting. When business has ended, conversation may become more earthy.

Although formally stated rules may be known to group members from the beginning, most group rules are learned through experience with a specific group, and because rules may vary from one group to the next, we have to constantly relearn them. Two particularly important areas of rule development are group interaction and group procedure. In one group, it may be acceptable to interrupt any speaker at any time; in another group, it may be forbidden for anyone to speak until he or she is recognized. Thus, Martha, who is used to raising her hand to be recognized at the business meetings of her social organization, may find herself unable to speak in a group meeting where the participants break in whenever they have a chance. In one group, it may be all right for someone to openly express anger or hostility toward a person or an idea; in another group, such displays may be frowned on. In one group, members' relative status may determine who speaks first, longest, or most often; in another group, the status of members may have no effect on interaction.

Rules help a group develop cohesiveness. As members conform to stated or implied guidelines of behavior, they find themselves relating to one another more effectively. One of the initial hurdles group members must surmount is *primary tension*—the anxieties of getting to know one another. As group members test out verbal and nonverbal behavior to see what will be accepted, they begin to become more comfortable with one another, primary tension is lessened, and the group is able to concentrate on its task.

Although rules are essential, some rules can be detrimental or destructive. Suppose that at the beginning of the first meeting, a few members of the group tell jokes and generally have a good time. If such behavior is allowed or encouraged, cutting up, making light of the task, and joke telling become a group norm. As a result, the group may become so involved in these behaviors that the task is delayed, set aside, or perhaps even forgotten. Participants may describe their experience by saying, "We don't do much, but it's fun." Even if some group members are concerned about such behavior, once it goes on for several meetings, it will be very difficult to change. As you participate in a group, you can try to be conscious of what rules seem to be in operation and whether or not those rules are helping the group's work. If you believe that certain rules are detrimental or destructive, make your position and the reasons for it known so that those rules do not become established and reinforced.

Consensus

If a decision is not a product of group thought and group interaction, the advantages of group decision making are lost. In addition, group members often feel more pleased about the process and more committed to the resulting decisions when such decisions are reached democratically, through group interaction.

Democratic decision making may be achieved through *consensus*, or total group agreement. After the group has discussed a point for a while, one member might pose a question that is phrased to capture the essence of the group's position. For example, someone might ask, "Are we in agreement that lack of direction is frustrating the efforts of department members?" If everyone agrees, the decision is reached by consensus. If the group does not agree, the group can continue to discuss the point until a statement can be made that incorporates differing viewpoints without compromising the principles behind them. But it takes the participation of most group members to arrive at a statement that represents the group position.

If consensus still cannot be reached, the group usually takes a vote. Suppose that after considerable discussion on the policy question "What measures should be taken to open lines of communication between the director and department employees?" it becomes obvious that the group cannot agree on whether to install a "gripe box" as one of the measures. The group should then take a vote. If in a seven-person group, the vote is six to one or five to two, the decision has been given solid support. If it is a four-to-three vote, however, there may be some questions about later group support of that decision. Nevertheless, the principle of majority rule is the only choice open.

Preparation

In most group deliberations, the better the quality of the information shared, the better the quality of the group decisions. And the quality of information is largely a function of how well prepared group members are when discussion begins.

Depending on the kind of problem being discussed, your preparation for group work may include one or more of the following:

1. *Read circulated information carefully before the meeting.* In some groups, the information necessary for decision making may be given to you before the meeting. But the whole point of starting a meeting with well-prepared members is short-circuited if you and other members of the group don't do the reading beforehand.

2. *Think about relevant personal experience.* Sometimes the topic to be considered is one that you have thought about or worked with before. For instance, if your group will be considering how to arrange available parking space so that it is equally distributed to administrators, faculty, and students, your own parking experiences may be useful to the group. Nevertheless, personal experience seldom constitutes complete preparation.

3. *Survey library sources.* Discussion of many questions requires solid, documented materials. Suppose your group will be considering changing college requirements. What are the requirements at similar colleges and universities? Your library should have catalogs from other schools that you can check. Or suppose you are considering instituting a class on media analysis. Your library has various magazines and journals that will have articles related to the issue. When you need to do library research, your reference librarian can suggest books, articles, government publications, newspapers, and other sources that contain useful data. Many specific library sources are discussed in Chapter 12.

4. *Poll public opinion.* For some topics, a public opinion poll is appropriate. For instance, on the question of campus parking, you may be able to take advantage of the experience and opinions of current students. What do they think of the present system? What would they like to see done? Prepare a few well-worded questions, go to the parking lots, and ask your questions. If a personal survey is not practicable, you may need to devise another means of eliciting responses from the relevant people. For the parking lot survey, you could put your survey questionnaire under the windshield wiper of every car and ask drivers to leave the completed questionnaires at the entry gate or drop them in the campus mail. Of course, in any survey, you need to make sure that you have polled a large enough group and that you have sampled different segments of the population before you attempt to draw any significant conclusions from your poll.

5. *Interview for information.* An effective but often overlooked means of preparation is the personal interview. One interview with a person with relevant expertise may be all that is needed for your subject, or you may have to interview several people. (We discuss interviewing for information in detail in Module A.)

Practice in Analyzing Group Characteristics

By Yourself

Select for analysis one of the most recent work groups in which you have participated. Which of the following had the greatest effect on group interaction or the quality of the group decision: environment, group size, presence or lack of cohesiveness, commitment to task, adherence to rules, methods of decision making, or group preparation? On what do you base your analysis?

Major Group Roles

Effective groups contain people who meet key role requirements. A *role* is a pattern of behavior that characterizes an individual's place in a group. Students of group dynamics have identified two key types of roles that are filled in productive groups: task roles and maintenance roles. *Task roles* pertain to the work a group must do to accomplish its goal; *maintenance* roles pertain to the group behaviors that keep the group working together smoothly.

In this section, we examine the major task and maintenance roles that are necessary for a group to function effectively; we also look at those negative roles that need to be kept to a minimum. The role of leadership is discussed in Chapter 10.

Task Roles

Some roles relate directly to the substance of the group's work. In effective groups, people will present information and opinions, ask for information and opinions, analyze data, create ideas, help keep the group focused on the topic, and record the group's key decisions.

Information or Opinion Giver. The information or opinion giver provides content for the discussion. Giving information actually constitutes about 50 percent of what is done in a group because without information (and well-considered opinions), the group will not have the necessary material from which to draw its conclusions. Chances are everyone in the group will fill this role at some time during the discussion.

Playing the information-giving role well requires solid preparation. The more material you have studied, the more valuable your contributions will be. As information giver, you will want to draw material from several different sources, and you will usually bring a record of your sources with you to the discussion.

Effective information givers present information clearly and objectively without getting emotionally involved. For instance, in answer to the question of whether dormitory theft is increasing, you might say, "According to statistics gathered by the campus police, theft has increased by at least 10 percent each of the last three years." Since you always want to be sure that any related information is presented, you might then add, "I wonder whether anyone else has found any other data that indicate the levels of theft?" Raising such a question tells the group that you welcome discussion of the information and that, whether it is substantiated or disproven, you have no personal investment in it.

The following are examples of ways that information givers might introduce their material:

"When the Jones Corporation considered this problem, they found . . ."

"The other day I ran across these figures that relate to your point."

"According to the Controller's analysis, it doesn't necessarily work that way. He presented material that shows . . ."

Information Seeker. Information seeking is just the opposite of information giving. Instead of presenting information, you probe for information from others. Although it is very important to have information to present, it is also important to help the group recognize when more information is needed.

Information seeking serves two important functions in a group. The most obvious is asking for information when the data the group has are insufficient for drawing a conclusion. For instance, a group that is discussing whether to raise fees for a club will need to know how raising fees is likely to affect membership. To ensure that the group does not fall back on unsubstantiated opinion, one member might ask whether anyone has relevant information. If not, the group can note that this information is needed before a decision can be made on this point.

A second function information seeking serves is to clarify group procedure. Thus, it can be relevant to ask for information about where in the decision-making process the group is at the moment, whether or not they are in agreement, and what they should be doing next.

Analyzer.   The analyzer probes both the content and the reasoning involved in the discussion. Analyzers know the steps a group must go through to solve a problem. They recognize when the group has skipped a point, has passed over a point too lightly, or has not considered relevant material. Analyzers help the group penetrate to the core of the problem they are working on.

First, analyzers probe the contributions of group members to determine whether information is accurate, typical, consistent, and otherwise valid. Suppose a group member reports that according to Paul Stewart, who oversees subscriptions to cable television, the number of new subscriptions dropped last month. An analyzer might ask such questions as "How many new subscriptions has the company been averaging each month over the past year? In how many months were new subscriptions below the average for this year? For last year? Has this drop been consistent?" The purpose of such questions is to test the data. If data are partly true, questionable, or relevant only to certain aspects of the issue, a different conclusion or set of conclusions might be appropriate.

Second, analyzers examine the reasoning of various participants. They make such statements as "Enrique, you're generalizing from only one instance. Can you give us some others?" or "Wait a minute, after symptoms, we have to take a look at causes," or "I think we're passing this possible solution too lightly. There are still questions about it that we haven't answered."

Idea Person.   The idea person is an imaginative individual who thinks originally, rattles off alternative ideas, and often comes up with an idea that serves as the basis for the ultimate decision. Although everyone in the group may provide information, usually only one or two people are truly inventive. When others seem unable to see past tried-and-true solutions, the idea person suggests a new one; when others think they have exhausted the possibilities, idea people come up with still another. As we might expect, not all these ideas are necessarily "world beaters." The creative mind is constantly mining ideas, but only a few are golden. Nevertheless, a good idea person is indispensable, and groups should not discourage their more creative members from advancing ideas.

Expediter.   The expediter keeps the group on track. Whether the group meets once or is ongoing, almost invariably some remarks will tend to sidetrack the group from the central point or issue. Sometimes apparent digressions are necessary to establish the background of the problem, enlarge its scope, or even give people an opportunity to air their feelings. Yet these momentary digressions can lead the group off on tangents that have little to do with the assignment. Expediters are the people who help the group stick to its agenda.

When the group has strayed, expediters will make statements like "I'm enjoying this, but I can't quite see what it has to do with resolving the issue," or "Let's see, aren't we still trying to find out whether these are the only criteria that we should be considering?" or "Say, time is getting away from us and we've considered only two possible solutions. Aren't there some more?"

Recorder.   People's perceptions and memories differ. Consider that in a one-hour group discussion about 9,000 words will be spoken. Unless special effort is made to record the group's procedure and decisions, much valuable information can be lost.

The record of a formal group meeting is called the *minutes.* Minutes include major motions, key debates, and conclusions agreed on by the group. The recorder types the minutes and circulates them to group members prior to the next meeting. The minutes then become a public record of the group's activities.

A good record of group proceedings is necessary for the following reasons:

1.   *To provide a formal statement of the group's decisions.* Statements such as "In the early portion of the discussion, the group decided to limit its analysis to activity in the southeastern states where declines in sales have been noted" summarize what took place and apprise every group member of the decision. If some controversy arises later, the group can be reminded of the decision.

2.   *To provide a record of all key information that serves as a basis for decisions.* Unless a group records the information that leads to decisions, the group's process is open to question. Others affected by the group's work cannot blindly accept that the group has done a comprehensive analysis of the question. A record of decisions shows others what was done.

3.   *To protect against misunderstanding and misperception by individual members.* As time goes by, people recall less and less of what was said unless they are reminded of it. At the end of a day's meeting, members may be able to summarize key decisions and key information; three weeks later, however, the substance of a meeting is likely to be a blur. A precise record shows the exact wording of what the group agreed on.

4.   *To serve as a running account of the group process.* An accurate record is also important to the group during discussion. It helps members find out where the group is, determine whether the discussion pertains to the group goal, and identify the foundation on which subsequent discussion should be built. Good discussion is a slow process, but anything that can be done to make the process more efficient without detracting from spontaneity should be encouraged. A written account keeps what is happening in front of the group and helps it avoid ambiguity.

Usually, the leader or another designated group member is responsible for keeping good records; occasionally, a person who is not a part of the group is solicited or hired to keep records. In either case, the recorder notes key comments of members, with special emphasis on decisions that the group has agreed on. Every person has the right to ask the recorder to read the last decision made or to read back a summary of information. As with any other skill, good recording takes a great deal of practice. You will find that when a person gets good at the job, the entire group prospers.

Maintenance Roles

Whereas task roles help the group deal with the content of discussion, maintenance roles help the group work together smoothly as a unit. In effective decision-making groups, people who fill maintenance roles will support one another, relieve tensions, control conflict, and give everyone a chance to talk.

Supporter.   People participating in groups are likely to feel better about their participation when their thoughts and feelings are recognized. Sometimes, however, people get so wrapped up in the discussion or in their own ideas that they may neglect to recognize and reward positive contributions. Supporters help provide this recognition.

Supporters respond nonverbally or verbally when good points are made. Supporters give such nonverbal clues as a smile, a nod, or a vigorous head shake and make statements like "Good point, Ming," "I really like that idea, Nikki," "It's obvious you've really done your homework, Janelle," and "That's one of the best ideas we've had today, Drew."

Tension Reliever.   According to folklore, all work and no play makes Jack a dull boy. When group members become immersed in their tasks, they sometimes get so involved and work so hard that they begin to wear themselves down. Nerves fray, vision clouds, and the machinery of progress grinds to a halt. Tension relievers recognize when the group process is stagnating or when the group is tiring. They have a sixth sense for when to tell a joke, when to take off on a digression, and when to get the group to loosen up a little before returning to the task. In some situations, a single well-placed one-liner will get a laugh, break the tension or the monotony, and jolt the group out of its lethargy. At other times, the group can be saved only with a real break—sometimes a minute or so will suffice; other times five, ten, or even fifteen minutes will be necessary.

Although task-oriented roles are obviously important, a group member who can fulfill a maintenance role such as "tension-reliever" is making a significant contribution to the group's success.

Tension relieving adds nothing to the content of the discussion, but it does improve immeasurably the spirits of the participants. Of all the roles, this one is the most difficult to play consciously. When people have to make a conscious effort to be tension relievers, they are likely to fail. Although not every group has a person who fills the bill completely, most groups include at least one person who can meet it well enough to be helpful. Even if a group can accomplish its task without a tension reliever, it certainly is not as much fun. You will know, recognize, and be thankful for the person who plays this role well.

Harmonizer.   The harmonizer brings the group together. It is a rare group that can expect to accomplish its task without some minor if not major conflict. Even when people get along well, they are likely to become angry over some inconsequential point in a heated discussion. Most groups experience some classic interpersonal conflicts caused by different personality types and by polarization. Norbert Kerr shows that when an issue is especially important, group members are likely to experience greater polarization and thus greater conflict.[4]

Harmonizers are responsible for reducing tensions and for straightening out misunderstandings, disagreements, and conflicts. They smooth ruffled feathers, encourage objectivity, and mediate between hostile or aggressively competing sides. A group cannot avoid some conflict, but if there is no one present to harmonize, participation can become an uncomfortable experience.

Harmonizers put into practice the skills discussed under "Guidelines for Managing Conflict" in Chapter 8. Harmonizers are likely to make such statements as "Brandon, I don't think you're giving Jana a chance to make her point," "Tom, Jack, hold it a second. I know you're on opposite sides of this, but let's see where you might have some agreement," "Lynne, I get the feeling that something Todd said really bugged you. Is that right?" or "Hold it, everybody, we're really coming up with some good stuff; let's not lose our momentum by getting into name-calling."

Gatekeeper.   Gatekeepers help keep communication channels open. In an effective group, all the members should have something to contribute. To ensure balanced participation, those who tend to dominate need to be held in check, and those who tend to be shy need to be encouraged. The gatekeeper is the one who sees that Juanita is on the edge of her chair, eager to speak but unable to break in, or that Don is rambling a bit and needs to be directed, or that Larry's need to talk so frequently is making Cesar withdraw from the conversation, or that Betty has just lost the thread of the discussion. Gatekeepers assume responsibility for helping interaction by making statements like "Joan, I see you've got something to say here," or "You've made a really good point, Todd; I wonder whether we could get some reaction on it," or "Amir and Kristen, it sounds as if you're getting into a dialogue here; let's see what other ideas we have."

Gatekeepers can also be sensitive to social, cultural, and gender factors that may affect group members' participation. For example, even within the same culture, group members may bring very different backgrounds, vocabularies, and stores of information to the discussion. Thus, some members may not understand some of the terms, historical allusions, or other information that other speakers take for granted—and they may be too embarrassed to ask for clarification. The same point

*In group meetings, your style of speaking can make the difference in whether you
are heard, no matter how good your ideas are. Certain communication habits often
put women at a disadvantage in groups.*

Cynthia was a member of a committee to raise funds for a political candidate. Most of the committee members were focused on canvassing local businesses for support. When Cynthia suggested that they write directly to a list of former colleagues, friends, and supporters of the candidate, inviting them to join an honorary board (and inviting them to contribute), her suggestion was ignored. Later the same suggestion was made by another committee member, Barry. Suddenly, the group came alive, enthusiastically embracing and planning to implement "Barry's idea."

Some of the men I spoke to—and just about every woman—told me of the experience of saying something at a meeting and having it ignored, then hearing the same comment taken up when it is repeated by someone else (nearly always a man).

Many people (especially women) try to avoid seeming presumptuous at meetings by prefacing their statements with a disclaimer such as, "I don't know if this will work, but . . ." or "You've probably already thought of this, but. . . . " Such disclaimers are even found on e-mail—the electronic conversation medium. An example given by linguist Susan Herring to illustrate the tone of messages typical of women who took part in an on-line discussion began, "This may be a silly naive question, but. . . ."

Some speakers (again, including many women) may also speak at a lower volume, and try to be succinct so as not to take up more meeting time than necessary. Barbara and Gene Eakins examined tape recordings of seven university faculty meetings and found that, with one exception, the

applies, only more so, when a group consists of people from different cultures.[5] Furthermore, some members may become frustrated because their ideas are not properly credited. (For a discussion of this point and its effect on women, see It's Her Idea, and He Gets the Credit. Why?)

Negative Roles

Just as the work group prospers when members fill the various task and maintenance roles, the group suffers when members play certain negative roles. The four most common negative roles that group members should try to avoid are those of aggressor, joker, withdrawer, and monopolizer.

men spoke more often and, without exception, spoke longer. The men's turns ranged from 10.66 to 17.07 seconds, the women's from 3 to 10 seconds. The longest contribution by a woman was still shorter than the shortest contribution by a man.

Herring found the same situation in electronic meetings. In the e-mail discussion she analyzed, she found that men's messages were twice as long, on average, as women's. And their voices sounded very different. All but one of the five women used an "attenuated/ personal" voice: "I am intrigued by your comment . . . Could you say a bit more?" The tone adopted by the men who dominated discussion was assertive ("It is obvious that . . ."; "Note that . . .").

All these aspects of how one speaks at a meeting mean that when two people say "the same thing," they probably say it very differently. They may speak with or without a disclaimer, loudly or softly, in a self-deprecating or declamatory way, briefly or at length, and tentatively or without apparent certainty. They may initiate ideas or support or argue against ideas raised by others. When dissenting, they may adopt a conciliatory tone, mitigating the disagreement, or an adversarial one, emphasizing it.

Before women decide to change their styles, though, they must realize the double bind they face. Geraldine Ferraro was called by Barbara Bush "the word that rhymes with witch." Ferraro's speech style was influenced by her Italian heritage, her New York City upbringing, and her working-class roots. Any woman who tries to become more "assertive" runs a risk of being sanctioned for being "too aggressive," just as men from the South may be seen as not masculine enough.

On the other hand, it may also be wise to decide that being seen as aggressive is a price worth paying for being listened to. Finally, we can all hope that if enough women adjust their styles, expectations of how a feminine woman speaks may gradually change as a result. ■

SOURCE: Deborah Tannen, *Talking From 9 to 5* (New York: William Morrow, 1994), pp. 277–289. © 1994 by Deborah Tannen, Ph. D. Reprinted by permission of William Morrow & Company, Inc.

Aggressor. Aggressors seek to enhance their own status by criticizing almost everything or blaming others when things get rough. The main purpose of aggressors seems to be to deflate the ego or status of others. One way of dealing with aggressors is to confront them. Ask them whether they are aware of what they are doing and of the effect their behavior is having on the group.

Joker. The behavior of jokers is characterized by clowning, mimicking, or generally disrupting by making a joke of everything. Jokers, too, are usually trying to call attention to themselves. The group needs to get jokers to consider the problem seriously; otherwise, they will be a constant irritant to other members. One way to proceed is to encourage them when tensions need to be released but ignore them when serious work needs to be done.

Withdrawer. Withdrawers refuse to be a part of the group. Sometimes they are withdrawing from something that was said; sometimes they are just showing their indifference. To get them involved in the group, try to draw them out with questions. Find out what they are especially good at, and rely on them when their skill is required. Compliments will sometimes bring them out of their shell.

Monopolizer. People who need to talk all the time are called monopolizers. Usually they are trying to make the impression that they are well read, knowledgeable, and of value to the group. They should, of course, be encouraged when their comments are helpful. However, when they are talking too much or when their comments are not helpful, the leader needs to interrupt them or draw others into the discussion.

Normal Group Behavior

You may be wondering about the proportion of time devoted in a "normal" group to the various functions described in this section. According to Robert Bales, one of the leading researchers in group interaction processes, 40 to 60 percent of discussion time is spent giving and asking for information and opinion; 8 to 15 percent of discussion time is spent on disagreement, tension, or unfriendliness; and 16 to 26 percent of discussion time is characterized by agreement or friendliness (positive maintenance functions).[6] Two norms we can apply as guidelines for effective group functioning, therefore, are (1) that approximately half of all discussion time is devoted to information sharing and (2) that group agreement far outweighs group disagreement.

Practice in Group Roles

By Yourself

Identify the role that is represented in each of the following examples as (A) information or opinion giver, (B) information seeker, (C) analyzer, (D) idea person, (E) expediter, (F) supporter, (G) tension reliever, (H) harmonizer, or (I) gatekeeper.

_____ **1.** "Shelby, I get the feeling that you have something you wanted to say here."
_____ **2.** "The last couple of comments have been on potential causes of the problem, but I don't think we've fully addressed the scope of the problem. If we've really identified the scope, perhaps we could draw a conclusion and then move on to causes."
_____ **3.** "Antoine, that was a good point. I think you've really put the problem in perspective."
_____ **4.** "Paul and Gwen, I know you see this issue from totally different positions. I wonder whether we might not profit by seeing whether there are any points of agreement; then we can consider differences."
_____ **5.** "Well, according to the latest statistics cited in the *Enquirer,* unemployment in the state has gone back up from 7.2 to 7.9 percent."
_____ **6.** "Sarah, you've given us some good statistics. Can we determine whether or not this is really an upward trend or just a seasonal factor?"

1. I 2. E 3. F 4. H 5. A 6. C

Problem Solving in Groups

Research shows that groups follow many different approaches to problem solving. Some groups move linearly through a series of steps to reach consensus, and some move in a spiral pattern in which they refine, accept, reject, modify, and combine ideas as they go along. Whether groups move in something approximating an orderly pattern or go in fits and starts, those groups that arrive at high-quality decisions are likely to accomplish certain tasks during their deliberations—namely, identifying a specific problem, arriving at some criteria that a solution must meet, identifying possible solutions to the problem, and determining the best solution or combination of solutions.

Defining the Problem

Groups are formed either to consider all issues that relate to a specific topic (a social committee, a personnel committee, or a public relations committee would be formed for this reason) or to consider a specific issue (such as the year's social calendar, criteria for granting promotions, or a long-range plan for university growth). Much of the wheel-spinning that takes place during the early stages of group discussion results from members' not understanding their specific goal. It is the duty of the person, agency, or parent group that forms a particular work group to give the group a clear goal. For instance, a group may be formed for the purpose of "determining the criteria for merit pay increases" or "preparing guidelines for hiring at a new plant." If the goal is not stated this clearly, it is up to the group leader or representative to find out exactly why the group was formed and what its purpose is. If the group is free to determine its goal, it should move immediately to get the goal down on paper; until everyone in the group agrees on the goal, they will never agree on how to achieve it.

Regardless of the clarity of its goal, the group may still want to reword or in some way modify it. A group should consider several criteria before finalizing the wording of its statement of purpose.

Dilbert reprinted by permission of UFS, Inc.

1. *Is the problem phrased as a question?* The group discussion format is one of inquiry. A group begins from the assumption that answers are not yet known. Although some decision-making groups serve merely as rubber-stamping agencies, the group ideally has freedom of choice. Phrasing the group's purpose as a question furthers the spirit of inquiry.

2. *Does the question contain only one central idea?* The question "Should the college abolish its foreign language and social studies requirements?" is poorly phrased because it contains two distinct problems. Either one would make a good topic for discussion, but they cannot both be discussed at once.

3. *Is the wording of the question clear to all group members?* Sometimes a topic question contains wording that is so ambiguous that the group may waste time quibbling over its meaning. For instance, a group that is examining a department's curriculum might suggest the following question: "What should the department do about courses that aren't getting the job done?" Although the question is well intentioned and participants may have at least some idea about their goal, such vague wording as "getting the job done" can lead to trouble in the discussion. Instead of waiting until trouble arises, reword questions in specific terms before the group begins discussions. Notice how this revision of the preceding question makes its intent much clearer: "What should the department do about courses that receive low scores on student evaluations?"

4. *Does the question encourage objective discussion?* The phrasing of a question may drastically affect a group's decisions. Consider the following: "How should our sexist guidelines for promotion be revised?" What kind of objective discussion is likely to occur when, right from the start, the group has agreed that the guidelines are sexist? Moreover, such a phrasing suggests that being sexist is the only problem that new guidelines will have to resolve. With such wording, not only are the scales tilted before the group even gets into the issues involved, but also the group's thinking is given a single direction. The phrasing of the question should neither prejudice the group's thinking nor indicate which direction the group will go in even before discussion commences.

5. *Is the question appropriate for group consideration?* One of the most common criticisms of the group process is that it tends to waste time on tasks best dealt with by individuals. How can you tell whether your group should be discussing a particular question? Victor Vroom, an industrial psychologist, and his associates have suggested guidelines for evaluating the appropriateness of a question for group discussion.[7] Among the most important considerations are whether a high-quality decision is required and whether acceptance by members of the group is necessary to put the decision into practice. A high-quality decision is one that is well documented. Often high-quality decisions are too much for one person to handle; gathering the data alone may require hours of work by several people. Moreover, because vigorous testing is necessary at every stage of the decision-making process, a group is more likely to ask the right questions. Likewise, individuals within the organization are the ones who must carry out the decision. If group members are involved in the decision, they will be motivated to see that the decision is implemented.

Other conditions can indicate that an individual decision is more appropriate than group discussion. If one person has the necessary information and authority to make a good decision, if a solution that has worked well in the past can be applied to this situation, or if time is limited and immediate action is necessary, group discussion is less appropriate.

6. *Can the question be identified easily as one of fact, value, or policy?* How you organize your discussion will depend on the kind of question. Later, we discuss organization; for now, let's consider the three types of questions.

Questions of *fact* concern the truth or falsity of an assertion. Implied in such questions is the possibility of determining the facts by way of directly observed, spoken, or recorded evidence. For instance, "Is Smith guilty of stealing equipment from the warehouse?" is a question of fact. Either Smith committed the crime or he did not.

Questions of *value* concern subjective judgments of quality. They are characterized by the inclusion of some evaluative word such as *good, reliable, effective, or worthy.* For instance, advertisers may discuss the question "Is the proposed series of ads too sexually provocative?" In this case, "too sexually provocative" stands as the evaluative phrase. Another group may discuss the question "Is the sales force meeting the goals effectively?" Although we can establish criteria for "too sexually provocative" and "effectively" and measure material against those criteria, there is no way to verify our findings objectively. The answer is still a matter of judgment, not fact.

Questions of *policy* ask whether or not a future action should be taken. The question is phrased to invite a solution or to test a tentative solution to a problem or a felt need. "What should we do to lower the crime rate?" seeks a solution that would best address the problem of increased crime. "Should the university give equal amounts of money to men's and women's athletics?" seeks a tentative solution to the problem of how to achieve equity in the financial support of athletics. The inclusion of the word *should* in all questions of policy makes them the easiest to recognize and the easiest to phrase of all discussion questions. Most issues facing work groups are questions of policy.

If you are discussing either a question of fact or a question of value, the remaining steps of problem solving (analyzing the problem, determining possible solutions, and selecting the best solution) are not relevant to your discussions. What kind of a structure, then, is appropriate for discussing questions of fact and value?

Discussions of questions of fact focus primarily on finding the facts and drawing conclusions from them. For instance, in discussing the question "Is Smith guilty of stealing equipment from the warehouse?" the group would decide (1) whether facts can be assembled to show that Smith did take equipment from the warehouse and (2) whether his taking the equipment constituted stealing (as opposed to, say, borrowing or filling an order for equipment).

Discussions of questions of value follow a similar format. The difference is that with questions of value the conclusions drawn from the facts depend on the criteria or measures used to weigh the facts. For instance, in discussing the question "Who is the most effective teacher in the department?" the group would decide (1) what the criteria for an "effective teacher" are and (2) which teacher meets those criteria better than other teachers in the department.

Analyzing the Problem

Analysis of a problem entails finding out as much as possible about the problem and determining the criteria that must be met to find an acceptable solution. If you were discussing the question "What should be done to equalize athletic opportunities for women on campus?" these two aspects of your analysis might be phrased as follows:

1. What has happened on campus that signifies the presence of a problem for women? (Nature of the problem)
   A. Have significant numbers of women been affected?
   B. Do women have less opportunity to compete in athletics than men?
   C. Has the university behaved in ways that have adversely affected women's opportunities?
2. By what means should we test whether a proposed solution solves the problem? (Criteria)
   A. Does the proposed solution cope with each of the problems uncovered?
   B. Can the proposed solution be implemented without creating new and perhaps worse problems?

Determining Possible Solutions

For most problems, many possible solutions can be found. At this stage of discussion, the goal is not to worry about whether a particular solution is a good one or not but to come up with a list of potential answers.

One way to identify potential solutions is to brainstorm for ideas. *Brainstorming* is a free-association procedure; that is, it involves stating ideas as they come to mind, without stopping to evaluate their merits, until you have compiled a long list. In a good ten- or fifteen-minute brainstorming session, you may think of several solutions by yourself. Depending on the nature of the topic, a group may come up with a list of ten, twenty, or more possible solutions in a relatively short time.

Brainstorming works best when the group postpones evaluating solutions until the list is complete. If people feel free to make suggestions—however bizarre they may sound—they will be much more inclined to think creatively than if they fear that each idea will be evaluated on the spot. Later, each solution can be measured against the criteria. For the question on equalizing athletic opportunities for women, a framework for determining possible solutions might be outlined as follows:

3. What can be done to equalize opportunities? (Possible solutions)
   A. Can more scholarships be allocated to women?

Brainstorming is a free-association procedure that involves stating ideas as they come to mind.

    B.   Can the time allocated to women's use of university facilities be increased to a level comparable with men's use?

Selecting the Best Solution

At this stage in the discussion, the group evaluates each prospective solution on the basis of how well it meets the criteria agreed on earlier. For the question on equalizing athletic opportunities for women, each solution would have to pass the following tests:

4.   Which proposal (or combination) would work the best? (Best solution)

    A.   How well would increasing women's scholarships solve each of the problems that have been identified? Would it create worse problems?

    B.   How well would increasing women's time for use of facilities solve each of the problems that have been identified? Would it create worse problems?

    C.   Based on this analysis, which solution is best?

In Groups

Divide into groups of about four to six. Each group has ten to fifteen minutes to arrive at a solution to one of the following: (1) What should professors do to discourage cheating on tests? (2) What should the college or university do to increase attendance at special events? (3) What should be the role of students in evaluating their curriculum?

After discussion, each group should determine (1) what roles were operating in the group during the discussion; (2) who was filling those roles; (3) whether the group considered the nature of the problem, criteria, and possible solutions before arriving at a solution; and (4) what factors helped or hurt the problem-solving process.

Summary

Effective groups meet several criteria: They work in a physical and psychological setting that facilitates good interactions, they are of an optimum size, they work as a cohesive unit, they show a commitment to the task, they develop and adhere to rules that help the group work, their members interact freely to reach consensus, their members are well prepared, and they contain people who have enough expertise and aggregate skills to meet key role requirements.

Group members may perform one or more of the task roles of giving information, seeking information, analyzing, being an idea person, expediting, and recording. They may also perform one or more of the maintenance roles of supporting, tension relieving, harmonizing, and gatekeeping. They should try to avoid the negative roles of aggressor, joker, withdrawer, and monopolizer.

Questions for group discussion may be questions of fact, value, or policy.

Effective work groups discussing questions of policy define the problem, analyze the problem, determine possible solutions, and then select the best solution.

Suggested Readings

Brilhart, John K., and Galanes, Gloria J. *Effective Group Discussion*, 8th ed. Madison, WI: WCB Brown & Benchmark, 1995. A very popular textbook. Includes an intercultural perspective.

Sher, Barbara, and Gottlieb, Annie. *Teamworks!* New York: Warner Books, 1989. Based on the premise that a group of people working together can provide a system of support that will enable each person to accomplish more than they could on their own. Written in an easy-to-read style that is supplemented with countless experiences of real people.

Verderber, Rudolph F. *Working Together*. Belmont, CA: Wadsworth, 1982. Provides a thorough treatment of analyzing and resolving various types of discussion questions.

Notes

1. A great deal of relevant research is summarized in Marvin E. Shaw, *Group Dynamics: The Psychology of Small Group Behavior*, 3d ed. (New York: McGraw-Hill, 1981) Cragan and Wright point out that very little research on these issues was done in the 1980s. See John F. Cragan and David W. Wright, "Small Group Communication Research of the 1980s: A Synthesis and Critique" *Communication Studies* 41 (Fall 1990): 216.

2. Paul Hare, *Handbook of Small Group Research,* 2d ed. (New York: Free Press, 1976), p. 214.

3. Shaw, p. 202.

4. For a review of research, see Norbert L. Kerr, "Issue Importance and Group Decision Making," in Stephen Worchel, Wendy Wood, and Jeffry A. Simpson, eds., *Group Process and Productivity* (Newbury Park, CA: Sage, 1992), pp. 69–74.

5. Arthur D. Jensen and Joseph C. Chilberg, *Small Group Communication: Theory and Application* (Belmont, CA: Wadsworth, 1991), pp. 367–371.

6. Robert F. Bales, *Personality and Interpersonal Behavior* (New York: Holt, Rinehart & Winston, 1971), p. 96.

7. V. H. Vroom and P. W. Yetton, *Leadership and Decision-Making* (Pittsburgh: University of Pittsburgh Press, 1973).

**After you have read
this chapter, you
should be able to:**

*List and explain
characteristics of leadership*

*Differentiate between task-
oriented and person-oriented
leadership styles*

Prepare for leadership

*Identify key leadership
functions*

*Evaluate group decisions,
participation, and leadership*

10

Leadership
in Groups

"C hapman, as you know, I'm concerned with the basic skills levels of the people we've been interviewing for jobs in manufacturing. The more I think about it, the more I believe we need to play a more active role in providing adult education that would not only be good for the community, but I think would benefit us in the long run. The reason I called you in here was to see whether you would take leadership in set-ting up a group whose goal it is to establish an adult literacy program that our company could sponsor. You can select the people you'd like to work with, and I'll give you full support."

Like Norm Chapman, you are likely to be called on to take a leadership role. As much as we may believe that we're up to the task, we are often uncertain exactly how we should go about exercising leadership in group decision making.

Our goal in this chapter is to show what it means to be the leader of a work group, how to proceed if you want to try for leadership, and what you are responsible for doing in the group after you get the job. Although much of this discussion is applicable to all leadership situations, we focus on the question of leadership in the decision-making or work-group context. Finally, we offer some guidelines for evaluating the process and outcomes of group communications.

What Is Leadership?

The definition of leadership varies from source to source, yet common to most definitions are the ideas of *influence* and *accomplishment*. Leadership means being in charge—exerting influence—and leadership results in reaching a goal.[1] Let's explore these two ideas.

1. *Leadership means exerting influence.* Influence is the ability to bring about changes in the attitudes and actions of others. Influence can be indirect (unconscious) or direct (purposeful). Many times we influence others without being aware of it. If you have a new hairstyle, or are wearing a new suit, or have purchased a flashy new car, you may well influence someone who sees you to try your hairstyle or to buy a similar suit or car. In a group, a leader can influence members indirectly by serving as a role model. In this chapter, we look at what you can do consciously to help guide your group through the decision-making process.

The exercise of influence is different from the exercise of raw power. When you exercise raw power, you force the group to submit, perhaps against its will; when you influence others, you show them why an idea, a decision, or a means of achieving a goal is superior in such a way that they will follow your lead of their own free will. Members will continue to be influenced as long as they are convinced that what they have agreed to is right or is in their best interest as individuals or as a group.

2. *Leadership results in reaching a goal.* In the context of task or problem-solving discussions, reaching the goal means accomplishing the task or arriving at the best solution available at that time.

In an organizational setting, a leader is usually appointed or elected. In a decision-making group, however, the struggle for leadership often proceeds without benefit of election or appointment. In fact, those involved may not perceive that a struggle takes place. In groups in which one individual has strong urges to control and the others have equally strong urges to be controlled, leadership will be established with no struggle at all. In most decision-making groups, however, leadership is shared, switches back and forth, or develops into power struggles in which people exercise their need to lead.

Becoming a Leader

Many times problem-solving groups select their own leader. But even if one person is the selected leader, another person may emerge as the actual leader. What factors are involved in becoming a group leader? Leaders are likely to be selected or to emerge on the basis of perceived traits, style of leadership, and behavior in the group.

Leadership Traits

Are there certain traits that make one person a more likely candidate for leadership than another? Studies conducted over the years seem to substantiate portions of the trait perspective of leadership.[2]

Research findings suggest that leaders exhibit traits related to ability, sociability, motivation, and communication skills to a greater degree than do nonleaders.[3] With regard to ability, leaders have been found to exceed average group members in intelligence, scholarship, insight, and verbal facility. Leaders exceed group members in such aspects of sociability as dependability, activeness, cooperativeness, and popularity. In the area of motivation, leaders exceed group members in initiative, persistence, and enthusiasm. And leaders exceed average group members in the various communication skills we have focused on in this text. This does not mean that people with superior intelligence, those who are most liked, those with the greatest enthusiasm, or those who communicate best will necessarily be the leaders. However, it probably does mean that people are unlikely to be leaders if they do not exhibit at least some of these traits to a greater degree than do those they are attempting to lead.

Do you perceive yourself as having many of these traits? If so, you are a potential leader. However, because several individuals in almost any grouping of people have the potential for leadership, which one ends up actually leading others depends on factors other than having these traits. One of the most important of these factors is a person's leadership style.

Leadership Styles

Although there is no one "right" way to lead, different group situations do often require different leadership styles. Thus if you want to become a leader, you need to understand the various styles of leadership, and which is likely to be more appropriate at a particular time. Even though people will tend to lead a group with a style that reflects their own personality, leaders who want to be effective in all kinds of situations need to learn how to adjust their style to the needs of the situation and the group.

What are the major leadership styles? Most recent studies look at leadership styles as either task-oriented (sometimes called authoritarian) or person-oriented (sometimes called democratic). As you read about these two major styles, notice that they correspond to the task and maintenance functions of groups described in Chapter 9.

Dilbert reprinted by permission of UFS, Inc.

The *task-oriented* leader exercises more direct control over the group. Task leaders will determine the phrasing of the question. They will analyze the problem and decide how the group will proceed to arrive at the solution. They are likely to outline specific tasks for each group member and suggest the roles they desire members to play.

The *person-oriented* or democratic leader may suggest phrasings of the question, suggest procedure, and suggest tasks or roles for individuals. Yet in every facet of the discussion, the person-oriented leader encourages group participation to determine what actually will be done. Everyone feels free to offer suggestions to modify the leader's suggestions. What the group eventually does is determined by the group itself. Person-oriented leaders will listen, encourage, facilitate, clarify, and support. In the final analysis, however, it is the group that decides.

Pioneer work by Ralph White and Ronald Lippitt suggests the following advantages and disadvantages of each style: (1) More work is done under a task-oriented leader than under a person-oriented leader. (2) The least amount of work is done when no leadership exists. (3) Motivation and originality are greater under a person-oriented leader. (4) Task-oriented leadership may create discontent or result in less individual creativity. (5) More friendliness is shown in person-oriented groups.[4]

So which style is to be preferred? Research by Fred Fiedler suggests that whether a particular leadership style is successful depends on the situation: (1) How good are the leader's interpersonal relations with the group? (2) How clearly defined are the goals and tasks of the group? (3) To what degree does the group accept the leader as having legitimate authority to lead?[5] Some situations will be favorable to the leader on all dimensions: The leader has good interpersonal relations with the group, the goal is clear, and the group accepts the leader's authority. Some situations will be unfavorable to the leader on all dimensions: The leader has poor interpersonal relations with the group, the goal is unclear, and the group fails to accept the leader's authority. Then, of course, there are situations that are partly favorable and partly unfavorable to the leader on the various dimensions.

Fiedler proposes that task leaders are most effective in favorable or extremely unfavorable situations. In positive situations, in which the leader has good interpersonal relations, a clear goal, and group acceptance, the leader can focus entirely on the task. Conversely, in very negative situations, there will be little that the leader can do to improve member perceptions, so the leader may as well storm forward on the task. Where people-oriented leadership is likely to be most effective is in those moderately good or bad situations in which the leader has the most to gain by improving interpersonal relations, clarifying the goal, and building credibility with the group.

Let's consider two specific examples—one of a mostly favorable situation, and one of a moderately unfavorable situation. Suppose you are leading a group of employees who are meeting to determine the recipient of a merit award. If you have good interpersonal relations with the group, if the criteria for determining the award are clearly spelled out, and if the group accepts your authority, you are likely to be highly effective by adopting a task-oriented style of leadership. The group will understand what it is supposed to do and will accept your directions in proceeding to accomplish the task. If, on the other hand, your interpersonal relations with two of the group's other four members has been shaky, the group is not sure how it is supposed to go about making the decision, and at least two members of the group are undecided about your ability to lead, a person-oriented style of leadership is necessary. Before the group can really begin to focus on the task, you will need to build your interpersonal relations with at least two members of the group, work with them to clarify the goal, and engage in behaviors that will help build your credibility. So, it isn't a matter of which style is always best; it is a matter of what kinds of circumstances are present.

Are leaders likely to be equally adept at task- and person-oriented styles? Although it is possible, many people show more skill at one style or the other. Thus in many groups, even those with a designated leader, more than one person is needed to fulfill all the leadership roles within the group. Nevertheless, throughout this book, we have discussed the kinds of skills that can enable you to function well in either a task- or a people-oriented style.

Leadership Preparation

Although having certain leadership traits and being able to adapt leadership style to the needs of the group are important in determining who will lead, your chances of selection or emergence as a leader are increased if you behave in the following ways during group deliberations:

1. *Be knowledgeable about the group task.* Although the leader is not the primary information giver in a group, group members are more willing to follow when the leader appears to be well informed. The more knowledgeable you are, the better you will be able to analyze individual contributions.

2. *Work harder than anyone else in the group.* Leadership is often a question of setting an example. When others in the group see a person who is willing to do more than his or her fair share for the good of the group, they are likely to support that person. Of course, such effort may involve personal sacrifice, but the person seeking to lead must be willing to pay the price.

3. *Be personally committed to the group's goals and needs.* To gain and maintain leadership takes commitment to the particular task. When you lose that sense of commitment, your leadership may wane and be transferred to others whose enthusiasm is more attuned to a new set of conditions.

4. *Be willing to be decisive at key moments in the discussion.* When leaders are unsure of themselves or unwilling to make decisions, their groups may ramble aimlessly or become frustrated and short-tempered. Sometimes leaders must make decisions that will be resented; sometimes they must decide between competing ideas about courses of action. Any decisions leaders make may cause conflict. Nevertheless, people who are unwilling or unable to be decisive are not going to maintain leadership for long.

5. *Interact freely with others in the group.* One way to show potential for leadership is to participate fully in group discussions. This does not mean that you should dominate the group's deliberations, but it does mean sharing your ideas, feelings, and insights concerning both the content of the group's work and, when appropriate, the group process as well. Too often people sit back silently, thinking, "If only they would call on me for leadership, I would do a really good job." But there is no reason for a group to turn to an unknown quantity. Moreover, by participating fully in the early stages of group work, you can find out whether you are able to influence others before you try to gain leadership.

6. *Develop skill in maintenance functions as well as in task functions.* Effective leaders make others in their groups feel good, contribute to group cohesiveness, and take care to give credit where it is due. Although a group may have both a task leader and a maintenance leader, the primary leader is often the one who shows maintenance skills.

Gender Differences in Leader Acceptability

A question that has generated considerable research is whether the gender of a leader has any effect on a group's acceptance of leadership. Research suggests that gender does affect group acceptance, but not because women lack the necessary traits or abilities. Negative perceptions are largely a result of sex-role stereotypes and devaluing.

Sex-role stereotypes influence how leaders' behaviors are perceived. A persistent research finding is that the same messages are evaluated differently depending on the source of the message.[6] Thus, whereas some women's behaviors will be considered bossy, dominating, and emotional, men exhibiting essentially the same behaviors will be judged as responsible, as offering high-quality contributions, and as showing leadership. So the problem that women face is not that they don't possess or exhibit leadership characteristics, but that their efforts to show leadership are misperceived.

Moreover, sex-role stereotypes lead to devaluing cooperative and supportive behaviors that many women use quite skillfully. As Sally Helgesen points out, many female leaders are successful *because* they respond to people and their problems with flexibility and *because* they are able to break down barriers between people at all levels of the organization.[7]

As a result of male bias and devaluing of female skills, some women get discouraged in seeking leadership roles. But changes in perception are occurring as the notion of "effective" leadership changes. Thus, as women continue to show their competence, they will be selected as leaders more often. As Jurma and Wright have pointed out, research studies have shown that men and women are equally capable of leading task-oriented groups.[8] Patricia Andrews supports this conclusion, noting that it is more important to consider the unique character of a group and the skills of the person serving as leader than the sex of the leader. She goes on to show that a complex interplay of factors (including how much power the leader has) influences effectiveness more than gender does.[9]

Practice in Analyzing Leadership

By Yourself

1. What leadership traits do you believe you have?
2. What is your leadership style? Are you more of a task-oriented leader or a person-oriented leader? What are the strengths and weaknesses of your style?
3. Under which leadership style do you work best? Why?

Functions of Group Leadership

Becoming a leader and carrying out leadership functions are two different things. Many people reach the top of the leadership pole only to slide slowly to oblivion. The effective group leader prepares the meeting place, plans the agenda, introduces the topic and establishes procedures, ensures that all group members have a chance to contribute, asks appropriate questions, is sensitive to cutural differences, and summarizes the discussion as needed.

Preparing the Meeting Place

We have already talked about the importance of a good working environment. If the environment is not good, the leader needs to take responsibility for improving it. As leader, you are in charge of such physical matters as heat, light, and seating. Make sure the temperature of the room is comfortable. Make sure that lighting is adequate, and most important, make sure the seating arrangements will promote spirited interaction.

Planning the Agenda

Recall that an agenda is an outline of the topics that need to be covered at a meeting. Figure 10.1 shows a well-planned agenda for a group discussing the question "What should be done to integrate the campus commuter into the social, political, and extracurricular aspects of student life?"

You may prepare the agenda yourself or in consultation with the group. When possible, the agenda should be in the hands of group members several days before the meeting. How much preparing any individual member will do is based on many factors, but unless the group has an agenda beforehand, members will not have an

March 1, 1996

To: Campus commuter discussion group

Fr: Janelle Smith

Re: Agenda for discussion group meeting

Date: March 8, 1996

Place: Student Union, Conference Room A

Time: 3:00 P.M. (Please be prompt.)

Please come prepared to discuss the following questions. Be sure to bring specific information you can contribute to the discussion of questions 1 through 4. We will consider question 5 on the basis of our resolution of the other questions.

Agenda for Group Discussion

Question: What should be done to integrate the campus commuter into the social, political, and extracurricular aspects of student life?

1. How many students commute?

2. Why aren't commuters involved in social, political, and extracurricular activities?

3. What criteria should be used to test possible solutions to the problem?

4. What are some of the possible solutions to the problem?

5. What one solution or combination of solutions will work best to solve the problem?

Figure 10.1   *Agenda for a discussion group meeting. Note that the agenda is distributed a week in advance and that the date, time, place, and specific questions for discussion are clearly indicated.*

opportunity for careful preparation. Too often, when no agenda is planned, the group discussion is a haphazard affair, often frustrating and usually unsatisfying.

Orienting Group Members

At the beginning of the group's first meeting, the leader needs to orient the group members. In a newly formed group, commitment may be low for some members, expectations may be minimal, and the general attitude may be skeptical. People may be thinking, "We know that many group sessions are a waste of time, so we'll take a wait-and-see attitude." A good leader will start the group process by answering such questions as Why are we here? Who got us together? What is our mission? To whom are we responsible? What kinds of responsibilities will each group member have? and How much will each member be expected to do? Some of these questions will already have been discussed with individuals, but the first meeting gives the leader a chance to put everything together.

Giving Everyone an Equal Opportunity to Speak

For the group process to work, group members need to be encouraged to express their ideas and feelings. Yet, without leader intervention, some people are likely to dominate and some people are likely to feel that they haven't been heard. For instance, in an eight-person group, left to its own devices, two or three people may tend to speak as much as the other five or six together; furthermore, one or two members may contribute little or nothing. At the beginning of a discussion, you must assume that every member of the group has something to contribute. You may have to hold in check those who tend to dominate, and you may have to work to draw reluctant members into the discussion.

At the beginning of the group's first meeting, the leader needs to orient the group members.

Accomplishing this ideal balance is a real test of the gatekeeping skill of a leader. If ordinarily reluctant talkers are intimidated by a member of the group, they may become even more reluctant to participate. Thus, you may have to clear the road for shy speakers. For example, when Dominique gives visual or verbal clues of her desire to speak, say something like "Just a second, Lennie, I think Dominique has something she wants to say here." Then, instead of "Dominique, do you have anything to say here?" you may be able to phrase a question that requires more than a yes or no answer, such as "Dominique, what do you think of the validity of this approach to combating crime?" When people contribute a few times, it builds up their confidence, which in turn makes it easier for them to respond later when they have more to say.

Similar tact is called for with overzealous speakers. If garrulous yet valuable members are constantly restrained, their value to the group may diminish. For example, Lennie, the most talkative member, may be talkative because he has done his homework; if you turn him off, the group's work will suffer. After he has finished talking, try statements such as "Lennie, that's a very valuable bit of material; let's see whether we can get some reactions from other members of the group on this issue." Notice that a statement of this kind does not stop him; it suggests that he should hold off for a while.

There are three common patterns of group communication, as depicted in Figure 10.2, in which the lines represent the flow of discussion among eight participants. Figure 10.2a shows a leader-dominated group. The lack of interaction often leads to a rigid, formal, and usually poor discussion. Figure 10.2b shows a more spontaneous group. Because three people dominate and two are not heard from, however, conclusions will not represent group thinking. Figure 10.2c shows something close to the ideal pattern. It illustrates a great deal of spontaneity, a total group representation, and—theoretically, at least—the greatest potential for reliable conclusions.

Asking Appropriate Questions

Although the members of any group bring a variety of skills, information, and degrees of motivation to the group, they do not always operate at peak efficiency without help from the leader. Perhaps one of the most effective tools of leadership is the ability to question appropriately. This skill requires knowing when to ask questions and what kinds of questions to ask.

By and large, the leader should refrain from asking questions that can be answered yes or no. To ask group members whether they are satisfied with a point that was just made will not lead very far, for after the yes or no answer you must either ask another question to draw people out or change the subject. The two most effective types of questions are those that call for supporting information and those that are completely open-ended and give members complete freedom of response. For instance, rather than asking John whether he has had any professors who were particularly good lecturers, you could inquire, "John, what are some of the characteristics that made your favorite lecturers especially effective?"

Knowing when to ask questions is particularly important. Although we could list fifteen to twenty circumstances, let's focus on four essential purposes of questioning:

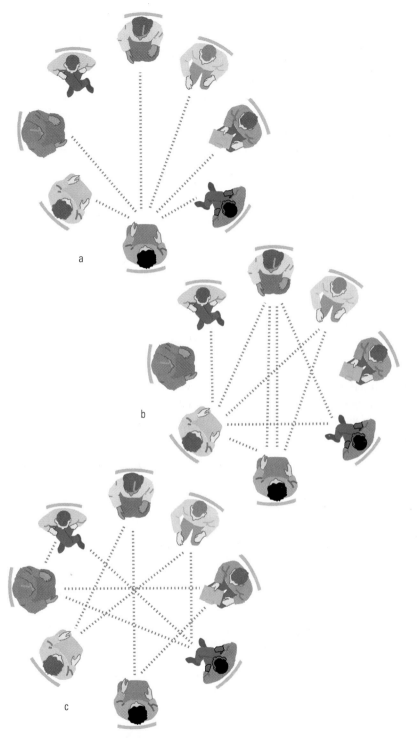

Figure 10.2 *Three common patterns of group communication*

1. *To focus discussion.* Individual statements usually have a point; the point of each statement relates to a larger point being made; and the general discussion relates to an issue or to an agenda item. You can use questions to clarify speakers' points or to determine the relationship of the points to the issue or agenda item. For instance, to relate a statement to the larger topic in a discussion of marijuana use, you might ask, "Are you saying that the instances of marijuana use leading to hard-drug use don't indicate a direct causal relationship?" Or, in response to what has just been said, "How does that information relate to the point that Mary just made?" Or, to ask about an issue or an agenda item, "In what way does this information relate to whether or not marijuana is a health hazard?"

2. *To probe for information.* Many statements need to be developed, supported, or in some way dealt with. Yet often members of a group apparently ignore or accept a point without probing it. When the point seems important, the leader should do something with it. For example, to test the support for an assertion, you can say, "Where did you get that information, Miles?" or "That seems pretty important; what do we have that corroborates the point?" To test the strength of a point, you might ask, "Does that statement represent the thinking of the group?"

3. *To initiate discussion.* During a discussion, there are times when lines of development are apparently ignored, when the group seems ready to agree before sufficient scrutiny of a point. At these times, it is up to the leader to suggest a question for further discussion. For instance, "OK, we seem to have a pretty good grasp of the nature of the problem, but we haven't looked at any causes yet. What are some of the causes?"

4. *To deal with interpersonal problems.* Sometimes the leader can use questions to help members ventilate personal feelings. For example, "Ted, I've heard you make some strong statements on this point. Would you care to share them with us?" At times, a group may attack a person instead of the information that is being presented. Here you can say, "Juan isn't the issue here. Let's look at the merits of the information presented. Do we have any information that runs counter to this point?"

Questions by themselves are not going to make a discussion. In fact, too frequent use of questions can hurt the discussion that is taking place. The effective leader, therefore, uses questions sparingly but incisively.

Dealing with Cultural Diversity

As John Brilhart and Gloria J. Galanes point out, every group discussion is "intercultural to some extent."[10] Thus it is important for a leader to recognize and accept differences within the group.

Most of us will see our group as comprised of individuals who, working hard enough together, can make changes. Thus we see things from an individualistic rather than a collectivist world view. According to Gudykunst and Kim, individualistic cultures promote self-realization for their members; collectivist cultures require that individuals fit into the group.[11] How might such differences in views affect a group and its work? From a collectivist point of view, the group is comprised of members that sacrifice for the good of the group. When a group does well, all members are praised; if a member stands out from the group, the group may feel an obligation to force the individual to conform. From an individualistic perspective, in contrast, a group is comprised of individuals, it is all right to praise an individual for his or her contribution to the group effort, and it is important for individuals to stand out.

To deal with such differences, Brilhart and Galanes suggest that before drawing inferences about group members when their behavior appears to be generally different, ask yourself whether you could be observing a cultural difference and, if so, try to adapt to different cultural practices.[12] Since this book is written from an individualist perspective, your task may prove to be even more difficult when you as a leader hold a collectivist perspective. Before a group with major cultural differences can work effectively, it is important for all members to recognize their differing perspectives and be willing to try to work through the differences.

Summarizing When Necessary

Often, a group talks for a considerable time, then takes a vote on how the members feel about the subject. A consensus is more likely to develop if the group moves in an orderly manner toward intermediate conclusions represented by summary statements that express the group's agreement. For instance, on the question "What should be done to lower the amount of employee theft?" the group should reach agreement on each of the following questions:

1. What is the problem?
2. What are the symptoms of the problem? (Draw intermediate conclusions; ask whether the group agrees.)
3. What are the causes? (Draw an intermediate conclusion on each cause separately or after all causes have been considered; ask whether the group agrees.)
4. What criteria should be used to test the solutions?
5. What is one criterion? (Draw conclusions about each criterion.)
6. What are some of the possible solutions? (Determine whether all worthwhile solutions have been brought up.)
7. How does each of the solutions meet the criteria? (Discuss each and draw conclusions about each; ask whether the group agrees.)
8. Which solution best meets the criteria? (The answer to this final question concludes the discussion; ask whether all agree.)

During the discussion, the group might draw six, eight, ten, or even fifteen conclusions before it is able to arrive at the answer to the topic question. The point is that the group is far more likely to agree on the final conclusion if each of the subordinate questions has been answered to the satisfaction of the entire group.

It is up to the leader to point up intermediate conclusions by summarizing what has been said and seeking consensus. Everyone in the group should realize when the group has arrived at some decision. If left to its own devices, a group may discuss a point for a while, then move on to another point before a conclusion is drawn. The leader must sense when enough has been said to reach a consensus. Then the leader must phrase the conclusion, subject it to testing, and move on to another area. Here are examples of phrases that can be used during the discussion:

"I think most of us are stating the same points. Are we really in agreement that . . ." (State the conclusion.)

"We've been discussing this for a while, and I think I sense an agreement. Let me state it, and then we'll see whether it does summarize the group's feeling." (State the conclusion.)

"Now we're getting into another area. Let's make sure that we are really agreed on the point we've just finished." (State the conclusion.)

"Are we ready to summarize our feelings on this point?" (State the conclusion.)

Practice in Exercising Leadership Responsibilities

In Groups

In groups of five, discuss a topic such as "What can be done to increase student motivation to keep classrooms free of litter?" Each person leads the group for approximately five minutes. After everyone has had a chance to lead, discuss efforts at giving people equal opportunity to speak, asking questions, and summarizing. Focus on behaviors that characterized successful efforts.

Evaluating Group Communication

You are likely to learn to increase your effectiveness in groups as you get feedback about individual and group performance. Groups can be evaluated on the quality of the decision, the quality of individual participation, and the quality of leadership.

The Decision

The questionnaire in Figure 10.3 gives you a framework for evaluating the quality of a group's decision. This questionnaire calls for you to consider three major questions:

1. *Did the group arrive at a decision?* That a group meets to discuss does not necessarily mean that it will arrive at a decision. As foolish as it may seem, some groups thrash away for hours only to adjourn without having come to a conclusion. Of course, some groups discuss such serious problems that a decision cannot be reached without several meetings. In such cases, it is important to ensure that the group adjourns with a clear understanding of what the next step will be. When a group "finishes" its work without arriving at some decision, however, the result is likely to be frustration and disillusionment.

2. *What action will be taken as a result of the decision?* Problem-solving decisions imply implementation. If the group has "finished" without considering means

Group Decision Analysis

Analysis of group characteristics: _____

_____

Did the group arrive at a decision? Explain. _____

_____

What action was taken as a result of that discussion? Explain. ____

_____

Was the group decision a good one? Explain. _____

_____

Was quality information presented? _____

_____

Were the data fully discussed? _____

_____

Did interim conclusions reflect group discussion? _____

_____

Were conclusions measured against some set criteria? _____

_____

Did the group arrive at the decision by consensus? _____

_____

Did the group agree to support the decision? _____

_____

Figure 10.3   *Form for evaluating group decisions*

for putting its decision into action, there is reason to question the practicality of the decision.

3.   *Was the group decision a good one?* This may be the most difficult question to answer. Of course, whether a decision is good or bad is a value judgment. The questionnaire suggests six criteria for such an evaluation:

a. Was quality information presented to serve as a basis for the decision?

b. Were the data discussed fully?

c. Did interim conclusions relate to information presented, or were they stated as opinions that had no relation to content?

d. Was the final decision measured against some set of criteria or objectives?

e. Did the decision seem to be the product of consensus, or was it determined by the persuasive or authoritarian power of the leader?

f. Did the group agree to support the decision?

Individual Participation

Although a group will struggle without good leadership, it may not be able to function at all without members who are willing and able to meet the task and maintenance functions of the group. The questionnaire in Figure 10.4 incorporates each of the elements considered in Chapter 9 on group participation and provides a simple checklist that can be kept for each individual.

Leadership

Although some group discussions are leaderless, no discussion should be without leadership. If there is an appointed leader—and most groups have one—evaluation can focus on that individual. If the group is truly leaderless, the evaluation should consider attempts at leadership by the various members or focus on the apparent leader who emerges from the group. Figure 10.5 contains a simple checklist for evaluating group leadership.

Practice in Analyzing Group Communication

In Groups

Divide into groups of about four to six. Each group should be given or should select a task that requires some research. Each group then has approximately thirty to forty minutes of class time for discussion. While group A is discussing, members of group B should observe and, after the discussion, analyze the proceedings. For practice in using the various questionnaires, some of the observers could be asked to do a decision analysis (Figure 10.3), some could be asked to do an individual member analysis (Figure 10.4), and some could be asked to do a leadership analysis (Figure 10.5). After the discussions, the observers could share their observations with the group. In the next class period, group B discusses and group A observes and analyzes. Sample questions for discussion include the following:

Individual's Group Participation Checklist

For each of the following questions, rate the participant on a scale of 1 to 5:
1 = high; 2 = good; 3 = average; 4 = fair; 5 = poor.

Preparation

	1	2	3	4	5
Seems to be well prepared	☐	☐	☐	☐	☐
Is aware of the problem	☐	☐	☐	☐	☐
Analyzes the problem	☐	☐	☐	☐	☐
Suggests possible solutions	☐	☐	☐	☐	☐
Tests each solution	☐	☐	☐	☐	☐

Carrying Out Roles

	1	2	3	4	5
As information or opinion giver	☐	☐	☐	☐	☐
As information seeker	☐	☐	☐	☐	☐
As analyzer	☐	☐	☐	☐	☐
As idea person	☐	☐	☐	☐	☐
As expediter	☐	☐	☐	☐	☐
As recorder	☐	☐	☐	☐	☐
As supporter	☐	☐	☐	☐	☐
As tension reliever	☐	☐	☐	☐	☐
As harmonizer	☐	☐	☐	☐	☐
As gatekeeper	☐	☐	☐	☐	☐

Avoiding Negative Roles

	1	2	3	4	5
As aggressor	☐	☐	☐	☐	☐
As joker	☐	☐	☐	☐	☐
As withdrawer	☐	☐	☐	☐	☐
As monopolizer	☐	☐	☐	☐	☐

Write an analysis of the person's group participation (two to five paragraphs) based on this checklist.

Figure 10.4 *Form for evaluating individual participation*

- What should be done to improve parking (advising, registration) on campus?
- What should be done to increase the participation of minorities in college or university teaching (governance, administration)?

Group Leadership Checklist

For each of the following questions, rate the participant on a scale of 1 to 5:
1 = high; 2 = good; 3 = average; 4 = fair; 5 = poor.

Preparation to Lead	1	2	3	4	5
Understands topic	☐	☐	☐	☐	☐
Works hard	☐	☐	☐	☐	☐
Shows commitment	☐	☐	☐	☐	☐
Interacts freely	☐	☐	☐	☐	☐
Is decisive	☐	☐	☐	☐	☐

Leading the Group					
Has group of optimum size	☐	☐	☐	☐	☐
Creates and maintains a suitable atmosphere	☐	☐	☐	☐	☐
Works to develop a cohesive unit	☐	☐	☐	☐	☐
Helps the group develop appropriate rules	☐	☐	☐	☐	☐
Has an agenda	☐	☐	☐	☐	☐
Promotes systematic problem solving	☐	☐	☐	☐	☐
Asks good questions	☐	☐	☐	☐	☐
Encourages balanced participation	☐	☐	☐	☐	☐
Refrains from dominating group	☐	☐	☐	☐	☐
Deals with conflict	☐	☐	☐	☐	☐
Arrives at decisions by means of consensus or voting	☐	☐	☐	☐	☐
Brings discussion to a satisfactory close	☐	☐	☐	☐	☐

Write an analysis (two to five paragraphs) based on this checklist.

Figure 10.5   *Form for evaluating group leadership*

Summary

Leadership means exerting influence to accomplish a goal. Although leaders may show higher levels of ability, sociability, motivation, and communication skills than others in the group, the presence of such traits does not guarantee that you will lead effectively.

How well you lead may depend on your style and how you put it into operation. Some leaders adopt the task-oriented style, focusing on what needs to be done and how to do it; others adopt the person-oriented style, focusing on interpersonal relationships of group members. As Fiedler's work has shown, how a leader performs depends on the interaction of task structure, leader–member relations, and position power. If you hope to earn the support of group members for leadership, you will want to be knowledgeable about the task, work harder than others in the group, be personally committed to group goals and needs, be willing to be decisive, interact freely with others in the group, and develop skill in maintenance and task functions.

Leaders have several specific functions. To lead a group well, you must prepare the meeting place, plan an agenda, introduce the topic and establish procedures, ensure that everyone has an equal opportunity to speak, ask appropriate questions, recognize the possibility of cultural differences, and summarize as needed.

Groups can be evaluated on the quality of the decision, the quality of individual participation, and the quality of leadership.

Suggested Readings

Bass, Bernard M. *Bass and Stogdill's Handbook of Leadership: Theory, Research, and Managerial Applications,* 3d ed. New York: Free Press, 1990. Provides reviews of historical and contemporary leadership theory and research. Focuses on the idea that leaders are agents of change.

Cohen, William A. *The Art of the Leader.* Englewood Cliffs, NJ: Prentice-Hall, 1990. Begins with the premise that many highly intelligent, well-educated, motivated people who want to be good leaders just don't know how to do it. Then focuses on specific methods of leadership that the author has learned from theory, observation, and his own experience, including his time as a reserve officer in the U.S. Air Force.

Covey, Stephen R. *Principle-Centered Leadership.* New York: Summit Books, 1991. Covey believes that leadership is the ability to apply principles, natural laws, and governing values that are universally valid to solving problems. He discusses application of leadership principles in interpersonal, managerial, and organizational settings.

Lawson, John D. *When You Preside,* 5th ed. Danville, IL: Interstate Printers and Publishers, 1980. Written as a handbook for leaders of many types of groups. A great deal of good, practical information.

Notes

1. See Bernard M. Bass, *Bass and Stogdill's Handbook of Leadership: Theory, Research, and Managerial Applications*, 3d ed. (New York: Free Press, 1990), pp. 19–20.

2. Ibid. See Chapter 5 for a review of studies up to 1970 and subsequent chapters for analysis of studies through the 1980s.

3. Marvin E. Shaw, *Group Dynamics: The Psychology of Small Group Behavior*, 3d ed. (New York: McGraw-Hill, 1981), p. 325.

4. Ralph White and Ronald Lippitt, "Leader Behavior and Member Reaction in Three 'Social Climates,'" in Dorwin Cartwright and Alvin Zander, eds., *Group Dynamics*, 3d ed. (New York: Harper & Row, 1968), p. 334. The point that groups are largely unproductive under laissez-faire leadership is reinforced by Bass, p. 559.

5. Fred E. Fiedler, *A Theory of Leadership Effectiveness* (New York: McGraw-Hill, 1967).

6. Doré Butler and Florence L. Geis, "Nonverbal Affect Responses to Male and Female Leaders: Implications for Leadership Evaluations," *Journal of Personality and Social Psychology* 58 (1990): 54.

7. Sally Helgesen, *The Female Advantage: Woman's Ways of Leadership* (New York: Doubleday, 1990).

8. William E. Jurma and Beverly C. Wright, "Follower Reactions to Male and Female Leaders Who Maintain or Lose Reward Power," *Small Group Research* 21 (1990): 110.

9. Patricia H. Andrews, "Sex and Gender Differences in Group Communication: Impact on the Facilitation Process," *Small Group Research* 23 (1992): 90.

10. John K. Brilhart and Gloria J. Galanes, *Effective Group Discussion*, 8th ed., Madison, WI: Brown & Benchmark, 1995, p. 107.

11. William B. Gudykunst and Young Yun Kim, *Communicating with Strangers: An Approach to Intercultural Communication*, 2d ed. (New York: McGraw-Hill, 1992), pp. 42–43.

12. Brilhart and Galanes, p. 107.

Group Communication
Chapters 9–10

What kind of a group communicator are you? The following analysis looks at ten specifics that are basic to a group communication profile. On the line provided for each statement, indicate the response that best captures your behavior: 1, never; 2, rarely; 3, occasionally; 4, often; 5, almost always.

_____ I enjoy participating in committee or other group discussions. (Ch. 9)

_____ I prepare well beforehand for group discussions. (Ch. 9)

_____ I analyze a problem to determine the questions that need to be asked in order to solve the problem. (Ch. 9)

_____ I contribute freely and openly in groups. (Ch. 9)

_____ My contributions are very helpful in the group's effort to accomplish its task. (Ch. 9)

_____ I help the group consider whether material presented is relevant. (Ch. 9)

_____ I am good at saying things that help the group work well together. (Ch. 9)

_____ I try to provide leadership for the group. (Ch. 10)

_____ When I am a leader, I provide the members of the group with a carefully thought-out suggested procedure. (Ch. 10)

_____ When I am a leader, I ask relevant questions that help the group move forward with its task. (Ch. 10)

Based on your responses, select the group communication behavior that you would most like to change. Write a communication improvement goal statement similar to the sample goal statement in Chapter 1 (page 24). If you would like verification of your self-analysis before you write a goal statement, have a friend or coworker complete this same analysis for you.

five

Public Speaking

B ill Clinton, Jesse Jackson, and Pat Schroeder are but three contemporary speakers who have sought to forge a national consensus on key issues facing our country. Whether or not we ever speak to a national audience, we may often be called on, by choice or by necessity, to speak our ideas in public. This part of the book considers the variables that affect public speaking.

In order to have the greatest chance for an effective speech in any situation, you need to have a plan—a strategy for achieving your goal. An effective speech plan is a product of six action steps that are covered in Chapters 11 through 15. In the final two chapters, we consider additional skills related specifically to speeches intended to inform and to persuade.

**After you have read
this chapter, you
should be able to:**

Brainstorm for topics

Compile audience data

*Predict level of audience
interest in, knowledge of, and
attitude toward a topic*

*Indicate physical and
psychological conditions
affecting the speech*

Test your speech goal

Phrase a thesis statement

11

Selecting a Topic,
Analyzing Audience and
Occasion, and Refining
the Speech Goal

A s a graduate student who has "made good" and is on scholarship at a major university, Ayanna has been invited to speak to an assembly at her old inner-city high school. She's excited by the invitation but also anxious about the speech. She feels vaguely that she might have a lot to say to the students coming up behind her, but she wonders whether they will be interested in her speech and isn't quite sure where to begin her preparation or exactly what her focus should be. She wonders, "Where do I start?"

Many of us find ourselves in situations like Ayanna's. We have a general idea of some of the kinds of things we might like to include in a speech but don't know how to put it all together.

ACTION STEP 1

Determine a specific speech goal that is adapted to your audience and occasion.

An effective speech plan is a product of six action steps, summarized in Figure 11.1. In this chapter, we consider the four elements that comprise the first step: selecting a topic, analyzing your audience, analyzing the occasion and setting, and articulating your goals in the form of a thesis statement. Although we discuss each element separately, they overlap and are sometimes accomplished in a different order.

Action Steps for Speech Plan

1. Determine a specific speech goal that is adapted to your audience and occasion. (Chapter 11)

   A. Select a topic from a subject area you know something about and that is important to you.

   B. Analyze your audience.

   C. Analyze your occasion.

   D. Articulate your goal by determining the response that you want from your audience.

2. Gather and evaluate verbal and visual material for use in the speech. (Chapter 12)

3. Develop a strategy for adapting material to your specific speech audience. (Chapter 13)

4. Organize and develop your material in a way that is best suited to your particular audience. (Chapter 14)

   A. Choose an organizational pattern that clearly communicates the material.

   B. Develop an introduction that both gets attention and leads into the body of the speech.

   C. Develop a conclusion that both summarizes the material and leaves the speech on a high note.

   D. Refine the speech outline.

5. Select clear, vivid, emphatic, and direct wording for the speech. (Chapter 15)

6. Practice delivering the speech. (Chapter 15)

   A. Use voice and bodily action to develop a conversational quality that shows enthusiasm, eye contact, and spontaneity.

   B. Rehearse the speech until you can deliver it extemporaneously within the time limits.

Figure 11.1 *Action steps for an effective speech plan*

Selecting a Topic

Sometimes, people are invited to speak on a specific topic; at other times, however, and especially in the classroom, selecting a topic is up to you. But selecting a topic can be a major stumbling block. We often hear people say, "Oh, I'm sure I can give a good speech—if only I could find a topic!" Yet finding a good topic should be quite easy if you choose from topics you know about and topics that interest you. Perhaps you are asking, "Why not select a topic that the audience wants to hear?" Although this approach sounds good, selecting topics solely on that basis, regardless of your own knowledge or interest, can lead to trouble. For instance, international students may try to select current events topics that they think their classmates will be familiar with rather than talking about experiences, values, and perceptions related to their own culture that they are well informed about and that would provide valuable new information for most of the class. What you'll find is that if you have knowledge about and interest in a topic, you will be able to adapt that topic to the audience.

Suitable topic areas are likely to include your school major (or prospective profession), your hobbies (or spare-time activities), and current events or social issues that concern you. Let's see how you can identify good specific topics from these topic areas.

To generate a list of topics, try brainstorming. As we discussed in the group communication section, brainstorming is an uncritical, nonevaluative process of generating ideas, much like the old word-association process. For example, in response to the word *music*, you might brainstorm *rock, new wave, dance, electronic, amplifiers.* When you start with a word or an idea related to a subject you know about and are interested in, you can often list twenty, thirty, or even fifty related words.

Start by dividing a sheet of paper into three columns. Label column 1 "Major" or "Vocation," column 2 "Hobby" or "Activity," and column 3 "Current Events" or "Social Issues." Then select a word to head each column and, one column at a time, brainstorm from each word. If, for instance, in column 2, "Hobby," you write "pocket billiards," you might brainstorm such related words as "cue," "English," "games," "tables," and "equipment." After you have worked for at least five minutes on a column, turn to the next column. Although you may not finish all three columns in one sitting, do not go to the next step of speech preparation until you have listed at least twenty items in each column.

Brainstorming allows you to take advantage of a basic commonsense principle: Just as it is easier to select the correct answer to a multiple-choice question than it is to think of the answer to the same question without the choices, so too is it easier to select a topic from a list than to come up with a topic out of the blue. So, when you believe your list for each heading is complete, read the entries and check the three or four words or phrases that sound most compelling to you. Instead of asking yourself "What should I talk about?" ask yourself "What are the one, two, or three best topics I have listed under each heading?" The computer buff whose brainstorming list is shown in Figure 11.2 will find it much easier to decide to talk about viruses, windows, or networks from the twenty-four topics listed than to think of a topic cold.

Hobby: Computers			
games	software	graphics	printers
spreadsheets	windows	hard disk	floppy disks
hardware	hacking	programming	memory
mouse	word processing	keyboards	color monitors
uses	networks	costs	CD-ROM
capabilities	viruses	databases	ethics

Figure 11.2 *Brainstorming a topic*

If the words or phrases you select still seem too general, start a new brainstorming list with one of these topics. When you have checked two or three topics from each of the three columns, you will have six to nine good topics, enough for all of your speeches this term!

Practice in Brainstorming for Topics

By Yourself

Divide a sheet of paper into three columns. Label column 1 with your major or vocation, such as "Art History"; label column 2 with a hobby or activity, such as "Chess"; label column 3 with a concern or issue, such as "Water Pollution." Working on one column at a time, brainstorm a list of at least twenty words or phrases for each column. Then check three of the words or phrases in each column that are most compelling—of special meaning to you or of potential interest to your audience.

Analyzing the Audience

How effective your speech will be is likely to depend on how well it arouses listeners' interest, complements and adds to their knowledge, and speaks to their particular attitudes. Consequently, before you can refine your choice of topic into a specific goal, you need to analyze your audience.

Audience analysis is a systematic study of your specific speech audience. An audience analysis includes (1) essential audience demographic data and (2) predictions of their level of interest in, knowledge of, and attitudes toward you and your topic. The results of this analysis will guide you in refining your goal, selecting supporting material, and organizing and presenting your speech.

Gathering Audience Data

The audience data necessary to help you predict how an audience will receive your speech can be gathered in one of three ways:

1. *Assemble data from observation.* If you are a member of the group to which you will be speaking, you already have access to significant data about your audience. For instance, since you are a member of the class that will be hearing your classroom speeches, you already have firsthand information to draw upon.

2. *Question the person who scheduled your speech.* If you are speaking to a community action group, for example, your contact person can answer your questions about the audience.

3. *Infer information on the basis of the nature of the audience.* If the contact person cannot answer all of your questions satisfactorily, you can make informed guesses based on indirect information. For instance, because a community action group is made up of people who live in a specific community, you can infer audience data based on observations about the people who are likely to belong to such a group and who live in such a community.

Now let us consider the specific areas in which it is most important to have accurate data: age, education, gender, occupation, income, race, religion, and nationality, geographic uniqueness, and group affiliation.

Age.   You will want data to confirm both the average age and the age range. Audience age has been used as a primary predictor of audience interests, knowledge, and attitudes for more than two thousand years. Aristotle drew conclusions about what he recommended for speakers based primarily on whether listeners were young, old, or in-between. He contended that young listeners have strong passions and exalted notions, are quick-tempered and courageous, love honor and victory, and that they overdo everything; whereas elderly listeners are skeptical, cynical, cowardly, and loquacious, lack confidence in the future, and guide their lives more by reason.[1]

Whether or not age actually predicts interests and attitudes, when you have an accurate picture of average age, you can select the most relevant examples and arguments. For example, in a speech to an audience dominated by teenagers, you will get only blank stares with allusions to the music of Glenn Miller and Tommy Dorsey; likewise, in a speech to an audience composed of older adults, you might be met with bewilderment and perhaps even hostility if you refer only to heavy-metal performers.

In the classroom, you may assume that your audience will be mostly people in their late teens and early twenties, but it's important to take a careful look: There may be more of a range than originally anticipated. Recent statistics show that a typical college class may have students in their thirties, forties, and beyond.[2]

Education.   You want data to confirm whether audience members have high school, college, or postgraduate educations or whether their education levels are mixed. For either informative or persuasive speeches, level of education is an excellent predictor of audience interest and knowledge. For informative speeches, the higher the educational level of your listeners, the more likely they will be interested in and able to understand literary, historical, and geographic references and allusions. Likewise, they are more likely to have the background necessary to understand complex explanations. For persuasive speeches, the higher the educational level of the audience, the more likely its members will be able to process complex arguments. You are also likely to find a well-educated audience more open-minded, more willing to at least listen to new proposals, and more accepting of social and technological changes than less well-educated groups. Your classmates are among these better-educated audiences.

Gender. For some topics, you will want data to confirm whether your audience will be primarily male, primarily female, or fairly well balanced. Although gender differences are less marked than they once were (for example, you cannot assume that women are generally homemakers or that men are primarily breadwinners), men and women still have different perspectives on many issues.

When your audience comprises mostly people of your gender, you are likely to have considerable experience that you can use to relate to them. When your audience is mostly of the opposite gender, however, it is crucial to choose language and illustrations that are relevant to them.

Occupation. If most members of your audience have a single occupation, such as nursing, banking, drill-press operating, teaching, or sales, it will be easier to predict the kinds of information that are of interest and value to them. Similarly, your choice of information and examples would probably be different when speaking to an audience made up mostly of students, blue-collar workers, or professionals such as doctors or lawyers. Unless you attend a highly specialized school or are in a section restricted to students from a particular college, program, or major, your classmates are likely to represent a cross section of occupational interests.

Income. If you have data to confirm that the average income level of your audience is high, low, or average, you can often predict how the audience might react to speeches with an economic focus. There is no sense in trying to convince an audience of people with below-average incomes of the value of investments, purchases, or recreational opportunities that require huge resources. On the other hand, people with lower incomes are sometimes more sympathetic to appeals to support the needy, even if the level of support they can afford is minimal. Moreover, whether any audience considers money an obstacle may well depend on its financial circumstances.

Culture. Determining such cultural elements as ethnicity, religion, or nationality is increasingly relevant as society becomes more multiracial and multicultural. Currently, for example, 25 percent of all people in the United States identify themselves as nonwhite, including Hispanic, Asian, and black. This percentage is likely to continue to increase.[3] Cultural data may affect the kinds of material used to illustrate or support your arguments and may help to provide a basis for predicting how audience members might stand on some issues. For instance, it might be a mistake to assume that everyone in a multicultural audi-

Effective speakers make awareness of the audience a central part of their thinking throughout the speech preparation process.

ence shares the same views on the roles of government, family, or school. Likewise, it is important to know whether an audience is homogeneous in a relevant respect. For instance, an all-Catholic audience is likely to hold a negative attitude toward abortion on demand.

Geographic Uniqueness.   The knowledge that an audience has a geographic bond—for example, the audience members are from the same state, city, or neighborhood—can help you select meaningful information, arguments, and examples. For instance, it is much easier to paint a vivid picture of the effects of littering or pollution if you can personalize the issue by relating these effects to the audience's own city or neighborhood. Most people are more inclined to support a project to improve the environment if they see the problem in "their own backyard."

Group Affiliation.   Another element that bonds people together is group affiliation. If the majority of audience members belong to the same group, you can predict with greater certainty the kinds of information and examples they will perceive as relevant. For example, a group of veterans will respond more favorably to combat or defense analogies than to literary parallels.

Predicting Audience Reactions

The next step in audience analysis is to use the previous data to assess the audience's potential interest in, knowledge of, and attitudes toward your topic and the goal for your speech. These predictions form a basis for the development of your speech strategy.

Audience Interest.   Your first goal is to assess whether the audience is likely to have an immediate interest in your topic or whether you will need to elicit that interest. Suppose you are planning to give a speech on cholesterol to an audience composed mostly of males between ages forty and sixty. In this case, you can predict significant audience interest. Why? Because the cholesterol and heart attack connection is of immediate concern to older men. In cases where you predict only mild interest in the topic, you will need to build interest by the way you develop your speech. We examine strategies for both building and maintaining interest in Chapter 13, Adapting to Audiences.

Audience Understanding.   Your second goal is to assess whether the audience has sufficient background to understand your information. This assessment is necessary because you don't want to try the patience of your listeners by elaborately explaining what they already know, nor lose their attention by using language and information they do not understand.

For some speech topics, significant background knowledge is unnecessary. Because most people are familiar with automobiles, for example, you can predict that an audience will have enough background information to understand the content of a speech explaining the special features of new models. For other topics, lack of background may require you to give some basic orientation information before the speech will make sense. For instance, if you are planning to speak on the importance of the corporate culture (the shared values of an organization) to productivity in an organization, you can predict that a typical classroom audience doesn't have the background to follow your speech without sufficient orientation.

Audience Attitude.   Finally, it is important to assess your audience's attitude. Audience attitude is a product of the direction and strength of feelings about (1) your topic and (2) your credibility.

Topic.   Knowledge of the direction and strength of the audience's attitudes about your topic is especially important when you seek to change a belief or move an audience to action. Audience attitudes are expressed by opinions that may be distributed along a continuum from highly favorable to hostile. Even though any given audience may have one or a few individuals' opinions at nearly every point of the distribution, in most audiences opinions will tend to cluster at a particular point on the continuum. That point represents the general audience attitude on that topic.

Except for polling the audience, there is no way to be sure about your assessment, but you can make reasonably accurate estimates based on demographic knowledge and published surveys. Unskilled workers, for example, are likely to look at minimum-wage proposals differently than are business executives; many men will look at women's rights proposals differently than most women will; a meeting of the local Right-to-Life chapter will look at abortion differently than will a meeting of NOW (National Organization for Women). The more data you have about your audience and the more experience you have in analyzing audiences, the better are your chances of accurately judging audience attitudes.

With minimal research, you can find published surveys that indicate how large segments of society regard certain issues. For instance, most libraries carry the *Gallup Report*, a monthly magazine that provides survey information gathered through Gallup polls. Your library may also carry books, such as *American Values*,[4] that include surveys of opinions on U.S. political, social, economic, and religious values. In addition, popular weekly newsmagazines (*Newsweek*, *Time*, and *U.S. News & World Report*) commission polls by professional polling agencies when they believe their topic is a "hot" one.[5]

Credibility.   Likewise, your success in informing or persuading an audience is likely to depend on their attitude toward you—whether they perceive you as a credible source of information. Although speech experts differ in listing the characteristics of credibility, most include knowledge and expertise, trustworthiness, and personality.

Knowledge and expertise includes your qualifications or capability—your "track record." Speakers who demonstrate knowledge and expertise are likely to be highly regarded. What is the extent of your knowledge level for your speech? Are you (or can you be) recognized as having necessary expertise? Do you have good material from reliable sources? Are you sure of your facts and figures? People who have a history of giving good information, being clear thinkers, and being able to demonstrate their expertise are usually respected by others.

Trustworthiness refers to both a person's apparent motives and that person's character. First, audiences will weigh a speaker's intentions. For instance, when an employee of your gas and electric company talks about testing your house or apartment for air leaks, you are likely to see his or her motives as "pure," because if you repair such leaks and thus lower your gas and electric use, the company stands to lose money. On the other hand, if representatives of a local home-repair business offer to give you a "free inspection for air leaks," you may suspect their motives, because if their inspection shows "major air leakage" they probably will want to sell you on having them do "necessary" repairs. The more positively your audience views your intentions, the more credible your words will seem.

Thus, when developing your speech and thinking about your audience, it's important to consider what your real intentions are. Are you presenting material that your listeners will perceive as informative, so that they will not suspect you of having ulterior motives?

Likewise, an audience will consider a speaker's character. *Character* refers to a person's mental and ethical traits. We are more likely to trust and believe a person whom we perceive to be honest, industrious, dependable, strong, and steadfast. We often will overlook what are otherwise regarded as shortcomings if a person shows character. Recall that in the 1992 presidential campaign character became a major issue. Then-President Bush attempted to portray then-Governor Clinton as shifty. Although Clinton won the election, many of those who voted for Ross Perot and George Bush cited their concerns about Clinton's character as a major reason for not voting for him.

Thus, when developing your speech and thinking about your audience, it's important to consider your character strengths. Are you presenting material in ways that will increase your audience's perception of your trustworthiness?

Personality refers to a person's behavior and emotions. In short, it is the impression a person makes on us. Sometimes, we have a strong gut reaction about a person based solely on a first impression. Based on such traits as enthusiasm, friendliness, warmth, a ready smile, and caring (or its absence), we take a natural liking or disliking to a person. Likewise, audiences perceive speakers as friendly, warm, and caring when they have a straightforward enthusiasm about their subjects. Because perception of personality weighs so much in determining a person's credibility, we'll focus on the elements of effective delivery in Chapter 15.

Information about your audience will be combined with information about your topic in order to adapt your speech to your specific audience. We will discuss how to use this information to increase audience adaptation in Chapter 13.

Practice in Analyzing your Audience

By Yourself

1. Analyze the audience for your next speech by completing the checklist shown in Figure 11.3.

2. In conducting an audience analysis, what factors related to culture and public speaking might be valuable for a speaker to discover? Why?

Analyzing the Occasion and Setting

Speeches are often given in conjunction with a particular occasion. When they are, knowledge of the occasion provides a speaker with guidelines for both meeting audience expectations and determining the tone of the speech. For example, a high school or college commencement is a formal occasion, calling for a formal and even elevated tone; moreover, the audience on this occasion will expect the speaker to address the needs of graduating students.

Analyzing occasion and setting is still important even when a speech does not commemorate a special event. Once you know more about the setting, you can prepare yourself to meet the physical and psychological conditions that cause unprepared speakers major difficulty.

Audience Analysis Checklist

Data

1. The audience educational level is ____ high school, ____ college, ____ postgraduate.

2. The age range is from ____ to ____. The average age is about ____.

3. The audience is approximately ____ percent males and ____ percent females.

4. My estimate of the income level of the audience is ____ below average, ____ average, ____ above average.

5. The audience is basically ____ the same race or ____ a mixture of races.

6. The audience is basically ____ the same religion or ____ a mixture of religions.

7. The audience is basically ____ the same nationality or ____ a mixture of nationalities.

8. The audience is basically of the same ____ state, ____ city, ____ neighborhood, or ____ other definable area.

Predictions

9. Audience interest in this topic is likely to be ____ high, ____ moderate, ____ low.

10. Audience understanding of the topic will be ____ great, ____ moderate, ____ little.

11. Audience attitude about the topic will be ____ in favor, ____ neutral, ____ opposed.

12. Audience attitude toward the speaker is likely to be ____ positive, ____ neutral, ____ negative.

Figure 11.3   *Form for analyzing an audience*

1. *How large will the audience be?* It is important to know whether the audience will be small (fewer than 50 people), medium (50 to 100), or large (more than 100). The size of the audience helps to determine the formality of the presentation. If you are anticipating an audience of 25 to 35 people, you can gear yourself for an informal setting in which you are close to all listeners. With a small audience, you can talk in a normal voice and feel free to move about. In contrast, if you anticipate an audience of 200 or more, in addition to needing a microphone, you probably will want to make your delivery, language, and even the nature of your development more formal.

2. *When will the speech be given?* The time of day and the timing of a speech relative to other events can affect how the speech is received. If a speech is scheduled after a meal, for instance, the audience may be lethargic, mellow, or even on the verge of sleep. In this case, it helps to insert more "attention-getters"—examples, illustrations, and stories—to counter potential lapses of attention.

3. *Where in the program does the speech occur?* If you are the featured speaker—the person the audience has come to hear—you have an obvious advantage: You are the focal point of audience attention. In the classroom, however, and at some rallies, hearings, and other events, there are many speeches, and your place on the schedule may affect how you are received. For example, speaking first or last can make a difference. If you go first, you may need to "warm up" the listeners and be prepared to meet the distraction of a few audience members strolling in late; if you speak last, you must counter the tendency of the audience to be weary from listening to several speeches.

4. *What is the time limit for the speech?* The amount of time you have to speak greatly affects the scope of your speech and how you develop it. Keep in mind that the time limit for classroom speeches is quite short. We often get overly ambitious about what we can accomplish in a short speech. "Three major causes of environmental degradation" can be discussed in five minutes, but "A history of human impact on the environment" cannot.

Problems with time limits are not peculiar to classroom speeches. Any speech setting includes actual or implied time limits. For example, a Sunday sermon is usually limited to about twenty minutes; a keynote speech for a convention may

Different occasions and settings call for different specific goals, speech language, and styles of delivery.

be limited to thirty minutes; a political campaign speech may be limited to forty-five minutes or an hour. Whatever the time limit, speakers must consider realistically how much can be covered within it. Particularly when you want your presentation to have depth, it's important to narrow your focus and not cover too broad an area.

5. *What are the expectations for the speech?* Every occasion provides some special expectations. For classroom speeches, one of the major expectations is meeting the assignment. Whether the speech assignment is defined by purpose (to inform or to persuade), by type (expository or descriptive), or by subject (book analysis or current event), your goal should reflect the nature of that assignment.

Meeting expectations is equally important for speeches outside the classroom. At an Episcopalian Sunday service, the congregation expects the minister's sermon to have a religious theme; at a campaign rally, listeners expect a speech on political issues; at a social dinner event, listeners often expect a lighthearted and entertaining talk.

6. *Where will the speech be given?* The room in which you are scheduled to speak also affects your presentation. If you are fortunate, your classroom will be large enough to seat the class comfortably. But classrooms vary in size, lighting, seating arrangements, and the like. Giving a speech in a room that is long and narrow creates different problems from speaking in one that is short and wide. In a long, narrow room, speech must be louder to reach the back row, but eye contact can be limited to a more narrow range. In a dimly lit room, try to get the lights turned up, especially if you are planning to use visual aids. Investigating the environment for the speech helps you to meet the demands of the situation.

Outside the school setting, speakers often encounter even greater variations. It's important to have specific information about the room in which you are scheduled to speak, including seating capacity, shape, number of rows, lighting, whether there is speaking stage or platform, distance between speaker and first row, and so on, before you make final speech plans. If possible, visit the place and see it for yourself.

7. *What facilities are necessary to give the speech?* For some speeches, you may need a microphone, a chalkboard, or an overhead or slide projector and screen. In most instances, speakers have some kind of speaking stand, but it's wise to not always count on it. If the person who has contacted you to speak has any control over the setting, be sure to explain what you need. But always have alternative plans in case what you have asked for is unavailable. It's frustrating to plan a slide presentation, for example, and then discover there is no place to plug in the projector!

Practice in Analyzing the Occasion and Setting

By Yourself

Analyze the occasion and setting for your next speech by answering the series of questions in Figure 11.4.

Figure 11.4 *Form for analyzing the occasion and setting*

Writing the Speech Goal and Thesis Statement

Once you have chosen your topic and analyzed the audience and occasion for your speech, you continue the preparation process by identifying the general goal you are hoping to achieve, crafting a specific speech goal, and ultimately refining your goal by writing a thesis statement.

General Goal

Most speeches can be organized under three major headings: entertaining, informing, and persuading. Because speech is a complex act that may affect an audience in different ways, these headings are useful only to show that in any public speaking act one overriding general goal is likely to predominate. Consider the following examples:

> Jay Leno's opening monologue on "The Tonight Show" is a speech that may give some information and may even contain some intended or

unintended persuasive message, but his general goal is to entertain his audience.

A history professor's lecture on the events leading to World War I may use humor to gain and hold attention, and the discussion of the events may affect the class's attitudes about war, but the professor's primary goal is to explain those events so that the class understands them.

Political candidates may amuse us with their anecdotes about life in politics and may give us some information that clarifies aspects of key political issues, but their general goal is to persuade us to vote for them.

Although some public speakers give speeches solely for the purpose of entertaining, in this text we focus attention on informative and persuasive speeches.

Specific Goal

The specific goal, or specific purpose, is a single statement that specifies the exact response the speaker wants from the audience. For a speech on the topic of "evaluating diamonds," the goal could be stated as "I would like the audience to understand the four major criteria for evaluating a diamond." For a speech on "supporting the United Way," the goal could be stated as "I would like the audience to donate money to the United Way." In the first example, the goal is informative: The speaker wants the audience to understand the criteria. In the second example, the goal is persuasive: The speaker wants the audience to donate money. Figure 11.5 gives further examples of specific goals that clearly state how the speakers want the audience to react to the specific topics.

Now let us consider a step-by-step procedure for writing the specific speech goal:

1. *Keep writing until your tentative speech goal is a complete sentence that states the specific response or behavior you want from your audience.* Suppose you want to talk about illiteracy. The topic "illiteracy" provides only the framework for a specific speech goal. "Illiteracy in the workplace" indicates the aspect of the topic you want to consider. "*Three effects* of illiteracy in the workplace" limits what you will say to a specific number. The topic is now clearly defined, but you still need to specify what response you intend to elicit from your audience. "*I would like the audience to understand* three effects of the problem of illiteracy in the workplace" represents a complete-sentence statement of your speech goal. Notice that this statement includes an infinitive form ("to understand") indicating the specific desired response.

2. *Write out at least three different wordings of the goal.* The clearer your specific goal, the more purposeful and effective your speech is likely to be. Even if you like your first sentence, write at least two additional ones. The second, third, or fourth version may be the clearest statement of your goal.

3. *Write the goal as a sentence rather than as a question or fragment.* "Is illiteracy a way of life in the workplace?" is a question that may be a good topic for dis-

Entertainment Goals

I would like my audience to be amused by my portrayal of an over-the-hill football player.

I would like my audience to laugh at my experience as a waiter.

Informative Goals

I would like my audience to understand the characteristics of the five common types of coastlines.

I would like my audience to understand the three basic forms of mystery stories.

Persuasive Goals

I would like my audience to believe that drug testing by business and industry should be prohibited.

I would like my audience to join Amnesty International.

Figure 11.5 *Specific speech goals*

cussion, but it is not a good speech goal, because it does not point in any direction that indicates the purpose of the speech. Likewise, "Illiteracy—a detriment to success" is a fragment that may be a good title, but it, too, fails as a speech goal for much the same reason: It does not give clear enough direction for identifying prospective main points of the speech.

4. *Write the goal so that it contains only one idea.* The statement "I would like the audience to understand three effects of illiteracy in the workplace and to prove how it is detrimental to both industry and the individual" includes two distinct ideas; either one can be used, but not both, because together they blur the focus of the speech. Make a decision. Do you want to focus your talk on specific effects of illiteracy? Then the goal "I would like the audience to understand three major effects of illiteracy in the workplace" is the better statement. Do you want to focus on how harmful it is? Then the goal "I would like to prove that illiteracy is detrimental to the individual and to industry" is preferable.

5. *Revise the infinitive or infinitive phrase until it indicates the specific audience reaction desired.* If you regard your ideas as useful but noncontroversial, then your intent is basically informative, and the infinitive that expresses your desired audience reaction should take the form "to understand" or "to appreciate." If, however, the main idea of your speech is controversial, a statement of belief, or a call to action, then your intent is persuasive and will be reflected in such infinitives as "to believe" or "to change."

Thesis Statement

Before you begin constructing your speech, you need to refine your goal by writing a thesis statement. Whereas the specific goal is a statement of how you want your audience to respond, the *thesis statement* is a sentence that specifies the key elements of the speech supporting that goal. For example, the speech goal "I would like the audience to understand the major criteria for evaluating a diamond" clearly states what you want the audience to do (understand the major criteria), but it does not identify the criteria. If you had worked in a jewelry store or had read several articles about jewelry, then you would have the information at your fingertips enabling you to specify the criteria. Your thesis statement might then be "Diamonds are evaluated on the basis of carat (weight), color, clarity, and cutting." Likewise, for the speech goal "I would like my audience to donate money to the United Way," you might have the information necessary to write the thesis statement "You should donate to the United Way because it covers a wide variety of charities with one contribution, it spends a very low percentage on overhead, and it allows you to designate specific agencies to receive your money if you so desire."

For many topics, however, you may not have the specific information necessary to write such a statement or you may not have thought about the topic enough to be specific. For instance, suppose Emming has written the specific speech goal "I would like the audience to understand the major causes of juvenile crime." If he has the necessary information at this stage of preparation, a useful way to identify potential causes is to brainstorm a *semantic map*—a visual diagram of ideas. Mapping is a kind of brainstorming session in which you verbalize associations to your goal statement and map them on paper.

The objective of the semantic-mapping process is to identify ideas without initial regard to whether they are main ideas, supporting details, or random ideas related to the speech goal. Once you get specific ideas down on paper, you can begin to evaluate them in order to select the most relevant ones for your thesis statement. For the juvenile crime topic, Emming could start with the idea "causes" and brainstorm, based on his reading and observation, as shown in Figure 11.6.

Emming has listed six potential major causes. Depending on the amount of information you have and the breadth of the subject area, you might brainstorm six, eight, or even a dozen specifics.

Representing the material in this form provides Emming a chance to get his thoughts down on paper without being concerned about weight, order, or appropriateness. Now he can study them to see which ideas have the most promise. If at this stage he still doesn't think he has enough information to make good choices, he can delay writing the specific thesis statement until after he has finished his research for the speech. If, however, he is sufficiently confident about his choices at this time, from these six he might choose poverty, broken homes, and peer pressure as the three most important. He can then write a thesis statement as follows: "The three major causes of juvenile crime are poverty, broken homes, and peer pressure."

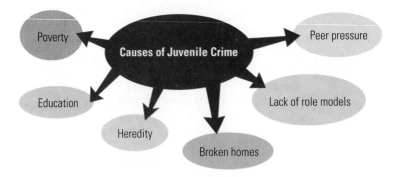

Figure 11.6 *Semantic-map brainstorming*

In Chapter 14, Organizing Speech Material, we will again use semantic mapping, not only to help us select main points for a speech but also to select and organize supporting material.

Relationship among Elements

As we have seen, there are many potential speech topics within a single subject area. Likewise, a given topic can be the basis for one of three general goals (to entertain, inform, or persuade) and many different specific goals. Finally, a specific goal can be elaborated in a thesis statement. This relationship among subject, topic, general goal, specific goal, and thesis statement is illustrated in Figure 11.7.

The process of refinement illustrated by these examples will pay big dividends as you research and develop your speech. How?

First, a clearly written goal helps you to limit your research. If you want the audience to understand "the effects of illiteracy in the workplace," you can limit your reading to "effects" with a focus on "the workplace," saving you many hours of research time on other aspects of illiteracy.

Second, a clearly written goal helps you to organize your ideas logically. The main points of a speech grow directly from the goal, and they are forecast in the wording of the thesis statement. Thus, the main points for the specific goal "I would like the audience to understand three major effects of illiteracy in the workplace" could be the following: (1) Illiteracy in the workplace locks people out of career advancement. (2) Illiteracy in the workplace prevents people from understanding even the simplest written instructions. (3) Illiteracy in the workplace leads to frustration that is manifested in chemical abuse and criminal activity.

When you can write a thesis statement incorporating your main points, you are well on your way to a complete and effective speech.

Subject Area: Career counseling

Topic: Networking

General Speech Goal: Informative

Specific Goal: I want the audience to understand the procedure for networking in career development.

Thesis Statement: You can use networking most effectively if you make networking a high priority, position yourself in places of opportunity, advertise yourself, and follow up on your contacts.

Subject Area: Finance

Topic: Debt

General Speech Goal: Informative

Specific Goal: I would like the audience to understand two major factors that are increasing the problem of personal debt in the United States.

Thesis Statement: Personal debt is facilitated by easy access to credit and need for instant gratification.

Subject Area: National Collegiate Athletic Association (NCAA)

Topic: Sanctions

General Speech Goal: Persuasive

Specific Goal: I would like the audience to believe that sanctions are an ineffective means of punishing colleges that violate NCAA rules.

Thesis Statement: NCAA sanctions do not deter colleges from violating rules, they do not make it difficult for schools to field winning teams, and they do not prevent sanctioned colleges from receiving financial support.

Figure 11.7 *Relationship among subject, topic, general goal, specific goal, and thesis statement*

Practice in Writing Speech Goals and Thesis Statements

By Yourself

1. Write three well-worded goal statements for a single speech (the topic may be taken from your brainstorming sheet). Using the five-step procedure outlined on pp. 279–280 as a guide, decide which of the three statements best states the goal.

2. If you can, write a complete thesis statement for the specific goal just selected. If you do not yet have enough information to complete your thesis statement, you can wait until you have found sufficient information on your topic. (Finding information is discussed in Chapter 12.)

Summary

The first step in effective speech preparation is to select a topic that you know something about and are interested in. Identify topics by listing general areas of interest, such as jobs, hobbies, and issues or concerns. Under each subject list specific topics. Brainstorming helps in generating a lot of topics.

The next step is to analyze the audience and occasion to decide how to shape and direct your speech. Audience analysis is the study of audience knowledge, interests, and attitudes. Gather specific data about your audience to determine how members of the audience are alike and how they differ. Use this information to tailor your speech to audience concerns and attitudes. Also, consider how the occasion of the speech and its physical setting will affect your overall speech plan.

Once you have a speech topic and have accounted for your audience and setting, you can determine your speech goal and write a thesis statement. The general goal may be to entertain, to inform, or to persuade. The specific goal is a complete sentence that specifies the exact response the speaker wants from the audience. The five-step procedure for writing the specific speech goal includes (1) writing until your tentative speech goal is a complete sentence that states the specific response or behavior you want from your audience, (2) writing out at least three different wordings of the goal, (3) writing the goal as a sentence rather than as a question or fragment, (4) writing the goal so that it contains only one idea, and (5) revising the infinitive or infinitive phrase until it indicates the specific audience reaction desired. The thesis statement is a sentence that outlines the specific elements of the speech supporting the goal statement. An effective thesis statement may not be written until the research for the speech is complete.

Suggested Readings

Bender, David L., ed. *American Values: Opposing Viewpoints.* San Diego, CA: Greenhaven Press, 1989. Presents analyses of American political, social, economic, and religious values.

Corbett, Michael. *American Public Opinion: Trends, Processes, and Patterns.* New York: Longman, 1991. Supplies information about both current views on public issues and methods of taking and interpreting opinion polls.

Notes

1. *The Rhetoric and Poetics of Aristotle,* trans. W. Rhys Roberts (New York: Modern Library, 1984), pp. 121–126.

2. *Digest of Educational Statistics,* 25th ed. (Washington, DC: U.S. Government Printing Office, 1989), p. 31.

3. William A. Henry III, "Beyond the Melting Pot," *Time* (April 9, 1990), p. 29.

4. David L. Bender, ed., *American Values: Opposing Viewpoints* (San Diego, CA: Greenhaven Press, 1989).

5. Weekly newsmagazines are indexed in *Readers' Guide to Periodical Literature.* Thus, if you are looking for an article in a weekly newsmagazine, you would look in *Readers' Guide* under the topic you were researching.

**After you have read
this chapter, you
should be able to:**

*Identify sources
of information*

*Differentiate between factual
and opinion statements*

*Use verbal and visual
material in your speech*

Record data

Cite sources in your speeches

12

Finding, Using, and Recording Information

T asha was upset. The Student Senate was beginning hearings on complaints about course registration, and since she represented an important segment of the student body she felt a need to speak. What was bothering her was that although she had some strong opinions, she felt that she didn't have any specific information to communicate.

Tasha's experience is not unlike that of many of us. We believe that our views on subjects are worth being heard, but we just don't know how to go about explaining or supporting what we want to say.

ACTION STEP 2

Gather and evaluate verbal and visual material that you can use in the speech.

Once we have determined a speech goal that is adapted to our audience and occasion, we begin looking for the information to develop that goal. In this chapter, we'll consider what kinds of information to look for, where to look for it, how to record information, and how to cite it in our speeches.

Where to Look: Sources of Information

Benjamin Franklin once said, "An empty bag cannot stand upright." Without solid material, your speech will fold like Franklin's empty bag. To help you in your quest for high-quality information, in this section we consider the kinds of material you will look for to give substance to your speech. Effective speakers start with their own knowledge and experiences and then work outward through observation, interviews, surveys, and research.

Personal Knowledge

If you have chosen to speak on a topic you know something about, you may already have sufficient material to lay a solid foundation for your speech. For instance, athletes have special knowledge about their sports, coin collectors about coins, detective-fiction buffs about mystery novels, "do-it-yourselfers" about home repairs and gardening, musicians about music and instruments, farmers about animals or crops and equipment, and camp counselors about camping. For many of your speeches, then, you are your first, and perhaps your best, source of information. Your firsthand knowledge will contribute to the development of unique, imaginative, and original speeches.

Observation

For many topics, you can get good, specific information through careful observation. If, for instance, you are planning to talk about how newspapers are printed, you can learn about printing operations by touring your local newspaper printing plant and observing the process in action. If you want to talk about urban renewal in your downtown area, you can go downtown and look around. Observation adds a personal dimension to your speeches that can make them more informative as well as more interesting.

Good observers focus their attention. Suppose you wanted to learn more about the duties of partners in a mixed-doubles tennis match. Instead of just watching the match, which for most people means trying to follow the ball, you might focus on the server's partner. You might follow his or her every move for a game, trying to see such things as how his or her net technique differs depending on which side he or she is playing, whether it is first serve or second serve, and so on.

It helps to take notes during observations so that you remember what you see. By focusing on such specifics as net play, receiving technique, serving technique, and positioning, you will discover detailed information that can be used in a speech on teamwork required in mixed-doubles tennis.

Interviews

When you can identify people who have firsthand information, you might consider interviewing them. An *interview* involves asking questions designed to encourage people to share their information with you. Much of the information appearing in your local newspaper is likely to come from interviews. Will people take the time to talk with you? You'll be surprised at how cooperative people can be if you approach them correctly. Be sure to call or write well in advance to make an appointment.

When you have selected the person to interview, prepare a good list of questions. If you have questions prepared beforehand, you can maximize the time available and take full advantage of the people who are willing to talk with you. (For guidelines on interviewing, refer to Module A.)

Surveys

The *survey* is a variation of the interview. As we mentioned in Chapter 9, a survey is a list of one or more questions that can be asked of a great number of people. For such diverse topics as student reaction to a particular course, the local football team's chances in an upcoming game, or how well the council is governing the city, you can obtain useful information through a survey.

Surveys are usually comprised of yes-or-no questions, scaled questions, or open-ended questions.

Yes-or-no questions are designed to give you clear, unambiguous answers. For example:

> Do you believe that the College of Arts and Sciences should require all its students to take a three-hour course in Fundamentals of Effective Speaking for graduation?
>
> ____ Yes ____ No

A series of yes-or-no questions can provide a great deal of specific information in a short time.

Scaled questions differ from yes-or-no questions in that they allow for recording gradations in subject reaction.

Do you agree or disagree with the following statement:

> The College of Arts and Sciences should require all its students to take the three-hour course Fundamentals of Effective Speaking for graduation.

Strongly agree	Mildly agree	Undecided	Mildly disagree	Strongly disagree

Not all research happens in the library. Interviews allow the information seeker to probe for details, anecdotes, observations, and expert opinion—all elements that can add vividness and credibility to a speech.

By allowing the respondent more leeway, they yield answers with more depth than yes-or-no questions. Again, with a series of scaled questions, you can get a great deal of information in a short period of time.

Open-ended questions are those that encourage statement of opinion.

> What would be your response to a decision of the College of Arts and Sciences to require all its students to take the three-hour course Fundamentals of Effective Speaking for graduation?

Open-ended questions give you the greatest amount of depth but, because of the likelihood of a wide variety of responses, are the most difficult to process.

A survey can, of course, be considerably longer than one question. But the shorter the survey, the more likely you are to get a large number of responses. You will want to make sure that you have polled a large enough group and that you have sampled different segments of the relevant population before you attempt to draw any conclusions from your poll.

Written Sources

Effective speakers often find that some of their best material comes from written sources. Any good library provides sources that will enable you to access information on virtually any topic. For many speeches, the best material will come from what you read. Written sources are available on almost any speech topic.

Books. Books are especially good sources for major topics on which large amounts of material are available. Although your library is likely to have books on most any topic, you must know how to find what you need. In the past, libraries featured a card catalog. Although some libraries may still have a card catalog, many of them have transferred records of their holdings to a computer system. For instance, at the University of Cincinnati, the traditional card catalog no longer exists. Whether you are looking for books in a card catalog or on a computer, books are listed by title, author, and subject.

You may need to exercise some creativity in discovering the categories and subject listings under which useful books are catalogued. Suppose you are researching the topic "illiteracy." You may find little or nothing under that heading in the card catalog or computer file. With a few minutes of creative thinking, however, you should be able to come up with such additional headings as "literacy," "education—comparative," "reading," "reading comprehension," "reading disabilities," and so forth. You will often have to turn to alternative headings to discover the extent of your library's listings.

Periodicals. Periodicals are magazines and journals that appear at fixed periods—weekly, biweekly, monthly, quarterly, or yearly. Material you get from weekly, biweekly, and monthly magazines is more current than anything you will find in books. A periodical is thus likely to be your best source when your topic focuses on information that is less than two years old. Because it usually takes one to three years for current topics to appear in books and encyclopedias, it may be a waste of time to search the card catalog or encyclopedias for information. Occasionally, a book is rushed into print within six months of an event, but such speed is rare—and the worth of such a hastily prepared work is questionable. A periodical is also your best source when the topic is so limited in scope that it is unlikely to provide enough material for a book or when you are looking for a very specific aspect of a particular topic.

The Readers' Guide to Periodical Literature is an index of articles in some 200 popular magazines and journals, such as *Business Week, Ebony, Newsweek, Reader's Digest,* and *Vital Speeches.* The *Humanities Index* and the *Social Sciences Index* will lead you to articles in more than 300 scholarly periodicals each, such as the *American Journal of Sociology,* the *Economist, Modern Language Quarterly,* and *Philosophical Review.* The *Education Index* will lead you to articles in 350 English-language periodicals, yearbooks, and monographs.

Although you can do manual searches through these indexes, most university and public libraries subscribe to services that use a CD-ROM system to provide computerized indexes of all the bound-volume indexes cited above. For instance, the University of Cincinnati library subscribes to Wilson Databases, which gives access to all the indexes mentioned above.

Periodical indexes are published each year and in monthly and quarterly supplements for the current year. If the index you want to use is computerized, just indicate the subject, and sources will appear on the computer screen with the most recent publication date first. If the index you want to use is not computerized, you will need to determine when the relevant events occurred or when the topic was actively discussed. For example, if you are preparing a speech on the effects of political infomercials like those used by Ross Perot during the 1992 presidential campaign, begin your research in the index for 1992 and work forward and backward from there until the supply of articles dries up. Similarly, if you are preparing a speech on what it was like to be a television writer during the McCarthy era and you want material published during that time period, begin your research in the index for 1953, the height of the McCarthy era.

Encyclopedias. Most libraries have a recent edition of *Encyclopedia Britannica, Encyclopedia Americana,* or *World Book Encyclopedia.* An encyclopedia can be a good starting point for research. There are also specialized encyclopedias in such areas as religion, philosophy, and science. Encyclopedias give an excellent overview of many subjects and also provide bibliographies, which are lists of sources of information on a particular subject. But because the material is usually very general and may be years out of date, never limit your research to an encyclopedia.

Statistical Sources. Statistical sources present numerical information on a wide variety of subjects. When you need facts about demography, continents, heads of state, weather, or similar subjects, refer to one of the many single-volume sources that report such data. Two of the most popular sources in this category are the *World Almanac and Book of Facts* and the *Statistical Abstract.*

Biographical Sources. When you need accounts of a person's life, from thumbnail sketches to reasonably complete essays, you can turn to one of the many biographical sources available. In addition to full-length books and encyclopedia entries, consult such books as *Who's Who in America* and *International Who's Who.*

Newspapers. Newspaper articles are excellent sources of facts about and interpretations of contemporary issues. Use newspaper research in much the same way as magazine research—to gather information on subjects from a particular time in history. Your library probably holds both an index of your nearest major daily and the *New York Times Index.*

United States Government Publications. The following two government publications are especially useful for locating primary sources:

Federal Register. The *Register* publishes daily regulations and legal notices issued by the executive branch and all federal agencies. It is divided into sections such as rules and regulations and Sunshine Act meetings. Of special interest are announcements of hearings and investigations, committee meetings, and agency decisions and rulings.

Monthly Catalog of United States Government Publications. The *Monthly Catalog* covers publications of all branches of the federal government. It has semiannual and annual cumulative indexes by title, author/agency, and subject.

Electronic Databases. An *electronic database* is information stored so that it can be retrieved from a computer terminal. The advantages of college library electronic databases are that they can be searched much more quickly than their print counterparts, results can be printed or downloaded onto a floppy disk, and at most schools the use of databases is free of charge.

Depending on the size of your library, you may have access to such self-service databases as ERIC (700 educational journals and thousands of research reports collected by the U.S. Department of Education); INFOTRAC Expanded Academic Index (more than 1,000 journals and newspapers, emphasizing communication, history, humanities, law, political science, psychology, religion, sciences, social sciences, sociology); MEDLINE (some 3,600 journals in biomedicine, health sciences, medicine); PSYCLIT (more than 1,400 English and foreign-language journals in education, psychology, sociology); SOCIOFILE (communication, criminal justice, demography, geography, political science, sociology, speech); and LEXIS/NEXIS (accounting, business, government, law, medicine), to name just a few.

By using these databases you can compile bibiolographies and view abstracts, or even full articles, on the computer screen. Reference librarians should know which databases your library subscribes to and can help you learn to access them. (For an illustration of the potential of a computer search, see Tips for On-Line Database Searches, on pages 294–295.)

National and International Networking.   Today, anyone with access to a personal computer also has access to national and international electronic networks. Most colleges and universities are now connected to Internet, an international electronic network of networks. This superhighway of information provides access to an ever-increasing number of information resources. Students and faculty use Internet to give them access to databases and bulletin boards, scholarly and professional electronic discussion groups, library holdings at colleges and universities across the United States and abroad, and exchange of e-mail (electronic mail).

Specialty Indexes.   Many libraries also contain specialty indexes of recent topics. Consult the reference librarian for a detailed account of your library's bibliographies, indexes, and special resources. Don't hesitate to ask library staff for help; helping library patrons is a major professional responsibility, and with very few exceptions, librarians will gladly offer their assistance. The best way to learn about all of your library's resources is with the help of its staff.

Skimming Sources

For most topics, you will uncover far more sources than you can use. How can you quickly evaluate a source to determine whether or not to read it in full? A method that can help you make this decision is *skimming,* or rapidly going through the work to determine what is covered and how. If you are evaluating a magazine article, spend a minute or two finding out what it covers. Does it really present information on the exact area of the topic you are exploring? Does it contain any documented statistics, examples, or quotable opinions? (We'll examine the kinds of information to look for in the next section.) Is the author qualified to draw valid conclusions? If you are evaluating a book, read the table of contents carefully, look at the index, and skim pertinent chapters, asking the same questions as you would for a magazine article. Skimming helps you decide which sources should be read in full, which should be read in part, and which should be abandoned. Minutes spent in such evaluation will save hours of reading.

*You've logged onto a remote database to begin an information search, and you dis-
cover thousands of potential sources on your topic. How do you cope with this
wealth of information—especially since you're paying for every second you spend
on-line? As shown by the following example (from a textbook for journalism students), the key is to plan your search strategy in advance.*

Databases most helpful to journalistic
researchers come in two forms: bibliographic and full-text. A *bibliographic*
database is an enormous index, or set
of indexes, that provides the information necessary to locate the actual
material. This kind of database can tell
you who wrote what article in which
issue of what journal. It might even
give you a two-sentence summary of
the article. But if you want to read the
article for yourself, you need to either
locate it in the library or plug into a
full-text database. There you will find
the entire contents of selected magazines, newspapers, reports, and documents. ...

For the purposes of this search, we
will log on to DIALOG, the country's
largest database vendor. Before we
turn on the computer (or ask an on-line
expert to do so), we plan our strategy,
focusing on answers to these vital
questions:

1. What kind of material are we
   looking for (articles in consumer
   publications, primary research,

government statistics, names of
experts)?

2. What keywords define and limit
   our topic?

3. What database or databases available from this vendor would be
   most likely to contain the kind of
   information we need?

Let's begin with a search on
domestic violence issues. First, we
answer the three vital questions:

1. *Kind of material.* Let's say
   we're looking for primary research on
   domestic violence, the kind found in
   journals that serve the fields of sociology, psychology, psychiatry, mental
   health, therapy, and the like.

2. *Keywords.* We know from
   past experience (and from looking at
   the Library of Congress Subject
   Headings) that a number of descriptors
   work with this topic: family violence,
   conjugal violence, domestic violence.

3. *Database.* Looking through
   the most recent DIALOG Database
   Catalog, we find a number of possibilities, among them a database called

If you are compiling a periodical bibliography on computer, you will discover
that the services your library subscribes to are likely to feature a short abstract for
each article that comes up on the computer screen. This will help you determine

"Family Resources." The description tells us that the database contains bibliographic references from more than 1,200 journals, books, newsletters, and government documents on research related to the family. Dating back more than twenty years, the database covers the disciplines of medicine, psychology, sociology, and education. This all sounds promising.

[Here is] how the search progresses:

a. We log on to the database and punch in our keywords (*conjugal* or *domestic* or *family* coupled with *vio*). Using all possible terms at once increases the efficiency of the search. After a second or two of searching, the computer responds by telling us that 1,751 items in the database contain these keywords.

b. We ask the computer to limit these items in several ways. First, we want only journal articles (not items from newsletters or government documents). The computer finds 920 references.

c. Now we limit the search to 1985–1990 (688 references).

d. Now we limit ourselves to the most current material, 1988–1990 (279 references).

e. Finally, to increase the chances of the articles' being on target for our search, we ask the computer to find references that actually have the keywords in the titles (23 references).

f. Now we ask the distant computer to send the titles of these references. (Asking for titles is free; asking for full citations costs per citation.) Looking at these titles, we find several that sound promising.

g. We ask the distant computer to send full citations plus abstracts of those articles that sound promising.

h. Because this database also includes "human resources" (otherwise known as "people"), we decide to use the computer to search for national experts on family violence. These people may make good interview subjects. Note that each listing gives the person's name, affiliation, phone numbers, present position, and areas of expertise. This search, from start to finish, took six minutes and cost about $10....

Perhaps someday databases will entirely replace library collections—but that day is still in the distant future. Today's journalistic information gatherers should begin to seriously educate themselves about computerized searching while continuing to hone their traditional searching methods. Computerized and traditional methods complement each other and can lead to faster, more efficient, more productive information gathering. ■

SOURCE: Lauren Kessler and Duncan McDonald, *The Search: Information Gathering for the Mass Media* (Belmont, CA: Wadsworth, 1992), pp. 83–84, 88–89, 98.

which sources you want to read in their entirety. Once you have the sources in hand, however, you'll still need to follow a skimming procedure.

By Yourself

For one of the three speech goals you wrote in Chapter 11 (see p. 283), answer the following questions:

1. What is your personal knowledge base for this topic?
2. What, if anything, could you observe to broaden your personal knowledge base?
3. Whom could you interview for additional information for this topic?
4. List three specific articles or books you have found that provide information for your topic.

What to Look for: Types of Speech Material

Whether you draw information from your own background or from interviews, surveys, or books, you will be looking for supporting information in various forms.

Supporting Information: Facts and Opinions

Most informative and persuasive speeches require information directly supporting your assertions and arguments. The two major types of supportive information for speeches are factual statements and expert opinions.

Factual Statements.   *Factual statements* are those that can be verified. "Compact disks are 'read' with a laser beam." "The Macintosh Performa comes with a CD-ROM port." "More than 4,000 people died and more than 22,000 were injured in Kobe, Japan, during the 1995 earthquake." "Johannes Gutenberg invented printing from movable type in the 1400s." These are all statements of fact that can be verified.

Statements of fact, including those made in the sciences, are really statements of probability. The probability may be so high as to be, for all practical purposes, certainty, or it may be a good deal less. For instance, "more than 4,000 people died and more than 22,000 were injured in Kobe, Japan, during the 1995 earthquake" means that at least 4,000 persons died (additional persons may have died but had not yet been identified at the time the statement was made) and that compilations of data suggest at least 22,000 were injured. Raymond Nickerson, in his book *Reflections on Reasoning,* says that when dealing with factual information you need to be concerned with its degree of confidence.[1] If you read a statement that asserts a fact you want to feature in your speech, one way to attempt to verify it (or to at least determine that its accuracy is highly probable) is to check it against material from another article or book on the same subject. Although checking accuracy may seem a waste of time, you'll be surprised at the difference in "facts" reported in two or more sources. If at least two sources say essentially the same thing, you can be more confident. On the other hand, if two or more sources give different slants on the material, you will know that what is being discussed may be a matter of opinion.

Still, verifying factual information is not always easy, and many times accepted "facts" turn out to be totally wrong. In her book *Who Stole Feminism?* Christina Hoff Sommers[2] gives several examples of misuse of factual statements. For instance, in January 1993 newspapers and television networks reported an alarming finding: incidents of domestic battery tended to rise by 40 percent on Super Bowl Sunday. NBC, which was broadcasting the game that year, made special pleas to men to stay calm. Journalists across the country accepted the 40-percent figure at face value. Ken Ringle, a reporter at the *Washington Post,* did not. He found that the story had no basis in fact. Sommers devotes almost a dozen pages to how this figure got originally presented and how a variety of studies show far different results. Yet, we continue to hear this figure taken as fact.[3]

Expert Opinion.　A second kind of useful supportive material is expert opinion. *Expert opinion* can range from qualified predictions to interpretations of facts made by authorities in a particular subject area. If a noted economist states that as a result of the increase in inflation figures for the previous two months, interest rates are likely to rise as well, that would be a qualified prediction. If the same economist concludes that illiteracy contributes to poverty, based on facts giving the numbers of illiterate Americans and the kinds of problems illiterate people face, that would be an interpretation.

While opinions cannot entirely take the place of documented facts, expert opinion can be used to interpret and give weight to facts that you have discovered. Moreover, in situations where you cannot get facts, where they are inconclusive, or where they need to be supplemented, you will have to further support your claims with expert opinion.

The quality of opinion depends on whether its source is an expert on the matter at hand. If an ophthalmologist or a police chief states an opinion about the relationship between drug abuse and birth defects, the statement is not evidence because their specific expertise lies in other areas. On the other hand, if a pediatrician specializing in the care of at-risk newborns asserts that such defects occur in higher numbers when the mothers are drug users, then that opinion is expert. Of course, opinions are most trustworthy when they are accompanied by factual data. If the physician can cite data from reputable scientific studies, the opinion is worth even more.

How do you choose experts? How do you tell an expert from a "quack"? First, the person should have high standing in his or her field. Second, the person must be an expert in the matter at hand. For instance, to give testimony in a trial determining whether a document was written by the person named, an attorney will seek the opinion of someone who is an acknowledged authority on handwriting analysis.

Moreover, the attorney will use the handwriting expert's opinion only on whether the person named wrote the document, not on whether the person who wrote the document committed a crime.

If you plan to use expert opinions in your speech, identify them as opinions and indicate to your audience the level of confidence that should be attached to the statement. For instance, an informative speaker might say, "The temperatures throughout the last half of the 1980s were much higher than average. Paul Jorgenson, a space biologist, believes that these higher-than-average temperatures represent the first stages of the greenhouse effect, but the significance of these temperatures is not completely accepted as fact."

Verbal and Visual Forms of Material

Factual statements, expert opinions, and other material gathered from your research may be presented in a variety of forms. Some material you find may be in a straightforward form that you can use just as it is. For instance, if you found that Joe Jones had graduated from high school without learning how to read, you might present that fact in your speech. Or you might present that fact as one in a series of examples or as part of a comparison, or you might develop it into a narrative.

Depending on your topic and speech goal, you may use research material verbally in any of the following ways: as examples, illustrations, statistics, anecdotes, narratives, comparisons, contrasts, quotable explanations and opinions, definitions, and descriptions.

Examples and Illustrations. *Examples* are specific instances that illustrate or explain a general statement. The generalization "The quality of American cars is beginning to rival that of foreign cars," for instance, may be illustrated or explained with the following specific example: "The frequency-of-repair records for 1993 and 1994 Ford Escorts and Pontiac Grand Ams are much closer than in previous years to those of cars made by Nissan and Toyota." Examples are a common mode of idea development because they are usually readily available or easily constructed. More important, they provide concrete detail that makes a general statement more meaningful to the audience.

You can use examples individually or in series. In the following passage, notice how Mario Cuomo, then governor of New York, uses a series of examples to support his point about the importance of family education.

> I learned to do all the basic things from my family before I ever went to school.... The real tough teaching jobs were left up to my mom and pop: things like tying my shoes, not playing with fire, learning my way to the potty, picking up my own toys and socks, not hitting my brother or sister, standing up to the bully down the block. In short, I learned to be a worker, a citizen, a neighbor, a friend, a husband and I hope a civilized human being all under the tutelage of this marvelous university called the family and all before I set foot in a school.[4]

Although you will want to develop most of the general statements in your speech with real examples, at times you may want to develop generalizations with hypothetical examples. Hypothetical examples are those drawn from reflections about future events; they develop the idea "What if … ?" In the following excerpt, John A. Ahladas presents hypothetical examples of what it will be like in the year A.D. 2039 if global warming continues.

> In New York, workers are building levees to hold back the rising tidal waters of the Hudson River, now lined with palm trees. In Louisiana, 100,000 acres of wetland are steadily being claimed by the sea. In Kansas, farmers learn to live with drought as a way of life and struggle to eke out an existence in the increasingly dry and dusty heartland. . . . And reports arrive from Siberia of bumper crops of corn and wheat from a longer and warmer growing season.[5]

When you plan to use only one example in your speech and you want to make the most of it, then cast the example in illustration form. An *illustration* is an example that has been developed with added detail. The following segment shows the difference between casting the same information in example form and in illustration form:

> *Generalization:* Most people want to accomplish an objective with the least amount of effort.
> *Example:* When entering a building, people will wait for an open door rather than use the energy to open a closed door.
> *Illustration:* "I remember watching the entrance of a large office building. There were five doors. The one on the far left was open, the rest closed. Most everybody used the open door, even waiting for people to come out before they could enter just because the door was easier than the effort of pushing another door open. This is true of much of life."[6]

Now let us consider guidelines for selecting and using examples. First, examples should relate directly to the generalization. If you say "American car manufacturers are becoming more sensitive to environmental issues" and then give the example "Chrysler Corporation has run a series of commercials urging drivers not to throw litter on the highways," the example may concern the environment, but it does not state how Chrysler Corporation is doing anything that shows sensitivity to environmental issues.

Second, the examples should be clear and specific enough to create a clear picture for the audience. Suppose you said "American car manufacturers give long warranties." Giving the examples that "Chrysler and General Motors are now giving five- to seven-year warranties on all models" would be specific. Saying "Chrysler and General Motors are now giving pretty long warranties on all models" would not be.

Third, the examples you use, even if true, should not be misleading. For instance, if Chrysler were the only manufacturer to give a long warranty, it would be

Use statistics from only the most reliable sources and double-check any startling statistics with another source.

unethical to support the generalization "American car manufacturers give long warranties" with the Chrysler example if you knew that it was the only American car company with such a warranty.

Because specifics both clarify and substantiate, it's a good idea to follow this rule of thumb: Never let a generalization stand without at least one example.

Statistics.   *Statistics* are compilations of examples. Just as two examples are better than one, statistics representing large numbers of examples are more powerful yet. Statistical statements, such as "Seven out of every ten local citizens voted in the last election" or "The cost of living rose 4.5 percent in 1991," enable you to pack a great deal of information into a small package. When statistics are well used, they can provide impressive support for a point; when they are poorly used, they may be boring and, in some instances, downright deceiving. Here are some guidelines on using statistics effectively:

   1.   *Use only statistics whose reliability you can verify.* Using statistics from only the most reliable sources and double-checking any startling statistics with another source will guard against the use of faulty statistics. For example, it is important to double-check statistics that you find in such sources as paid advertisements or publications distributed by special-interest groups. Be especially wary if your source does not itself provide documentation of the statistics it reports.

   2.   *Use recent statistics so that your audience will not be misled.* For example, if you used the statistic that only 2 of 100, or 2 percent, of U.S. Senators are women (true in 1992), you would be misleading your audience. If you wanted to make a point about the number of women in the Senate, you would want the most recent figure (8 in 1995). When citing statistics, check that your source gives the year or range of years to which the statistics apply.

3. *Use statistics comparatively whenever possible.* By themselves, statistics are hard to interpret, but when used comparatively, they have much greater impact. In a speech on chemical waste, Donald Baeder points out that whereas in the past chemicals were measured in parts per million, today they are measured in parts per billion or even parts per trillion. Had he stopped at that point, the audience would have had little sense of the immensity of the figures. Notice how he goes on to use comparisons to put the meaning of the statistics in perspective:

> One part per billion is the equivalent of one drop—one drop!—of vermouth in two 36,000 gallon tanks of gin and that would be a very dry martini even by San Francisco standards! One part per trillion is the equivalent of one drop in two thousand tank cars.[7]

In your comparisons, be careful not to present a misleading picture. If you say that during the past six months Company A doubled its sales while its nearest competitor, Company B, improved by only 40 percent, the implication would be misleading if you did not indicate the size of the base; Company B, with a larger base of sales, could have more sales and proportionately more impressive sales growth than Company A.

4. *Do not overuse statistics.* Although statistics can be an excellent way to present a great deal of material quickly, be careful not to overuse them. A few pertinent numbers are far more effective than a battery of statistics. When you believe you must use many statistics, try preparing a visual aid, perhaps a chart, to help your audience visualize them.

Anecdotes and Narratives. *Anecdotes* are brief, often amusing stories; *narratives* are tales, accounts, personal experiences, or lengthier stories. Each presents material in story form. Do you remember the last time one of your professors said, "That reminds me of a story"? Probably more people listened to the story than to any other part of the lecture. Because holding audience interest is so important in a speech and because audience attention is likely to be captured by a story, anecdotes and narratives are worth looking for, creating, and using. For a two-minute speech, you have little time to tell a detailed story, so one or two anecdotes or a very short narrative would be preferable. In longer speeches, however, including at least one longer anecdote or narrative will pay dividends in holding audience attention as well as in fostering audience understanding.

The key to using stories is to make sure that the point of the story states or reinforces the point you make in your speech. In a speech about telecommunication, Randall Tobias, vice chairman of AT&T, made a point about the promise and the threat of technology.

A lighthearted story I heard from a scientist-colleague illustrates the point.

A theologian asked the most powerful supercomputer, "Is there a God?" The computer said it lacked the processing power to know. It asked to be connected to all the other supercomputers in the world. Still, it was not enough power. So the computer was hooked up to all the mainframes in the world, and then all the minicomputers, and then all the personal computers. The theologian asked for the final time, "Is there a God?" And the computer replied: "There is now."[8]

Neither the anecdote nor the narrative needs to be humorous to be effective. In a speech on the subject of blacks and women in universities, Patti Gillespie told the following story to show the inaccuracy of perceptions even among university faculty:

I recently heard a male senior professor say with considerable pride that on his faculty there were now an equal number of men and women. His observation was quickly affirmed by one of the junior men in the department. Because I knew the department and could not get the figures to tally, I asked that we go through the faculty list together. Both men were surprised when we discovered that, by actual count, the current faculty consisted of nine men and five women, that is almost two men for each woman.[9]

Comparisons and Contrasts. One of the best ways to give meaning to new ideas is through comparison and contrast. *Comparisons* illuminate a point by showing similarities. Although you can easily create comparisons using information you have found, you should still keep your eye open for creative comparisons developed by the authors of the books and articles you have found.

Comparisons may be literal or figurative. Literal comparisons show similarities of real things: "The walk from the lighthouse back up the hill to the parking lot is equal to walking up the stairs of a thirty-story building." Figurative comparisons express one thing in terms normally denoting another: "I always envisioned myself as a four-door sedan. I didn't know she was looking for a sports car!"

Comparisons make ideas not only clearer but also more vivid. Notice how Stephen Joel Trachtenberg, in speech to the Newington High School Scholars' Breakfast, used a figurative comparison to demonstrate the importance of being willing to take risks, even in the face of danger:

The eagle flying high always risks being shot at by some harebrained human with a rifle. But eagles and young eagles like you still prefer the view from that risky height to what is available flying with the turkeys far, far below.[10]

Whereas comparisons show similarities, *contrasts* show differences. Notice how this humorous contrast dramatizes the difference between "participation" and "commitment":

If this morning you had bacon and eggs for breakfast, I think it illustrates the difference. The eggs represented "participation" on the part of the chicken. The bacon represented "total commitment" on the part of the pig![11]

Quotations.   When you find an explanation, an opinion, or a brief anecdote that seems to be exactly what you are looking for, you may quote it directly in your speech. Bear in mind that audiences want to listen to your ideas and arguments; they do not want to hear a string of long quotations. Nevertheless, a well-selected quotation might be perfect in one or two key places.

Quotations can both explain and vivify. Often another person has made a point in a way that is far clearer or more vivid than we could make it. For example, in her speech "The Dynamics of Discovery," Catherine Ahles, vice president for college relations at Macomb Community College, used the following quote from Helen Keller to show the detrimental effects of pessimism: "No pessimist ever discovered the secrets of the stars . . . or sailed to an uncharted land . . . or opened a new heaven to the human spirit."[12]

Frequently, historical or literary quotations can reinforce a point vividly. In his introduction to a speech on "Integrity," for example, Ronald W. Roskens quoted Sir Harold Macmillan, the former British prime minister, as having said, "If you want to know the meaning of life . . . don't ask a politician."[13] C. Charles Bahr, chairman of Bahr International, in a speech on telling the truth to sick companies, quoted Mark Twain on the importance of telling the truth: "Always do right. It will amaze some people and astonish the rest."[14]

To take advantage of such opportunities, you need access to one or more of the many available books of quotations. One is the *International Thesaurus of Quotations,* compiled by Rhoda Thomas Tripp.[15] Another is *Bartlett's Familiar Quotations,* which came out in a new edition in 1992.[16] Library reference sections carry several books of quotations. These books are often organized by topic, which helps in finding a particularly appropriate quote to use in your speech.

Keep in mind that when you use a direct quotation, it is necessary to credit the person who formulated it. Using any quotation or close paraphrase without crediting its source is plagiarism.

Definitions and Descriptions.   Information is clearer to audiences when words are defined carefully and material is described completely. Often research will turn up definitions and descriptions that you can quote or adapt to suit your speech.

A *definition* is a statement that explains what something is or what a word means. Our communication is based on the assumption that we, as members of a culture, share common meanings of words. Nevertheless, many of the words we use in our speeches, especially when they concern specialized or technical knowledge, may not be understood by our audiences. As a result, we must define words carefully when they are important to audience understanding. For instance, if you said that your computer comes with a mouse, you would add, "a hand-operated device that lets you easily control the location of the pointer on your screen."

A *description* is a verbal picture or an account in words. We can describe a room, a city, a park, a dog, a computer system, or any other object, place, person, or thing, with the goal of enabling the audience to form a mental picture that corresponds to the actual thing. For example, a classroom might be described as twenty by twenty feet, with five rows of wooden chairs bolted to the floor and a single center aisle as the only way of getting to the seats.

Visual Aids.   So far, all of our discussion of developmental material has focused on verbal material, but many speeches gain in effectiveness from the use of visual aids. A visual aid is a form of speech development that allows the audience to see as well as to hear about the material. Visual aids are likely to serve one of two functions in a speech: (1) as a means of showing information so that, as the speech progresses, members of the audience will gain visual as well as auditory impressions, or (2) as a means of creating moods, emotions, and attitudes that supplement or take the place of verbal information.

The major rationale for the use of visual aids in any speech is that audiences are more likely to understand and retain information when it is presented to more than one sense. Whether or not a picture is literally worth a thousand words, research has shown that people learn considerably more when ideas appeal to both the eye and the ear than when they appeal to the ear alone.[17] As you prepare your speeches, you should consider graphic visuals, including charts, diagrams, maps, drawings, flipcharts, photographs, films, slides, overheads, and the chalkboard. (Detailed discussions of definitions, descriptions, and visual aids can be found in Chapter 16.)

Practice in Using Research Material

By Yourself

Develop one of the following three statements with any three of the following types of material: an example or illustration, an anecdote or a narrative, a comparison or contrast, statistics, or a quotable explanation or opinion.

a.   Women are more careful (careless) drivers than men.

b.   _____ has a very good team this year.

c.   SAT scores have risen (fallen) during the past five years.

Recording Data and Citing Sources

Whether the research materials you find are facts, opinions, quotations, or other forms of information, you need to record the data accurately and keep a careful account of your sources so that they can be cited appropriately.

Recording Data

It is important to record data so that you can provide the information and its source in a speech or report the documentation to anyone who might question the information's accuracy. When question periods are provided at the end of a speech, members of an audience will often ask for sources of information. Whether or not there is a question period, however, listeners need the assurance that they can find the material used in your speech if they should decide to look for it.

How should you record these materials you uncover in your research (including not only research into printed sources but also personal knowledge, observation, interviews, and surveys)? Because most speakers use only some of their research material and are never sure of the final order in which it will be used, it's best to record the material so that it can be easily selected and moved around. The note-card method is probably the best.

In the note-card method, each factual statement or authoritative opinion, along with bibliographical documentation, is recorded on a separate four-by-six-inch or larger index card. Although it may seem easier to record all material from one source on a single sheet of paper (or to photocopy source material), sorting and arranging material is much easier when each item is recorded separately. On each card, indicate the topic of the recorded information, the information, and the publication data. Any part of the information that is quoted directly should be enclosed with quotation marks. Publication data will differ depending on whether the information is from a book or from a periodical or newspaper. For a book write the name of the author, the title, the publisher, the date, and the page number from which the information was taken. For a periodical or newspaper, write the name of the author if one is given, the title of the article, the name of the periodical or newspaper, the date, and the page number from which the information was taken. List bibliographical information in enough detail so that the information can be found later if needed. Figure 12.1 illustrates a useful note-card form.

As your stack of information grows, you can then sort the material. Each item goes under a heading to which it is related. For instance, the card in Figure 12.1 might be indexed under the heading "Poverty in America," if you had more than one card with information related to poverty. Likewise, if you had evidence cards related to ongoing problems throughout the economy, you would make another copy of this card and sort it under the heading "Stagnant Economy."

The number of sources that you should use depends in part on the type of speech. For a narrative of a personal experience, you obviously will be the main, if not the only, source. For reports and persuasive speeches, however, speakers ordinarily use several sources. One-source speeches often lead to plagiarism; furthermore, a one- or two-source speech simply does not provide sufficient breadth of material. By selecting, combining, adding, cutting, and revising, you can develop an original approach to your topic.

Citing Sources in Speeches

In your speeches, as in any communication in which you use ideas that are not your own, try to work the source of your material into your presentation. Such efforts to

Topic: Number of Americans in Poverty

The Census Bureau released a report showing that the number of Americans living below the poverty line last year—defined as an income of $14,763 for a family of four—climbed to more than 39 million, or 15% of the nation's population.

"America, the Poorer," _Time_, October 17, 1994, p.21.

Figure 12.1 *A useful note-card form*

include sources not only help the audience evaluate the content but also add to your credibility. In addition, citing sources will give concrete evidence of the depth of your research. Failure to cite sources, especially when you are presenting information that is meant to substantiate a controversial point, is unethical.

In a written report, ideas taken from other sources are designated by footnotes; in a speech these notations must be included within the context of your statement of the material. Your citation need not be a complete representation of all the bibliographical information. Figure 12.2 gives examples of several appropriate source citations.

Although you do not want to clutter your speech with bibliographical citations, make sure to mention the sources of your most important information.

Practice in Using Note Cards

By Yourself

1. Pick at least three different sources that you identified under Practice in Identifying Sources (p. 296). Then complete six note-cards, four of factual state-

> "According to an article about Japanese workers in last week's <u>Time</u> magazine . . .
>
> "In the latest Gallup poll, cited in the February 10th issue of <u>Newsweek</u> . . .
>
> "But to get a complete picture we have to look at the statistics. According to the 1992 <u>Statistical Abstract</u>, the level of production for the European Economic Community rose from . . .
>
> "In a speech on business ethics delivered to the Public Relations Society of America last November, Preston Townly, CEO of the Conference Board, said . . .

Figure 12.2 *Examples of source citations*

ments and two of expert opinions. On your note-cards cite the name of the author if one is given, the title of the article or book, and the publication data. If the source is a book, include the publisher, the year it was published, and the page number of the information; if the source is a periodical, include the date of the publication and the page number of the information.

    2.   Practice ways of citing each of these sources.

Summary

Effective speaking requires high-quality information. You need to know where to look for information, what kind of information to look for, how to record it, and how to cite your sources in your speeches.

    To find material, begin by exploring your own knowledge and work outward through observation, interviews, surveys, and written sources. Look for material in books, periodicals, encyclopedias, statistical sources, biographical sources, newspapers, government publications, computer databases, Internet, and specialty indexes. By skimming material you can quickly evaluate sources to determine whether or not to read them in full.

It is quite likely that many of the catalogs and indexes that you would like to use can be accessed electronically. You will want to check with your reference librarian to see which materials are on-line.

Two major types of supporting material for speeches are factual statements and expert opinions. Factual statements report verifiable occurrences. Expert opinions are interpretations of facts made by qualified authorities. Although you will use some of your material as you find it, you may want to present the information in a different form. Depending on your topic and speech goal, you may use facts and opinions orally as examples, illustrations, anecdotes, narratives, statistics, quotations, comparisons, contrasts, definitions, and descriptions. Likewise, you may show information with visual aids.

A good method for recording material that you may want to use in your speech is to record each item of information, along with necessary bibliographical documentation, on a separate note-card. As your stack of information grows, sort the material under common headings. During the speech, cite the sources for the information.

Suggested Readings

Kessler, Lauren, and McDonald, Duncan. *The Search: Information Gathering for the Mass Media.* Belmont, CA: Wadsworth, 1992. In addition to a thorough review of written sources, has chapters on finding and using expert opinion and methods of evaluating evidence.

Rubin, Rebecca B.; Rugin, Alan M.; and Piele, Linda J., *Communication Research: Strategies and Sources,* 3d ed. Belmont, CA: Wadsworth, 1993. Includes a description of research sources as well as specific guidance for research projects in the field of communication.

Notes

1. Raymond S. Nickerson, *Reflections on Reasoning* (Hillsdale, NJ: Erlbaum, 1986), 13.
2. Christina Hoff Sommers, *Who Stole Feminism? How Women Have Betrayed Women* (New York: Simon & Schuster, 1994).
3. Ibid., pp. 188–198.
4. Mario M. Cuomo, "The Family," *Vital Speeches,* February 15, 1980, p. 268.
5. John A. Ahladas, "Global Warming," *Vital Speeches,* April 1, 1989, p. 382.
6. Guernsey Jones, "How Deep Are Your Convictions?" *Vital Speeches,* June 1, 1987, p. 493.
7. Donald L. Baeder, "Chemical Wastes," *Vital Speeches,* June 1, 1980, p. 497.
8. Randall L. Tobias, "In Today Walks Tomorrow: Shaping the Future of Telecommunication," *Vital Speeches,* February 15, 1993, p. 273.
9. Patti P. Gillespie, "Campus Stories, or the Cat Beyond the Canvas," *Vital Speeches,* February 1, 1988, p. 237.
10. Stephen Joel Trachtenberg, "Five Ways in Which Thinking Is Dangerous," *Vital Speeches,* August 15, 1986, p. 653.
11. G. Michael Durst, "The Manager as a Developer," *Vital Speeches,* March 1, 1989, pp. 309–310.
12. Catherine B. Ahles, "The Dynamics of Discovery: Creating Your Own Opportunities," *Vital Speeches,* March 15, 1993, p. 352.
13. Ronald W. Roskens, "Integrity," *Vital Speeches,* June 1, 1989, p. 511.
14. C. Charles Bahr, "Sick Companies Don't Have to Die," *Vital Speeches,* September 1, 1988, p. 685.
15. *The International Thesaurus of Quotations,* compiled by Rhoda Thomas Tripp (New York: Harper & Row, 1987).
16. Justin Kaplan, general editor, *Bartlett's Familiar Quotations* (Boston: Little, Brown, 1992).
17. Bernardette M. Gadzella and Deborah A. Whitehead, "Effects of Auditory and Visual Modalities in Recall of Words," *Perceptual and Motor Skills* 40 (February 1975): 260.

After you have read this chapter you should be able to:

Create or build audience interest

Adapt to your audience's level of understanding

Develop information

Reinforce or change an audience's attitude toward your topic

Build the audience's perception of you as a speaker

Write an audience adaptation strategy

13

Adapting
to Audiences

Dan had gathered a wide variety of information for his speech. As he pondered which information he should use and how he should use it, he began to get frustrated. When he shared his frustrations with his friend Gloria, she looked at him and asked, "Well, Dan, doesn't what you include and how you use it depend on who you're going to be talking with?" Dan slowly shook his head and said, "Of course—I forgot all about the audience!"

ACTION STEP 3

Develop a strategy for adapting material to your specific speech audience.

Aristotle, whose rhetorical writings provide the base for much of our public-speaking theory, wrote that the audience was the end and object of a speech.[1] Thus, the third action step of an effective speech plan is audience adaptation. Regardless of the goal of your speech, the success of that speech will depend on how it is adapted to the specific audience you are addressing.

Audience adaptation is the active process of relating material to audience interests, knowledge, and attitudes. Because members of each audience you face will present different profiles, you will need to consider a strategy for adapting to them by creating or building their interest, by relating to their level of understanding, and by reinforcing or changing their attitude toward you or your information. Adaptation is central to all of the remaining steps of speech preparation. In this chapter, we lay the groundwork for that strategy; in the following chapters, we continue means of adapting through organization and presentation.

Creating or Building Audience Interest

An audience analysis can help you determine potential audience interest in a topic (see Figure 11.2, Audience Analysis Checklist, on p. 275). If you predict that your audience will have an immediate interest in your topic, then your goal is to maintain or build that interest; if you predict that your audience may not have an initial interest, then your goal is to create interest. What determines whether an audience will find information interesting? Most people's interest is determined by whether they believe that the information has personal impact—that it relates specifically to *them*.

One strategy for showing personal impact is to stress the timeliness of the information—how listeners can use the information *now*. For some speeches, the timeliness of the information may be obvious. Suppose you are a company division manager giving a speech to employees about the specific changes in the newly installed version of their word-processing system. Because employees need to understand these changes now, you need only briefly mention the importance of the changes to them.

The test of your creativity comes when your audience doesn't recognize the timeliness of your information. Suppose you are giving a speech on the criteria for evaluating the quality of diamonds. Without your prompting, the majority of the audience may not view diamond evaluation as high-priority information. If, however, you can get them to acknowledge that on some special occasion (a wedding, birthday, or anniversary) they may be considering buying a diamond ring, earring, or necklace, your listeners are more likely to see information on evaluating diamonds as personally relevant.

A second strategy for demonstrating personal impact is to show how the information relates to the audience's personal space. Saying "Let me bring this closer to home by showing you. . . ." is a direct attempt to show spatial impact. The strategy works because people see information as important when they perceive it as affecting "their own backyard." If, for instance, you were giving a report on the difficulties that the EPA is having with its environmental cleanup campaigns, people will listen more closely if you give examples in their own community rather than examples from other parts of the country. If you don't have local information, take time to find it. For the EPA topic, a telephone call to the local or regional EPA office or the local newspaper will get you the information you need to make the connection.

A third strategy for demonstrating personal impact is to stress the seriousness of the information. Information that has a direct physical impact (toxic waste affects the health of all of us), economic impact (waste cleanup and disposal are expensive—they raise our taxes), or psychological impact (toxic waste erodes the quality of our life and the lives of our children), will be given more attention than information that does not. For instance, think of how classroom attention picks up when the professor reveals that a particular piece of information is going to "be on the test." This economic impact (not paying attention can *cost* us a lower grade) is often enough to jolt us into attention. Most of us just don't put our attention into high gear unless we see the seriousness of information.

By showing your audience that the issues you raise are timely, affect their personal space, and are serious, you can reinforce the relevance of almost any topic. The more remote the impact appears to be, the harder you will have to work to show that impact.

For example, suppose you want to help your classmates understand how they can determine readability levels of books and magazines. Think for a minute: What could you say that might show timeliness? or impact on personal space? or seriousness? The following passage illustrates effective use of these strategies:

> Have you complained recently that a reading assignment was giving you fits? Have you ever said, "I just can't seem to understand this stuff even though I'm spending hours going over it"? Most of us have experienced this kind of frustration. Although we may have a gut reaction that it's the reading material that's at fault, we may still question our lack of concentration or ability. Yet, many times your gut reaction is correct.
>
> How can you tell whether it's you or the reading material that is at fault? Perhaps the best way is by taking a few minutes to determine its readability level. Today, I'm going to share with you how you can quickly and easily test the readability level of books and magazines.

Notice how the speaker has shown timeliness ("complained recently") and economic impact ("spending hours"). Notice also how the speaker emphasizes "you" and "we" and uses questions throughout. We'll consider these stylistic means of building adaptation in Chapter 15.

In addition to an overall strategy for creating and building interest, you also need strategies for jump-starting attention in the midst of the speech. To deal with lapses in attention, you need to prepare yourself with anecdotes, examples, and startling information. Think of the times that your mind wandered until the speaker said, "Let me tell you a story." Immediately attention picks up. For example, in the middle of a speech on toxic waste you may see attention flagging as you cite technical informa-

Anecdotes, examples, and startling information will help you deal with lapses in audience attention.

tion. Don't wait until you've lost your audience; now is the time to say, "Let me share with you a story that illustrates the gravity of toxic waste."

Just because you have a great number of attention-getting stories, examples, and illustrations does not mean that you have to use all of them. The effective speaker is sensitive to audience reaction at all times. When the audience is really with you, there's no need to break the rhythm. But when you sense the audience is not following your ideas, that's the time to lighten up with material that will pique attention. Keep in mind, however, that such information must pertain directly to the point you are making or it will be counterproductive. Also remember that there is almost no way to keep audience members on the edge of their seats throughout the entire speech. Some sections of a speech may demand more from an audience. Any speech, regardless of how good, has highs and lows. The difference between an excellent speech and a mediocre one is that its highs are much higher and its lows are not as low.

Adapting to Audience Level of Understanding

An audience analysis can help you determine what your audience already knows about your topic. If you predict that your audience has sufficient information to understand you with little difficulty, then your goal is to present your information in a way that will ensure continuous understanding; if, however, you predict that your listeners may not understand the information very well, then your goal is to give enough background information to orient them.

Giving Background Information

Your success with any topic depends on your audience's having sufficient background information at the outset of a speech. If it does, then you can assume most of your listeners will follow the ideas you present in the body of your speech. If you and your audience don't start out with the same core of background information, then your listeners may soon lose track of any further ideas you want to develop in your speech. A good rule of thumb is to err on the side of expecting too little knowledge rather than expecting too much. So, if there is any reason to believe that some people may not have much knowledge, take time to define terms and review necessary facts. For instance, suppose your speech is about changes in political and economic conditions in Eastern Europe. Although you can be reasonably sure that everyone in your audience is aware of the breakup of the Soviet Union, they may not remember all the specifics. Before launching into your speech, remind the audience of the specific background information that is necessary to understanding the ideas in your speech. For example, you may need to review the names of the nations that were once part of the Soviet Union.

Next you need to determine how to present that information without insulting the intelligence of some or all of your audience. One effective way to present information that the audience may already be familiar with is to preface it with a phrase such as "As you will remember," "As we have come to find out," or "As we all learned in our high school courses." For instance, in your speech on Eastern Europe, you might say, "As you will recall, the old Soviet Union now consists of the following separate states." If listeners already know the information, they will see your summary as a reminder; if they do not know it, they are getting the information in a way that doesn't call attention to their information gaps; they can act as if they do, in fact, remember.

Even if you believe your audience has the necessary background information, it may still be helpful to review key points in the speech introduction. For instance, in explaining the main features of your company's new word-processing package, you may still want to review features of the old package that employees are used to. The review brings relevant information to a conscious level and suggests that they should keep that information in mind as you present new information.

How much orientation you can give depends on how much time is available. When you don't have the time to give a complete background, determine where a lack of information will impinge on your ability to get through to your audience and fill in the crucial information that closes those gaps.

Developing Information

Even when you predict that your audience has the necessary background information, you still need to work on ways of developing information that ensures continued understanding. You can use such devices as defining, describing, exemplifying, and comparing to help clarify information that may be confusing or difficult for some audience members. Keep in mind that an audience is made up of individuals with different comprehension styles. As you plan your speech, ask yourself the following questions:

1. *Have I defined all key terms carefully?* For instance, if you are discussing the problems of the functionally illiterate, have you included a clear definition of "functionally illiterate"?

2. *Have I supported every generalization with at least one specific example?* For instance, if you are planning to say that the functionally illiterate have difficulty reading simple directions, you'll want to exemplify the statement by saying "For instance, a person who is functionally illiterate might not be able to read a label that says 'Take three times a day after eating.'"

3. *Have I compared new information to information my audience already understands?* Suppose you want to introduce the audience to the sport of badminton. You might consider opening your speech by saying

> Badminton is a fast-paced racket game. You'd be surprised at how fast the bird flies from one side of the court to the other. Let's look at the dynamics of the game.

But such an opening might lose many members of the audience. They may not have a series of images, rules, and practices that come to mind when they hear "badminton"; you need to help them get oriented. One way of doing this might be to associate badminton, an unfamiliar sport, with tennis, a sport for which most Americans have a reasonably well-developed set of procedures. Thus, you might revise your opening as follows:

> Today we begin our study of badminton, a fast-paced racket game. To give you an idea of what badminton is like, think of the sport of tennis. Badminton is played on a court that is about two-thirds the size of a tennis court. As with tennis, players hit an object across a net with their rackets. The major contrasts with tennis are as follows: A badminton racket has a hitting surface that is less than half that of a tennis racket; the net is five feet high instead of three feet six inches; and instead of the object being a ball that may be hit on the bounce, badminton players hit a shuttlecock, often called a bird, which must be kept in the air at all times. The shuttlecock looks like a small ball about one inch in diameter with feathers stuck into the top half.

By associating badminton with tennis, the audience can begin to build a mental badminton script, including information about equipment and the rules for playing, that allows them to visualize the game.

In short, at any point in a speech where there appears to be any difficulty in understanding an idea or a concept, be prepared to define, exemplify, and compare. This advice is based on a sound psychological principle: The more different kinds of explanations a speaker gives, the more listeners will understand. Each of us learns information in slightly different ways. For instance, some people can learn by listening to an explanation, whereas others learn better when they physically go through the steps. In other words, while one person might understand a concept that is presented with no additional supporting information, a second person may not understand until an example is presented, a third person may not understand until a comparison is presented, and a fourth person might require all three types of developmental material to get a clear understanding. Consequently, effective speakers must present information that adapts to the different learning styles of individual audience members.

Now let's see how this works in practice. Suppose that a speaker says, "A significant number of Americans are functionally illiterate." A few audience members may understand the extent of illiteracy in America on the basis of that statement alone. Notice, however, how much clearer the statement becomes after the speaker says, "That is, large numbers of Americans cannot read well enough to understand simple cooking instructions, directions on how to work an appliance, or rules on how to play a game." With just the addition of three examples, many more people are likely to completely understand. Now notice how the extent of the problem is clarified with the addition of comparative statistics: "During the past twenty years the number of Americans who are functionally illiterate has increased by 15 percent."

The value of such multiple methods of development goes beyond responding to individual learning styles. The first statement, "A significant number of Americans are functionally illiterate," consists of eight words that are likely to be uttered in slightly less than five seconds! A listener who coughs, drops her pencil, or happens to remember an appointment she has during those five seconds will miss the entire message. The reiteration with examples adds thirty words and takes an additional ten or more seconds to utter. Now, even in the face of some distractions, it is likely that most listeners will have heard and registered the information.

Because another way of presenting information is to show it as well as talk about it, in Chapter 15 we will consider various visual aids that can affect both audience interest and audience understanding.

Reinforcing or Changing Audience Attitude toward You or Your Topic

An audience analysis can help you determine the audience's attitude toward your topic and toward you as a speaker. If you predict that your audience will have a positive attitude toward you and your topic, then your goal is to build on that positive attitude; if you predict that your audience may have a negative attitude toward you or your topic, then your goal is to create a positive attitude.

Audience Attitude toward Your Topic

Although audience attitude toward the topic is most relevant with persuasive speeches, it can affect informative speeches as well. An *attitude* is a predisposition for or against people, places, or things. An attitude is usually expressed in evaluative terms—you like or dislike something. So, if you plan to give a speech on refinishing wood furniture, a person in the audience may start out with a positive or negative attitude. "I think refinishing furniture is too hard" expresses a negative attitude toward your topic.

As you consider your audience, you are likely to classify their attitude toward you or your topic as no opinion (either no information or no interest), in favor (already holding a particular belief), or opposed (holding an opposite point of view). You will then want to develop a strategy that adapts to that attitude.

At this point in the course, you should proceed with your chosen topic if you predict that your audience has no opinion, is in favor, or is only slightly opposed to your topic; if you believe that your audience is likely to be very much opposed to your topic or speech goal, you may want to select one that is less challenging at this stage. (In Chapter 17, Persuasive Speaking, we consider strategies for dealing with audiences that are very much opposed to the speaker's topic or goal.) Often an audience's negative attitude toward a topic results from not understanding why they need to know the information. Your efforts to create and build interest, stressing the personal impact of the topic, and to adapt the information to their level of understanding will go a long way toward improving audience attitude.

Audience Attitude toward You as a Speaker

If you predict that the audience has a positive attitude toward you as a speaker, then you need only try to maintain that attitude; if, however, you predict that the audience has no opinion or for some reason has a negative attitude toward you, then you will want to create, build, or change that attitude.

Audience attitude toward you relates to your credibility with the audience—the level of trust that an audience has or will have in you. For instance, when an audience listens to a speaker discuss the economic factors that are most likely to affect the stock market in the coming year, how much weight they give to that speaker's information will depend in part on their perception of his or her credibility. As you recall from the discussion in Chapter 11, speaker credibility is based primarily on the audience's perception of the speaker's knowledge/expertise on the particular subject and his or her trustworthiness and personality.

What can you do to improve your audience's attitude toward you? You can encourage the person who will be introducing you to build your credibility, and you can build your own credibility during the speech.

First, you can work with the person introducing you (for speeches you give outside the classroom there is usually someone assigned to introduce you). Well before the day of the speech, provide the person with information that establishes your expertise on the topic. In some cases, the introducer will ask you to write an introduction for him or her to present. If so, by all means take advantage of that opportunity. In the statement, explain the nature of your expertise; if possible, include information that shows your practical experience in the subject area. If, for example, you are speaking about literacy to a Parents and Teachers Association meeting, include accounts of your experience in tutoring children and adults.

Regardless of what the introducer says or how well known you are to your audience, their reaction to you is likely to depend on their perception of your expertise, trustworthiness, and personality as revealed by your behavior during the speech. Let's look at each of these key areas.

Building Audience Perception of Your Knowledge and Expertise.   The first step in building a foundation of knowledge and expertise is to go into the speaking situation fully prepared. Audiences have an almost instinctive knowledge of when a speaker is "winging it," and most audiences lose respect for a speaker who hasn't thought enough of them or the situation to have a well-prepared message.

As a measure of the depth of your knowledge, your audience will expect you to have a wealth of high-quality examples, illustrations, and personal experiences. Recall how much more favorably you perceive those professors who have an inexhaustible supply of supporting information as opposed to those professors who present, and seem to have, only the barest minimum of facts.

Your speech should show the audience any direct involvement you have had with the topic area. In addition to increasing the audience's perception of your depth of knowledge, your personal involvement increases the audience's perception of your practical understanding of the issues and your personal concern for the subject. For example, if you are speaking on toxic waste, your credibility will increase manifold by sharing with the audience your personal experiences in petitioning for local environmental controls.

Building Audience Perception of Your Trustworthiness.   The audience's perception of your trustworthiness results from their assessment of your character and your apparent motives for presenting the information. Early in the speech, it's important to emphasize why the audience needs to know the information. Then, throughout the speech, emphasize your sincere interest in the well-being of the audience. In a

Your audience will expect you to have a wealth of high-quality examples, illustrations, and personal experiences in your speech.

speech on toxic waste, for example, you could explain how a local dumpsite affects the community. As you present documented facts and figures showing the extent of danger to individuals, your audience is likely to form the belief that you have a sincere interest in the well-being of the community.

Building Audience Perception of Your Personality.   A speaker's personality is another key ingredient in how an audience perceives credibility. Audience perceptions of personality are often based on first impressions of such characteristics as attractiveness. Although physical attractiveness is a genetic quality over which we have little control, you can behave in ways that will increase audience perception of your attractiveness. For instance, you can dress, groom, and carry yourself in an attractive manner. The old compliment "He/she cleans up really good" is one to remember. It is surprising how much an appropriately professional dress and demeanor will increase audience perception of attractiveness.

In addition, audiences react favorably to a speaker who acts friendly. Friendliness is an important component of personality. A smile and a pleasant tone of voice go a long way in developing a quality of warmth that will increase an audience's comfort with a speaker and her or his ideas.

Three key behaviors that increase an audience's favorable perception of a speaker's personality are enthusiasm, eye contact, and vocal expressiveness. These keystones of a strong speech delivery will be discussed in detail in Chapter 15.

Special Problems of Speakers from Different Cultures

This chapter has been written from the perspective of a speaker raised in the United States. Even though such speakers may have to adapt to cultural differences, their task is still relatively easy because the majority of their audiences are likely to have had many common cultural experiences. For instance, even though Mexican-Americans or Japanese-Americans raised in the United States may maintain a strong sense of their Mexican or Japanese heritage, they still have many cultural similarities with members of their audience.

But, the chances of a student in this course coming from a totally different culture have increased dramatically. Suppose, for a minute, that you are a person who has recently emigrated to the United States or has moved here for your higher education. Being less familiar with the general United States culture, you would have a more difficult time adapting to your classroom audiences than other students in the class.

Two of the problems with adaptation are difficulty with the English language and lack of a common set of experiences to draw from. Difficulty with the language includes both difficulty with pronunciation and difficulty with vocabulary and idiomatic speech. Both of these could make you feel self-conscious. But the lack of a common set of experiences to draw form may be even more significant. So much of our information is gained through comparison examples that the lack of common experiences may make drawing comparisons and using appropriate examples much more difficult.

What can you do to help yourself through the public-speaking experience? Difficulty with language may require you to speak more slowly and to articulate as clearly as possible. Also, make sure that you are comfortable with your topic. As suggested in Chapter 11, it may be wise for you to talk about aspects of your homeland. Since you will be providing new information, your classmates will likely look forward to hearing you speak. It would be useful for you to practice at least once with a person raised in the United States. You can ask the person to help you make sure that you are using language, examples, and comparisons that the audience will be able to relate to.

On the other hand, you'll find that most American students are much more tolerant of mistakes made by people who are speaking in what is for them a second or even third language than they are of mistakes made by American-born students. Also, keep in mind that the more practice you can get speaking to people from this culture, the more comfortable you will become with the language and with your ability to adapt to an American audience.

A Plan of Adaptation

Now that you have considered how to adapt speech information to a given audience, it is time to determine a specific plan of adaptation. Adaptation is relatively easy when the majority of the audience members are like you—that is, similar to you in age, race, religion, academic background, and so forth. As you face more diverse audiences, however, problems of adaptation become more complex. As a result, you must think through the basis for your predictions very carefully and speak to each of them completely. Even experienced speakers find that it helps to write out a governing strategy.

First, assemble a specific audience analysis for each speech situation (see Figure 11.3, p. 275). Analyze your information on audience age, education, gender, occupation, income, race, religion, nationality, group affiliation, and geographic uniqueness, to determine the significant characteristics of your audience. Recall that you are predicting whether or not your audience is interested in the topic, likely to understand your material, and likely to have a positive attitude toward you and your material. When you have reviewed your predictions, you can consider strategies for adaptation.

1. *Consider strategies for adapting to audience level of interest.* Determine whether or not the audience is likely to have an immediate interest in your speech information. Write down what you will do early in the speech to show timeliness, spatial impact, and seriousness. Also indicate what attention-getting techniques you plan to use during the speech to rebuild or heighten interest.

2. *Consider strategies for adapting to audience level of understanding.* Determine whether and how much background information needs to be given. Determine what you can do to clarify difficult concepts. Be specific about your use of such informative modes as definitions, examples, comparisons, and contrasts.

3. *Consider strategies for building audience attitude toward you and your topic.* Write how you will attempt to show your knowledge/expertise, trustworthiness, and appealing personality. If you will be introduced by another speaker, list what you hope will be the result of that introduction. The majority of your analysis should focus on what you will do in the speech.

Let us consider two specific examples—one in which audience factors are known and in your favor, and one in which audience factors have to be inferred from the data available and are less favorable to speaker success.

Case 1.   Suppose the speaker is the immediate supervisor for all clerical staff at her company. Her goal is to inform them about the installation of a new word-processing program on all computers. Because she is the supervisor, she knows that the audience will be comprised of about twenty-five Cincinnati women and men of mixed race, religion, and nationality, ages from nineteen to forty, with educational levels ranging from high school graduate to graduates of two-year college programs. Based on that information, her analysis might include the following predictions:

- Their interest is likely to be high because they will have to become proficient with the new program in a short period of time.
- Because of their familiarity with the company, the types of computers, and the previous package, their level of understanding of the information about the new package is likely to be high.
- Although their attitudes about changing programs may vary, they are likely to be open to the information if they can be convinced that the new package provides improvements that will enable them to accomplish their goals more easily.

Based on these predictions, the speaker might write the following strategy:

Interest.   Because interest is likely to be high, I will place my emphasis on maintaining that interest. Since the staff are familiar with word-processing packages, I can focus on several of the features that will enable them to produce better copy more easily; thus, I can emphasize timeliness and economic impact (saving time and money).

Understanding.   To adapt to their knowledge level, I will use comparisons of the key features of the new package to operations they are familiar with.

Attitude.   Although their attitude toward the information is likely to be favorable, I will still attempt to feature improvements so that they will understand why they need to spend their time and energy learning the new system. I will show them that the improvements are significant. On the other hand, their attitude toward me may be skeptical. Because I am "management," they may be a little cynical about my intentions. I will have to stress that what is good for the company is also good for them.

Case 2.   Suppose now that the same person has been asked to talk about computer software packages at the monthly meeting of a local community organization comprised of adults. She's been asked to because members of the speaker committee of this organization want to be "up to date." They think it would be worthwhile to have a speech on this topic so that their members can learn something about how they can make greater use of a computer if they own or have access to one. If the only information the speaker has about the audience is that they are adult members of a community organization who have agreed to scheduling a speech on computer software, she can still infer data about them that will help her determine a speech strategy. Because it is an adult organization, she can infer that the audience will be comprised of both males and females of mixed race, religion, and nationality, with a mixed educational background, and ages ranging from about twenty-five upward. Moreover, she can infer that many have homes and families, and because they are members of a local community organization, they will have a geographic bond.

Even though her data are inferred, the speaker can still make the following predictions about the interests, level of understanding, and attitudes of her audience:

- Their interests are likely to vary, based on curiosity rather than any immediate need for information about computer packages. Still, they wouldn't come if they didn't have some interest.
- Because their background knowledge probably ranges widely, it is likely that their level of understanding of the specifics of software packages is relatively low.
- Their attitude about software packages is likely to range from favorable to neutral or even slightly negative. Some will be very positive about what the software can do for them; others will be fearful and will see the computer as an intrusion into their privacy.

Based on these predictions, the speaker might develop the following strategy:

Interest. Because interest levels will vary, I will have to begin the speech with an anecdote or a personal experience that will capture initial interest. Very early in the speech I will also try to develop a need to gain information about computer software packages. I will stress those software packages that would be useful immediately to a general adult audience and would have a real impact on them. I should limit my speech to packages that would help them manage finances—including those providing investment information.

Understanding. Because the audience members are unlikely to share the same background information on computers, I will need to provide background information about the usefulness of computers and computer packages in general to all adults. I must keep information on an elementary level, and I must define all terms carefully. I must also take into account the perceptions of people of different races and cultural backgrounds. I will need a variety of examples, illustrations, and anecdotes that relate to a racially and culturally diverse audience. To adapt to their level of understanding, I will compare computer package information to other operator manuals and directions they are familiar with.

Attitude. Because their attitudes are also likely to vary, I will use examples and illustrations of "average Americans" who have found computer packages to be interesting and useful. Because they know little about me, I will have to demonstrate my expertise and assure them that my intentions are to help them learn more about technology that could be useful to them. I will try to keep the speech light and somewhat humorous.

By Yourself

1. Working with the predictions that you prepared in Chapter 11, under Practice in Analyzing Your Audience (p. 274) and Practice in Analyzing the Occasion and Setting (p. 277), write an audience adaptation strategy in which you include specifics about how you will adapt to audience interest, level of understanding, and attitude toward you and your topic.

2. If a multicultural audience is expected, what difference will that make in your audience adaptation strategy?

Summary

Speakers adapt to their audiences by planning strategies that create or build audience interest, adapt to audience levels of understanding, reinforce or change audience attitudes toward the topic and the speaker.

Most people's interest is determined by whether they believe the information relates specifically to them. Strategies include stressing the timeliness of the information, its impact on the audience's personal space, and the seriousness of the personal impact. To deal with lapses in attention, prepare some amusing anecdotes or startling examples. Strategies for adapting to audience members' level of understanding depend on their existing knowledge and background. If the audience lacks specific topic knowledge, then fill in necessary background information. During the remainder of the speech use definitions, examples, and comparisons.

Audience attitudes—predispositions for or against people, places, or things—are classified as no opinion, in favor, or opposed. If the audience has no opinion, is in favor, or is only slightly opposed to your topic, efforts to create and build attention and adapt to their level of understanding will also work to improve attitude. If the audience is strongly opposed to the topic or goal, select another one that is less challenging.

If the audience has a positive attitude toward you, try to maintain that attitude; if, however, it has no opinion or for some reason is negative, then work to change that attitude. Attitude toward the speaker is based on audience perception of speaker credibility—the level of trust an audience has. Although a positive introduction by another person can help, speakers build their own credibility by going into the speech fully prepared, by emphasizing sincere interest in the audience's well-being, by dressing, grooming, and presenting themselves attractively, and by smiling and talking in a pleasant tone of voice.

For your first few speeches, it may help to write out a governing strategy that specifies how you plan to adapt your speech to the specific audience.

Suggested Readings

Gudykunst, William B., and Young Yun Kim. *Communicating with Strangers: An Approach to Intercultural Communication,* 2nd ed. New York: McGraw-Hill, 1992.
Samovar, Larry A., and Richard E. Porter, *Communication Between Cultures.* Belmont, CA: Wadsworth, 1995.
Both of these books offer insight into analyzing and adapting to multicultural audiences.

Note

1. *The Rhetoric and the Poetics of Aristotle,* trans. W. Rhys Roberts (New York: Modern Library, 1984), p. 32.

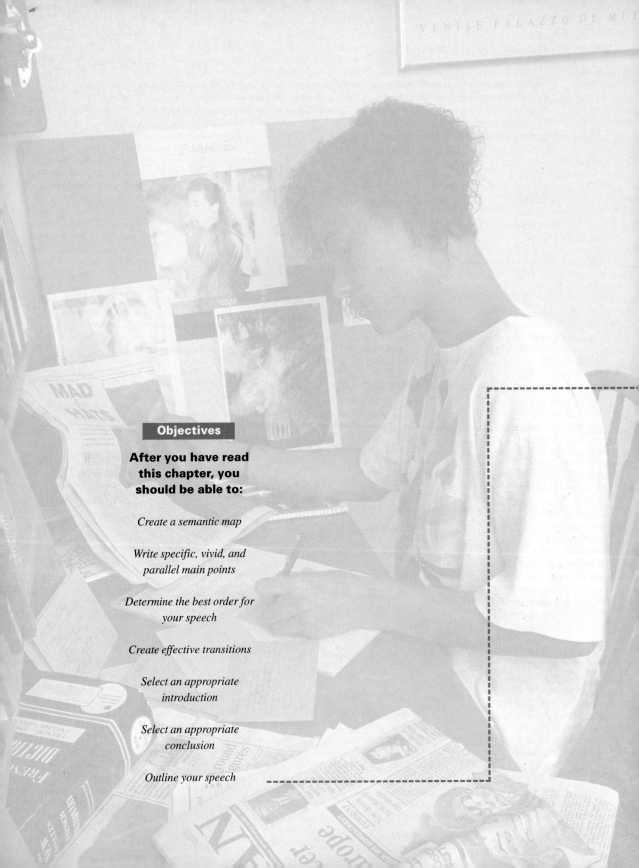

Objectives

After you have read this chapter, you should be able to:

Create a semantic map

Write specific, vivid, and parallel main points

Determine the best order for your speech

Create effective transitions

Select an appropriate introduction

Select an appropriate conclusion

Outline your speech

14

Organizing
Speech Material

"Troy, that was a terrific speech. I haven't heard so many good stories in a long time."

"You're right, Brett, the stories were interesting, but, you know, I had a hard time following it."

"Well, he was talking about ways that we can help save the environment—but, you're right, I can't seem to remember anything but that one point about recycling. Let's see, what were the other key points?"

Amazingly enough, Troy and Brett's experience is not that unusual, for many speakers don't seem to take the time to work out a basic structure.

Plato, the famous classical Greek philosopher, was one of the first people to recognize the organic nature of a speech. He wrote, "Every discourse, like a living creature, should be put together that it has its own body and lacks neither head nor feet, middle nor extremities, all composed in such a way that suit both each other and the whole."[1] Or to put it in a way that follows the old military guideline: First you tell them what you're going to tell them, then you tell them, then you tell them what you told them.

ACTION STEP 4

Organize and develop material in a way that is best suited to your particular audience.

In this chapter, we begin with an overall approach to organizing the the body of the speech. Then we discuss the development of the body, transitions, introduction, and conclusion. We conclude with some basic guidelines for outlining an entire speech.

Preparing the Body of the Speech

Many speakers assume that because the introduction is the first part of the speech to be heard by the audience, they should begin outlining with the introduction. When you think about it, however, you realize that it is difficult to work on an introduction until you have considered the material to be introduced. Moreover, the plan for your speech is likely to change as you develop the outline. Accordingly, unless you know exactly what will be in the speech, outline the body first.

To do so, select and state the main points, determine the best order, and then select and develop the examples, quotations, and other elements that explain or support the main points. We begin with a visual, or graphic view, of organization and then consider refining the visual picture into outline form.

Semantic Mapping

A useful way to begin organizing your speech is to brainstorm a semantic map—a visual diagram of ideas. In Chapter 11, you'll recall, we defined semantic mapping as a kind of brainstorming session in which you verbalize associations to your goal statement and map them on paper. The objective of this process is to identify ideas without initial regard to whether they are main ideas, supporting details, or random ideas related to the speech goal.

As you begin to organize your speech, you may already have a clearly written thesis statement that specifies the main points of your speech, or you may not yet have achieved that goal. At this stage, brainstorming ideas will help you get enough information down on paper so that you can begin to organize the random information and then write an outline from the completed map.

Suppose Janeen has written the specific goal "I want the audience to understand the major roles of the president of the United States." If she has not yet decided on her thesis statement, she can start with the idea "roles of the president" and brainstorm based on her reading and observation. The result might look like Figure 14.1. Representing the material in this form provides Janeen a chance to get thoughts down on paper without being concerned about wording, order, or even appropriateness. Then she can begin analysis to see which ideas have the most promise.

Selecting and Stating Main Points

Main points are the key building blocks of a speech—the ideas you want your audience to remember if they remember nothing else. Because main points are so important, they should be carefully selected and worded so that the audience immediately recognizes them.

For instance, in the mapping example just given, Janeen has six ideas to work with. As she examines these six, she decides that "greeter of foreign dignitaries" is a role that is not important enough to talk about in a short speech. Likewise, she may see "example for the people" as too vague to work with. Now she's left with "head of executive branch," "chief of a political party," "boss of armed forces," and "responsible for foreign relations."

Because she has a well-written goal, the main points are already suggested—the speech will be about roles. Had the thesis statement been determined early in the

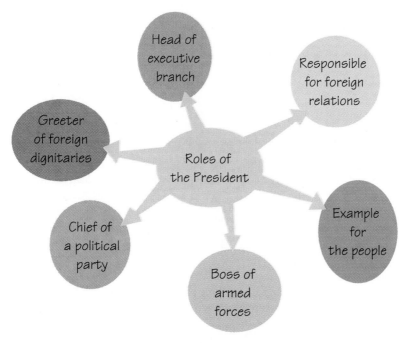

Figure 14.1 *Brainstorming for main ideas*

preparation process, the selection of main points would have been even easier. If Janeen had already arrived at the thesis statement "The president is chief of foreign relations, commander in chief of the armed forces, head of a political party, and head of the executive branch," writing out the main points would have been no problem whatsoever. Written in outline form, the main points would be as follows:

I.   The president is chief of foreign relations.

II. The president is commander in chief of the armed forces.

III. The president is the head of a political party.

IV. The president is the head of the executive branch.

Once you have selected the main points, the next step is to state them in complete sentences that are specific, vivid, and parallel in structure.

Main points are *specific* when their wording is likely to call up the same images in the minds of all audience members. For her speech, suppose that Janeen had written the first main point as follows:

I.   The president is responsible for things related to foreign countries.

This wording is so general that the audience is unlikely to understand what she means: The idea is not phrased in a way that is likely to create a clear mental image. Thus, as Janeen revises the main point for clarity, she seeks wording that will increase the likelihood of audience understanding. She substitutes "chief of" for "responsible for" and substitutes "foreign relations" for "things related to foreign countries," with the following result:

I.   The president is the chief of foreign relations.

Main points are *vivid* when their wording produces strong sensory impressions on the audience. Often the more specific the sentence, the stronger the sensual impression will be. Thus, the revised wording of point I is more vivid as well as more specific than the first draft. But vividness goes beyond being specific. Suppose that Janeen had written her second main point as follows:

II. The president is the boss of the army, navy, and air force.

The wording of this point is reasonably clear and specific. In reference to hierarchy, "boss" is likely to denote "in charge of," and "army, navy, and air force" are specific, clearly understood words. Still, "boss" is not a vivid word and "army, navy, and air force" don't state the point very powerfully. As Janeen revises her main points for vividness, she seeks words that will strike sharper images. The end result is the following:

II. The president is commander in chief of the armed forces.

"Commander in chief" is more striking than "boss," and "armed forces" is likely to create a sharper visual image than naming three branches. In Chapter 15, Presenting Your Speech, we will further develop the ideas of clarity, vividness, emphasis, and appropriateness of language.

Main points are *parallel* when their wording follows the same structural pattern, often using the same introductory words. Parallel structure helps the audience recognize main points, and it is especially effective when the points are of equal value or importance. For example, each main point in the speech about the roles of the president begins with the words "The president is."

Sometimes parallelism is achieved by less obvious means. One method is to start each sentence with an active verb. For instance, suppose Kenneth wants his audience to understand the steps involved in antiquing a table. He might write the following main points in the first draft of his outline:

I. Clean the table thoroughly.

II. The base coat can be painted over the old surface.

III. A stiff brush, sponge, or piece of textured material can be used to apply the antique finish.

IV. Then you will want to apply two coats of shellac to harden the finish.

Note that the wording of these points does not present a clear, parallel structure. The first point is stated as an imperative; the next two use passive verbs; the last one refers to "you." If Kenneth revises the wording to make it parallel, the result might be as follows (parallel active verbs are italicized):

I. *Clean* the table thoroughly.

II. *Paint* the base coat over the old surface.

III. *Apply* the antique finish with a stiff brush.

IV. *Harden* the surface with two coats of shellac.

Notice how the similarity of structure clarifies and strengthens the message. The audience can immediately identify the key steps in the process.

Why, in a preparatory outline, is it important to use complete sentences? To answer this question, let us examine two contrasting ways of stating the same main points, as shown in Figure 14.2

Specific Goal: I want the audience to understand the major roles of the president of the United States.

Thesis Statement: The president is chief of foreign relations, commander in chief of the armed forces, head of a political party, and head of the executive branch.

Key Word Outline	Sentence Outline
I. Foreign relations	I. The president is chief of foreign relations.
II. Armed forces	II. The president is commander in chief of the armed forces.
III. Political party	III. The president is the head of a political party.
IV. Executive branch	IV. The president is the head of the executive branch.

Figure 14.2 *Key word versus sentence outline*

The items in the key word outline indicate the subject areas only. Although the words *foreign relations, armed forces, political party,* and *executive branch* relate to the purpose and indicate the subject areas of the thesis statement, how they are related is unknown. These labels might be useful as key words on note cards, but they will not work at this stage of preparation because the ideas they represent, and the relationship among them, need to be clarified and sharpened.

Notice the significant improvement in the sentence outline. The main points not only include each classification but also explain the relationships of the categories to the goal sentence. In addition, starting each item with "The president is" sets up parallel main points. If the listeners remember only the main points of the sentence outline, they will still know exactly what the speaker claims the major roles of the president are. Moreover, by writing the main point as sentences, the speaker is also more likely to think of them as sentences and present complete-sentence main points during speech practice.

As you begin to phrase prospective main points, you may find your list growing to five, seven, or even ten points that seem to be main ideas. A list that long is usually a clue that some points are really "sub" points or repeat other points. Because every main point must be developed in some detail, it is usually impractical to have more than two to five main points. If you have more than five, rework your speech goal to limit the number of main points, group similar points under a single heading, or determine whether some points are subpoints that can be included under main points.

Determining the Best Order

A speech can be organized in many different ways. Your objective is to find or create the structure that will help the audience make the most sense of the material and so achieve your speech goal. There are several organizational patterns that can help an audience understand and remember main points better: time, space, topic, causality, logical reasons, and problem–solution. Which of these is optimal for your speech is determined by the nature of the information and the perception of the information you want to leave with your audience.

Time or Chronological Order.   Time order follows a chronological sequence of ideas or events. When you select a chronological arrangement of material, the audience understands that there is a particular importance to both the sequence and the content of those main points. Time order is most appropriate when you are explaining how to do something, how to make something, how something works, or how something happened, as if you were indicating step 1, step 2, step 3. In the following example, notice that the order of main points is as important to the logic of the speech as the wording.

Specific Goal: I want the audience to understand the four steps involved in preparing an effective résumé.

Thesis Statement: The four steps in preparing a résumé are gathering relevant information, deciding on an appropriate format, planning the layout, and polishing the statements of information.

    I.   Gather relevant information.

   II.   Decide on an appropriate format.

  III.   Plan the layout.

  IV.   Polish the statements of information.

Space Order.   Space order follows a spatial relationship among the main points. It is most appropriate when you want the audience to understand that there is a special significance to the positioning of the information. Space order is likely to be used in descriptive informative speeches where you might be explaining a scene, a place, a person, or an object. To form a coherent, logical description, you can proceed from top to bottom, left to right, inside to outside, or in any constant direction that the audience can picture. In the following example, notice how the spatial order helps us visualize the three layers of the atmosphere:

Specific Goal: I want the audience to picture the three layers that make up the earth's atmosphere.

Thesis Statement: The earth's atmosphere comprises the troposphere, the stratosphere, and the ionosphere.

    I.   The troposphere is the inner layer of the atmosphere.

   II.   The stratosphere is the middle layer of the atmosphere.

  III.   The ionosphere is the succession of layers that constitute the outer regions of the atmosphere.

Topic Order.   Topic order emphasizes categories or divisions of a subject. Because any subject can be subdivided or categorized in many different ways, a topic order allows you to select those divisions or categories that are most informative for an audience. The order of the topics may go from general to specific, least important to most important, or in some other logical sequence. If all the topics are of equal weight and level of generality, their order is unimportant. For example, in a speech on extrasensory perception, the three topics of telepathy, clairvoyance, and precognition are of equal weight and thus can be placed in any order on the outline.

    If topics vary in weight and importance to the audience or the goal of the speech, how you order them may influence your audience's understanding or acceptance of them. Because audiences will often perceive the last point as the most important, you will want to present topics in the order of importance that is most suitable for the audience and speech goal, as shown in the following example.

Specific Goal: I want the audience to understand the insights our clothes give us into our society.

Thesis Statement: Our clothing gives insight into our society's casual approach, its youthful look, the similarity in men's and women's roles, and the lack of visual distinction between rich and poor in our society.

    I.   Our clothes indicate our casual approach.

   II.   Our clothes indicate our emphasis on youthfulness.

  III.   Our clothes indicate the similarity in men's and women's roles.

  IV.   Our clothes indicate the lack of visual distinction between rich and poor.

Causal Order.   Causal order emphasizes the cause-and-effect relationship between main points and the subject of the speech. That is, it shows that something results from specific conditions. When you use a causal order, you are telling the audience that one thing or event is instrumental in bringing about another, as in the following example.

Specific Goal: I want the audience to understand the major causes of juvenile crime.

Thesis Statement: Juvenile crime is a result of poverty, lack of discipline, and broken homes.

    I.   One major cause of juvenile crime is poverty.

   II.   A second major cause of juvenile crime is lack of discipline in the home.

  III.   A third major cause of juvenile crime is broken homes.

Logical Reasons Order.   An organization based on logical reasons emphasizes why you believe an audience should believe in a statement or behave in a particular way. Unlike the first four arrangements of points, the logical reasons order is most appropriate for a persuasive speech. (In Chapter 17, we will consider additional ways of phrasing and ordering reasons for persuasive speeches.)

Specific Goal: I want the audience to donate money to the United Way.

Thesis Statement: Donating to the United Way is appropriate because your one donation covers many charities, you can stipulate which specific charities you wish to support, and a high percentage of your donation goes to charities.

    I.   You should donate to the United Way because one donation covers many charities.

   II.   You should donate to the United Way because you can stipulate which charities you wish to support.

  III.   You should donate to the United Way because a high percentage of your donation reaches the charities.

Problem–Solution Order.   Problem–solution order organizes main points to show that (1) there is a problem requiring a change in attitude or behavior (or both), (2) the solution presented will solve the problem, and (3) the solution is the best way to solve that problem. The problem–solution order is effective when you want to prove to the audience that a new solution is needed to remedy a problem; consequently, this type of organization works best for a persuasive speech. Notice how the three points of the problem–solution order are presented in the following example.

Specific Goal: I want the audience to believe that business and industry should be allowed to conduct random drug tests on all employees.

Thesis Statement: Businesses should be allowed to conduct random drug tests on employees because drug abuse creates major problems in the workplace, random drug testing lowers instances of drug abuse, and random drug testing is the best solution to the problem.

I. Businesses should be allowed to conduct random drug tests because drug abuse is creating major problems in the workplace.

II. Businesses should be allowed to conduct random drug tests because random drug tests lower instances of drug abuse.

III. Businesses should be allowed to conduct random drug tests because random drug testing is the best solution to the problem.

In summary, then, (1) state each main point as a complete sentence, (2) state each main point so that it develops the key words in the speech goal, (3) make each main point specific, (4) state each main point vividly, (5) state each main point in parallel language, (6) limit the number of main points to five, and (7) organize the main points in the pattern best suited to your material and specific goal.

Selecting and Outlining Supporting Material

The main points outline the structure of your speech. Whether your audience understands, believes, or appreciates what you have to say usually depends on how well those main points are developed and embellished with supporting material.

As we saw in Chapter 12, factual statements and expert opinions are the principal types of research information used in speeches. Once the main points are in place, you can select the most relevant of those materials and decide how to develop each main point.

List Supporting Material.   First, using the semantic-mapping technique, write down each main point and under it state the information that develops that main point. Don't worry if ideas don't seem to relate to each other as you write them

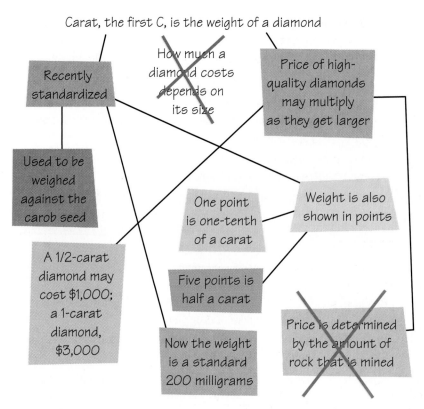

Figure 14.3 *Semantic mapping of supporting material*

down. For example, for the first main point of a speech with the goal "I want the audience to understand the four C's that determine the value of a diamond," your semantic map might resemble Figure 14.3.

Subordinate the Material.   Once you have listed the relevant items of information, look for relationships among ideas and draw lines that connect information logically. Sometimes you'll find you have stated the same point two different ways ("How much a diamond costs depends on its size" and "Price of high-quality diamonds may multiply as they get larger"). Often two or more items can be grouped under a more general heading. Occasionally you will have listed some information that you decide not to include in the outline ("Price is determined by the amount of rock that is mined"). When you are finished, your main point will have two or more subdivisions, and each subdivision may have two or more sub-subdivisions. These items of information can now be grouped and subordinated in outline form, as follows:

    I. Carat, the first C, is the weight of the diamond.

        A. Diamond weight has been standardized only recently.

1. Originally, merchants measured the carat of diamonds against the carob seed.
2. Now the carat has been standardized as 200 milligrams.
3. Partial weight of a carat is shown in points.
   a. One point is one-tenth of a carat.
   b. Five points is half a carat.

B. As diamond weights increase, the costs multiply.
1. A high-quality 1/2-carat stone may cost $1,000.
2. A high-quality 1-carat stone may cost $3,000.

In this speech, each subpoint might be developed with additional examples, illustrations, anecdotes, and other supporting material. The outline only needs to include enough supporting information to ensure that you can explain and clarify the point you are making.

Determining Transitions

Transitions are complete sentences that link major sections of a speech. They summarize what has gone before and/or show movement to the next main idea. Transitions act like a tour guide leading the audience through the speech and are helpful when you do not want to take a chance that the audience might miss something. At breaks from one part of the speech to another or from one main point to another, effective speeches contain appropriate transition statements, as in the following examples.

At the start of the body of a speech on how to antique a table: Antiquing a table is a process that has four steps.

After finishing the first step in antiquing a table: Now that we see what is involved in cleaning the table, let's move on to the second step.

Note the transition between the two main points in the sample outline provided at the end of this chapter (pp. 348–349).

Practice in Outlining the Speech Body

By Yourself

1. Map the potential main points of your next speech. After selecting the points that best reflect your speech goal, write the main points in outline form. Determine whether the main points best follow a time, space, topic, causal, logical reasons, or problem–solution order. Revise the wording of the main points so that each is written in specific, vivid language and all are parallel in structure.
2. Map the factual statements, expert opinions, and other material that develop each main point. Group the points that relate to each other. Subordinate material so that each subpoint contains only one idea.
3. Write transitions that you could use before each main point.

Preparing the Introduction

At this stage of preparation, the body of the speech is sufficiently well developed that you can concentrate on how to begin your speech. Here we consider what a speech introduction should accomplish and how to craft effective ones.

Goals of the Introduction

A good introduction (1) gains attention, (2) sets the tone for a speech, (3) creates a bond of goodwill between speaker and audience, and (4) leads into the content of the speech.

Getting Attention. Although an audience is generally captive (few members will get up and leave), their physical presence does not guarantee that they will listen. They hope they will like the speech, but if they do not, they can always daydream their way through it. The speaker's first goal, therefore, is to create an opening that will win the listeners' undivided attention by arousing their interest and providing them a need to know the information that will be presented.

Some speakers fail to realize that attention must be accompanied by involvement or else the attention may be short-lived. For instance, a speaker may get momentary attention by pounding on the stand, by shouting "Listen!" or by telling a joke, but if an attention-getting device does not relate to the subject matter of the speech and the tone a speaker wishes to establish, the audience's attention may be lost as soon as the impact of the attention-getter has passed. The attention-getter comprises one or more sentences that direct audience attention to the subject matter of the speech and reinforce their need to know. In the following section, we discuss several types of attention-getting devices you may use.

Setting a Tone. How a speaker approaches a topic, the audience, and the occasion varies from speech to speech. For example, some speeches may examine a grave problem, whereas others may look lightheartedly at the foibles of humankind. Each intention will be carried out through the tone set in the speech. Although the occasion (a funeral or an awards banquet) may suggest a tone, in many speeches the tone is established by what the speaker says, particularly in the introduction.

Cathy copyright 1983 Cathy Guisewite. Reprinted with permission of Universal Press Syndicate. All rights reserved.

If you want to set a lighthearted tone, then a humorous opening is appropriate; if you want to set a serious tone, then the opening of the speech should be serious. A speaker who starts with a rib-tickling ribald story is putting the audience in a lighthearted, devil-may-care mood; if that speaker then says, "Now let's turn to the subject of AIDS (or nuclear war or drug abuse)," the audience will be confused and the speech is probably doomed.

Creating a Bond of Goodwill.   If your listeners have heard you before, they may be looking forward to hearing you again. Often, however, they will not know you at all. Or they may even view you as a person who will tell them things they do not want to hear, who will make them feel uncomfortable, or who will make them think about things they do not want to think about. If they are going to invest time in listening to you, they must be assured that you are worth listening to.

For some topics you may want to begin building your credibility during the introduction. Although credibility and goodwill can be created with a separate statement, in short speeches it is conveyed through the sincerity of your voice and your apparent concern for individual audience members as shown by personal pronouns and direct forms of address. Active efforts at creating goodwill and building credibility are especially important in persuasive speeches.

Leading into Content.   Too often introductions fail to focus the audience's attention on the goal of the speech. In most speech introductions, it is appropriate to tell listeners what the speech is about. For instance, in an informative speech on campaigning, after your attention-getter you may say directly, "In this speech, I'll explain the four stages of a political campaign." In a persuasive speech, you may proceed less directly and keep the audience in suspense until its attention is firmly established.

Because the thesis statement is a forecast of main points, it can be used to lead into the speech. Position it as the last point in the outline of the speech introduction (as shown in the sample outline on pp. 348–349), even if there is some strategic reason for not stating the thesis statement in the speech.

How long should the introduction be? For most speeches, the introduction ranges from 5 to 10 percent of the speech. Thus, for a five-minute speech (approximately 750 words), an introduction of 35 to 75 words is appropriate; for a thirty-minute speech, an introduction of two to four minutes is appropriate. Whether your speech introduction meets all four of the goals directly, it should be long enough to put listeners in a frame of mind that will encourage them to hear you out but not so long that it leaves too little time to develop the substance of the speech. Of course, the shorter the speech, the shorter the introduction.

Types of Introductions

Ways to begin a speech are limited only by your imagination. To find the most effective opening, try three to five different introductions in practice and pick the one that seems best suited to your purpose and meets the needs you have identified in your analyses of the audience and the occasion. We will describe briefly several methods of getting attention that work for short and long speeches: startling statements, questions, stories, personal references, quotations, suspense, and compliments.

As with all parts of a speech, the key to a good introduction is preparation. What will you say when you reach the podium to reinforce the goodwill of your audience and focus attention on the goal of your speech?

Startling Statement.   Especially in a short speech, the kind you are likely to give in your first assignment, you must grab your listeners' attention and focus on the topic quickly. One excellent way to do that is to open with a startling statement that will override the various competing thoughts in your listeners' minds. The following example illustrates the attention-getting effect of a startling statement:

> If I pointed a pistol at you, you would be justifiably scared. But at least you would know the danger to your life. Yet every day we let people fire away at us with messages that are dangerous to our pocketbooks and our minds, and we seldom say a word. I'm talking about television advertisers.

Rhetorical Question.   Asking a rhetorical question (one that elicits a mental response rather than a spoken one) is another way to get listeners to think about your ideas. Like the startling statement, this opening is also suitable for a short speech. Whether a question works as an opening depends on how the audience perceives it. The question has to have enough importance to be meaningful to the audience. Notice how this student begins her speech on counterfeiting with a series of short questions:

> What would you do with this twenty-dollar bill if I gave it to you? Take your friend to a movie? Treat yourself to a pizza and drinks? Well, if you did either of these things, you could get in big trouble. This bill is counterfeit!

Story.   Nearly everyone enjoys a good story, so an introduction that includes story material will get an audience's attention. Keep in mind that an effective opening must lead into the speech as well as get attention. If you have a good story that does both, you probably have an unbeatable opening. If your story is not related to the subject, save it for another occasion.

Because most good stories take time to tell, they are usually more appropriate for longer speeches; however, you will occasionally come across a short one that is just right for your speech, as was this one from the introduction to a speech on making money from antiques:

> At a recent auction, bidding was particularly brisk on an old hand-blown whiskey bottle, and finally a collector on my left was the successful taker at fifty dollars. When the purchase was handed over to him, an aged but sharp-eyed farmer standing nearby leaned over and took a good look at the bottle. "My God," he gasped to his friend. "It's empty!"
>
> To that farmer an empty bottle wasn't worth much. But in today's world anything that's empty might be worth a fortune, if it's old enough. Today I want to talk with you about what might be lying around your basement or attic that's worth real money—a branch of antiques called "collectibles."

Personal Reference.   Although any good opening should engage the audience, the personal reference is directed solely to that end. In addition to getting attention, a personal reference can be especially effective at building goodwill between speaker and audience, and it can draw in listeners as active participants in a speech. A personal reference opening like this one on exercise may be suitable for a speech of any length:

> Say, were you panting when you got to the top of those four flights of stairs this morning? I'll bet there were a few of you who vowed you're never going to take a class on the top floor of this building again. But did you ever stop to think that maybe the problem isn't that this class is on the top floor? It just might be that you are not getting enough exercise.

Quotation.   A particularly vivid or thought-provoking quotation makes an excellent introduction to a speech of any length. You will need to use your imagination to develop the quotation so that it yields maximum benefits. For instance, in the following introduction the speaker starts with a familiar Shaw quote. By itself it wouldn't be related to the speech or necessarily focus audience attention. But notice how William McCormick uses the quotation as a preface to material that would be less attention-getting without the quotation.

> George Bernard Shaw once wrote, "The road to hell is paved with good intentions." Probably no statement better describes the state of our tort system in this country. With the best of intentions, the scales of a system designed to render justice have been tipped. The balance has moved so far toward the desire to compensate all injuries and all losses that the overall cost to society has become too high. We have reached a point where

exposure to liability is becoming almost limitless and incalculable, making everyone—governments, businesses and individuals—a victim.[2]

Suspense. An extremely effective way to gain attention is through suspense. If you can start your speech in a way that gets the audience to ask "What is she leading up to?" you may well get them hooked for the entire speech. The suspense opening is especially valuable when the topic is one that the audience might not ordinarily be willing to listen to if the speech were opened less dramatically. Consider the attention-getting value of the following:

> It costs the United States more than $116 billion per year. It has cost the loss of more jobs than a recession. It accounts for nearly 100,000 deaths a year. I'm not talking about cocaine abuse. The problem is alcoholism.

Notice that by putting the problem "alcoholism" at the end, the speaker encourages the audience to try to anticipate the answer. And since the audience may well be thinking "drugs," the revelation that the answer is alcoholism is likely to be that much more effective.

Compliment. It feels good to be complimented. We like to believe we are important. Although politicians often overdo the compliment, it is still a powerful opening when used well. Consider the following opening on the free-enterprise system:

> Thank you, ladies and gentlemen. I am honored to be speaking to such a fine group of concerned Americans. Your membership in the United States Industrial Council, and your presence at today's National Issues Seminar, affirm your belief in the central role played by millions of individual businesses in creating jobs, wealth and managerial skills for a world that desperately needs all three.[3]

This method encourages listeners to take pride in their accomplishments and thus gives them a warmer feeling toward the speaker.

Selecting an Introduction

Because the introduction is critical in establishing your relationship with your audience, it's worth investing the time to compare different openings. Try working on three or four different introductions; then pick the one you believe will work best for your specific audience and speech goal.

For example, if you were giving a speech on computer innovation, you might prepare the following three introductions:

> In 1946 it took an entire room filled with vacuum tubes to power the ENIAC computer. Today the capacity of that entire room filled with vacuum tubes can be duplicated in one single chip. In this speech I'd like to talk with you about the next round of innovation in computer technology, a round that will have at least an indirect effect on all of us.

During the past ten years, all of us have marveled at the innovations that have brought highly sophisticated computers into a price range that makes a computer network possible for even the smallest of businesses. What could possibly be in store for the future? My experience with computer technology suggests that "You ain't seen nothing yet." Today I'd like to talk with you about the next round of innovation in computer technology, a round that will have at least an indirect effect on all of us.

Computers are a common part of our everyday life. We get our groceries checked out by computer at our local food market, our purchases are recorded by computer at any clothing store, and the kid who cuts our grass is likely to have our account on computer at home! But as amazing as the recent past has been, future potential is unlimited. Today I'd like to talk with you about the next round of innovation in computer technology, a round that will have at least an indirect effect on all of us.

Which introduction would you prefer if you were giving a speech on computers to your classmates? Why? Although each of the three is satisfactory, each has its special advantages. The first one focuses on size of the early computers, the second focuses on cost, the third focuses on uses. Moreover, none of the three completely meets all four of the goals of a speech introduction.

Although each type of introduction has been discussed separately, they may be used either alone or in combination, depending on the time you have available and the attitude of your audience. The introduction will not make your speech an instant success, but it can get an audience to look at and listen to you and to focus on your topic. That is about as much as a speaker can ask of an audience during the first minute or two of a speech.

Practice in Writing Speech Introductions

By Yourself

For the speech you have outlined (see p. 337), prepare three separate introductions that would be appropriate for your classroom audience. Which is the best for your audience and your specific goal? Why?

Preparing the Conclusion

Shakespeare said, "All's well that ends well," and nothing could be truer of a good speech. The conclusion offers you one last chance to hit home with your point. Too many speakers either end their speeches so abruptly that the audience is startled or ramble on aimlessly until they exhaust both the topic and the audience. A weak conclusion—or no conclusion at all—can destroy much of the impact of an otherwise effective speech. Even the best conclusion cannot save a poor speech, but it can heighten the impact of a good speech.

Goals of the Conclusion

A conclusion has two major goals: (1) to wrap up the speech so that it reminds the audience of what you have said and (2) to hit home so that the audience will remember your words or consider your appeal. Even though the conclusion will be a relatively small part of the speech—seldom more than 5 percent (35 to 40 words of a five-minute speech)—it is worth the time and effort to make it effective.

Types of Conclusions

Now let us look at several of the most common types of conclusions.

Summary.   By far the easiest way to end a speech is to summarize the main points. Thus, the shortest appropriate ending for a speech on the warning signs of cancer would be "So remember, if you experience a sudden weight loss, lack of energy, or blood in your urine or bowels, then you should see a doctor immediately." Such an ending restates the key ideas the speaker wants the audience to remember. Summaries are appropriate for either informative or persuasive speeches.

Although effective speakers often summarize to achieve the first goal of wrapping up the speech, reminding the audience of what they have said, they are likely to supplement their summaries with material designed to achieve the second goal: hitting home so that the audience will remember their words or consider their appeal. The following represent several ways to supplement or replace the summary.

Story.   Storylike, or anecdotal, material that reinforces the message of the speech works just as well for the conclusion as for the introduction. In a speech on banking, Edward Crutchfield ends with a personal experience showing that bankers must be ready to meet competition coming from any direction:

> I played a little football once for Davidson—a small college about 20 miles north of Charlotte. One particularly memorable game for me was one in which I was blindsided on an off-tackle trap. Even though that was 17 years ago, I can still recall the sound of cracking bones ringing in my ears. Well, 17 years and 3 operations later my back is fine. But, I learned something important about competition that day. Don't always assume that your competition is straight in front of you. It's easy enough to be blindsided by a competitor who comes at you from a very different direction.[4]

Storylike conclusions will work for either informative or persuasive speeches.

Appeal to Action.   The appeal to action is a common way to end a persuasive speech. The appeal describes the behavior that you want your listeners to follow after they have heard the arguments. Notice how Marion Ross, professor of economics at Mills College, concludes her speech on living a full and creative life with a memorable figure of speech that captures the appeal she is making to her students:

> We, the faculty, want you to grow wings that won't melt in the sun as did those of Icarus. We want to give you the materials to make your own

wings, and we are bold enough to say the thoughts of great thinkers, works of great art and, in some cases, musings of tinkerers of the past are wrought of gold. They won't melt. Use them. It is you who must take these materials, forge them with your own energy and burnish them with your own imagination to make your own wings.[5]

By their nature, appeals are most relevant for persuasive speeches, especially when the goal is to motivate an audience to act.

Emotional Impact.   No conclusion is more impressive than one that drives home the most important points with real emotional impact. Consider the powerful way in which General Douglas MacArthur used plain, strong language to conclude his speech when he ended his military career:

> But I still remember the refrain of one of the most popular barrack ballads of that day, which proclaimed most proudly that "Old soldiers never die; they just fade away."
> And like the old soldier of that ballad, I now close my military career and just fade away—an old soldier who tried to do his duty as God gave him the light to see that duty.
> Goodbye.[6]

Like the appeal to action, the emotional conclusion is likely to be used for a persuasive speech where the goal is to reinforce belief, change belief, or motivate an audience to act.

Selecting a Conclusion

Speakers select the type of conclusion for their speeches on the basis of the speech goal and the likely appeal to the audience. As we have seen, summaries and story-like conclusions are appropriate for informative or persuasive speeches; appeals and emotional conclusions are more appropriate for persuasive speeches. To determine how you will conclude your speech, try out several conclusions, then choose the one that you believe will best reinforce your speech goal with the particular audience you are addressing.

Practice in Writing Speech Conclusions

By Yourself

For the speech you have outlined (see p. 337), prepare three separate conclusions that would be appropriate for your classroom audience. Which is the best for your audience and your specific goal? Why?

Refining the Complete Outline

From the moment you begin organizing your material, the goal is to develop a complete outline for your speech—a short representation of the speech with key points expressed in complete sentences. Think of an outline not as a complete speech written in outline form but as a blueprint to follow. The value of working with an outline is that you can test the logic, development, and overall strength of the structure of your speech before you prepare the wording or begin practicing its delivery.

Does a speaker really need to write such an outline? Some speakers do not prepare outlines; they have learned, through trial and error, alternate means of planning speeches and testing structures that work for them. Some accomplish the entire process in their head and never put a word on paper, but they are few indeed. Most of us—beginners and experienced speakers alike—need to perfect the outline so that the speech has a solid, logical structure and meets its goal. There is often a direct relationship between the quality of the outline and the effectiveness of the speech.

The basic techniques for constructing outlines are straightforward. In this section, the techniques are adapted to the specific task of developing a speech. The following six guidelines help to test logic and development and will produce a better speech.

1. *Use a standard set of symbols to indicate structure.* Main points are usually indicated by roman numerals, major subdivisions by capital letters, minor subheadings by Arabic numerals, and further subdivisions by lowercase letters. Thus, an outline for a speech with two main points might look like this:

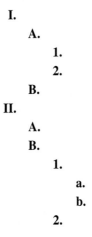

Whether an outline is broken down to the 1, 2, 3 level or a, b, c level depends on the amount of material you have and want to use for those portions of the speech. Although further breakdown of ideas can be shown, a speech outline is rarely subdivided beyond the level shown here.

2. *Use complete sentences for main points and major subdivisions.* Complete sentences help you to see (1) whether each main point actually develops the thesis of your speech goal and (2) whether the wording makes your intended point. Although an outline of phrases or key words works best when the outline is to be used as a speaker's notes, in the planning stage—constructing the blueprint of the speech—complete sentences are preferable. Unless the key ideas are written out in full, it will be difficult to follow the rest of the guidelines.

3. *Make sure that each main point and major subdivision contains only one idea.* This guideline ensures that the development of each part of the speech will be relevant to the point. Let us examine an incorrect and a correct phrasing:

Incorrect	*Correct*
I. The park is beautiful and easy to get to.	**I.** The park is beautiful.
	II. The park is easy to get to.

Trying to develop the incorrect example will lead to confusion because both ideas cannot be developed at the same time. The correct procedure sorts out distinct ideas so that the speaker can line up supporting material with confidence that the audience will see and understand its relationship to the main points.

4. *Make sure that major subdivisions relate to or support major points.* This principle is called *subordination.* Consider the following example:

> **I.** Proper equipment is necessary for successful play.
>
> **A.** Good gym shoes are needed for maneuverability.
>
> **B.** Padded gloves will help protect your hands.
>
> **C.** A lively ball provides sufficient bounce.
>
> **D.** And a good attitude doesn't hurt.

Notice that the main point deals with equipment. A, B, and C (shoes, gloves, and ball) relate to the main point. But D, attitude, is not equipment and should appear somewhere else, if at all.

5. *Limit main points to a maximum of five.* A speech usually contains from two to five main points. Regardless of the length of time available, audiences will have difficulty assimilating a speech that has more than five points. If a speech does seem to have more than five points, either try to group points under broader headings to limit them to five or fewer, or consider eliminating some points. Audiences will remember two main points each with four subdivisions more easily than they will remember eight main points.

6. *Limit outline length to one-third the total number of words anticipated in the speech.* An outline is only a skeleton of the speech—not a manuscript with letters and numbers. The outline provides a logically sound structure for a speech while still allowing the speaker to experiment with methods of development during practice periods and to adapt to audience needs during the speech itself. One way to determine optimum outline length is to compute the total number of words you will speak during the time limit and then to limit your outline to approximately one-third of that total. Because approximate figures are all that are needed, you can use a speaking rate of 150 words per minute for your computation. Thus, for a two- to three-minute speech, which would include roughly 300 to 450 words, the outline should be limited to 100 to 150 words. The outline for an eight- to ten-minute speech, which would include roughly 1,200 to 1,500 words, should contain about 400 to 500 words.

Now that we have considered the various parts of an outline, let us put them all together for a final look. The sample outline in Figure 14.4 (pp. 348–349) illustrates the various principles and guidelines presented in this chapter, as indicated by the notations in the Analysis column to the right.

Outline	Analysis
Speech Goal: I want the audience to understand the two factors that determine the relationship between cholesterol and heart attacks.	*Written at the top of the page, the speech goal is used to remind the speaker of the goal and to test the relevance of the outline's points.*

Introduction

I. During the last few years a new word has become a major part of our health vocabulary—cholesterol.

II. Cholesterol is a type of fat that can build up plaque in the arteries and restrict the flow of blood.

The word Introduction *sets this section apart as a separate unit. The introduction gets attention and often, by stating the thesis of the speech, leads into the body.*

Thesis: Risk of heart attack is predicted by both total cholesterol levels and the ratio between "good" and "bad" cholesterol.

The thesis outlines the elements that were forecast in the speech goal.

Body

I. The first factor in predicting the risk of heart attack is overall cholesterol score.

  A. Most Americans have blood cholesterol levels of between 115 and 300 mg/dl (milligrams per deciliter).

  B. These overall levels predict three levels of risk.

    1. Scores of over 240 are considered high risk.

    2. Scores of 200 to 240 are considered moderate risk.

    3. Scores of below 200 are considered low risk.

The word Body *sets this section apart as a separate unit. Main point I reflects a topical relationship of main ideas. It is stated as a complete substantive sentence. The main point could be developed in many ways. The subdivisions explain range and levels of risk.*

(Now that we have considered the overall cholesterol score, let's consider the second prediction.)

The transition reminds the listeners of the first factor and forecasts discussion of the second.

Figure 14.4   *A complete speech outline*

Outline	Analysis

II. The second factor in the prediction of the risk is the cholesterol ratio.

  A. Blood cholesterol is measured in terms of its LDLs (low-density lipoproteins) and its HDLs (high-density lipoproteins).

    1. LDLs are called "bad" cholesterol because they carry the fat that is deposited in the arteries.

    2. HDLs are called "good" cholesterol because they carry fat from the arteries.

  B. The higher the ratio between LDLs and HDLs, the higher the risk of heart attack.

    1. Ratios of 6 and above (6 parts LDL to 1 part HDL) indicate a higher-than-average risk.

    2. Ratios of 4 to 6 indicate an average risk of heart attack.

    3. Ratios of 4 and below indicate a lower-than-average risk.

Main point II continues the topical relationship. Notice that each main point considers one major idea. Ordinarily, subordination is shown by the following sets of symbols: Major points—I, II, III, etc.; subdivisions—A, B, C, etc.; subdivisions of subdivisions—1, 2, 3, etc.

The substance of the outline should be tested by asking:

1. Is the speech goal a clear, concise statement?

2. Are the main points stated as clear, substantive sentences?

3. Do the main points develop the speech goal directly?

4. Does each main point consider only one idea?

5. Do the various subpoints really support or develop the division they are subordinate to?

Conclusion

I. Cholesterol levels indicate risk of heart attack.

II. Accurate predictions, however, require a knowledge of both overall levels and ratios.

The word Conclusion *sets this section apart as a separate unit. This conclusion is cast as a summary. The conclusion may take any form that ties the speech together and leaves a lasting impression.*

Bibliography

Conti, C. Richard, and Tonnessen, Diana. *Heart Disease and High Cholesterol: Beating the Odds.* Reading, Mass.: Addison-Wesley, 1992.

Cooper, Kenneth H. *Controlling Cholesterol.* New York: Bantam Books, 1988.

Fisher, Hans, and Boe, Eugene. *The Rutgers Guide to Lowering Your Cholesterol.* New York: Warner Books, 1985.

Figure 14.4 *Continued*

By Yourself

Complete your speech outline, using Figure 14.4 as a model. Test the outline to make sure that it conforms to the guidelines discussed in this chapter.

Summary

A speech is organized with an introduction, a body, and a conclusion.

First, organize the body of the speech. One way to begin is with a semantic map, a visual diagram of ideas for the main points of the speech. When you have the potential main points, select the ones you will use. Main points are written as complete sentences that are specific, vivid, and written in parallel language.

A speech can be organized in many different ways depending on the type of speech and the nature of the material. Some of the most common organizational patterns are time, space, topic, causality, logical reasons, and problem–solution.

Main points are embellished with supporting material. A useful process is to begin by mapping the potential material, then subordinating the material in a way that clarifies the relationship between and among subpoints and main points.

Prepare transitions to be used between points. Transitions are complete sentences that link major sections of a speech.

Second, outline the introduction to gain attention, set the tone for the speech, create goodwill, and lead into the body of the speech. Typical speech introductions include startling statements, questions, stories, personal references, quotations, suspense, and compliments.

Third, outline the conclusion. A well-designed speech conclusion ties the speech together and ends it on a high note. Typical conclusions include summaries, stories, appeals to action, and emotional impact.

Finally, to refine the outline, use a standard set of symbols, use complete sentences for main points and major subdivisions, limit each point to a single idea, relate minor points to major points, use no more than five main points, and make sure the outline length is no more than one-third the number of words in the final speech.

Suggested Readings

Boyd, Stephen D., and Renz, Mary A. *Organizing and Outlining: A Workbook for Students in a Basic Speech Course.* New York: Macmillan, 1985. A short (58-page) paperback that allows for hands-on experience in creating outlines.

Haynes, Judy L. *Organizing a Speech: A Programmed Guide,* 2d ed. Falls Church, VA: Speech Communication Association, 1981. A programmed approach that enables you to systematically check your understanding of organization.

Notes

1. Plato, *Phaedrus* (Indianapolis: Bobbs-Merrill, 1956), p. 53.
2. William M. McCormick, "The American Tort System," *Vital Speeches,* February 15, 1986, p. 267.
3. Based on Rafael D. Pagan, Jr., "A System That Works," *Vital Speeches,* July 15, 1980, p. 594.
4. Edward E. Crutchfield, Jr., "Profitable Banking in the 1980's," *Vital Speeches,* June 15, 1980, p. 537.
5. Marion Ross, "Go, Oh Thoughts, On Wings of Gold," *Vital Speeches,* February 15, 1989, p. 284.
6. Douglas MacArthur, "Address to Congress," in William Linsley, ed., *Speech Criticism: Methods and Materials* (Dubuque, IA: Brown, 1968), p. 344.

After you have read
this chapter, you
should be able to:

*Test the wording of your
speech for clarity, vividness,
emphasis, and directness*

*Present your speech with
enthusiasm, eye contact,
and spontaneity*

*Practice your speech
effectively*

Prepare useful speech notes

Cope with nervousness

Evaluate a speech objectively

15

Presenting
Your Speech

"That was really good," Keisha said to Derek as Mikala finished her speech. "She didn't seem to be giving a speech—she was just talking with us."

"True," Derek replied, "but the way she described the procedure you could tell that she had worked to make sure the steps were clear."

"Maybe, but it just seemed so easy for her—I wish I could be so smooth."

Easy? Maybe, but the fact is that in addition to the hours she spent finding and organizing her material, Mikala also practiced the speech many times until she was sure that the main points were clear, well developed, and well presented.

Good presentation involves putting into practice the final two action steps of an effective speech plan:

ACTION STEP 5

Select clear, vivid, emphatic, and direct wording for the speech.

ACTION STEP 6

Practice the speech delivery.

In this chapter, we will focus on aspects of verbal and nonverbal communication that are most relevant to speech presentation. We will also consider how to practice your speech for maximum effect and how to cope with nervousness.

Wording Your Speech

If you were preparing a paper, a newspaper article, or a magazine story, you would write out drafts of the work, criticize what you had written, and rewrite until you were satisfied. "Writing out" a speech in a similar way may help you sharpen both your focus and your language. However, good writing and good speaking are not necessarily the same; good speech is measured not by the eye but by the ear.

Written and oral language are not totally different, but if you compare tapes of what people say with sections of books and magazines, you will find that oral language has more personal pronouns, more contractions, shorter sentences on average, more simple sentences, greater use of one- and two-syllable words, and a greater proportion of common or familiar words.

In this section, we consider what criteria you can use to measure whether your words contribute to an effective oral style. In our analysis, we build on the information presented in Chapter 3, Verbal Communication, and adapt it to the public-speaking setting, focusing on clarity, vividness, emphasis, and directness of language.

Clarity

You will recall that using clear language helps the listener receive the same meanings as the speaker intended. *Clarity* eliminates ambiguity and confusion. Suppose a teacher recommended a student to a prospective employer by saying, "He does pretty well on tests, he gets his other stuff done in pretty good order, and he talks in class—no complaints." If you were the prospective employer, how much would you really know about that student's work? Suppose instead the teacher said, "He gets B grades or better on tests, he completes all of his homework and turns it in on time, and his class discussion shows his understanding of basic theory—he's a pleasure to have in class." Note how the second phrasing gives a much clearer picture of the student's behavior through the use of precise, specific words.

Precision. Words are *precise* when they create a meaning in the minds of an audience that is as close as possible to the meaning intended. Thus, to convey the idea of a large body of running water, you say "river"; when you are thinking of a small body of running water, you say "stream" or "creek."

Specific and Concrete Words. Specific and concrete words call up a single image. The more vague or general the words you select, the more choice you give a listener and the more likely it is that the listener will select an image different from the one you intended. To be specific and concrete, we say "books, paper, and pencils" instead of "things"; "two maples, an oak, and four evergreens" instead of "trees"; and "a '94 Volvo" instead of "a foreign car."

Simple Words. In addition to precise and specific/concrete words, you can improve clarity by selecting simple words over more difficult or less common equivalents. When handling complex ideas, speakers sometimes go overboard and use words that seem pompous, affected, or stilted. When you have a choice, select the simplest, most familiar word that expresses your precise meaning. Figure 15.1 gives some examples of needlessly fancy words and simpler equivalents.

Vividness

Although speaking clearly ensures that audiences understand your meaning, effective public speakers also make their points vividly. *Vivid* means full of life, vigorous, bright, intense. A baseball announcer might portray a center fielder's catch by saying "Jackson made a great catch." This is an evaluation that states the announcer's opinion but evokes no images. Saying "Jackson made a great one-hand catch against the wall" would be more vivid. And saying "Jackson, racing with his back to the infield, leaped and made a one-hand stab just as he crashed into the center field

To simplify your language, use:		
building	instead of	edifice
clothing	instead of	apparel
bury	instead of	inter
engagement	instead of	betrothal
begin	instead of	commence
avoid	instead of	eschew
wedding	instead of	nuptials
predict	instead of	presage
beauty	instead of	pulchritude
home	instead of	residence
view	instead of	vista

Figure 15.1
Using simple words

wall" is even more vivid. The words *racing, leaped, stab,* and *crashed* paint an intense verbal picture of the action.

Speakers through the ages have experimented with various language techniques to enhance the vividness of their speeches. Two of the most frequently used techniques are similes and metaphors.

A *simile* is a direct comparison of dissimilar things. Similes usually contain the word *like* or *as.* Many expressions that have become clichés are similes. We may say "He runs like a turtle" or "She's slow as molasses" to make a point about lack of speed, or "He swims like a rock" or "She's built like a pencil" to dramatize a negative description. Similes are vivid when the basis for the direct comparison is imaginative or different: "Trucks are like monstrous boxcars that eat highways for breakfast" is a vivid simile.

A *metaphor* is a comparison that establishes a figurative identity between objects being compared. Instead of saying that one thing is like another, a metaphor says that one thing is another. Thus, problem cars are "lemons"; a team's porous infield is a "sieve." In a speech delivered in Fulton, Missouri, in 1946, Winston Churchill spoke of an "iron curtain" that had descended upon Europe. Describing Russian-dominated countries as those "behind the iron curtain" served as a vivid metaphor of political reality for more than forty years until the Berlin Wall came tumbling down in 1989.

Although similes and metaphors usually add vividness to a speech, speakers sometimes reach for a figure of speech where the comparison or identity is forced. For the figure to really work, it must be appropriate. For instance, a zealous speaker might say, "Without the ignition of advertising, the engine of our economy would run much more slowly," but after a moment's thought, we realize that without ignition, the engine wouldn't run at all!

Vivid speech begins with vivid thought. You must have a striking mental picture before you can communicate one to your audience. If you cannot feel the bite of the wind and the sting of the freezing rain, if you cannot hear the thick, juicy sirloin steak sizzling on the grill, if you cannot feel the empty yet exhilarating feeling as the jet climbs in takeoff, you will not be able to describe these sensations vividly. The more imaginatively you can think about your ideas, the more likely you are to state them vividly.

Emphasis

A third important element of wording is *emphasis.* In a 500-word speech, all 500 words are not of equal importance. You neither expect nor want an audience to remember every word spoken. Still, if you leave it up to listeners to decide which words and ideas are most important, they may select the wrong ones. You are the speaker; you know what you want to emphasize. How can you do it? Although you can emphasize with your voice and body, in this section we consider how you can emphasize with wording by means of placement and sequencing, proportion, repetition, and transition.

Emphasizing through Placement and Sequencing. *Placement* and *sequencing* mean constructing a list of items in such a way that the most important comes last. If a speaker says that the president is the chief of foreign relations, commander in chief of the armed forces, head of a political party, and head of the executive branch, there is a natural tendency for the audience to perceive the last role as the most important. Unfortunately, many speakers list items with no consideration of order. If the last item turns out to be the most trivial, the audience will perceive that item as anticlimactic. To take advantage of the natural tendency to look for the most important idea to come last, emphasize by building a sequence that moves from least important to most important.

Emphasizing through Proportion. *Proportion* means spending more time on one point than on another. If a speaker devotes five minutes to the president's role as head of the executive branch and only two minutes each to the president's roles as head of a political party and commander in chief of the armed forces, the audience will assume that the president's role as head of the executive branch is the most important.

Emphasizing through Repetition. If you say "The federal budget deficit this year is over 400 billion dollars—that's 400 billion," a listener will perceive the repetition as an indication that the point must be important and should be remembered. Repetition is widely used because it is easy to practice and quite effective. If you want the audience to remember your exact word, you can repeat it once or twice: "The number is 572638, that's 5, 7, 2, 6, 3, 8" or "A ring-shaped coral island almost or completely surrounding a lagoon is called an atoll—the word is *atoll.*"

If you want the audience to remember an idea but not necessarily the specific language, you will probably restate it rather than repeating it. Whereas *repetition* is the exact use of the same words, *restatement* means echoing the same idea but in different words: "The population is 975,439—that's roughly one million people" or "The test will comprise about four essay questions; that is, all the questions on the test will be the kind that require you to discuss material in some detail."

Emphasizing through Transition. *Transitions* are the words, phrases, and sentences that show relationships between ideas. Transitions summarize, clarify, forecast, and in almost every instance, emphasize.

Our language contains a number of words that show idea relationships. Words such as "also," "likewise," and "moreover" forecast additional material; words such as "therefore," "all in all," and "in short" bring ideas together to show results; words such as "but," "however," and "on the other hand" indicate changes in direction; and words such as "in other words," "for example," and "that is to say" explain or exemplify. The list in Figure 15.2 contains some common transitional words and phrases and explains their uses.

Moreover, as we discussed in the last chapter, you can make statements that call special attention to words and ideas. Such special-attention statements function as a "tour guide" leading the audience through the speech. At the start of the body of the speech, you might say, "My analysis will have three major parts." To bridge between points in a speech explaining a process, you might say, "Now that we see what the ingredients are, let's move on to the second step: stripping the surface."

In addition to acting as a tour guide, special-attention transitions can announce the importance of a word or idea. You might say, "Now I come to the most important point" or "If you forget everything else, be sure to remember this" or "Let me say this again because it is so important." These examples represent only a few of the

Transitions	Uses
■ also ■ and ■ likewise ■ again ■ in addition ■ moreover ■ similarly ■ further	■ Use these words to add material.
■ therefore ■ and so ■ so ■ finally ■ all in all ■ on the whole ■ in short ■ thus ■ as a result	■ Use these expressions to add up consequences, to summarize, or to show results.
■ but ■ however ■ yet ■ on the other hand ■ still ■ although ■ while ■ no doubt	■ Use these expressions to indicate changes in direction, concessions, or a return to a previous position.
■ because ■ for	■ Use these words to indicate reasons for a statement.
■ then ■ since ■ as	■ Use these words to show causal or time relationships.
■ in other words ■ in fact ■ for example ■ that is to say ■ more specifically	■ Use these expressions to explain, exemplify, or limit.

Figure 15.2 *Common transitional words and phrases*

possible expressions that interject keys, clues, and directions to stimulate the audience's memory or understanding.

Directness

The final aspect of an effective oral style is directness. *Directness* means using language that is adapted to the needs, interests, knowledge, and attitudes of the audience. Direct language cements the bond of trust between speaker and audience and the requirements of the occasion. In most situations, the more direct you can make your language, the more appropriate it will be. To increase directness, you can use personal pronouns, ask rhetorical questions, share common experiences, and speak hypothetically.

Using Personal Pronouns.   Often, merely by speaking in terms of "you," "us," "we," and "our," you will give the audience a verbal clue to your interest in them. In a speech on football defenses, for example, instead of saying "When people go to a football game, they often wonder why defensive players change their position just before the ball is snapped," try saying "When you go to a football game, you may often wonder why defensive players change their position just before the ball is snapped." Al-though this pronoun change may seem a very small point, by involving the listeners it can mean the difference between the audience's attention and indifference.

Asking Rhetorical Questions.   Although public speaking is not direct conversation with your audience, you can create the impression of direct conversation by asking rhetorical questions. *Rhetorical questions* are questions phrased to stimulate a mental response rather than a spoken one. Rhetorical questions encourage mental participation; once audiences start participating, they become more involved with the content of the speech. For instance, one more change in the football example we used previously would increase audience mental participation. Instead of saying "When you go to a football game, you may often wonder why defensive players change their position just before the ball is snapped," you might ask, "When you go to a football game, have you ever asked yourself, 'I wonder why Kessel moved to the other side of the line before the snap?' or 'I wonder why Jones started to rush the passer and then all of a sudden stepped back'?"

Sharing Common Experiences.   If you think your audience has had experiences like yours, share them in the speech. Talking about common experiences will allow your audience to identify more with you. If you were talking to a group of Girl or Boy Scouts, to drive home the point that worthwhile tasks require hours of hard work you might say, "Remember the hours you put in working on your first merit badge? Remember wondering whether you'd ever get the darned thing finished? And do you remember how good it felt to know that the time you put in really paid off?" (Notice how this example incorporates common experience along with personal pronouns and rhetorical questions to heighten the sense of shared experience.) When members of an audience identify with you, they will pay more attention to what you have to say.

Speaking Hypothetically.   When you cannot involve the audience directly with your topic, you can often relate to them by speaking hypothetically. If you were talking to a garden club about chartering an airplane for a group vacation, you might use the following hypothetical discussion:

> Let's say that for your club trip this month you wanted to go to the Tulip Festival in Holland, Michigan. Now, you could drive, but 500 miles is a long way to drive. You could fly commercially, but individual passage from here to Holland, Michigan, would be pretty expensive, plus you'd have to make two intermediate stops. Now, if you chartered an airplane, you could fly directly to Holland for a lot less.

Even though the example is only hypothetical, for purposes of getting the audience involved, it would work quite well.

Practice in Clarity, Vividness, Emphasis, and Directness

By Yourself

In each of the following sentences, circle words and phrases that are needlessly general, vague, or uncommon. Then restate the ideas in clear, precise, concrete/specific, simple, and vivid language.

> The course I took out of the history department in the most recent past was by far one of the most interesting courses I ever took.

> Our society tolerates a lot of things that don't go very well with our professed ideal of equality.

> We won't have clean air until we do something decisive about the terrible stuff our vehicles and industries are continually putting into the atmosphere.

> The reason Martin Luther King became so important historically was that he was a really great speaker.

> Experts say that our institutions of higher education are rapidly approaching a condition of financial extremity.

In Groups

1.   Divide into groups of three. A talks with B on topics such as those suggested in the previous exercise, while C observes. During the discussion, C should try to keep track of the way ideas are expressed, noting uses of vivid versus dull and clear versus vague language. After five minutes of discussion, the observers share their comments, then switch roles and repeat the process.

2.   Divide into groups of three. Each person prepares a one-minute statement containing at least five facts on a topic. In the presentation, the speakers should practice the use of sequencing, proportion, repetition, and transition to emphasize the five facts. After the presentation, the two listeners indicate the order of importance of the facts. Each person should be given one or two opportunities to speak.

3. What direct-language methods could you use to relate the following ideas to your class? Share methods with other members of your group.

People are afraid to report venereal disease to authorities.

Pitching horseshoes is fun.

The average American watches a lot of television.

The Amazon basin is a dense jungle.

Elements of Speech Delivery

Delivery is the use of voice and body to communicate the message of the speech. We often hear people say, "It's not what you say but how you say it that counts." Why is delivery so important? Primarily because delivery is the source of our contact with the speaker's mind. Delivery is what we see and what we hear. Think of delivery as a window through which we see a speech: When it is cracked, clouded over, or dirty, it obscures the content, organization, and language of the speech; when it is clean, it allows us to appreciate every aspect of the speech more fully.

Three elements of delivery are especially important in communicating effectively with an audience: conversational quality, vocal characteristics, and bodily action.

Conversational Quality

We say that a speaker has *conversational quality* when the delivery sounds like conversation. Although a speech is not a two-way conversation, using certain techniques characteristic of conversation will give listeners the feeling that you are conversing with them directly. In particular, you can enhance the conversational quality of your speeches through enthusiasm, eye contact, and spontaneity.

Enthusiasm. Interesting conversationalists and public speakers alike are enthusiastic about what they have to say. In fact, a review of speech research shows that enthusiasm is by far the most important element of effective speaking. This should come as no surprise. A speaker who looks and sounds enthusiastic will be listened to, and that speaker's ideas will be remembered.

If you are an outgoing person who displays feelings openly, you may find it easy to sound enthusiastic in your speeches. If you are rather reserved, however, your delivery is more likely to be perceived as lacking enthusiasm. To counteract this perception, you may have to work to intensify your feelings about your information so that your voice reflects those feelings.

How can you increase your own enthusiasm? First, select a topic that really excites you. Choosing an uninspiring topic will make it that much harder to care about communicating with your audience. Second, get involved in the material. Don't settle for being reasonably clear and organized; try to develop vivid mental pictures of what you are trying to say. Mental activity (thinking vividly) will lead to physical activity, the kinds of facial expressions, gestures, and movement that are

Effective delivery doesn't mean striving for theatrical effects. A conversational speaking style allows the speaker's sincerity and conviction to come through.

associated with enthusiasm. Third, remind yourself that your speech has a goal that in some way benefits the audience. Whether you are speaking to inform, to persuade, or to entertain, there is a reason your audience ought to listen to you. If you are convinced that you have something worthwhile to communicate, you are likely to feel and show more enthusiasm.

Eye Contact.   Both in conversation and in speeches, we expect speakers to look at us while they are talking. If they do not, they may lose our attention or cause us to lose eye contact with the speaker. In speeches, eye contact helps audience members concentrate, increases their confidence in the speaker, and contributes to their perception of the speaker as sincere. By the same token, speakers who fail to maintain eye contact with audiences are almost always perceived as ill at ease and often as insincere or dishonest.[1]

Being perceived as having eye contact involves looking at individuals and small groups in all parts of your audience throughout your speech. So long as you are looking at people and not at your notes or at the ceiling, the floor, or out the window, everyone in the audience will perceive you as genuinely trying to communicate. Try not to spend all of your time looking front and center. Shift your gaze from time to time so that you establish eye contact with the people at the ends of the aisles and those in the back of the room.

Spontaneity.   Both in conversation and in speeches, we expect people to speak spontaneously. A *spontaneous* speech is one that seems as fresh as a lively conversation, even though it has been well practiced. Remember how painful it was to listen to class members who were required to recite bits of prose or poetry they had memorized? Because they were struggling so hard to remember the words, they were not communicating any sense of meaning. The words sounded stilted and forced, not spontaneous. Although accomplished actors can make lines they have spoken literally thousands of times sound spontaneous, most public speakers cannot. Instead of trying for a forced spontaneity, avoid memorizing a speech word for word. If you allow some variation in your wording each time you practice or give a speech, you will automatically be more spontaneous.

Vocal Characteristics

The effective use of voice in speech delivery depends on several factors. To begin with, you need to become aware of the pitch, volume, rate, and quality of your voice. Then you can strive for variety, emphasis, and clear articulation.

Pitch, Volume, Rate, and Quality.   Recall that a person's voice includes pitch (highness and lowness on a scale), volume (loudness), rate (speed of speech), and quality (tone of voice). Problems with any of these characteristics can detract from your delivery. For instance, if audience members perceive the speaker's pitch as too high on the scale or the volume as too loud, they may become irritated and lose concentration on what the speaker is saying. If you speak too softly, many people in the audience may not be able to hear you. If you speak too fast, members of the audience may not be able to fully understand you, and you may slur sounds to the point that parts of your speech become unintelligible. If you speak too slowly, members of the audience may become restive and lose interest in what you have to say.

Variety and Emphasis.   Have you ever listened to a speech or a lecture that was delivered in a flat monotone? Effective speakers strive for vocal variety and emphasis—the contrasts in pitch, volume, rate, and quality that hold attention and lead the audience to distinguish the relative importance of words.

To illustrate the effect of variety and emphasis, take the simple sentence "I am not going to the movie." The meaning this sentence conveys to listeners depends on how you say it. If you create emphasis by the way you say "not," the sentence means you are answering the question of *whether* you are going; if you emphasize "movie," the sentence means you are answering the question of *where* you are not going. If you speak the sentence in a monotone—all the words at the same pitch, volume, and rate—listeners cannot be sure which question you are answering. Using variety and emphasis appropriately contributes to the meaning you communicate.

If you want to test your use of variety and emphasis, have someone listen as you read short passages aloud. Ask the person to tell you which words were higher in pitch, or louder, or slower. When you find that you can give a speech in such a way that the person recognizes which words you were trying to emphasize, you will be showing improvement in using vocal variety to clarify meaning.

Vocal Interferences.   As we discussed in Chapter 4, vocal interferences are the sounds that interrupt or intrude into fluent speech, causing distraction and, occasionally, total communication breakdown. In that chapter, we referred to such interferences as

"LADIES AND GENTLEMEN... IS *THAT* MY VOICE?... I NEVER HEARD IT AMPLIFIED BEFORE. IT SOUNDS SO WEIRD. HELLO. HELLO. I CAN'T BELIEVE IT'S ME. WHAT A STRANGE SENSATION. ONE, TWO, THREE... HELLO. WOW..."

© 1993 by Sidney Harris.

the "uh's," "er's," "well's," and "OK's" that creep into our speech, as well as those nearly universal interrupters of many Americans' conversation, "you know" and "like."

If you discover that vocal interferences are a problem in your public speaking, you will want to refer to that section of Chapter 4 for suggestions you can try in order to learn to hear and eventually limit your usage.

Articulation.   The shaping of speech sounds into recognizable oral symbols that combine to produce a word is called *articulation.* Many speakers suffer from minor articulation problems, such as adding a sound to a word (ath*a*lete for athlete), leaving out a sound (li*b*ary for lib*r*ary), transposing sounds (re*va*lent for re*lev*ant), and distorting sounds (tru*f* for tru*th*). Although some people have consistent articulation problems that require speech therapy (such as consistently substituting *th* for *s*), most of us are guilty of carelessness that is easily corrected.

Articulation is often confused with *pronunciation,* the form and accent a speaker gives to the syllables of a word. In the word *statistics,* articulation refers to the clear shaping of the ten sounds (*s, t, a, t, i, s, t, i, k, s*); pronunciation refers to how the sounds are grouped and accented (*sta tis' tiks*). Thus, you can clearly articulate an incorrect pronunciation. If you are unsure of how to pronounce a word you are going to use in your speech, be sure to look it up in a dictionary.

Although major articulation problems need to be corrected by a speech therapist, the most common faults of most speakers can be improved during a single term. The two most common faults are slurring sounds (running sounds and words together) and leaving off word endings. Spoken English will always contain some running together of sounds. For instance, most people say "tha-table" for "that table"; it is just too difficult to make two *t* sounds in a row. But many of us slur sounds and drop word endings to excess. "Who ya gonna see?" for "Who are you going to see?" illustrates both these errors. If you have a mild case of "sluritis," you can make considerable improvement by trying to overarticulate speech sounds as you read passages aloud. Some teachers advocate "chewing" your words—that is, making sure that you move your lips, jaw, and tongue very carefully for each sound you make. As with most problems of delivery, it takes conscientious practice—perhaps taking ten to fifteen minutes three days a week for a few months—to bring about significant improvement.

Because constant mispronunciation and misarticulation suggest that a person is ignorant or careless (or both), you will want to try to correct any mistakes that you make. Figure 15.3 lists a number of common problem words that students are likely to mispronounce or misarticulate in their speeches.

Word	Incorrrect	Correct
arctic	*ar' tic*	*arc' tic*
athlete	*ath' a lete*	*ath' lete*
family	*fam' ly*	*fam' a ly*
February	*Feb' yu ary*	*Feb' ru ary*
get	*git*	*get*
larynx	*lar' nix*	*lar' inks*
library	*ly' ber y*	*ly' brer y*
nuclear	*nu' klee er*	*nu' kyu ler*
particular	*par tik' ler*	*par tik' yu ler*
picture	*pitch' er*	*pic' ture*
recognize	*rek' a nize*	*rek' ig nize*
relevant	*rev' e lant*	*rel' e vant*
theater	*thee ay' ter*	*thee' a ter*
truth	*truf*	*truth*
with	*wit* or *wid*	*with*

Figure 15.3

Some common problem words

Cultural Concerns with Accents.   A major concern of speakers from other cultures is their *accent*—the inflection, tone, and speech habits typical of a particular country or region. The accents of people from foreign cultures tend to reflect the articulation and rhythm of their first language.

But one doesn't have to be from a foreign culture to have an accent; in reality, nearly everyone speaks with some kind of an accent. For most of us, an "accent" means any tone or inflection that differs from the way we and our neighbors speak. For instance, natives of a particular city or region will speak with inflections and tones that they believe are "normal" North American speech. But when they visit a different city or region, they will be accused of having an "accent," because the people living in the city or region they visit hear inflections and tones that they perceive as different from their own speech.

If you are from a "foreign" culture, can you easily get rid of your accent? The answer to that question depends on how old you are and how much you are willing to work at it. Suppose a family with a two-year-old, a twelve-year-old, and two adults moves from Italy to the United States. With no conscious effort, the two-year-old will learn to speak English with no Italian accent. The twelve-year-old will in time get rid of most of his or her accent. But the adults are likely to maintain much of their accent unless they work very hard at changing their speech habits.

When should people work to lessen or eliminate their accents? Only when their accents are so "heavy" or different from people's expectations that they have difficulty in communicating effectively. People who expect to go into teaching or other professions where how they speak will have a major effect on their performance will want to consider taking lessons from speech professionals.

Bodily Action

Bodily action includes facial expressions, gestures, posture, and movement. Since we discussed bodily actions in Chapter 4, in this section we will focus on aspects of those nonverbal behaviors that are particularly relevant to public speaking.

Your *facial expression* includes your eye and mouth movements. Audiences will respond negatively to deadpan expressions and perpetual grins or scowls; they will respond positively to honest and sincere expressions that reflect your thoughts and feelings. Think actively about what you are saying, and your face probably will respond accordingly.

Your *gestures* are the movements of your hands, arms, and fingers that describe and emphasize. If gesturing does not come easily to you, it is probably best not to force yourself to gesture in a speech. To encourage gestures, leave your hands free at all times to help you "do what comes naturally." If you clasp your hands behind you, grip the sides of the speaker's stand, or put your hands into your pockets, you will not be able to gesture naturally even if you want to.

Your *posture* is the position or bearing of your body. In speeches, an upright stance and squared shoulders communicate a sense of confidence to an audience. Speakers who slouch may give an unfavorable impression of themselves, including the impression of limited self-confidence and an uncaring attitude.

Your *movement* refers to motion of your entire body. Some speakers stand still throughout an entire speech. Others are constantly on the move. In general, it is probably better to remain in one place unless you have some reason for moving. A little movement, however, adds action to the speech, so it may help hold attention. Ideally, movement should help focus on transitions, emphasize ideas, or call attention to particular aspects of the speech. Avoid such unmotivated movement as bobbing and weaving, shifting from foot to foot, or pacing from one side of the room to the other. At the beginning of your speech, stand up straight on both feet. If you find yourself in some peculiar posture during the speech, return to the upright position with your weight equally distributed on both feet.

Poise refers to assurance of manner. A poised speaker is able to avoid mannerisms that distract the audience such as taking off or putting on glasses, smacking the tongue, licking the lips, or scratching the nose, hand, or arm. As a general rule, anything that calls attention to itself is negative, and anything that helps reinforce an important idea is positive. Likewise, a poised speaker is able to control speech nervousness. As we will discuss later in this chapter, all speakers show varying amounts of nervousness. Poised speakers have learned to push the thought of their nervousness aside and concentrate on communicating with the audience.

If you are thinking actively about what you are saying, your bodily action will probably be appropriate. If you use either too much or too little bodily action, your instructor can give you some pointers for limiting or accenting your normal behavior. Although you may find minor faults, you should not be concerned unless your bodily action calls attention to itself. In that case, you should determine ways of controlling or changing the behavior.

During practice sessions, you can try various methods of monitoring your bodily action. You can practice a portion of your speech in front of a mirror to see how you look to others when you speak. (Although some speakers swear by this method, others find it a traumatic experience.) If you have access to a video camera, you can record your speech and replay it for analysis. Or you can enlist a willing listener to critique how your bodily action contributes to or detracts from your delivery. This method is especially helpful for improving problems of delivery. Once you have identified a behavior you want to change, you can tell your helper what to look for as you speak. For instance, you might say "Raise your hand every time I begin to rock back and forth." By getting specific feedback when the behavior occurs, you can learn to become aware of it and make immediate adjustments.

Practice in Voice and Bodily Action

By Yourself

Indicate what you regard as your major problem of voice and articulation (such as speaking in a monotone or slurring words). Outline a plan for working on the problem.

In Groups

Divide into groups of three to six. Each person should have at least two minutes to tell a personal experience. The other members of the group should observe the speaker for any problems in vocal variety and emphasis, articulation, and bodily action.

Rehearsing Your Speech

Once your speech is outlined, you are ready to begin rehearsing. In this section, we consider methods of delivery, guidelines for practicing, and the use of notes.

Methods of Delivery

How you proceed with rehearsing depends on your method of delivery. Speeches may be delivered impromptu, by manuscript, by memorization, or extemporaneously.

Impromptu.   An *impromptu* speech is given without previous specific preparation. Although most people prefer to prepare their thoughts carefully before they face an audience, there are times when you will be called on to speak on the spur of the moment. For instance, at a meeting, Janet, an account representative, may be asked to justify an expenditure, explain the rationale behind a campaign, or respond to a previous speaker. In each of these cases, she will have to speak intelligently on the spot. Since such occasions can be important ones, professionals prize the ability to speak impromptu.[2]

You can become a more effective impromptu speaker by adapting the skills you are learning for formal speeches. As you gain facility with speech preparation skills, you'll find that you can mentally determine a speech goal, outline the key points you want to make, and think of the kind of material you want to present as quickly as the occasion demands.

Regardless of how well spoken you are on impromptu occasions, however, it would be foolhardy to leave preparation of formal speeches to the last minute. Audiences expect to hear a speech that has been well thought out beforehand.

Manuscript.   A common and often misused mode of delivery is the *manuscript* speech. Because the manuscript speech is written out in full and then read aloud, the wording can be planned very carefully. Presidents and other heads of state sometimes have good reason to resort to the manuscript because even the slightest mistake in sentence construction could cause a national or international outcry.

In the absence of a compelling need for exact phrasings, most speakers have little need to prepare a manuscript. Often, the only excuse for doing so is the apparent sense of security that the written speech provides. This security comes at a high price. As you can attest from your listening experience, manuscript speeches are unlikely to be spontaneous, stimulating, or interesting. Most important, because manuscript speeches give the speaker little opportunity to adapt to the specific audience, the audience usually feels spoken at rather than spoken with. Because of these disadvantages, you should usually avoid manuscript speaking, except as a special assignment.

Memorization.   A *memorized* speech is merely a manuscript committed to memory. Like the manuscript, it gives the speaker the opportunity to stick to an exact wording, while allowing the speaker to look at the audience instead of at the manuscript. Unfortunately for most speakers, however, memorization has most of the same disadvantages as the manuscript speech. Few individuals are able to memorize so well that their speech sounds spontaneous; moreover, the speaker cannot easily adjust to the specific audience. Like a manuscript speech, a speech that sounds memorized will come across more as a performance than as a communication. For these reasons, you should also avoid memorization, especially for your first speech assignment.

Extemporaneous.   The most effective method of delivery for most speeches you give, in class and elsewhere, is extemporaneous. An *extemporaneous* speech is carefully prepared and practiced, but the exact wording is determined at the time of utterance. Why should most of your speeches be given extemporaneously? Extemporaneous speaking permits you to draft an effective, well-planned speech while maintaining the conversational spontaneity of the impromptu speech. It also gives you much more flexibility to adapt to the audience than does the manuscript or memorized speech. Moreover, as a result of practicing your speech, you develop a fluency that limits the number of vocal interferences that can detract from the audience's perception of your expertise.[3] Because extemporaneous delivery combines most of the advantages of the other methods of delivery, experienced speakers generally prefer the extemporaneous method.

Now let's consider how a speech can be carefully prepared without being memorized.

Guidelines for Practicing the Speech

Novice speakers often believe that their preparation is complete once they have finished their outline. Nothing could be further from the truth. Only through rehearsing the speech can you can find effective, economical wording and hone your delivery. If you are scheduled to speak at 9 A.M. Monday and you do not finish the outline until 8:45, the speech will probably be far less effective than it would have been had you allowed yourself sufficient practice time. In general, you should try to complete your outline at least two days before the speech is due so that you have sufficient practice time to revise, evaluate, and mull over all aspects of the speech.

A good rehearsal period involves going through the speech, analyzing what you did, and then going through the speech again.

First Practice.   To make the most of your practice time, complete the following steps:

1. Read through your outline once or twice to get the ideas in mind. Then put the outline out of sight.

2. Stand up and face your imaginary audience. You want to make the practice as similar to the speech situation as possible. If you are practicing in your room, pretend that the chairs, lamps, books, and other objects in your view are people.

3. Write down the time that you begin.

4. Begin speaking. Keep going until you have presented your conclusion.

5. Write down the time you finish. Compute the length of the speech for this first practice.

6. Look at your outline again. Did you leave out any key ideas? Did you talk too long on any one point and not long enough on another? Did you really clarify each of your points? Did you try to adapt to your anticipated audience?

If you can get a friend or relative to listen to your practices and help you with your analysis, so much the better.

Second Practice.   During the same rehearsal period, go through the entire process again. By practicing a second time right after your analysis, you are more likely to make the kind of adjustments that begin to improve the speech.

In practice sessions, stand up and face your imaginary audience. You want to make the practice as similar to the speech situation as possible.

Subsequent Practices.   After you have completed one full rehearsal consisting of two sessions of practice and analysis, put the speech away for a while. Although you may need to go through the speech three, four, or even ten times, there is no value in cramming all the practices into one long rehearsal time. You may find that an individual practice right before you go to bed will be very helpful; while you are sleeping, your subconscious will continue to work on the speech. As a result, you are likely to find significant improvement in your mastery of the speech when you practice again the next day.

Using Notes

Should you use notes during practice or in giving the speech itself? The answer depends on what you mean by notes and how you plan to use them. It is best to avoid using notes at all for your first short speech assignments. Then, when assignments get longer, you will be more likely to use notes properly and not as a crutch. Of course, there is no harm in experimenting with notes to see what effect they have on your delivery.

Appropriate notes comprise key words or phrases that help trigger your memory. Notes will be most useful to you when they consist of the fewest words possible written in lettering large enough to be seen instantly at a distance. Many speakers condense their full-sentence speech outline into a brief speaking outline consisting of words or phrases. Figure 15.4 (p. 372) shows a set of notes made from the speech outline shown in Figure 14.4 (pp. 348–349).

For a speech in the five-to-ten-minute category, one or two 3-by-5-inch cards should be enough to hold your notes. When your speech contains a particularly good quotation or a complicated set of statistics, you may want to write them out in full on separate 3-by-5-inch cards.

During practices, you should use notes the way you plan to use them in the speech. Either set them on the speaker's stand or hold them in one hand and refer to them only when you have to. Speakers often find that the act of making a note card is so effective in helping cement ideas in the mind that during practice, or later during the speech itself, they do not need to refer to the notes at all.

Whether or not you use notes, practice the speech until you master the order and development of ideas. Don't try to memorize the words. When people memorize, they repeat the speech the same way until they can recite the words; when they stress the learning of ideas, they practice the speech a little differently each time. For instance, practice 1 may have this wording: "A handball court is a large rectangular box 20 feet wide, 40 feet long, and 20 feet high." In practice 2, the same content may be phrased this way: "A handball court is 20 by 40 by 20—a lot like a large rectangular box." When you are not tied to a particular phrasing, you can adapt to your audience's reactions at the time of delivery. For example, if you sense puzzlement, you can restate or repeat a point. Moreover, because each experience builds on the last, the speech itself often contains wording better than any used during practice.

Cholesterol and Heart Attacks

Cholesterol risks
    Overall levels
        Most Americans between 115 and 300
        Three levels of risk
            Over 240 high
            200 to 240 moderate
            Under 200 low

    Ratios
        LDLs bad; HDLs good
            LDLs deposit fat
            HDLs carry away
        Ratios predict risk
            Higher than 6 bad
            4-6 average
            Lower than 4 good

Figure 15.4 *Notes for a speech*

Practice in Analyzing Your Speech Rehearsals

By Yourself

Keep a log of your rehearsal program for your next speech. How many times did you practice? At what point did you feel you had a mastery of substance? How long was each of your practice periods?

For your second speech practice, indicate where in the speech you made changes to improve clarity, vividness, emphasis, and directness. Be specific in describing those changes.

Likewise, indicate where in the speech you made changes to improve enthusiasm, eye contact, and spontaneity. Be specific in describing those changes.

Finally, indicate what aspects of language and delivery you will pay special attention to in the final practice and in the speech itself. Again, be specific.

Coping with Nervousness

All speakers feel nervous as they approach their first speech. Whether you label your feeling as nervousness, stage fright, speech fright, shyness, reticence, speech apprehension, or some other term, the meaning of that feeling is essentially the same: a fear or anxiety about public speaking.

People's public-speaking nervousness is usually a function of either a trait or a state. A *trait* is a relatively ongoing characteristic of an individual; a *state* is the state of mind that a person experiences for a period of time. Nervousness is a trait when a person experiences a fear of any kind of communication. Those of us with trait nervousness are likely to experience similar fears in friendly conversations, group meetings, and public speaking, as well as in such mass media situations as television, radio, or film. Research has shown that up to 20 percent of the population may experience trait communication nervousness.[4]

In contrast, public-speaking nervousness is a state when it is directed only to public speaking. For instance, many people who experience no apprehension at communicating on a one-to-one basis with peers, relatives, or authority figures may experience considerable fear of public speaking. State apprehension, especially public-speaking apprehension, is quite common. As much as 80 percent of the population admits to at least some public-speaking nervousness. If you have no major problems in interacting with people in other communication situations, your nervousness at the thought of giving a speech is likely to be less of a problem than you might think.

Public-speaking nervousness may be *cognitive* (in the mind) or *behavioral* (physically displayed). Cognitively, speaker nervousness comes at the thought of speaking in public. People who say they are fearful of talking in public make negative predictions about the results of their speaking. People who experience fear may recognize the importance of having their ideas heard, but in their mind, any benefits that might come from giving a speech are far outweighed by the fear itself. Behaviorally, speaker nervousness is represented by such physical manifestations as stomach cramps, sweaty palms, dry mouth, and the use of such filler expressions as "um," "like," and "you know." At times the behavior is an avoidance of speaking in public or speaking for the shortest period of time possible when required to speak.

To help cope with this nervousness, keep in mind that fear is not an either–or matter—it is a matter of degree. A relatively few people may experience such a small degree of nervousness about public speaking that they don't even seem to notice it; likewise, an even smaller number are so afraid of speaking in public that they become tongue-tied, break out in hives, or hyperventilate at the very thought. Most of us are somewhere between these two extremes.

So, we can see that the fear of speaking in public is normal. The more important question is whether it is harmful. In all the years I have been teaching, I have had one case of a person who began his speech normally, but after the first sentence literally ran back to his seat. Speaker nervousness a real problem only when it becomes debilitating—when the fear is so great that a person is unable to go through with giving a speech.

Over the years I have also had students who were obviously suffering discomfort at having to stand in front of the audience. Many of us wish that we could speak without these obvious reactions. But would we really be better off if we could be totally free from nervousness? Gerald Phillips, a speech scholar who has been studying public-speaking nervousness for more than twenty years, says no. Phillips has noted that "learning proceeds best when the organism is in a state of tension."[5] In fact, it helps to be a little nervous to do your best: If you are lackadaisical about giving a speech, you probably will not do a good job.

Because at least some tension is constructive, our goal is not to get rid of nervousness but to learn how to cope with our nervousness. Phillips cites results of studies that followed groups of students with speaker nervousness for one- and three-year intervals after instruction in dealing with their nervousness. Almost all the students had learned to cope with the nervousness, even though they still experienced the same level of tension. Phillips goes on to say that "apparently they had learned to manage the tension; they no longer saw it as an impairment, and they went ahead with what they had to do."[6]

So, we can conclude that nearly everyone who speaks in public, whether for the first or fiftieth time, experiences some nervousness. Now let's look at some things to consider as you prepare your first speech:

1. *Despite nervousness, you can make it through your speech.* Very few people are so bothered that they are unable to function. You may not enjoy the "flutters" you experience, but you can still deliver an effective speech.

2. *Listeners are not as likely to recognize your fear as you might think.* The thought that audiences will notice an inexperienced speaker's fear often increases that fear. Thoughts that an audience will be quick to laugh at a speaker who is hesitant or that it is just waiting to see how shaky a person appears can have devastating effects. But the fact is that members of an audience, even speech instructors, greatly underrate the amount of stage fright they believe a person has.[7]

3. *The better prepared you are, the better you will cope with nervousness.* Many people show extreme nervousness either because they are not well prepared or because they think they are not well prepared. According to Gerald Phillips, a positive approach to coping with nervousness is "(1) learn how to try, (2) try, and (3) have some success."[8] All of Part Five is devoted to helping you become well prepared for your speeches so that you will have more successful efforts. As you learn to recognize when you are truly prepared, you will find yourself paying less attention to your nervousness.

4. *The more experience you get in speaking, the better you can cope with nervousness.* Beginners experience some fear because they do not have experience speaking in public. As you give speeches, and see improvement in those speeches, you will gain confidence and worry less about any nervousness you might experience. A recent study of the impact of basic courses on communication apprehension indicates that experience in a public-speaking course can reduce students' communication apprehension scores.[9]

In addition, experienced speakers learn to channel their nervousness. The nervousness you feel is, in controlled amounts, good for you. It takes a certain amount of nervousness to do your best. What you want is for your nervousness to dissipate once you begin your speech. Just as athletes are likely to report that their nervousness disappears once they begin play, so too should speakers find nervousness disappearing once they get a reaction to the first few sentences of their introduction.

Specific Behaviors

The following are some specific behaviors that you can use to control nervousness. Coping with nervousness begins during the preparation process and extends to the time you actually begin a speech. In addition to the following suggestions, see Taking the Terror Out of Talk on pages 376–377.

1. *Pick a topic you are comfortable with.* The best way to control nervousness is to pick a topic you know something about, one that is important to you, and one that you know your audience is likely to respond to. Public speakers cannot allow themselves to be saddled with a topic they do not care about. An unsatisfactory topic lays the groundwork for a psychological mind-set that almost guarantees nervous-

Picking a topic you know something about and is important to you will help you control your nervousness.

Scared to death of speaking? In this article, Michael T. Motley, a professor of com-
munication and rhetoric who also works as a communication consultant, suggests
that one key to reducing your anxiety is to think of a speech as communication
rather than as a performance.

Surveys show that what Americans fear most—more than snakes, heights, disease, financial problems or even death—is speaking before a group. This is surprising, in a way, since even a dreadful speech isn't as serious as illness, poverty or the grave. Yet about 85 percent of us feel uncomfortably anxious speaking in public. Even professionals aren't immune. Some of our most successful politicians, evangelists, and entertainers suffer extreme stage fright, or, to use its more formal label, "speech anxiety."

While it's comforting to realize that such anxiety is almost universal, a magic formula to dispel it would be even more comforting. There is no such formula, but recent research that helps us understand speech anxiety better also suggests ways to control it....

Excessive anxiety is especially common among people who view speeches as performances, in which they must satisfy an audience of critics who will carefully evaluate gestures, language and everything else they do. Though they can't describe precisely what these critics expect, people with a performance orientation assume that formal, artificial behavior is somehow better than the way they usually talk. Research has shown that expecting to be evaluated or being uncertain about the proper way to behave arouses anxiety in almost any situation.

A much more useful orientation, and a more accurate one, is to view speeches as communication rather than performance. The speakers' role is to share ideas with an audience more interested in hearing what they have to say than in analyzing or criticizing how they say it—a situation not very different, at least in this regard, from everyday conversation....

Once people genuinely view making a speech as communication, they

ness at the time of the speech. By the same token, having a topic you know about and that is important to you lays the groundwork for a satisfying speech experience.

2. *Take time to prepare fully.* If you back yourself into a corner and must find material, organize it, write an outline, and practice the speech all in an hour or two, you almost guarantee failure and destroy your confidence. On the other hand, if you do a little work each day for a week before the assignment, you will experience considerably less pressure and increased confidence.

can think of it in terms of their normal, everyday conversation rather than in terms of past anxiety-ridden performances. I have found that with this approach, speech anxiety almost always subsides and the speeches almost always improve....

A nonperformance orientation helps speakers realize that their real objective is to communicate. Unlike our school classmates who counted the number of times we said "uh" during book reports, most audiences are more interested in hearing what we have to say than in evaluating our speech skills....

By far the most important quality of a speaker's delivery is to make the members of the audience feel that they are truly being spoken with rather than spoken at. People who perform at concerts, plays and dance recitals are expected to have unusual skills and to show them off. But if a speaker's purpose is to communicate, all he or she needs are the gestures, vocal inflections and facial expressions used in everyday conversation....

There is an exercise I use to demonstrate the point: As the speaker approaches the podium, I dismiss the audience temporarily and begin a "one-way conversation" with the speaker. I tell him or her to forget about giving a speech and simply talk spontaneously to me, using the speech-outline notes as a guide. In this situation, most people feel rather silly orating, so they start to speak conversationally, using natural language, inflections and gestures. I ask the speaker to maintain this conversational style while the audience gradually returns, a few people at a time.

The speakers usually do this successfully as the audience returns. When they don't, the transition from talk to speech is invariably identified later by the audience as the point when effectiveness began to decrease and by the speaker as the point when anxiety began to increase....

For most of us, giving a speech is an important and novel event. It's natural and appropriate to feel some anxiety. A speaker's aim should be to keep this natural nervousness from cycling out of control: not to get rid of the butterflies but to make them fly in formation. ■

SOURCE: Michael T. Motley, "Taking the Terror Out of Talk," *Psychology Today,* January 1988, pp. 46–49. Copyright 1988 Sussex Publishers, Inc. Reprinted by permission.

Experience in preparation and the length and difficulty of the speech will affect your schedule. For instance, experienced speakers often begin research a month before the date they are to give the speech; they then reserve an entire week for rehearsal and revision.

Giving yourself enough time to prepare fully includes sufficient time for rehearsal. Practice your first speech at least two or three times. Your goal is to build habits that will control your behavior during the speech itself. If our national love affair with big-time athletics has taught us anything, it is that careful preparation enables athletes (or speakers) to meet and overcome adversity. Among relatively equal opponents, the winning team is the one that is mentally and physically prepared for the contest. When an athlete says "I'm going into this competition as well prepared as I can possibly be," he or she is more likely to do well. In this regard, speechmaking is like athletics. If you assure yourself that you have carefully prepared and practiced your speech, you will do the kind of job of which you can be proud.

3. *Try to schedule your speech at a time that is psychologically best for you.* When speeches are being scheduled, you may be able to choose the time. Are you better off "getting it over with"—that is, being the first person to speak that day? If so, volunteer to go first. But regardless of when you speak, do not spend time thinking about yourself or your speech. At the moment the class begins, you have done all you can do to be prepared. Focus your mind on the other speeches and become involved with what each speaker is saying. Then when your turn comes, you will be as relaxed as possible.

4. *Visualize successful speaking experiences. Visualization* involves developing a mental strategy and picturing yourself implementing that strategy. How many times have you said to yourself, "Well, if I had been in that situation I would have . . ."? Such statements are a form of visualizing. Joe Ayres and Theodore S. Hopf, two scholars who have conducted extensive research on visualization, have found that if people can visualize themselves going through an entire process, they have a much better chance of succeeding when they are in the situation.[10] Successful visualization begins during practice periods. For instance, if during a practice you not only say "So, you can see how the shape of the wing gives a plane lift," but you also see members of the audience nodding, you are visualizing successful response.

Finally, when your turn comes, walk to the speaker's stand confidently. Research indicates that your fear is most likely to be at its greatest right before you walk forward to give your speech and when you have your initial contact with the audience.[11] As you walk to the speaker's stand, continue to visualize success: Remind yourself that you have good ideas, that you are well prepared, and that your audience wants to hear what you have to say. Even if you make mistakes, the audience will profit from your speech.

5. *Pause for a few seconds before you begin.* When you reach the stand, stop a few seconds before you start to speak. Take a deep breath while you make eye contact with the audience; that may help get your breathing in order. Try to move about a little during the first few sentences; sometimes a few gestures or a step one way or another is enough to break some of the tension.

Persistent Nervousness

What if after doing everything suggested here you still experience what you believe are abnormal fears about speechmaking? Recent research has shown that a small number of students may need more help than the ordinary speech course provides.

Unfortunately, many students respond by dropping the course. But that is not an answer to speech anxiety. In all areas of life, people have to give speeches; they have to get up before peers, people from other organizations, customers, and others to explain their ideas. Although it is never too late to get help, a college speech course is the best time to start working on coping with speech nervousness. Even if your fears prove to be more perception than reality, it's important to take the time to get help.

To start, see your professor outside class and talk with him or her about what you are experiencing. Your professor should be able to offer ideas for people you can see or programs you can attend. As Virginia Richmond and James McCroskey have shown as a result of years of research in communication apprehension, for some people there is a need for special programs.[12] One of the most popular programs is *systematic desensitization,* which repeatedly exposes people to the stimulus they fear, associating it each time with something pleasant. Another program is *cognitive restructuring,* which helps people to identify the illogical beliefs they hold and provides individualized instruction in formulating more appropriate beliefs. Over time, people can condition themselves to overcome their fears and take a more positive approach to their communication. Many communities offer such programs.

But keep in mind that there are very few speech students who have been so hurt by fear that they can't deliver a speech. The purpose of a speech course is to help you learn and develop the skills that will allow you to achieve even when you feel extremely anxious.

Practice in Analyzing Nervousness

By Yourself

Interview one or two people who give frequent speeches (a minister, a politician, a lawyer, a businessperson, a teacher). Ask about what is likely to make them more or less nervous about giving a speech. Find out how they cope with their nervousness. Which behaviors do you believe might work for you?

Critical Analysis of Speeches

In addition to learning to prepare and present speeches, you are learning to critically analyze the speeches you hear. From a pedagogical standpoint, critical analysis of speeches not only provides the speaker with feedback on where the speech went right and where it went wrong but also gives you, the critic, insight into the methods that you want to incorporate or, perhaps, avoid in presenting your own speeches.

Although speech criticism is context specific (analyzing the effectiveness of an informative demonstration speech differs from analyzing the effectiveness of a persuasive action speech), in this section we look at criteria for evaluating public speaking in general. Classroom speeches are usually evaluated on the basis of how well the speaker has met specific criteria of effective speaking.

In these last five chapters, you have been learning not only steps of speech preparation but also the criteria by which speeches are measured. The critical assumption is that if a speech has good content, is well organized, is well worded, and is well delivered, it is more likely to achieve its goal. Thus, the critical apparatus for evaluating any speech comprises questions that relate to the basics of content, organization, language, and delivery.

The following series of questions can be adapted to the evaluation of any speech. Notice that each question is followed by a reference to the pages in this text where relevant factors and guidelines are discussed.

Content

1. Was the goal of the speech clear? (pp. 279–280)
2. Did the speaker have high-quality information? (pp. 288–295)
3. Did the speaker use a variety of kinds of developmental material? (pp. 296–304)
4. Did the speaker adapt the content to the audience's interests, knowledge, and attitudes? (pp. 312–323)

Organization

5. Did the introduction gain attention, gain goodwill for the speaker, and lead into the speech? (pp. 338–343)
6. Were the main points clear statements? (pp. 329–335)
7. Did the conclusion tie the speech together? (pp. 343–345)

Language

8. Was the language clear? (pp. 62–66; 354–355)
9. Was the language vivid? (pp. 355–356)
10. Was the language emphatic? (pp. 356–359)
11. Was the language direct? (pp. 359–360)

Delivery

12. Did the speaker sound enthusiastic? (pp. 361–362)
13. Did the speaker look at the audience? (pp. 85; 362)
14. Was the delivery spontaneous? (pp. 362–363)
15. Did the speaker show sufficient vocal variety and emphasis? (p. 363)

16. Were the pronunciation and articulation acceptable? (pp. 364–365)

17. Did the speaker have good posture? (p. 366)

18. Did the nonverbal elements of the speech complement the speech content? (pp. 366–367)

19. Did the speaker show sufficient poise? (p. 367)

By Yourself

Use the preceding list of nineteen questions to evaluate a speech you have listened to in or out of class. Then write a two- to five-page paper explaining your evaluation.

Summary

Speech presentation involves a number of verbal and nonverbal skills. The wording of the speech is more effective if it is clear, vivid, emphatic, and directed to the audience.

In addition to being well worded, effective speeches are well delivered. For most speeches, good delivery begins with a conversational quality achieved through enthusiasm, eye contact, and spontaneity. Vocal characteristics that can affect the delivery include pitch, volume, rate, and quality; variety and emphasis; and articulation. Bodily actions can sometimes detract from delivery but usually are appropriate if the speaker is focused on communicating with the audience.

Rehearsal is a key aspect of speech preparation. Although your speeches may be delivered impromptu, as manuscript speeches, or as memorized speeches, for most situations the extemporaneous method works best, because it combines careful presentation with spontaneity.

To rehearse an extemporaneous speech, complete the outline at least two days in advance. Between the time the outline is completed and the time the speech is to be given, you will want to practice the speech several times, weighing what you did and how you did it after each practice. You may wish to use brief notes, especially for longer speeches, as long as they do not interfere with your delivery.

All speakers feel nervous as they approach their first speech. Such nervousness may be traitlike, a relatively ongoing characteristic of an individual, or statelike, a state of mind that a person experiences for a period of time. Likewise, public-speaking nervousness may be cognitive (in the mind) or behavioral (physically displayed). Rather than being an either–or matter, nervousness is a matter of degree.

Because at least some tension is constructive, the goal is not to get rid of nervousness but to learn how to cope with it. Bear in mind that you can make it through your speech, despite nervousness, and that listeners are not nearly as likely to recognize your fear as you might think. In addition, the more experience you get in speaking and the better prepared you are, the better you will cope with nervousness. In fact, experienced speakers learn to channel their nervousness in ways that help them to do their best.

Even though nervousness is normal, you can use several specific behaviors to help control it: (1) Pick a topic you are comfortable with. (2) Take time to prepare fully. (3) Try to schedule your speech at a time that is psychologically best for you. (4) Visualize successful speaking experiences. (5) Pause for a few seconds before you begin.

If nervousness is truly detrimental to your performance, see your professor outside class and talk with him or her about what you are experiencing. Your professor should be able to offer ideas for people you can see or programs you can attend.

Speeches are evaluated on how well they meet the guidelines for effective content, organization, language, and delivery.

Suggested Readings

Clevenger, Theodore, Jr. "A Synthesis of Experimental Research in Stage Fright." *Quarterly Journal of Speech* 45 (April 1959): 134–145. Draws eleven conclusions about stage fright that are still consistent with recent data.

Mayer, Lyle V. *Fundamentals of Voice and Articulation,* 11th ed. Dubuque, IA: Wm. C. Brown, 1996 (paperback). A short, and very popular, book.

McCroskey, James C. "Oral Communication Apprehension: A Summary of Recent Theory and Research." *Human Communication Research* 4 (1977): 78. A companion article to the Clevenger article.

Notes

1. Judee K. Burgoon, Deborah A. Coker, and Ray A. Coker, "Communicative Effects of Gaze Behavior: A Test of Two Contrasting Explanations," *Human Communication Research* 12 (1986): 495–524.

2. John R. Johnson and Nancy Szczupakiewicz, "The Public Speaking Course: Is It Preparing Students with Work-Related Skills?" *Communication Education* 36 (1987): 131–137.

3. Lawrence A. Hosman, "The Evaluative Consequences of Hedges, Hesitations, and Intensifiers: Powerful and Powerless Speech Styles," *Human Communication Research* 15 (1989): 400.

4. James C. McCroskey, "Oral Communication Apprehension: A Summary of Recent Theory and Research," *Human Communication Research* 4 (1977): 78.

5. Gerald M. Phillips, "Rhetoritherapy Versus the Medical Model: Dealing with Reticence," *Communication Education* 26 (1977): 37.

6. Ibid.

7.   Theodore Clevenger, Jr., "A Synthesis of Experimental Research in Stage Fright," *Quarterly Journal of Speech* 45 (April 1959): 136.

8.   Gerald Phillips, *Communication Incompetencies: A Theory of Training Oral Performance Behavior.* (Carbondale, IL: Southern Illinois University Press, 1991), p. 6.

9.   Heidi M. Rose, Andrew S. Rancer, and Kenneth C. Crannell, "The Impact of Basic Courses in Oral Interpretation and Public Speaking on Communication Apprehension," *Communication Reports* 6 (Winter 1993): 58.

10.   Joe Ayres and Theodore S. Hopf, "The Long-Term Effect of Visualization in the Classroom: A Brief Research Report," *Communication Education* 39 (1990): 77.

11.   Larry W. Carlile, Ralph R. Behnke, and James T. Kitchens, "A Psychological Pattern of Anxiety in Public Speaking," *Communication Quarterly* 25 (Fall 1977): 45.

12.   Virginia P. Richmond and James C. McCroskey, *Communication: Apprehension, Avoidance, and Effectiveness,* 2d ed. (Scottsdale, AZ: Gorsuch Scarisbrick, 1989), pp. 94–101.

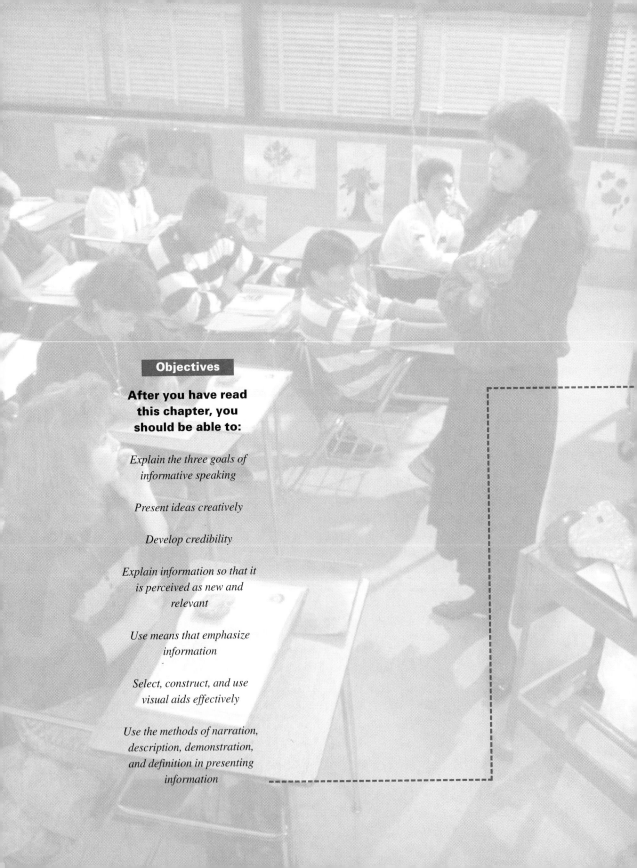

**After you have read
this chapter, you
should be able to:**

*Explain the three goals of
informative speaking*

Present ideas creatively

Develop credibility

*Explain information so that it
is perceived as new and
relevant*

*Use means that emphasize
information*

*Select, construct, and use
visual aids effectively*

*Use the methods of narration,
description, demonstration,
and definition in presenting
information*

16

Informative
Speaking

For several months, a major architectural firm had been working on designs for the arts center to be built in the middle of downtown. Members of the city council and guests from various constituencies in the city, as well as a number of concerned citizens, were taking their seats as the long anticipated presentation was about to begin. As Linda Garner, mayor and presiding officer of the city council, finished her introduction, Donald Harper, the principal architect of the project, walked to the microphone to begin his speech.

This type of scenario is played out every day as speakers struggle to help us increase our understanding of complex issues. Over a century ago, Ralph Waldo Emerson succinctly captured the challenge of presenting information effectively when he said, "Any piece of knowledge I acquire to-day has a value at this moment exactly proportioned to my skill to deal with it."[1]

In this chapter, we build on the steps of general speech preparation by focusing on speeches meant primarily to inform. First, we consider the nature of informative speeches and the factors involved in achieving your speech goal; second, we consider principles of informative speaking that are particularly relevant to achieving your speech goals; and finally, we look at four methods of informing. In the next chapter, we build on the steps of general speech preparation by focusing on speeches meant primarily to persuade.

The Nature of Informative Speeches

The primary goal of an informative speech is to create understanding. When the occasion calls for a speech that is informative rather than persuasive or entertaining, the audience expects the speaker to present the material in language that shows an informative intention and fulfills an informative function.

Speaking Intent

Whether a speech will be perceived as informative depends in part on the way speakers word their intent or goal. A speaker whose speech goal is phrased "to have the audience understand the components of impressionistic painting" is more likely to produce an informative speech than a speaker whose goal is phrased "to have the audience believe that Renoir is the best of the French impressionist painters." The phrase "to understand the components" suggests the presentation of objective information; the phrase "to believe that Renoir is the best" suggests affecting the audience's attitude—an intention that goes beyond simply imparting understanding.

Function of Information

Whether a speech is perceived as informative also depends on how the speaker uses the information in the speech. All speeches are likely to contain facts, opinions, and other information. In an informative speech, the speaker uses the material to clarify and explain. If, for instance, a speaker presents examples of how computers can be used to create graphic displays, those examples would serve an informative function; if, however, a speaker uses examples to build arguments supporting a company's need to upgrade its computer technology, the examples function persuasively.

In summary, then, when your speech is meant to inform, or create understanding, you will want to make sure that your specific goal is phrased with an informative intent and that you use information so that it functions informatively.

Factors in Achieving Your Informative-Speaking Goal

In informative speeches, you expect that your audience will learn from your presentation. Learning is generally a result of three factors: attending to or showing interest in the information being presented, understanding that information, and retaining the information in a form that results in the ability to recall it on demand. Your rhetorical challenge is to support these three factors in your speech.

1. *Generate enough interest in the information to arouse the audience's attention.* Whether or not they should, people are quick to make value judgments about whether they will listen to information you present. Thus, generating interest in the information is especially important.[2] For example, in a speech in which your intent is to teach your audience how to install a CD player in an older car, you must show audience members why this information is useful to them. Otherwise, the audience may "tune out" without benefiting from the material you've prepared. Moreover, as the speech continues, you must use your creativity to maintain that attention.

2. *Explain the information in ways that will enable the audience to understand.* If audience members don't fully understand key parts of the information, they will not learn it. For example, in your speech on how to install a CD player, if you use technical terms without carefully defining them, the audience will be unable to assimilate the instructions.

3. *Discuss information in ways that will enable the audience to remember it.* The minute we hear information, we begin to forget some of it. Within a relatively short time, we may lose anywhere from one-third to all of what we have heard. Consequently, as a speaker, you must present your information in such a way that audience members will be able to retain it and recall it on demand. In your speech on how to install a CD player, for example, you need to organize the process under a small number of headings so that the audience will be able to recall the main steps.

Practice in Identifying Informative Factors

By Yourself

In addition to taking content notes in class during your professors' lectures, make notes of the methods they use (1) to gain attention, (2) to create understanding, and (3) to ensure retention. Be prepared to share particularly good examples of different professors' methods.

Principles of Informative Speaking

The three factors that are involved in learning have suggested general strategies to follow in informative speaking. Now we turn to specific principles that you can follow to capitalize on these factors. Each principle is stated in a way that suggests which factors are incorporated. This discussion of principles assumes that you already have a tentative specific goal; that you have completed your research; and that you have a tentative time, space, topic, causal, reasons, or problem–solution order for your speech (patterns of organization that are relevant to informative speeches). The challenges you now are trying to meet are (1) how to create interest so the audience will listen, (2) how to explain in a way that will help the audience understand, and (3) how to discuss the information in a way that will help the audience remember. Accomplishing these goals involves the principles of creativity, credibility, newness, relevance, emphasis, and using visual aids.

Creativity

PRINCIPLE 1

Audiences are more likely to show interest in, understand, and remember information that is presented creatively.

Creativity underlies all the other principles discussed in this chapter because it affects every part of the learning process.

The Nature of Creativity.   Creativity in informative speaking involves using your material in an imaginative way—a way that is in keeping with John Haefele's belief that a creative person makes "new combinations."[3] Although you may be thinking "I'm just not a creative person," in reality everyone can be creative in their speeches if they are willing to work at it.

Creativity in speaking is a result of depth of information, time, receptivity, and availability of choices.

1.   *Gather enough quality information to give you a broad base from which to work.* Creativity is far more likely to be the product of perspiration than inspiration. The more you know, the more likely you are to approach the topic creatively.

2.   *Give yourself enough time for the creative process to work.* Once you have completed your outline, you need time, perhaps two or three days, for your mind to reflect on the material. For instance, you may find that the morning after an uninspiring practice, you suddenly have two or three fresh ideas. While you were sleeping, your mind was still going over the material; when you awoke, the product of unconscious or subconscious thought reached your consciousness. Had there been no intervening time between the unrewarding practice session and the actual speech delivery, your mind would not have had the time to work through the material. So, you can facilitate creativity simply by giving your mind time to process the material you have.

3.   *Be prepared for a creative thought whenever it comes.* Have you ever noticed how some fascinating ideas come to you while you are washing dishes or shining your shoes or watching television or waiting at a stop light? Have you also noticed that when you try to recall those ideas later, they are likely to have slipped away? Many speakers, writers, and composers carry a pencil and paper with them at all times, and when an idea comes, they make a note of it. Not all these flights of fancy are flashes of creative genius, but some of them are good, or at least worth exploring. If you do not make a note of your ideas, you will never know whether they were good.

4. *Force yourself to practice sections of the speech in different ways.* If you do not practice in different ways, you allow yourself to be content with the first way of presenting material that comes to mind rather than considering alternatives that might be better. If, however, you purposely phrase key ideas in different ways in each of the first few practices, you give yourself choices. Although some of the ways you express a point may be similar, trying new ways will stretch your mind, and chances are good that one or two of the ways will be far superior and much more imaginative than any of the others.

Creating Alternative Choices.   Start with the premise that an infinite number of lines of development are possible from any body of factual material. When you create choices, you can select the one that will work best in the speech.

To illustrate the technique of creating alternative choices, suppose you are planning to give a speech on climatic variation in the United States and that your research has uncovered the data shown in Figure 16.1. We will use these data to show that (1) one set of data can suggest several lines of development on one topic and (2) the same point can be made in many different ways.

City	Temperature (in Degrees Fahrenheit)				Precipitation	
	January		Yearly			
	High	Low	High	Low	July	Annual
Chicago	32	12	93	-6	3.4	33
Cincinnati	41	26	96	2	3.3	39
Denver	42	15	100	-5	1.5	14
Los Angeles	65	47	88	39	T*	14
Miami	76	58	96	44	6.8	59
Minneapolis	22	2	96	-21	3.5	24
New Orleans	64	45	98	23	6.7	59
New York	40	17	97	11	3.7	42
Phoenix	64	35	114	27	T	7
Portland, Maine	32	12	93	-6	3.9	42
St. Louis	40	24	97	2	3.3	35
San Francisco	55	42	86	33	T	18
Seattle	44	33	91	15	.6	38

*Trace

Figure 16.1 *Climatic data*

1. *One set of data can suggest several lines of development.* Before you read the following material, study Figure 16.1. What conclusions can you draw from it? By thinking creatively, you could draw the following conclusions:

    a. Yearly high temperatures in U.S. cities vary far less than yearly low temperatures.

    b. It hardly ever rains on the West Coast in the summer.

    c. In most of the major cities cited, July, a month thought to be hot and dry, produces more than the average one-twelfth of annual precipitation.

Thus, this one set of data produces conclusions that suggest at least three different lines of development for a single speech on climate.

2. *The same point can be made in different ways.* Let us consider the statement "Yearly high temperatures in U.S. cities vary far less than yearly low temperatures."

    a. *Statistical development:* Of the thirteen cities selected, ten (77 percent) had yearly highs between 90 and 100; three (23 percent) had yearly lows above freezing, six (46 percent) had yearly lows between zero and 32, and four (31 percent) had low temperatures below zero.

    b. *Comparative development:* Cincinnati, Miami, Minneapolis, New York, and St. Louis, cities at different latitudes, all had yearly high temperatures of 96 or 97; in contrast, the lowest temperature for Miami was 44, and the lowest temperatures for Cincinnati, Minneapolis, New York, and St. Louis were 2, -21, 11, and 2, respectively.

Can you find another way of making the same point?

Credibility

PRINCIPLE 2

> *Audiences are more likely to attend to your speech if they like, trust, and have confidence in you.*

Most of us tend to have more confidence in some people's explanations of information than in others'. In fact, people are more inclined to listen and pay attention to speakers they like and trust. As we saw in Chapter 13, we call this trust and confidence in a speaker *credibility.* Thus, to increase the likelihood that your audience will listen to you, make sure that you are perceived as being credible.

You'll recall that speaker credibility is based on knowledge/expertise (qualifications or capability), trustworthiness (apparent motives and moral and ethical traits), and personality (sum total of a person's behavioral and emotional tendencies).

Credibility is not something you can gain overnight or turn on or off at will. Nevertheless, there are several things you can do to avoid damaging your credibility and perhaps even to strengthen it during a speech or a series of speeches.

1. *Be well prepared.* If you are confident that you have prepared completely, your audience will accept your authority and listen carefully to you. If the audience recognizes your knowledge and expertise before you begin, that is a plus. For instance, if your audience knows that you are on the student senate, when they learn that you are speaking about how the student senate works to influence university decisions, they are even more likely to accept your information as authoritative. But even if you do not come into the speech with a reputation, if you talk knowledgeably and fluently, with command of your information and without stumbling and making a variety of misstatements, you will build credibility during your speech.

2. *Emphasize your interest in the audience.* Show your good intentions by emphasizing the benefits your particular audience can gain from your ideas. You want your listeners to understand that you care about them and what happens to them. For example, suppose you are planning to speak to an audience of young adults about methods of monitoring cholesterol levels. To show that your speech is directed to them, you might stress such information as "recent studies have revealed that high cholesterol levels are being discovered in large numbers of people in their teens and early twenties."

3. *Look and sound enthusiastic.* As we emphasized in Chapter 15, if you have a positive attitude about your topic, your audience is likely to become enthusiastic as well. If listeners suspect that you do not really care, however, they certainly are not going to.

You probably will see the cumulative effect of credibility during this term. As your class proceeds from speech to speech, some speakers will grow in stature in your mind and others will diminish. Let us look at two more behaviors that relate primarily to building your credibility in class.

4. *Be ready to speak on time.* Your credibility is enhanced by a positive attitude toward the schedule. Being ready to speak on time shows the class that you are willing to assume responsibility.

5. *Evaluate others' speeches thoughtfully.* If you can explain why a speech was effective and apply that understanding of speech principles to your own speeches, classmates will develop a respect for your public-speaking capabilities. Then they will be more likely to respect your ideas when you present your speech.

Intellectual Stimulation

PRINCIPLE 3

Audiences are more likely to listen to information they perceive to be intellectually stimulating.

Because audience members are less likely to pay attention to material they think they already know or consider peripheral to their needs, it is up to the speaker to find information that will be intellectually stimulating. Information will be perceived as intellectually stimulating when the information is new to audience members and when it meets deep-seated needs to know. It is up to the speaker not only to find new information but also to feature its newness.

At the same time, speakers need to take care not to overestimate an audience's familiarity with specific information. Even the most intelligent people in your classroom audience will know a great deal more about some subjects than others. Recently, a young woman speaking in her class referred to Adolf Hitler as a twentieth-century example of extreme oppression. She was quite surprised when many of her listeners responded to the mention of Hitler with vaguely unknowing expressions.

The goal, then, is to be sure to give enough details about the information that you regard as key to audience understanding of your topic without boring your listeners by telling them what they already know. Your ability to do this depends on how well you have analyzed your audience and how accurately you predict the audience's knowledge of your topic. Clearly, the more specialized your topic, the more you will need to take time to familiarize an audience with essential concepts and terms.

Even when you are talking about a topic that most of the people in your audience are familiar with, you can uncover new angles, new applications, or new perspectives on the material. For example, in our society, most people probably know what the game of football is and how points are scored. But an interesting speech could be built around a topic such as zone defenses that may provide new information and insights even to fans who think they have a pretty good grasp of the game. When your topic is a familiar one, keep thinking about the topic in different ways until you have uncovered an aspect that will be new to most of the audience.

New information has even greater impact when you can feature its novelty. *Novelty* is newness with a twist—something unexpected that commands our attention. In a speech on the perils of cliff diving, for example, an audience is likely to listen because of the novelty of the topic itself. But even if a topic is not novel, you can identify specific features of the topic that will be perceived as novel. For instance, for a segment of a speech on computers, you might focus on a novel application such as advancements in voice-activated word processing that will enable users to input data and commands simply by speaking to the computer.

But being new is not enough. The information must also be intellectually stimulating. All people have a deep-seated hunger for knowledge and insight. Part of the job of the informative speaker is to feed that hunger. Every day we are touched by ideas and issues that we don't fully grasp. Often it is easy to ignore these ideas and issues, partly because we don't have sufficient motivation to find additional information for ourselves. For instance, scientists recently discovered an "ice man," a well-preserved body of a man who lived between four and five thousand years ago, buried in the glacier of the southern Alps. Newspaper headlines announced the significance of the discovery, and while readers were likely excited by the information, they probably did not pursue the topic. The informative speaker who seizes this topic and links the significance of the ice man to an understanding of our own history and development may well stimulate our natural intellectual curiosity.

Let's consider another example. Suppose you are planning to talk about new cars. From just the data that you could draw from the April issue of *Consumer Reports*—the month in which comparative statistics and ratings are given for all new cars—you could select some interesting lines of development that would be intellectually stimulating. For instance, we are aware that during the past decade Japanese-made cars have captured an increasingly large share of the market, at least partly because of perceived quality issues. How are American companies responding to those issues? Are American-made cars achieving higher quality ratings? Are American-made cars "competitive"? Are sales increasing? Equally stimulating speeches could feature information on safety features, mileage data, and styling.

Relevance of Information

PRINCIPLE 4

Audiences are more likely to listen to and understand information they perceive to be relevant.

Rather than acting like a sponge to absorb every bit of information that comes our way, most of us act more like filters: We listen only to that information we perceive to be relevant. *Relevance* is the personal value that people see in information because it relates to their needs and interests. Relevance might be measured by an audience's "need to know."

Vital information—information the audience sees as a matter of life or death—is the ultimate in relevance. Police cadets, for instance, will see information explaining what they should do when attacked as vital. The same is true of information that bears on other significant personal concerns. For instance, students may perceive information that is necessary to their passing a test as vital. If you can show your listeners that your speech information is critical to their well-being, they will have a compelling reason to listen.

Of course, information does not have to be vital to be perceived as relevant. But you should always ask yourself in what way the material you plan to present is truly important to the audience and emphasize that connection in your speech. With some topics, you won't need to work very hard to show people how the information

Even when you are talking about a topic that most people in your audience are familiar with, you can uncover new angles, new applications, or new perspectives on the material.

affects them personally. For example, in Cincinnati, the Labor Day fireworks have attracted national attention. On that day, some 300,000 to 500,000 people attempt to see the fireworks in person, and at least that many more watch them on television. Thus, a speaker talking a few weeks before the event about creative or little-known strategies for seeing the fireworks would not need to spend much time establishing the relevance of the information.

Developing relevance is more of a challenge when your information seems far removed from the audience's experience or felt needs and concerns. Still, you can usually establish relevance. For example, a speech on Japan can focus on the importance of Japanese manufacturing to our economy, including local jobs; a speech on the Egyptian pyramids can relate them to the motives behind contemporary examples of monumental public or private buildings. Unless you establish relevance, your speech will be more of a performance than a communication. It is up to you to show how your information relates to the needs and interests of your audience.

Although relevance is important throughout the speech, be sure to emphasize it in your introduction. Suppose you are giving a speech on high-speed rail transportation. As you begin your speech, class members are sure to ask themselves, "Why should I listen to a speech on rail transportation?" The following opening explains the need to know:

> Have you been stuck in a traffic jam lately? Have you started what you had hoped would be a pleasant vacation only to be trampled at the airport or, worse, to discover when you got to your destination that your luggage hadn't? We're all aware that every year our highways and our airways are getting more congested. At the same time, we are facing a rapidly decreasing supply of petroleum. Today, I'm going to tell you about one of the most practical means for solving these problems: high-speed rail transportation.

Emphasis of Information

PRINCIPLE 5

> *Audiences are more likely to understand and to remember information that is emphasized.*

As we discussed in connection with speech delivery, a number of oral and verbal cues can establish emphasis. The important point here is that emphasis not only creates variety but helps audiences retain information. Remember, audiences will retain only some of the content you present; the rest is likely to be lost over time. To make the best use of emphasis, then, you must determine what it is that you want the audience to retain and prioritize your information accordingly.

The highest-priority information includes your specific goal, the main points of your speech, and key facts that give meaning to the main points. If you were giving a speech on evaluating diamonds, you would want to make sure that the audience remembered (1) that it heard a speech on the four criteria for evaluating a diamond (the goal) and (2) that the four criteria are carat (the weight of the diamond), clarity (the purity of the diamond), color (the tint of the diamond), and cutting (the shaping of the diamond). These are the main points. In addition, you might hope that the audience would remember (1) that a carat weighs 200 milligrams; (2) that clarity is marred by internal blemishes, such as bubbles, feathers, clouds, and inclusions, all of which detract from a diamond's purity; (3) that the most expensive diamonds are without color; and (4) that diamonds can be cut into six common shapes: emerald, oval, marquise, brilliant, heart, and pear.

Once you have prioritized your information, you can plan a strategy for increasing the audience's retention of the most important information. We have already discussed several language strategies that you can use: placement and sequencing, proportion, repetition, and external transitions. So, your emphasis strategy may include sequencing points so that the most important idea is last, spending more time on a point, repeating the exact words or the ideas, or announcing that the point is particularly important.

Three additional devices to aid retention of information are clarifying the framework, suggesting memory aids, and using humor. A final device, using visual aids, will be discussed in greater detail in the next section.

1. *Clarify the framework.* Speakers often construct their speeches the way they would if listeners could read them. But listening and reading are different in many ways, one of the most telling of which is that the reader who is lost can go back to the start of the sentence, paragraph, or article—the listener cannot. So, the effective speaker constantly clarifies the framework of the speech to help listeners see where they are, where they have been, and where they are going. Thus, in the introduction of the speech, you tell the audience what you will cover: "In this speech, we will look at the four criteria for evaluating a diamond." Then, as you proceed through a long main point, you might remind your listeners where you are: "So we've seen that color of the diamond affects its value; now let's consider the conditions that affect color." This tells your listener that you're still on the second main point, color, but you're moving to a different aspect of that main point. Even if listeners' attention strays momentarily, this clarifying statement helps them get back on track. And, as we have said previously, you will want to use a transition when you move from one main point to another. These directions make it *sound* as if the speech will be tremendously redundant. And, indeed, five or six references to structure in a short, two- to three-minute speech will be. But as you move to five-, seven-, or ten-minute speeches in class and twenty-, forty-five-, or sixty-minute speeches in the community, you will see that without these clarifications many listeners will lose the structure and retain less information.

The value of such clarifying structure is tremendous. From the speaker's standpoint, every word may be considered a gem. But from the listeners' standpoint, each sentence you utter is just another group of words. And because listeners' minds may wander, you must exercise control in how you want the audience to perceive what you say. I have heard listeners swear that a speaker never stated the second main point of the speech when in reality the point was stated, but in a way that had no effect on the audience. Clarifying structure, often through transitions, helps your audience recognize where you are in the speech and why your point is significant.

2. *Suggest memory aids.* Skilled listeners create memory aids for themselves when they really want to remember. You can help all of your listeners take advantage of this technique by suggesting memory aids for them to use. In describing the criteria for evaluating diamonds, suppose you say "There are four criteria: weight, clarity, tint, and shape." Chances are most listeners will have trouble remembering all four criteria. One way to help the audience remember is to label the four with words that all start with the letter *C:* "There are four C's of evaluation: carat, clarity, color, and cutting."

Another kind of a memory aid is association. *Association* is the tendency of one thought to stimulate recall of another similar thought. Suppose you are trying to help the audience remember the value of color in a diamond. Because blue is the most highly prized tint and yellow or brown tints lower a diamond's value, you might associate blue tint with "the blue ribbon prize" and yellow (or brown) tint with "a lemon." Thus, the best diamond gets the "blue ribbon," and the worst diamond is a "lemon." It is quite likely that these two associations will help your audience's retention immensely.

Figurative associations like these naturally fall into the two categories of similes and metaphors we discussed in the last chapter. Recall that a simile is a comparison using the word *as* or *like:* "A computer screen is like a television monitor." A metaphor states an identity: "Laser printers are the Cadillacs of computer printers." I still remember vividly a metaphor I heard a student use in a speech more than twenty years ago. The student explained the functioning of a television tube by saying, "A television picture tube is a gun shooting beams of light." If you make your associations striking enough, your audience will long remember your point.

3.   *Use humor.* Another way to emphasize is through humor. Audiences are likely to remember the point of a humorous story. For instance, suppose you were giving a speech on the importance of having perspective. Your highest-priority point might be that because a problem that seems enormous at the moment might turn out to be minor in a few days, being able to put events into perspective saves a great deal of psychological wear and tear. To cement the point, you might tell the following story:

> A first-time visitor to the races bet two dollars on the first race on a horse that had the same name as his elementary school. The horse won, and the man was ten dollars ahead. In each of the next several races he bet on horses such as "Apple Pie," his favorite kind of dessert, and "Kathie's Prize," his wife's name, and he kept winning. By the end of the sixth race, he was 700 dollars ahead. He was about to go home when he noticed that in the seventh race, "Seventh Veil" was scheduled in the number-seven position and was currently going off at odds of seven to one. The man couldn't resist—he bet his entire 700 dollars that the horse would place first. And sure enough, the horse came in seventh. When he got home, his wife asked "How did you do?" Very calmly he looked at his wife and said, "Not bad. I lost two dollars."

That's perspective.

Visual Aids

PRINCIPLE 6

Audiences are more likely to understand and to remember information that is presented visually.

In addition to the verbal modes of development we have discussed, you can also consider visual means of development. Audiences are more likely to understand and retain information when they can see it as well as hear it. For instance, memory for pictures is often remarkable, even over long periods. The details may not be well retained, but more general features are remembered. Mandler and Ritchey studied retention and found that some pictorial information was retained without any loss of accuracy for more than four months.[4]

Skill in using visual aids is an integral part of many real-life speaking situations. In business, for example, such data as sales trends and the results of market research are often presented with the help of visuals. Let's begin by looking at the various kinds of visual aids and then consider how to use those visual aids in a speech.

Types of Visual Aids. A wide variety of visual aids can be used in speeches. Keep the following suggestions in mind as you decide what types of visual aids you want and how you can best use them.

Yourself. Sometimes, through your gestures, movement, and personal attire, you can become your own best visual aid. Through descriptive gestures, you can show the size of a soccer ball and the height of a tennis net; through your posture and movement, you can show the motions involved in the butterfly swimming stroke and methods of artificial respiration; through your own attire, you can illustrate the native dress of a foreign country, the proper outfit for a cave explorer, or the uniform of a firefighter.

Objects. The objects you are talking about make good visual aids if they are large enough to be seen and small enough to carry around with you. A vase, a basketball, a braided rug, or a sword is the kind of object that can be seen by the audience and manipulated by the speaker.

Charts. A *chart* is a graphic representation of information in easily interpreted form. The most common types are word charts, flow charts, bar charts, line charts, and pie charts.

Word charts are used frequently to preview material that will be covered in the speech, to summarize material, and to remind the audience of where you are in the speech.

Flow charts are diagrams consisting of a set of symbols and connecting lines that shows step-by-step progression through a complicated procedure or system.

Bar charts, graphs with vertical or horizontal bars, can be used to show relationships between two or more variables at the same time or at various times on one or more dimensions.

Line charts can be used to show changes in one or more variables over time.

Pie charts may be used to show the relationship among parts of a single unit.

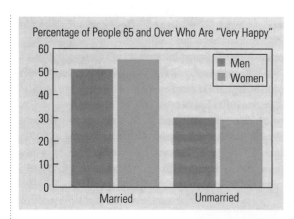

Percentage of People 65 and Over Who Are "Very Happy"

Magazine Costs: Where the Revenue Dollar Goes

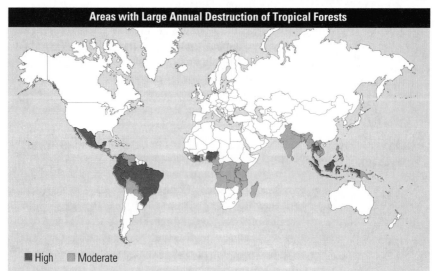

Areas with Large Annual Destruction of Tropical Forests

Visual aids of many types can make it easier for audiences to assimilate, comprehend, and retain information.

A popular way to display charts is to use a *flipchart*—a large pad of paper mounted on an easel. Today, you can get flipcharts (and easels) in any of several sizes. For a presentation to four or five people, you can use a small tabletop version; for a larger audience, you would be wise to use a larger size, such as the widely used 30-by-40-inch chart.

In designing your flipcharts, you will want to leave several pages between each chart in the pad. If you discover a mistake or decide to revise a chart, you can tear out that sheet without disturbing the order. After you have finished all the charts, you can tear out all but one sheet between each chart. The one sheet serves both as a transition page and as a cover sheet. Since you want your audience focusing on your words and not on visual material that is not being used, when you finish a chart you can flip to the empty page while you talk about material not covered by charts. Further, the empty page between charts assures that heavy lines or colors from the next chart will not show through.

Pictorial Representations.   In addition to charts, other types of graphic visuals include pictorial representations such as diagrams, drawings, maps, and photographs.

Diagrams and drawings are popular visual aids because they are easy to prepare. If you can use a compass, a straightedge, and a measure, you can draw well enough for most speech purposes. If your prospective drawing is too complicated for you to handle personally, you may need professional help. A major advantage of drawings is that you can often sketch cartoon figures to help you make a point humorously.

Maps are pictorial representations of a territory. Well-prepared maps allow you to focus on key physical details such as mountains, rivers, and valleys; or on the location of cities, states, nations, parks, and monuments; or on automobile, train, boat, and airplane routes. Maps are also a good way to display data in relation to geographic regions. For example, different colors can be used to show ranges for such data as average rainfall, population density, crime rates, or voting patterns. For many purposes, you may need to prepare a map that includes only the details you wish to show.

Photographs can be useful visual aids because they give you an exact reproduction. The problem with photographs is that they are seldom large enough to be seen from more than a few rows away. Moreover, they often include more detail than you need to make your point.

Projections.   Almost any kind of graphic or pictorial visual aid can be prepared for projection onto a screen. Your choices of projection media are films, slides, and overhead transparencies.

Although films may be beautifully done, they are seldom appropriate for informative speeches, mostly because films so dominate that the speaker loses control. Occasionally, it is possible that during a longer speech you will want to use short clips of a minute or two each. Still, because it requires darkening the room for that portion of time, using film in an informative speech is often disruptive.

Slides are mounted transparencies that can be projected individually. The advantage of slides over film is that you can control when each image will be shown. By using a remote control device, you can pace your showing of slides, and you can talk about each of them as long as necessary. But as with films, because their use requires darkening the room, it is easy for less accomplished speakers to lose control of their audience.

Perhaps the biggest potential problem is finding that your slides are out of order. When you have finished rehearsing your speech (be sure to rehearse using the slides as you plan to use them in your speech), double-check to make sure that the slides are in the right order.

Overhead transparencies are projected onto a screen via an overhead projector. Overheads are often the first choice in professional presentations because they can be made easily and inexpensively either by hand (traced or hand-lettered) or by machine (copy machine, thermographic, color lift, or computer drawn). They work well in nearly any setting, and unlike other kinds of projections, they don't require dimming the lights in the room. Overheads are especially useful for showing how formulas work, for illustrating various computations, or for analyzing data because you can write, trace, or draw on the transparency while you are talking.

When you make overheads yourself, you will probably want to mount the transparencies to avoid light leak, to make them easier to store, and to provide a place for notes to yourself. For a really professional appearance, you may want to consult a book on making and using overhead transparencies. One that I recommend is Lee Green's *501 Ways to Use the Overhead Projector.*[5]

Chalkboard.   As a means of displaying simple information, the chalkboard, a staple in every college classroom, is unbeatable. Unfortunately, the chalkboard is also easy to misuse and to overuse. Moreover, it is unlikely that the chalkboard would be your first choice for any major analysis of process or procedure because of its limitations in displaying complex material. Nevertheless, since effective use of the chalkboard should be a part of the professional speaker's repertoire, let's analyze its strengths and its weaknesses.

One common error in using the chalkboard is to write too much material while you are talking, an error that often results in displays that are either illegible or partly obscured by your body as you write. A second common error is to spend too much time talking to the board instead of to the audience.

The chalkboard is best used for short items of information that can be written in a few seconds. If you plan to draw or to write while you are talking, practice doing it. If you are right-handed, stand to the right of what you are drawing. Try to face at least part of the audience while you work. Although it may seem awkward at first, your effort will allow you to maintain contact with your audience and will allow the audience to see what you are doing while you are doing it.

Handouts.   Among the first visual aids that come to mind for many speakers are handouts. On the plus side, you can prepare handouts quickly, and all the people in the audience can have their own professional-quality material to refer to and take with them from the speech. On the minus side is the distraction of distributing handouts and the potential for losing the audience's attention when you want the audience to be looking at you. Before you decide on handouts, consider each of the other types of visual aids we have discussed. If you do decide on handouts, distribute them at the end of the speech.

Computer Graphics. The availability of software designed especially for producing "presentation graphics" is rapidly changing the way many speakers prepare charts, diagrams, and other visual aids. For very small audiences of up to four or five people, software is available that allows users to display the graphics directly on a monitor as a computer slide show. For larger audiences, graphics prepared on a computer can be projected with special equipment, printed out and enlarged, photographed to make slides, or used to create overhead transparencies or handouts. Except for complex multimedia presentations, then, computer graphics are not so much a new type of visual aid as a new way of producing the kinds of visuals already discussed.

The ever-growing capabilities of personal computers and popular software packages are rapidly making computer graphics a regular part of many speakers' repertoire. If you experiment with computer graphics, though, keep in mind that all the guidelines for using visual aids still apply. In particular, be wary of the temptation to produce overfancy graphics that actually obscure the information you want the audience to assimilate. With the ability the computer gives to manipulate graphics—for example, to easily create complex three-dimensional bar charts or combine several images and typefaces in a single display—it is all too easy to let the medium overpower the message (see A Bill of Rights for Presentation Audiences on pages 402–403).

Guidelines for Using Visual Aids. Clearly, visual images are useful in getting attention, facilitating understanding, and increasing retention. Yet many speakers who understand the value of "visual" sometimes forget the meaning of "aid." Visuals do not take the place of a well-prepared speech, nor should they be the primary focus of a speech. Visuals supplement the speech by serving the speaker's goal of helping the audience understand and retain information. With this point in mind, here are several guidelines for using visual aids effectively.

1. *Plan carefully when to use visual aids.* As you practice your speech, indicate on your outline when and how you will use each visual aid.

2. *Carefully consider audience needs.* Your use of visual aids is determined not only by the nature of your material but also by the needs of your audience. If your audience would find a graphic helpful in understanding and remembering a portion of your speech, then a visual aid at that point is appropriate. On the other hand, regardless of how exciting a visual may be, if it does not contribute directly to the audience's attention to, understanding of, or retention of information on your topic, then reconsider its use.

3. *Show visual aids only when you are talking about them.* You are competing with visual aids for attention. When you are using a visual aid to make a point, you expect the audience's attention to be directed to it. But if your visual aids are still in view when you are talking about something else, the audience will be inclined to continue to look at them. So, when the visual aid is not contributing to the point you are making, keep it out of sight.

4. *Talk about the visual aid while you are showing it.* Although a picture may be worth a thousand words, you know what you want your audience to see in the picture. Tell your audience what to look for; explain the various parts; interpret figures, symbols, and percentages.

Especially in business settings, more and more speakers are using "presentation graphics" software to create slides and other visual aids. But as Michael Kolowich argues, speakers can easily go astray if they focus on their graphic creations instead of on their audience and message. His points are well worth heeding whether you create your visuals by computer or by hand.

As I squinted through the darkness at a parade of 35mm images, I found myself becoming indignant.

Slide after slide was unreadable, failed to communicate, or detracted from the central message. "And I paid for this abuse," I muttered. Three consecutive lousy presentations.

This scene wasn't some two-bit small-business seminar, either. This was a gathering of software industry leaders. These were men and women with nearly unlimited access to technology that is capable of dazzling audiences. But in the end, technology was a hindrance rather than a help, as presenters tried to use every color, fill all empty space on the screen, and apply every typeface in their libraries.

We should be accustomed to this by now. For all the good PCs have done, every major new business-productivity tool has introduced a regression in the art it attempts to automate. Spreadsheets brought us bad business models and a false sense of security about how our businesses work. Desktop publishing brought us ugly documents and multiplied the number of people who could fill our in-boxes with junk. And now, presentation-graphics programs give millions the means by which they, too, can fail to communicate.

It's time that we stood up for the rights of presentation audiences, who sacrifice money and time to be informed, instructed, or entertained. It's time that we offered a Bill of Rights, which should be stuck to all the presentation designers' monitors before they start mousing merrily around the screen.

Here are some simple considerations every audience member has the right to expect from a presenter:

1. *The message of each slide will be concise, clear, and memorable.* If the message cannot be articulated in

5. *Display visual aids so that everyone in the audience can see them.* If you hold the visual aid, hold it away from your body and point it toward the various parts of the audience. If you place your visual aid on a chalkboard or easel or mount it in some way, stand to one side and point with the arm nearest the visual aid. If it is necessary to roll or fold the visual aid, bring some transparent tape to mount it to the chalkboard or wall so that it does not roll or wrinkle.

6. *Talk to your audience, not to your visual aid.* You may need to look at the visual aid occasionally, but you want to maintain eye contact with your audience as a single, straightforward sentence that can be remembered easily, then the slide may be trying to accomplish too much.

2. *Every word on a slide will be legible to every person in the room.* A speaker will not need to apologize to those in the back who may not be able to read the labels. Every presentation will be designed for the back row.

3. *All text will be horizontal.* We will not have to cock our heads to read axis labels and bar names; it's better to rotate the bars than to make members of the audience turn their heads.

4. *Color will be used to contrast, highlight, or symbolize, not merely to decorate.* The fewer colors on a slide, the better. Every color will be used purposefully.

5. *Slide titles will make a point, if they're used at all.* Merely describing the data ("U.S. Population, 1776 to 1992") wastes valuable space on a slide, but using that space to make a point ("Population Growth Is Slowing Dramatically") tells the audience what to look for. If the title doesn't advance the message, drop it.

6. *Proportions will be represented honestly.* Bar charts that exaggerate differences by starting the axis at a number other than zero are inex-cusable. They deceive the eye and often the mind.

7. *Three-dimensional charts will be used sparingly.* While the effect is state of the art, [3-D] charts are at best distracting and difficult to interpret (Does the axis line up with the front surface or the rear?), and at worst they are downright deceptive. . . .

8. *Pie charts will not be used to make comparisons.* Can you tell which slice is growing and which is shrinking? The eye and the mind are not designed for this kind of work.

9. *Every slide will support the message or make it more memorable.* A single slide can have a greater impact than a whole tray of them.

These rules are just a start. They all begin with one principle: Focus on what you want your audience to remember, not what you want to see. . . .

Remember that your audience has a right to clarity and a fair chance to absorb your message. Technology is seductive, but the real measure of a successful presentation is how much your audience takes away. ■

SOURCE: Michael Kolowich, "A Bill of Rights for Presentation Audiences Is Long Overdue," *PC Computing,* April 1992, p. 70. © 1992 Ziff-Davis Publishing Company, L.P.

much as possible, in part so that you can gauge to see how they are reacting to your visual material. When speakers become too engrossed in their visual aids, they tend to lose contact with the audience entirely.

7. *Pass objects around the audience with caution.* People look at, read, handle, and think about whatever they hold in their hands, and while they are so occupied, they may not be listening to you. Keep control of audience attention by telling them what they should be looking at and when they should be listening to you.

8. *Practice using the visual aids so that you use them well.* Many people think that once they have prepared good visual aids they will have no trouble using them in the speech. Nothing could be further from the truth. Many a good speech with good visual aids has become a shambles because the speaker had not planned carefully when he or she would use the visual, how the visual would be introduced, and most important, how it would be shown.

Practice in Recognizing Informative-Speaking Principles

By Yourself

Analyze a classroom lecture that you heard this week. Which of the principles of informative speaking (creativity, credibility, newness, relevance, emphasis, using visual aids) did the professor use to get attention? Create understanding? Increase retention? Which were used most effectively? Least effectively? Explain.

Methods of Informing

When you think about how you will present information in a speech, you can plan to use any of several methods of conveying information. In this section, we focus on four methods of informing: narrating, describing, demonstrating, and defining. Each of these represents both a technique of informing and a type of informative speech. Thus, you can use one or all of the methods as you prepare a single speech, or you can construct an informative speech based primarily on one of the methods. For instance, you could give a single informative speech on tornadoes in which you *narrate* an experience as part of the opening, then *define* tornadoes by contrasting them with hurricanes and typhoons, then *demonstrate* how a tornado develops, then *describe* the destruction that a single tornado can wreak on a city. Alternatively, you could give an entire speech narrating an experience with a tornado or focusing on one of the other methods.

Narrating

Recall from Chapter 12 that a narrative is a story, a tale, or an account. The primary goal of a narrative is to make a point in such a unique or interesting way that the audience will remember it because of the way it was presented. Suppose you were giving a speech on listening in which you wanted to make a point about the costs of faulty listening to personal well-being. You might exemplify this point with the following narrative statement: "Abraham suffered great personal cost by working all day to finish a report for the five o'clock deadline, only to find as he turned it in that he was a day early." As worded, the one-sentence narrative about Abraham isn't particularly interesting and is not likely to be remembered. But this short statement can be developed to be both interesting and memorable. Let's consider the elements of the narrative in general and how this particular narrative can be enhanced.

1. *Usually a narrative has a point—a climax to which the details build.* A joke has a punch line; a fable has a moral; other narratives have some climactic ending that makes the stories interesting. The point of this one-sentence narrative is the unnecessary cost that Abraham suffered by working all day to finish a project that didn't have to be done that day.

2. *A narrative is developed with supporting details.* A narrative can be long or short, depending on the number and the development of supporting details. Supporting details give background, but more important, they build the story so that its point will have maximum effect. For instance, in the narrative of Abraham's report, you could introduce such details as that Abraham got to work at 6 A.M., more than two hours earlier than usual, in order to find the time to work on the report and that he had to turn down a lunch invitation from a man he'd been trying to see for three weeks about an important issue of company policy.

3. *A narrative is often developed with suspense in mind.* The power of a narrative can be increased by withholding the punch line until the end. If you can tease the audience, you will hold their attention. They will be trying to see whether they can anticipate what you are going to say. Vocally, a slight pause before the punch line will heighten the effect: "Abraham worked all day to finish his report for the five o'clock deadline, only to discover when he turned it in [pause] that it was one full day early!"

4. *A narrative should include dialogue whenever possible.* A story will be much more enjoyable to an audience if they can hear it unfold through dialogue. For instance, notice how our one-line story improves with this presentation:

> As Abraham burst into his boss's office with report in hand, the boss's secretary stared at him, dumbfounded. When he said breathlessly "Here's the report, right on the dot!" she replied, "But, Abraham, the report isn't due until tomorrow!"

5. *A narrative should develop the humor of the situation whenever possible.* Not all narratives are funny, but more often than not, they will have an element of humor, and humor both holds attention and makes the story memorable.

Describing

"What does it look like?" "How do the parts fit together?" Questions like these are answered by describing. At least some of the informative communicating we do every day is descriptive. As with any of the skills of information exchange, however, descriptions must be carefully worded to be effective.

Suppose you listened to a speaker say "I was led into a huge family room with an enormous fireplace." What would you be able to tell about the room or the fireplace? Can you see the fireplace? Can you picture its immensity? Speech is descriptive when it provides word pictures that enable the audience to mentally picture what you are talking about. Now consider the following passage:

> I was led into a family room so large that people at the far end seemed constructed on a smaller scale than I. The dominant feature of the room was a huge flagstone fireplace that was a good ten feet wide and at least

twelve feet high—higher than a basketball net. The opening was the size of a normal picture window. The fireplace comfortably held logs a yard long. As I stood before it, I got a sense of what a fireplace must have been like in a medieval castle.

How do you describe accurately and vividly? Effective description requires at least two skills: (1) observing and (2) communicating the observation. Description is very much a product of alert, detailed observation. Only if you know what to look for and observe attentively can you create ways of reporting the essentials that will be accurate and vivid. Characteristics to be conscious of when you observe a place or an object are size, shape, weight, color, composition, age and condition, and the relationship among various parts.

How large is the place or object? If it's an object, how heavy is it? Both size and weight are most descriptive when they are presented comparatively. "The book is the same length and width as your text, but about twice as thick" and "The suitcase weighed seventy pounds, about twice the weight of a normally packed suitcase" are both descriptive.

What is the place or object's shape? What color is it? Simple shapes are easily described by words such as *round, triangular, oblong, spherical, conical, cylindrical,* and *rectangular.* Complex objects are best described as a series of simple shapes. Color, an obvious component of description, is difficult to describe accurately. Although most people can visualize black and white, the primary colors (red, yellow, and blue), and their complements (green, purple, and orange), very few objects are exactly these colors. Perhaps the best way to describe a color is to couple it with a common referent. For instance, "lemon yellow," "brick red," "green as a grape," and "sky blue" give rather accurate approximations.

What is the object made of? What is its age or condition? The composition of an object helps us visualize it. A ball of aluminum does not look the same as a ball of yarn. A pile of rocks gives a different impression than does a pile of straw. A brick building looks different from a steel, wood, or glass building. Whether an object is new or old can make a difference in its appearance. Because age by itself may not be descriptive, an object is often discussed in terms of condition. Books become ragged and tattered, buildings become run-down and dilapidated, land becomes eroded. Age and condition together often prove valuable in developing informative descriptions.

How does an object fit together? If the object you want to describe is complex, its parts must be fitted into their proper relationship before a mental picture emerges. Remember the story of the blind men who described an elephant in terms of what each felt? The one who felt the trunk said the elephant was like a snake; the one who felt a leg said the elephant was like a tree; and the one who felt the body said the elephant was like a wall. When it is relevant to your description, be sure audiences understand how the parts fit together.

Because the purpose of description is to enable the audience to visualize, it is better to give too much detail than too little. Moreover, if some particular aspect is especially important, you might describe it in two or three different ways to make the image as vivid as possible.

Description occurs in many speeches; for practice, your instructor may assign a speech exercise that focuses entirely on description.

Demonstrating

Many informative speeches involve explaining processes—telling how to do something, how to make something, or how something works. A *demonstration* involves going through the complete process that you are explaining—for example, how to get more power on a forehand table-tennis shot, how to make fettuccine noodles, or how to purify water.

When the task is relatively simple, such as how to get more power on a forehand table-tennis shot, you may want to try a complete demonstration. If so, practice until you can do it smoothly and easily under the pressure of facing an actual audience. Since the actual demonstration is likely to take longer than in practice (you are likely to have to make some modifications during the speech to enable everyone in the room to see the demonstration), you may want to make sure that the final practice is somewhat shorter than the maximum time limit you will have for the speech.

For a relatively complicated process, you may want to consider the *modified demonstration.* For a modified demonstration, you complete various stages of the

Demonstrations need to be carefully prepared and organized if audiences are to retain the information the speaker wants to convey.

demonstration at home and do only part of the actual work in front of the audience. Suppose you were going to demonstrate construction of a floral display. Actually performing the construction from scratch is too complex and time-consuming for a speech-length presentation. Instead, you could prepare a complete set of materials to begin the demonstration, a mock-up of the basic floral triangle, and a completed floral display. During the speech, you would describe the materials needed and then begin demonstrating how to make the basic floral triangle. Rather than trying to get everything together perfectly in a few seconds, you could remove, from a bag or some concealed place, a partially completed arrangement illustrating the floral triangle. You would then use this in your demonstration, adding flowers as if you were planning to complete it. Then from another bag, you could remove the completed arrangement to illustrate one of the effects you were discussing. Conducting a modified demonstration of this type is often easier than trying to complete an entire demonstration in a limited time.

Throughout a demonstration, speak slowly and repeat key ideas often. We learn best by doing, so if you can include audience participation, you may be even more successful. In a speech on origami, or Japanese paper folding, you could explain the principles, then pass out paper and have audience members each make a figure. Actual participation will increase interest and ensure recall. Finally, through other visual aids, you could show how these principles are used in more elaborate projects.

Although your audience may be able to visualize a process through vivid word pictures (in fact, in your impromptu explanations in ordinary conversation, it is the only way you can proceed), you will probably want to make full use of visual aids in a demonstration speech. Perhaps more than with any other kind of informative speech, when your goal is to demonstrate or explain a process, carefully prepared visual material may be essential to listeners' understanding.

Defining

Because we cannot solve problems or learn or even think without meaningful definitions, the ability to define clearly and vividly is essential for the effective communicator. Recall from our discussion of verbal communication that the meanings we give to words are learned and frequently vary in both denotation and connotation. For this reason, misunderstandings often occur because speakers and some or all of the listeners attach different meanings to the same words.

Ever since Plato first attacked the Sophists for their inability to define and classify, rhetoricians have seen definition as a primary tool of effective speaking. For example, Richard Weaver, representing the view of many modern scholars, has named definition as the most valuable of all lines of development.[6] In fact, an entire speech can be built around a definition of such terms as *freedom, equality, justice,* or *love.*

Although they differ in type, both of the following are examples of definition in speeches that show how the speaker is going to use a key word:

Let's talk for a moment about humanity. By humanity, I really mean "people skills"—our ability to work with each other.[7]

And I know something about humility. For example, I was born in Nebraska, and my apologies to any of you here today who were born in Nebraska, but many Californians feel that Nebraskans are virtually brain-dead. It came home to me the other day when I saw a bumper sticker that read: "Committing suicide in Nebraska is redundant."[8]?

How can you define words when giving them an exact meaning is important to the goal of your speech? The following are the five most common methods of defining: classification and differentiation, synonym and antonym, use and function, etymology and historical example, and example and comparison. In some cases, the goal of definition is solely to get the audience to share and remember an exact meaning. In other cases, the definition also serves the function of illustration or development to add color to the meaning. These methods can be used separately or in combination.

Classification and Differentiation.   When you define by *classification,* you give the boundaries of the particular word and focus on the single feature that differentiates that word from other words with similar meanings. Most dictionary definitions are of the classification/differentiation variety. For instance, a dog may be defined as a carnivorous, domesticated mammal of the family Canidae. "Carnivorous," "mammal," and "family Canidae" limit the boundaries to dogs, jackals, foxes, and wolves. "Domesticated" differentiates dogs from the other three.

Synonym and Antonym.   Synonym and antonym may be the most popular means of defining. Both enable the speaker to indicate approximate, if not exact, meaning in a single sentence; moreover, because they are analogous to comparison and contrast, they are often vivid as well as clear. *Synonyms* are words that have the same or nearly the same meanings; *antonyms* are words that have opposite meanings. Synonyms define by comparison. For instance, synonyms for *arduous* would be *hard, laborious,* and *difficult.* Antonyms define by contrast. Antonyms for *arduous* would be *easy* and *simple.* Synonyms are not exact duplicates of the word being defined, but they do give a good idea of what the word means. Of course, the synonym or antonym used must be familiar to the audience, or it will be self-defeating.

Use and Function.   Another way to define is to explain the use or function of the object a particular word represents. Thus, when you say "A plane is a hand-powered tool that is used to smooth the edges of boards" or "The operating system is the software that coordinates the computer's input, storage, processing, and output functions and enables the user to access other programs," you are defining objects by indicating their use. Because the use or function of an object may be more important than its classification, this is often an excellent method of definition.

Etymology and Historical Example.   *Etymology* is the derivation or history of a particular word. Because meanings of words change over time, origin may reveal very little about modern meaning. In some instances, however, the history of a word lends additional insight that will not only help the audience remember the meaning but also bring the meaning to life. For instance, a "censor" originally was one of two Roman magistrates appointed to take the census and, later, to supervise public morals. The best source of word derivations is the *Oxford English Dictionary.*

Example and Comparison.   Regardless of the way you define, you are likely to have to supplement your definitions with examples or comparisons to make them understandable and memorable, especially when you are defining abstract words. Consider the word *just* in the following sentence: "You are being just in your dealings with another when you deal honorably and fairly." Although you have defined by synonym, listeners may still be unsure of your exact meaning. If you add, "If Paul and Mary both do the same amount of work and we reward them by giving them an equal amount of money, our dealings will be just; if, on the other hand, we give Paul more money because he's a man, our dealings will be unjust," you are clarifying the definition with both an example and a comparison.

Practice in Preparing Informative Speeches

By Yourself

1.   Prepare an informative speech. An outline and a bibliography are required. Criteria for evaluation include means of generating audience interest, conveying understanding, ensuring retention, and building credibility. As an addendum to the outline, you may wish to write a plan for adapting the speech to your audience based on predictions you made using the audience analysis checklist on page 275. In the plan include four short sections discussing strategies for (1) building credibility, (2) getting and maintaining interest, (3) facilitating understanding, and (4) increasing retention. You may wish to discuss how you will use your creativity to ensure that the speech will be perceived as intellectually stimulating, relevant, clear, and memorable. Where appropriate, comment on the use of visual aids and the role of language and delivery techniques in implementing your plan. (For an example of an informative speech, see "In Search of Noah's Ark," pages 471–473 of the Appendix.)

2.   Prepare a speech in which you show how something is made, how something is done, or how something works. Evaluation will focus on quality of the topic; selection, construction, and use of visual aids; and skill in organization and presentation. Some topics that would be appropriate for this assignment are as follows: how to hit a racquetball killshot; hanging wallboard; grading meat; making a spinach soufflé; tying fishing flies; making a wood carving; demonstrating how a helicopter, a compact disc, or a photocopier works.

3.   Prepare a description of a structure, a place, an object, or a person. Evaluation of your description will focus on clarity and vividness of the description.

Informative Speech Checklist

Check all items that were accomplished effectively.

Specific Goal

_____ 1. Was the specific goal clear?

_____ 2. Was the specific goal designed to increase audience information?

Content

_____ 3. Was the speaker effective in establishing his or her credibilty on this topic?

_____ 4. Did the speaker get and maintain audience interest in the information throughout the speech?

_____ 5. Did the speaker show the relevance of the information?

_____ 6. Was the information intellectually stimulating?

_____ 7. Did the speaker show creativity in idea development?

_____ 8. Was the information explained in a way that helped the audience understand it?

_____ 9. To help the audience understand and/or retain the information, did the speaker use
_____ repetition? _____ transition? _____ association? _____ humor?
_____ visual aids?

Organization

_____ 10. Did the introduction _____ gain attention? _____ gain goodwill for the speaker?
_____ lead into the speech?

_____ 11. Did the speech follow a _____ time order? _____ space order? _____ topic order?
_____ causal order? _____ problem/solution order?

_____ 12. Was the order appropriate for the intent and content of the speech?

_____ 13. Did the conclusion _____ tie the speech together? _____ leave the speech on a high note?

Language

_____ 14. Was the language _____ clear? _____ vivid? _____ emphatic? _____ appropriate?

Delivery

_____ 15. Was the speech delivered _____ enthusiastically? _____ with good eye contact?
_____ spontaneously? _____ with appropriate vocal variety and emphasis?
_____ with good articulation? _____ with effective bodily action?

Evaluate the speech as (check one)
_____ excellent, _____ good, _____ average, _____ fair, _____ poor.
Use the information from your checklist to support your evaluation.

Figure 16.2 *Evaluating an informative speech*

Some suitable topics are as follows: Gateway Arch, a fisherman's skein, racing ice skates, Golden Gate Bridge, a ballet dancer, a college professor.

4. Prepare an extended definition of a word. Evaluation will focus on the definition's clarity and on the organization and quality of the developmental material. Examples of the kinds of general or abstract words for which extended definitions are appropriate are as follows: expressionism, rhetoric, logic, existentialism, Epicurean, acculturation, myth, fossil, extrasensory perception, and epistemology.

5. Prepare a report on some aspect of communication in a specific culture or on an individual speaker from that culture. Topics in the area of culture and communication might include Native Americans: language and culture; storytelling as public speaking in Jewish culture; call and response in public speaking in African-American culture; Japanese–American business relations: communication differences. Examples of individual speakers might include Barbara Jordan, Sagoyewatha, Sojourner Truth, Malcolm X, Elie Wiesel.

6. Write a critique of at least one of the informative speeches you hear in class. Outline the speech. As you outline, answer the questions on the informative speech checklist (Figure 16.2).

Summary

A speech will fulfill the audience's expectations of an information-sharing occasion if the intent uses language that is perceived as informative and if the facts and other developmental material function informationally. Factors in achieving an informative-speaking goal include getting the audience to listen to, understand, and retain as much of the information as possible.

Audiences are more likely to show interest in, understand, and remember information if (1) it is presented creatively, (2) they like, trust, and have confidence in the speaker, (3) they perceive the information to be intellectually stimulating, (4) they perceive it to be relevant, (5) it is emphasized, and (6) it is presented visually. Creativity involves using material in an imaginative way. Speakers are perceived to be credible if they demonstrate competence, good intentions, good character, and a pleasant personality. Information is perceived as intellectually stimulating if it is new to audience members and piques their curiosity. Information is perceived as relevant if it is vital or important. Information is likely to be remembered if it is repeated, if it is introduced with external transitions, if it is associated, or if it is presented humorously. Visual aids include the speaker, objects, charts, pictorial representations, projections, chalkboard, handouts, and computer graphics. Visual aids have the greatest impact if they are used in ways that best reinforce the points of the speech.

Methods of informing include narrating, describing, demonstrating, and defining. Narrating is telling a story, usually one with a point or climax related to the theme of the speech. Describing means creating a verbal picture through vivid depictions of size, shape, weight, color, composition, age and condition, and the relationship among parts. Demonstrating involves showing how to do something, how to make something, or how something works. Both full and modified demonstrations often are enhanced by visual aids. Defining is giving the meaning of a word or concept through classification and differentiation, synonym and antonym, use and function, or etymology and historical example, and is enhanced with the use of examples and comparisons.

Suggested Readings

Baine, David. *Memory and Instruction.* Englewood Cliffs, NJ: Educational Technology Publications, 1986. Contains excellent sections on mnemonic strategies.

Lesgold, Alan, and Glaser, Robert, eds. *Foundations for a Psychology of Education.* Hillsdale, NJ: Erlbaum, 1989. Includes excellent chapters on learning theory and learning skills that lay a foundation for informative speaking.

Petrie, Charles. "Informative Speaking: A Summary and Bibliography of Related Research." *Speech Monographs* 30 (June 1963): 79–91. Still quite a useful source.

Rorabacher, Louise. *Assignments in Exposition,* 9th ed. New York: Harper & Row, 1987. Although a book on writing, contains chapters on narration, definition, description, and analyses of processes that present material that can be adapted to the study of informative speaking.

Verderber, Rudolph. *The Challenge of Effective Speaking,* 9th ed. Belmont, CA: Wadsworth, 1994. Includes student examples using methods of informing discussed in this chapter.

Notes

1.   Ralph Waldo Emerson, *Natural History of Intellect and Other Papers,* vol. 12 (New York: AMS Press, 1979), p. 91.

2.   Mary Jo Nissen and Peter Bullemer, "Attention Requirements of Learning: Evidence from Performance Measures," *Cognitive Psychology* 19 (1987): 2.

3.   John W. Haefele, *Creativity and Innovation* (New York: Reinhold, 1962), p. 6.

4.   Jean M. Mandler and Gary H. Ritchey, "Long-Term Memory for Pictures," *Journal of Experimental Psychology: Human Learning and Memory* 3 (1977): 386–396.

5.   Lee Green, *501 Ways to Use the Overhead Projector* (Littleton, CO: Libraries Unlimited, 1982).

6.   Richard Weaver, "Language Is Sermonic," in James L. Golden et al., eds., *The Rhetoric of Western Thought,* 5th ed. (Dubuque, IA: Kendall Hunt, 1993).

7.   Vince Kontney, "Business and Education, A Crucial Connection," *Vital Speeches,* May 1, 1986, p. 438.

8.   Ibid.

After you have read this chapter, you should be able to:

Identify similarities and differences between informative and persuasive speaking

Write a proposition of belief or action

Analyze audience attitudes

Find reasons to justify the proposition

Find facts and opinions to support reasons

Organize reasons to meet audience attitudes

Phrase key ideas with emotional appeal

Build personal credibility

Deliver a speech with conviction

Refute ideas of an opponent

TARDEADA con
CESAR CHAVEZ
Calles 5 y B DAVIS CA
11 AGOSTO 3 PM ESPERANZA
COMIDA Y MUSICA GRATIS

17

Persuasive
Speaking

As she finished her speech, the entire audience rose as a body and cheered. Over the din, the chair shouted, "All those in favor, say aye" and as one, everyone roared "aye" as a testament to her lucid and persuasive argument. As she walked to her seat, people reached to pat her on the back, and those who could not touch her chanted her name: "Sheila . . . Sheila . . . !"

"Sheila! Wake up," Denny said as he shook her shoulder, "you're supposed to be working on your speech."

Perhaps you've imagined yourself giving such a stirring speech that your audience cheered wildly at your persuasive powers. Although everything works well in our fantasies, our real-life attempts at changing attitudes or modifying behavior are not always so successful. Speaking persuasively is perhaps the most demanding of speech challenges.

In the previous six chapters, we have discussed the steps involved in preparing and delivering any kind of speech, and the goals, principles, and methods of informative speaking. In this chapter, we build on these concepts as we examine those principles that are especially relevant to persuasive speaking. As you will see, we are not suggesting a new approach to speech preparation—only giving a focus to principles you have already learned.

Just as informative speaking involves a basic knowledge of how people learn, effective persuasive speaking makes use of knowledge about people's attitudes and behavior. In this chapter, we build on those concepts as we focus on the principles of persuasive speaking. We begin by examining similarities and differences between persuasive and informative speaking. Then we present and discuss a number of specific principles.

Persuasive and Informative Speaking: Similarities and Differences

Because effective persuasive speaking builds on informative-speaking skills, we first look briefly at how a persuasive speaker's procedure is related to the informative speaker's.

1. *Both informative and persuasive speakers design their speeches to achieve a specific goal.* Informative speakers seek to increase understanding; persuasive speakers design speeches to change beliefs and move audiences to action. Just as with an effective informative speech, a stirring persuasive speech does not simply happen. For every story of people who were so moved by a situation that they rose to deliver inspiring, spontaneous orations that brought immediate success, there are hundreds of stories of long hours of preparation in which people struggled to shape their messages to achieve maximum effect.

2. *Both informative and persuasive speakers attempt to generate enough interest in their information to arouse audience attention.* In any speech situation, people make value judgments about whether they will listen to the material a speaker presents. Suppose your specific speech goal is to have the audience support a tax increase to fund programs designed to increase basic skill levels of high school students. If your listeners do not attend to your speech because they are not interested in programs to increase such skill levels, they cannot be persuaded. In your speech, then, consider effective means of generating and maintaining interest.

3. *Both informative and persuasive speakers attempt to explain their information in ways that enable the audience to understand it.* If members of an audience do not truly comprehend the information, it is unlikely to affect their beliefs or move them to action. In your speech on funding an educational program, for example, your audience will be unmoved if it does not understand the nature of the funding or how the funding will be used to increase skills. The speech, then, must clarify the specific ideas and programs that you support.

4. *Both informative and persuasive speakers attempt to discuss information in ways that enable the audience to remember it.* In your speech on funding an educational program, gaining your audience's belief in the importance of a tax program will have little effect if the audience cannot remember what it was to believe or why. As in informative speaking, you must use strategies that emphasize ideas and make them vivid.

5. *Whereas informative speakers use their material solely to further understanding, persuasive speakers also use their speech material to support reasons for change or action.* In a persuasive speech advocating support for a tax increase for education, for example, it would be effective if you used examples and statistics to support the reason that high schools are not able to meet the educational needs of an increasingly diverse student population.

6. *Both informative and persuasive speakers seek to be perceived by their listeners as having their best interests in mind.* Although the audience members will recognize that you are trying to influence their attitudes or behavior, they should not perceive you as manipulating or taking advantage of them. All speakers must be sensitive to the legal and ethical considerations that guide effective speaking.

7. *Both informative and persuasive speakers assume that listeners have the power to act.* Thus, candidates running for office assume that people will act upon their choice at the ballot box. In this sense, persuasive speaking—even the classroom variety—is very "real"; when you give a speech, an audience is present—and that audience can act upon your recommendations.

8. *Although both informative and persuasive speakers consider audience attitudes toward them and their information, persuasive speakers must also understand where the audience stands on a specific goal so they can develop speech strategies to adapt to audience attitudes.* For instance, in your speech advocating an increase on taxes, once you identify the attitude of your audience toward a tax increase, you can prepare a strategy that addresses that specific attitude.

Principles of Persuasive Speaking

Having suggested that many factors in informative speaking are also relevant to persuasive speaking, we now turn to specific principles that you can follow when your goal is to persuade.

Writing a Specific Goal

PRINCIPLE 1

You are more likely to persuade an audience when the reaction that you hope to achieve is clearly defined.

How you write your persuasive speech goal may well determine the degree of success you attain with the speech. Although any random statement may influence another person's actions (for instance, merely saying "I see the new Penney's store opened in Western Woods" may "persuade" another person to go to Penney's for some clothing need), the successful persuader does not leave the effect of the message to chance. You want to write a highly specific persuasive goal.

In Chapter 11, you learned to write speech goals as complete sentences containing only one idea; moreover, the goal should include an infinitive or infinitive phrase that indicates the specific response you want from your audience. At this stage, then, you need to be sure that your persuasive speech, often called a *proposition,* states what you want your audience to believe or do. The following are examples of well-worded belief and action goals:

Propositions of Belief

I want my audience to believe that mandatory drug testing of air traffic controllers is necessary.

I want my audience to believe that state lotteries should be outlawed.

I want my audience to believe that Social Security taxes should be lowered.

Propositions of Action

I want my audience to donate money to this year's Fine Arts Fund.

I want my audience to write to their representatives in Congress to support gun control legislation.

I want my audience to attend the school's production of *A Chorus Line.*

When you believe you have a well-worded persuasive speech goal, review the goal with the following two additional tests in mind:

1. *Consider rewording the proposition if it calls for a dramatic change in audience attitude.* Much of this advice is based on Sherif and Hovland's social judgment theory.[1] *Social judgment theory* says that people have differing frames of reference that affect how they perceive information. These frames of reference will serve as anchor positions to which related messages are then compared. As a result, people will react to incoming information by placing it in one of three categories, or latitudes: (1) the latitude of acceptance (the position that is most acceptable to them), (2) the latitude of rejection (the position that is most objectionable), and (3) the latitude of noncommitment (statements people make that are neither accepted nor rejected). In addition to hypothesizing that people will place statements in one of these three categories, social judgment theorists also emphasize the issue of *ego involvement*—that is, how involved people are with an issue and how important their attitude is to them (*salience*).

Social judgment theory offers at least three guidelines for the persuasive speaker: (1) The more compatible a person's speech goal is to the listeners' latitude of acceptance, the better the chances are of affecting those listeners' attitudes. (2) The more a person's speech goal appears to contrast with listeners' latitude of acceptance, the less the chances are of positively affecting listeners' attitudes. (3) The more ego-involved listeners are in their attitudes, the less likely it is that those listeners' attitudes will be changed by any contrasting message.

In addition, to expect a substantial shift in attitude or behavior as a result of one speech is probably unrealistic. Major attitude change is more likely to come over time in a campaign involving many speeches. William Brigance, one of the great speech teachers of this century, used to speak of "planting the seeds of persuasion."

If you present a modest proposal seeking a slight change in attitude, you may be able to get an audience to at least consider the value of your message. Later, when the idea begins to grow, you can ask for a greater change. For instance, if your audience believes that taxes are too high, you will have trouble convincing them taxes should be increased. However, you may be able to influence them to see that taxes are not really as high as they originally thought or not as high as the prices of other goods and services.

2. *Consider rewording the proposition if it seems impractical.* Put yourself in your audience's place and ask whether the course of action you are proposing will seem practical to them. When an audience perceives that what you want them to do is impractical, they are likely to ignore your appeal regardless of its merits. For instance, if your goal is to have your classmates write letters to their representative in Congress, the act of writing a letter may seem too time-consuming to most of the class. If, on the other hand, you suggest writing a short message on a postcard and you can give your audience preaddressed postcards, they may be more inclined to dash off a few lines if they agree with the merits of your appeal.

Does this mean you should never ask an audience to believe something that seems preposterous to them or to do something that is difficult? No. The point is, the greater the demand you place on your audience, the more prepared you must be to meet resistance.

Analyzing Your Audience

PRINCIPLE 2

You are more likely to determine the most effective speech strategy when you understand your audience's interest and knowledge levels and attitude toward your goal.

Because much of the success of a speech depends on determining how an audience is likely to react to the material, you must analyze audience data carefully to make reasonable assessments. As we established in Chapter 11, you can make reasonably accurate estimates of audience interest, knowledge, and retention of material based on demographic information. The more data you have about your audience and the more experience you have in analyzing audiences, the better are your chances of judging its attitudes with accuracy, although a precise differentiation of opinion is seldom necessary. Knowledge gained from your analysis is processed in two ways: You assess your audience's position and attitudes and then develop a strategy for adapting to that position.

Audience Interest, Understanding, and Retention.   The issues of interest, understanding, and retention were discussed fully in Chapter 16, Principles of Informative Speaking. We will review them here in the context of persuasive speaking.

Audience Interest.   Persuasion is more likely to take place when you engage audience interest in your speech. Therefore, you need to assess whether the audience is likely to have enough immediate interest in your goal to listen to your information, and determine what you can do during the speech to build or maintain such interest.

Audience Understanding.   Persuasion is more likely to take place when your audience is able to understand both your arguments and your information. Therefore, you need to assess whether these are likely to be understood, and find a way of explaining information and arguments that facilitates audience understanding.

Audience Retention.   Persuasion is more likely when your audience remembers what it is supposed to believe or do, and why. Thus, you must assess the likelihood of audience retention, and if it is not high, consider how to emphasize key points more vividly.

Audience Attitude.   Persuasion is more likely to take place when your audience has a positive attitude toward your goal. Thus, it is crucial to assess the direction and strength of audience attitudes about your topic in general and your specific goal in particular. An *attitude,* you will recall, is a predisposition for or against people, places, or things. An attitude is usually expressed in evaluative terms—you like or dislike something. If, for example, a person is predisposed to favor the idea of physical fitness, we could say that the person has a positive attitude toward physical fitness.

In persuasive speaking, you are trying to influence people's beliefs. But how do beliefs relate to attitudes? Most psychologists see a *belief* as the cognitive, or mental, aspect of an attitude; that is, we believe something to be true if someone can prove it to our satisfaction. On the subject of physical fitness, I might believe that keeping in good physical condition increases my chances of avoiding heart disease. If I have a favorable attitude toward physical fitness in general, it will be easier for me to hold this belief.

Students of persuasion realize that people's attitudes or beliefs can be expressed as opinions. An *opinion* is a verbal expression of an attitude or a belief. Saying "I think physical fitness is important" is an opinion that reflects a favorable attitude toward physical fitness. Saying "I think keeping in good condition lowers my chances of heart disease" is an opinion reflecting my belief.

There is a difference between an opinion and a behavior. A *behavior* is an action related to or resulting from an attitude or a belief. As a result of their attitudes or beliefs, people behave in certain ways. For instance, a person who has a positive attitude toward physical fitness and believes in its health benefits may work out three or more times a week to stay in good physical condition. Exercise is the behavior that results from the attitude and/or the belief.

Often there is harmony among these elements. For instance, a person may have a favorable attitude toward physical fitness; the person may then state the opinion that good physical conditioning is important; and as a result of this attitude the person may work out at least three times a week. Of course, it is possible for discrepancies to occur: A person may voice the opinion that physical conditioning is important, but then never work out.

Audience attitudes are expressed by opinions, which may be distributed along a continuum from highly favorable to hostile (see Figure 17.1). Even though any

Hostile	Opposed	Mildly opposed	Neither in favor nor opposed	Mildly in favor	In favor	Highly in favor

Figure 17.1 *Opinion continuum*

given audience may contain one or a few individuals with opinions at nearly every point along the distribution, audience opinion tends to cluster at a particular point. That cluster point represents the general audience attitude on that topic. Because it would be impossible to direct your speech to all the shades of attitudes held by the members of your audience, you must classify audience attitude as predominantly "no opinion" (either no information or no interest), "in favor" (already holding a particular belief), or "opposed" (holding an opposite point of view) and then develop a strategy that adapts to that attitude.

Now let us consider specific strategies for adapting to audiences based on the classifications of no opinion, in favor, or opposed. Suppose your goal is to have your listeners believe that they should alter their intake of saturated fats so as to lower their overall cholesterol levels.

No Opinion. An audience that has no opinion is either uninformed, neutral, or apathetic. The most appropriate speech goals for audiences with no opinion are goals that establish a belief or goals that move the audience to action.

If you believe your audience has no opinion because it is uninformed, the strategy should be to give enough information to help your audience understand the subject before you develop persuasive appeals directed toward establishing a belief or moving your listeners to action. For instance, if you believe your audience has no opinion about lowering cholesterol levels because it is uninformed, then only a few members of your audience will know what cholesterol is, how it is formed, and what effects it has on blood composition. Even those who know what cholesterol is may not know enough about it to form an opinion about its effects. In the early part of the speech, then, you would define cholesterol, talk about how it is formed, and share medical evidence about its effects on the human body. Be careful about how much time you spend on this informative part of the speech. If it takes more than half of your allotted time to explain what you are talking about, you may not have enough time to do much persuading.

If you believe your audience has no opinion because it is neutral, then you see your audience as being able to reason objectively and accept sound reasoning. In this case, then, your strategy will involve presenting the best possible arguments and supporting them with the best information you can find. If your assessment is correct, then you stand a good chance of success with that strategy.

If you believe your audience members have no opinion because they are apathetic, all of your effort may be directed to moving them out of their apathy. Your audience may know what cholesterol is, how it is formed, and even understand the medical information regarding negative effects, but may not seem to care. Instead of emphasizing the information with this audience, you would emphasize motivation.

You will need less material that proves the logic of your arguments and more material that is directed to your listeners' personal needs.

Do not expect too much even from a neutral audience. Major attitude change is more likely to come from a series of speeches over a period of time than from a single speech. Because your classroom speaking allows for only one effort, however, you will want to make the most of it.

In Favor. If you believe your listeners favor your position, you will focus on motivating them to take action.

Although having a favorable audience sounds like an ideal situation, it carries hazards. When an audience already favors the proposal, it will look for more than a rehash of familiar material. For instance, if members of your audience already favor lowering their cholesterol levels, it would be a mistake to give them reasons why they should do so. What keeps people who have a favorable attitude from acting is their lack of agreement on what to do. Your job is to provide a specific course of action around which they can rally. When you believe your listeners are on your side, try to crystallize their attitudes, recommit them to a particular direction, or suggest a specific course of action that will serve as a rallying point. If you focus the speech on a specific way of reducing saturated fat intake, you can perhaps get audience attitudes going in the same direction. The presentation of a thoughtful and specific solution increases the likelihood of audience action.

Even when audience members are on your side, they may perceive what you want them to do as impractical. If so, they are likely to ignore your appeal regardless of its merits. For instance, if your goal is to have class members increase their exercise, taking the extra time necessary to exercise more may seem impractical given their workloads. However, if your campus facility has a weight room, you may be able to show them how they can increase their exercise by using otherwise "wasted" time between classes or before or after lunch, in which case they may see the practicality of your goal.

Opposed. An audience that is opposed will have attitudes ranging from slightly negative to thoroughly hostile. The most appropriate speech goals for audiences that are opposed are those arguments that change a belief.

If you believe your listeners are slightly opposed to your proposal, you can approach them rather directly with your argument, hoping that its weight will swing them to your side. If your audience is slightly opposed to lowering their saturated fat intakes, you can present good reasons and evidence in support of the proposal.

Another part of your strategy should concern the presentation of arguments in ways that lessen your listeners' negative attitudes without arousing their hostility. With a negative audience, take care to be objective with your material and make your case clearly enough that those members who are only mildly negative will consider the proposal and those who are very negative will at least understand your position.

If you believe that your audience is hostile toward your goal, you may want to approach the topic indirectly or you may want to consider a less ambitious goal. To expect a complete shift in attitude or behavior as a result of one speech is probably unrealistic. If you present a modest proposal that seeks a slight change in attitude, you may be able to get an audience to at least consider the value of your message. Later, when the idea begins to grow, you can ask for a greater change. For instance, the audience may be comprised of people who are "fed up" with appeals to monitor their diets. If you believe your goal is important to them regardless of their negative attitude, then develop a strategy that will be more subtle. That will involve recognizing their hostility and talking about the topic in a way that will not arouse that hostility.

Figure 17.2 summarizes the strategy choices appropriate to audiences with different attitudes toward your topic. Audience attitudes may also affect how you organize your speech; this aspect of audience adaptation is considered under Principle 4.

Practice in Assessing Audience Attitudes

By Yourself

In reference to your specific persuasive speech goal, is your audience's attitude likely to be in favor, neutral, or opposed? What speech strategies will you use to adapt to that attitude?

Giving Logical Reasons and Evidence

PRINCIPLE 3

You are more likely to persuade an audience when you give them logical reasons and solid evidence in support of your speech goal.

The main points of a persuasive speech are usually stated as *reasons*—statements that tell why a proposition is justified. Human beings take pride in being rational; we seldom do anything without some real or imagined reason. One way of persuading your audience is thus to provide sound, well-supported reasons in support of your proposition.

Does giving reasons and evidence result in attitude change and/or action? One school of thought is that changes in people's attitude come as a result of a "learning experience." This perspective, inspired by the work of Carl Hovland, a professor of psychology at Yale, and his colleagues, suggests that people seek out arguments or reasons in a message that provide rational or logical support for conclusions.[2] The Yale theorists proposed that this learning comes about through an essentially cognitive sequence of attending to, comprehending, and accepting a persuasive message. From a learning theory perspective, then, a persuasive speaker is effective to the extent that members of the audience adopt the speaker's arguments as their own cognitive responses.

Although recent analysis has shown that the new attitudes and behaviors people adopt are based on several cognitive elements, research confirms that people's attitudes are affected at least in part by the reasons and evidence in persuasive messages.[3]

Audience Attitudes and Strategy Choices		
If audience members are . . .	then they may . . .	so that you can . . .
Highly in favor	■ be ready to act	■ provide practical suggestions ■ put emphasis on motivation rather than on on information and reasoning
In favor	■ already share many of your beliefs	■ crystalize and reinforce existing beliefs and attitudes to lead them to a course of action
Mildly in favor	■ be inclined to accept your view, but with little commitment	■ strengthen positive beliefs by emphasizing supporting reasons
Neither in favor nor opposed	■ be uninformed be neutral be apathetic	■ emphasize information relevant to a belief or move to action ■ emphasize reasons relevant to belief or action ■ concentrate on motivating them to see the importance of the proposition or seriousness of the problem
Mildly opposed	■ have doubts about the wisdom of your position	■ give them reasons and evidence that will help them to consider your position
Opposed	■ have beliefs and attitudes contrary to yours	■ emphasize sound arguments ■ concentrate on shifting beliefs rather than on moving to action ■ be objective to avoid arousing hostility
Hostile	■ be totally unreceptive to your position	■ plant the seeds of persuasion try to get them to understand your position

Figure 17.2 *Adapting persuasive speech strategies to audience attitudes*

Finding Reasons.   How do you go about drawing up a list of reasons to consider? You can identify some good reasons simply by taking a little time to think about the subject of your speech. Suppose you wanted to persuade your friends to increase their level of exercise. You might begin by asking yourself, "Why should my friends increase their level of exercise?" You might then think of the following three reasons: (1) to help them control their weight, (2) to help them strengthen their cardiovascular system, and (3) to help them feel better. For most speeches, however, you will need to supplement your own thoughts with reasons you discover by observing, interviewing, and reading. Find as many reasons as you can through research, and then choose the best ones, remembering that for most speeches you want about three or four main points.

For example, for a speech goal phrased "I want the audience to believe that the United States should overhaul its welfare system," you might think of or find at least six reasons:

- The welfare system costs too much.
- The welfare system is inequitable.
- The welfare system does not help those who need help most.
- The welfare system has been grossly abused.
- The welfare system does not encourage seeking work.
- The welfare system does not encourage self-support.

Once you've compiled a list of possible reasons, select the three or four best reasons based on the following criteria:

1. *Good reasons can be supported.* Some reasons that sound impressive cannot be supported with facts. For example, the fourth reason, "The welfare system has been grossly abused," sounds like a good one, but if you cannot find facts to support so strong a statement, you should modify it or not use it in your speech. You'll be surprised how many reasons mentioned in various sources have to be dropped from consideration for a speech because they can't be supported.

2. *Good reasons are relevant to the proposition.* Sometimes, statements look like reasons but don't supply much evidence. For instance, "The welfare system is supported by socialists" may sound like a reason for overhauling it to people who dislike socialism, but it doesn't offer any direct evidence that the system needs overhauling.

3. *Good reasons will have an impact on the intended audience.* Suppose that you have a great deal of factual evidence to back up the statement "The welfare system does not encourage seeking work." Even though it is a well-supported, logical reason, it would be a weak reason to use in the speech if the majority of your audience did not see "seeking work" as a primary criterion for evaluating the welfare system. Although you cannot always be sure about the potential impact of a reason, you can make a decent estimate of its possible impact based on your audience analysis. For instance, on the topic of welfare reform, most audiences would be more concerned with costs, equity, and abuses of the system.

Finding Evidence to Support Your Reasons. By themselves, reasons are only unsupported statements. Although some are self-explanatory and occasionally even persuasive without further support, most require development before listeners will either accept or act on them.

Reasons can be supported by major kinds of evidence we introduced in Chapter 12: factual statements and expert opinion. There are times when facts are not available or are inconclusive. In these situations, you can further support your reasons with opinion. Recall that the quality of opinion as evidence depends on whether the source of the opinion is an expert on the subject in question and that opinions are most reliable when accompanied by factual data.

Let's illustrate evidence by supporting a proposition with fact and opinion.

Speech Goal: I want the audience to believe that capital punishment should be abolished.

Reason: Because capital punishment discriminates.

Evidence by Fact: For instance, as reported in an April 1990 issue of *Time,* "Since 1976, not a single white killer has been sentenced to death for the murder of any black victim, while 33 blacks have been executed for killing whites."

Evidence by Expert Opinions: According to Bryan Stevenson, an attorney for Amnesty International, "If the defendant is black and the victim is white, you're 22 times more likely to get the death penalty than if the defendant is white."

At this stage, your persuasive speech will have a logical structure: a clear speech goal, reasons in support of that goal, and support for the reasons.

Testing the Validity of Reasons. So far, we have concentrated on presenting good reasons. To test the validity of our reasoning more completely, however, we need to look at the relationship between the reasons and evidence and the conclusion drawn from them. Suppose that in support of the proposition that the world is beginning to experience the "greenhouse effect," you said (1) the average temperature for the 1980s was more than one degree higher than the average temperature for the 1970s and (2) during the past ten years we have experienced far greater extremes of temperatures than during the previous fifty years. To examine the reasoning, you would need to determine the logical relationship between the proposition and the information presented in support of it. An examination of the argument shows that you are asserting that the one-degree increase in average temperature and the fluctuations are indicators or "signs" of the greenhouse effect. Once you can describe or explain the relationship between the information (reasons and evidence) presented and the conclusion drawn from them (proposition), you can ask questions to test the logic of the reasoning. For example, in the following section, we see that an argument based on signs should be evaluated differently from an argument based on analogy or causation.

Several kinds of reasoning links can be established between evidence and propositions. Let's consider the five major forms—generalization, causation, analogy, definition, sign—that will work for you in most circumstances.

Generalization. You are reasoning by *generalization* when you argue that what is true in some instances (evidence) is true in all instances (conclusion). Generalization links are the basis for polls and predictions. Take, for example, the fact "Tom, Jack, and Bill studied and got A's" and the conclusion based on it, "Anyone who studies will get an A." The reasoning link can be stated, "What is true in these representative instances will be true in all instances." To test this kind of argument, you should ask,

"Were enough instances cited? Were the instances typical? Are negative instances accounted for?" If the answer to any of these questions is no, the reasoning is not sound.

Causation.   You are reasoning by *causation* when your conclusion is presented as the effect of a single circumstance or set of circumstances. Causation is one of the most prevalent types of arguments you will encounter. An example is "We've had a very dry spring" (evidence); "The wheat crop will be smaller than usual" (conclusion). The reasoning link can be stated, "The lack of sufficient rain causes a poor crop." To test this kind of argument, you should ask, "Are the conditions described by the data (evidence) alone important enough to bring about the particular conclusion? If we eliminated these conditions, would we eliminate the effect?" If the answer to one of these questions is no, the reasoning is not sound. You can also ask, "Do some other conditions that accompany the ones cited in the evidence cause the effect?" If so, the reasoning is not sound.

Analogy.   You are reasoning by *analogy* when your conclusion is the result of a comparison with a similar set of circumstances. Although reasoning by analogy is very popular, it is regarded as the weakest form of reasoning. The analogy link is often stated, "What is true or will work in one set of circumstances is true or will work in a comparable set of circumstances." An example is "Off-track betting has proved very effective in New York" (evidence); "Off-track betting will prove effective in raising state revenues in Ohio" (conclusion). The reasoning link can be stated, "If something works in New York, it will work in Ohio, because Ohio and New York are so similar." To test this kind of argument, you should ask, "Are the subjects really comparable? Are the subjects being compared really similar in all important ways?" If the answer to these questions is no, the reasoning is not sound. You can also ask, "Are any of the ways that the subjects are dissimilar important to the conclusion?" If so, the reasoning is not sound.

Definition.   You are reasoning by *definition* when your conclusion is a definition or a descriptive generalization that follows from agreed-on criteria. Again, this is a very popular form of reasoning. An example is "She takes charge; she uses good judgment; her goals are in the best interests of the group" (evidence); "She is a good leader" (conclusion). The reasoning link could be stated, "Taking charge, showing good judgment, and considering the best interests of the group are the characteristics that constitute good leadership." To test this kind of argument, you should ask, "Are the characteristics mentioned the most important ones in determining the definition? Are those characteristics best labeled with the stated term?" If the answer to these questions is no, the reasoning is not sound. You can also ask, "Is an important aspect of the definition omitted in the statement of the characteristics?" If so, the reasoning is not sound.

Sign.   You are reasoning by *sign* when your conclusion is based on the presence of observable data that usually or always accompany other, unobserved variables. If, for example, you see longer lines at the downtown soup kitchen, and the presence of that condition (longer lines) is usually or always an indicator of something else (the worsening of the recession), then you can predict the existence of the other, unobserved variable. Signs are often confused with causes, but signs are indications and sometimes effects, not causes. Longer lines at soup kitchens are a sign of the worsening recession. The longer lines may be an effect of a recession, but they do not cause the recession. To test this kind of argument, you should ask, "Do the data cited always or usually indicate the conclusion drawn? Are sufficient signs present?" If not, the reasoning is not sound.

Organizing Material to Meet Audience Attitudes

PRINCIPLE 4

You are more likely to persuade an audience when you organize your material according to the expected audience reaction.

Although the nature of your material and your own inclination may affect how you organize a persuasive appeal, the most important consideration is the expected audience reaction or attitude. The specific organizational pattern to select depends on whether your audience favors your proposition and, if so, to what degree.

The following organizational patterns—statement of logical reasons, problem–solution, comparative advantages, criteria satisfaction, residues, and motivational—may prove useful to adopt as stated, or they may suggest an organization that you believe will work for your audience given the material you have to work with. Although your selection depends in part on audience attitude, it also depends on the nature of your material. With some topics and some material, one organiza-

How you organize your speech will depend in part on expected audience reaction or attitude.

tional pattern may be naturally better than another; the forms are not entirely inter-changeable. For instance, for some proposals, your audience will have to be shown the nature of the problem before they will even listen to a course of action. For others, the problem may be readily apparent, and the emphasis can be placed on the superiority of your particular proposal for dealing with the problem. For purposes of illustrating persuasive organizational patterns, however, we will use the same proposition and the same (or similar) arguments. By applying each method to essentially the same arguments, you can contrast the forms and better understand their use.

Statement-of-Logical-Reasons Pattern. The statement-of-logical-reasons pattern is a straightforward organization in which you present the best supported reasons you can find following an order of second strongest first, strongest last, and other reasons in between. Although the pattern doesn't show a great deal of creativity and doesn't reflect any particular content or audience strategy, it will work when your listeners have no opinion on the subject, are apathetic, or are perhaps only mildly in favor or opposed. A statement-of-logical-reasons organization for a school tax levy proposition might look like this:

> *Proposition:* I want my audience to vote in favor of the school tax levy on the November ballot.

> **I.** Income will enable the schools to restore vital programs (second strongest).

> **II.** Income will enable the schools to give teachers the raises they need to keep up with the cost of living.

> **III.** The actual cost to each member of the community will be very small (strongest).

Problem–Solution Pattern. Recall from Chapter 14 that the problem–solution pattern provides a framework for clarifying the nature of the problem and for illustrating why a given proposal is the best one. This order is a logically sound one, for it begins by establishing that a problem exists and continues by showing that the proposition is a sound solution. The problem–solution pattern often is organized around three main points: (1) There is a problem that requires action; (2) the proposal will solve the problem; and (3) the proposal is the best solution to the problem. Since this pattern is also a straightforward presentation of reasons, it is likely to work best for a topic that is relatively unfamiliar to an audience—they are unaware that a problem exists—or for an audience that has no opinion or is mildly pro or con. A problem–solution organization for the school tax levy proposition might look like this:

> *Proposition:* I want my audience to vote in favor of the school tax levy on the November ballot.

> **I.** The shortage of money is resulting in serious problems for public education (statement of problem).

> **II.** The proposed increase is large enough to solve those problems (solution).

III. For now, a tax levy is the best method of solving the schools' problems (consequences).

Comparative-Advantages Pattern.   The comparative-advantages pattern places all the emphasis on the superiority of the proposed course of action. Rather than presenting the proposition as a solution to a grave problem, it presents the proposition as one that ought to be adopted solely on the basis of the advantages of that proposition over the status quo. Although this pattern can work for any audience attitude, it works best when the audience understands that there is a problem that must be solved. It also works for propositions that are based solely on the superiority of a particular choice. For instance, most people eat out occasionally; thus, their choice of restaurant is unrelated to any particular problem. A comparative-advantages approach to the school tax levy proposition would look like this:

Proposition: I want my audience to vote in favor of the school tax levy on the November ballot.

    I.   Income from a tax levy will enable schools to raise the standards of their programs.

   II.   Income from a tax levy will enable schools to hire better teachers.

  III.   Income from a tax levy will enable schools to better the educational environment.

Criteria-Satisfaction Pattern.   The criteria-satisfaction pattern seeks audience agreement on criteria that should be applied when considering a particular proposition and then shows how the proposition satisfies those criteria. When you are dealing with audiences that are opposed to your ideas, you need a pattern of organization that will not aggravate their hostility. The criteria-satisfaction pattern is an effective one to use with such audiences because it focuses on developing a "yes" response to criteria before you introduce the proposition and reasons. A criteria-satisfaction organization for the school tax levy proposition would look like this:

Proposition: I want my audience to vote in favor of the school tax levy on the November ballot.

   I.   We all want good schools (a community value).

      A.   Good schools have programs that prepare our youth to function in society (one criterion of good schools).

      B.   Good schools are those with the best teachers available (a second criterion of good schools).

  II.   Passage of the school tax levy will guarantee good schools.

      A.   Passage will enable us to increase the quality of vital programs (satisfaction of one criterion).

      B.   Passage will enable us to hire and to keep the best teachers (satisfaction of the second criterion).

Residues Pattern. The residues pattern is one in which you show that of the several possible courses of action that are reasonable to consider in the face of a felt need, only one will work. This pattern is another one that may be used with an audience that opposes your proposition. The reason it is likely to be effective is that before you state the proposal that you support, you show how the other reasonable proposals are flawed. Then you conclude with "the only method that is likely to have a chance of working." To persuade a hostile audience to vote for a school tax levy, you might use this organizational pattern:

> *Proposition:* I want my audience to vote in favor of the school tax levy on the November ballot.

   I. Saving money by reducing services and programs will not help the schools.

  II. The federal government will not increase its help to the schools.

 III. The state government will not increase its help to the schools.

  IV. All we have left is to pass the tax levy.

Motivational Pattern. The motivational pattern combines problem solving and motivation: It follows a problem–solution pattern but includes required steps designed to heighten the motivational effect. Much of the thinking behind motivational patterns is credited to Alan Monroe, a professor at Purdue University. Motivational patterns usually include a five-step, unified sequence that replaces the normal introduction–body–conclusion model: (1) an *attention* step, (2) a *need* step that fully explains the nature of the problem, (3) a *satisfaction* step that explains how the proposal solves the problem in a satisfactory manner, (4) a *visualization* step that provides a personal application of the proposal, and (5) an *action-appeal* step that emphasizes the specific direction listener action should take. A motivational approach to the school tax levy proposition would look like this:

> *Proposition:* I want my audience to vote in favor of the school tax levy on the November ballot.

   I. Comparisons of worldwide test scores in math and science have refocused our attention on education (attention).

  II. The shortage of money is resulting in cost-saving measures that compromise our ability to teach basic academic subjects well (need, statement of problem).

 III. The proposed increase is large enough to solve those problems in ways that allow for increased emphasis on academic need areas (satisfaction, how the proposal solves the problem).

  IV. Think of the contribution you will be making not only to the education of your future children but to efforts to return our educational system to the world level it once held (personal application).

V. Here are "Vote Yes" buttons that you can wear to show that you are willing to support this much-needed tax levy (action appeal showing specific direction).

Using Language to Motivate

PRINCIPLE 5

You are more likely to persuade an audience when your language motivates them.

Whether your speech is designed to affect people's beliefs or to move then to action, the audience's response is likely to depend on your motivational efforts. *Motivation* is defined as "forces acting on or within an organism to initiate and direct behavior."[4] From the time of Aristotle's *Rhetoric,* the first complete book on persuasion (written more than 2,000 years ago), students of public speaking have been aware of the power of arousing emotions to motivate. In the words of Richard Weaver, "A speech intended to persuade achieves little unless it takes into account how people are reacting subjectively to their hopes and fears and their special circumstances."[5]

Incentives as Motivation. Motivation is often a product of providing incentives. An *incentive* is simply "a goal objective that motivates."[6] Thus, if a speaker says that in addition to helping clean up the environment by collecting aluminum cans and glass and plastic bottles, you can earn money by turning them in to a recycling center, you might see earning money for your efforts as an incentive to recycling.

For an incentive to have value, it must be meaningful. Meaningfulness involves an emotional reaction. Eric Klinger, a leading researcher in motivation, believed that people pursue those objects, events, and experiences that are emotionally important for them.[7] Recycling would be a *meaningful* goal for someone looking for ways to participate in cleaning up the environment but not for someone who doesn't care about the environment or about earning small amounts of money. An incentive is most powerful when it is part of a meaningful goal.

Evaluating the Force of Incentives. People are more likely to perceive incentives as meaningful if the incentives present a favorable cost–reward ratio. As we discussed in Chapter 8, John Thibaut and Harold Kelley explain social interactions in terms of rewards received and costs incurred by each member of an interaction. Recall that rewards are such incentives as economic gain, good feelings, prestige, or any other positive outcome; costs are units of expenditure such as time, energy, money, or any negative outcome of an interaction.

Let's apply this idea to a speech setting. Suppose you are asking your audience to volunteer an hour a week to help adults learn to read. The time you are asking them to give is likely to be perceived as a cost rather than an incentive; however, you may be able to describe volunteering in such a way that it is perceived as a reward—a meaningful incentive. That is, you may be able to get members of the audience to feel civic-minded, responsible, or helpful as a result of volunteering time for such a worthy cause. If, in your speech, you can show that those rewards or incentives outweigh the cost, you can increase the likelihood of the audience's performing the desired action.

Use of Incentives to Meet Basic Needs. Many theorists who take a humanistic approach to psychology have argued that incentives are most powerful when they meet basic needs. One of the most popular needs theories is Abraham Maslow's. His theory suggests that people are more likely to act when a speaker's incentive satisfies a strong unmet need in members of the audience.

Maslow devised a hierarchy of needs that is particularly useful in providing a framework for needs analysis. Maslow divided basic human needs into seven categories arranged in a hierarchy that begins with the most fundamental needs. These seven categories, illustrated in Figure 17.3, are physiological needs, including food, drink, and life-sustaining temperature; safety and security needs, including long-term survival and stability; belongingness and love needs, including the need to identify with friends, loved ones, and family; esteem needs, including the quest for material goods, recognition, and power or influence; cognitive needs, including the need for knowledge and understanding; aesthetic needs, including the need for order and beauty; and self-actualization needs, including the need to develop one's self to realize one's full potential.[8] By placing these needs in a hierarchy, Maslow suggested that one set of needs must be met or satisfied before the next set of needs emerges. In theory, then, a person will not be motivated to meet an esteem need of gaining recognition until basic physiological, safety, and belongingness and love needs have been met.

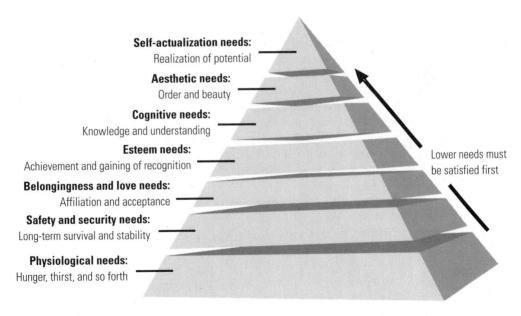

Figure 17.3 *Maslow's hierarchy of needs*

What is the value of this analysis to you as a speaker? First, it suggests the kinds of needs you may appeal to in your speeches. Second, it allows you to understand why a line of development will work on one audience and fail with another. For instance, in hard economic times, people are more concerned with physiological and safety needs and so will be less responsive to appeals to affiliation and altruism. Thus, in the past few years fund raisers for the arts have experienced far more resistance to giving than they did in the previous decade. Third, and perhaps most crucial, when your proposition conflicts with a felt need, you will have to be prepared with a strong alternative in the same category or in a more fundamental category. For instance, if your proposal is going to cost people money (say, higher taxes), you will have to show how the proposal satisfies some other comparable need (perhaps by increasing their security).

Revising Language to Arouse Emotions.   Even with good incentives directed to basic needs, to motivate an audience to act you must appeal to their emotions. What is an emotion? An *emotion* is experienced subjectively as a strong feeling and physiologically involves changes that prepare the body for action. Many of our emotions are triggered by physical happenings. For instance, when a dog jumps out from behind a tree, you may feel fear. Emotions are also triggered by words. For instance, when a friend says "Go to the play—don't worry about me, I'll be all right alone," you may feel guilt. In this section, we are interested in the conscious effort of a speaker to phrase ideas in ways that appeal to the emotions of the listeners.

Effective persuasive speech development entails both logical and emotional elements that act interdependently. Thus, you should not look for one set of materials that gives logical support and a separate set that arouses such emotions as fear or pity or joy. Instead, you should look for good reasons and for support that will, if properly phrased, arouse these emotions.

Suppose you are to give a speech calling for more humane treatment of the elderly in our society. As part of your appeal, you want to make the point that older people often feel alienated from the society that they worked so many years to support and develop. To make your case, you can present facts and figures to show how many older citizens are not employed, how many are relegated to nursing homes, and how many have skills and talents that are lost to society. These are all good reasons to improve the treatment of the elderly. If, in addition, you can cause your listeners to feel sad, angry, or guilty about that treatment, you can add an emotional dimension to the material.

The role of emotional appeal is to compel listeners to feel as well as to think about what is being said. You can achieve this goal by identifying the emotions you want your listeners to experience, by selecting information that will stimulate those emotions, by building key ideas with vivid, emotional pictures, and by putting special effort into building emotional appeal into the introduction and the conclusion.

1.   *Clearly identify the emotions you want your listeners to experience.* What emotion or emotions do you want your audience to experience as a result of your speech? If you are giving a speech designed to get the audience's support for more humane treatment of the elderly, you may want your listeners to feel sadness, anger, grief, caring, or perhaps guilt. If you are giving a speech designed to get the audience to attend your school's production of a musical, you may want your listeners to feel joy, excitement, or enthusiasm. If you are not sure what it is that you want your audience to feel, any speech effectiveness is likely to be accidental.

2. *Select information that will stimulate those emotions in your listeners.* Suppose you have determined that you want your listeners to feel sad about the lack of positive goals or aspirations among the elderly. What information do you have that will show the lack of goals or aspirations? Perhaps you have data from interviews with elderly people in which their only talk of the future is the inevitability of death. Perhaps you have accounts of social workers saying that many elderly people live totally in the past and are reluctant to talk about or even think about the future. Or perhaps you have information to show that many nursing homes do very little to give their clients anything to look forward to. These are all examples of the kinds of information that are likely to cause another person to feel sad.

3. *Build key ideas with vivid, emotional pictures.* The driving force of motivation will be your wording of key ideas. You should look for ways to increase their emotional impact. If you want your audience to support more humane treatment of elderly people, one of your reasons might be that "elderly people are often alienated from society." If you have material to support that reason, you can then ask yourself, "How can I phrase the material in a way that will motivate the audience to actually feel its impact?" You could respond with the following:

> Currently elderly people are alienated from society. A high percentage live in nursing homes, live on small fixed incomes, and exist out of the mainstream of society.

This states the facts but provides little emotional impact. Contrast the following statement of the same material:

> Currently, elderly people are alienated from the society that they worked their entire lives to support. What happens to elderly people in America? They become the forgotten segment of society. They are often relegated to "old people's homes" so that they can live out their lives and die without being "a bother" to their sons and daughters. Because they must exist on relatively small fixed incomes, they are confined to a life that for many means separation from the very society they helped to create.

With just the addition of an audience question and language that creates more vivid pictures, the same material takes on considerably more emotional strength.

4. *Put special effort into building emotional appeal into the introduction and conclusion.* Perhaps your greatest opportunities for meaningful emotional appeal occur in the introduction and conclusion of your speech. In the introduction, you capture and heighten audience interest, and you set the tone for the speech; in the conclusion, you try to cement the message of the speech in the minds of the listeners so that they cannot shake it. Betsy Burke's speech on euthanasia illustrates excellent use of emotional appeal in both her introduction and conclusion.[9] She began her speech as follows:

Let's pretend for a moment. Suppose that on the upper right-hand corner of your desk there is a button. You have the power by pushing that button to quickly and painlessly end the life of one you love: your brother or father. This loved one has terminal cancer and will be confined to a hospital for his remaining days. Would you push the button now? His condition worsens. He is in constant pain and he is hooked up to a life-support machine. He first requests, but as the pain increases he pleads for you to help. Now would you push that button? Each day you watch him deteriorate until he reaches a point where he cannot talk, he cannot see, he cannot hear—he is only alive by that machine. Now would you push that button?

After giving reasons for changing our laws on euthanasia, she concluded her speech as follows:

I ask again, how long could you take walking into that hospital room and looking at your brother or father in a coma, knowing he would rather be allowed to die a natural death than to be kept alive in such a degrading manner? I've crossed that doorstep—I've gone into that hospital room, and let me tell you, it's hell. I think it's time we reconsider our laws concerning euthanasia. Don't you?

Notice how the speaker creates a situation in which each member of the audience becomes personally involved with the decision. Instead of using abstract concepts, she uses specific, concrete terms selected for their emotional impact in order to help the audience feel what she is saying. Regardless of your beliefs about euthanasia, you would likely experience sadness as you empathize with this speaker.

Developing Credibility

PRINCIPLE 6

You are more likely to persuade an audience when they view you as a credible source.

In Chapter 16 on informative speaking, we outlined the nature of credibility and the characteristics that you need to develop to be perceived as credible. Credibility is as important, if not more important, in persuasive speaking. Almost all studies confirm that the speaker's credibility has a major effect on audience belief and attitude.[10]

In addition to the steps reviewed in Chapter 16—being well prepared, emphasizing your interest in the audience, looking and sounding enthusiastic, being ready to speak on time, and evaluating others' speeches thoughtfully—to demonstrate credibility in persuasive speeches, you must behave ethically.

Ethics are the standards of moral conduct that determine our behavior. Ethics include both how we ourselves act and how we expect others to act. Although ethical codes are personal, society has codes of ethics for communication and many other behaviors that are implicitly understood even if they are not written down anywhere.

Especially when we believe strongly in the righteousness of our cause, we may be tempted to believe that the end justifies the means, and to bend or even break moral rules to achieve our goals. We are all well aware of people who have ridden roughshod over society's moral or ethical principles. In the public-speaking context, the concerns voiced in recent years about negative, misleading, false, or irrelevant statements in political campaigns are in part concerns about ethics.

How a speaker handles ethical questions says a great deal about the speaker as a person, and thus bears directly on credibility. What ethical standards apply to speaking? The following six guidelines reflect the standards of hundreds of college students and provide an excellent foundation for a set of ethical standards in persuasive speaking.[11]

1. *Tell the truth.* Of all the guidelines, this may be the most important. Communication depends on a bond of trust between the parties involved. An audience that consents to listen to you is extending you its trust. Consequently, if people believe you are lying to them, they will reject you and your ideas. If during your speech they believe you are telling the truth, but later learn that you have lied, you are likely to lose your credibility with them for later speeches.

But telling the truth means more than avoiding deliberate, outright lies. Credible communicators do not twist facts. When the facts are well documented, they make the most of them; when the facts are weak, they acknowledge their potential weakness. Many times an honest "I really don't know, but I'll find out" will enhance credibility far more than trying to deflect a comment or use somewhat irrelevant information to try to make points. And if you are not sure whether information is true, don't use it until you have verified it. Ignorance is seldom accepted as an excuse.

If audiences detect misstatements of fact or ethical lapses, they are unlikely to be persuaded.

2. *Keep your information in perspective.* Many people get so excited about their information that they exaggerate its importance. Although a little exaggeration might be accepted as a normal product of human nature, when the exaggeration is perceived as distortion, most people will consider it the same as lying. For instance, suppose you discover that capital punishment has lowered the murder rates in a few states, but in many other states the statistics are inconclusive. If in your speech you assert that statistics show that capital punishment deters crime, you would be distorting the evidence. Because the line between some exaggeration and gross exaggeration or distortion is often difficult to distinguish, most people see any exaggeration as unethical.

3. *Resist personal attacks against those who oppose your ideas.* There seems to be an almost universal agreement that name-calling and other irrelevant personal attacks are detrimental to a speaker's trustworthiness. Responsible listeners recognize that such tactics do not contribute to the speaker's argument and represent an abuse of the privileged status the speaker enjoys.

4. *Give the source for all damning information.* Where ideas originate is often as important as the ideas themselves, especially when a statement is damning. If you are going to discuss wrongdoing by individuals or organizations, or condemn an idea by relying on the words or ideas of others, provide the sources of your information and arguments. Moreover, since the mention of wrongdoing brings communication to the edge of what is legally defined as slander, speakers should be aware of the legal as well as ethical pitfalls of making damning statements without proof.

5. *Disclose the complete picture.* Speakers can try to manipulate audience's perceptions by phrasing points in such a way as to ignore or put a positive spin on information that is damning to their case. Although they may console themselves with the thought that they have not told outright lies, knowingly suppressing unfavorable information does misrepresent the facts and violates the audience's trust.

6. *Be sensitive to cultural differences.* Although speakers seldom purposely attack members of the audience, thoughtlessness can be just as demeaning and, as a result, can defeat the very goal the speaker is attempting to achieve. First, avoid addressing members of an audience from a different culture as "you people." Separating yourself from the audience is often perceived as a put-down. Second, avoid using ethnic or sexist jokes for any reason. Even when we think we're saying something "just in fun," the joke will be perceived as demeaning. As David Kale, Academic Dean of Olivet Nazarene University, points out, "Verbal and psychological abuse can damage the human spirit in the same way that physical abuse does damage to the body."[12]

Delivering the Speech Convincingly

PRINCIPLE 7

You are more likely to persuade an audience if your delivery is convincing.

Effective delivery for persuasive speeches is no different from effective delivery for any speech. But because delivery is so important, it is worth a moment to focus on one key aspect of delivery that is especially relevant to persuasion: The effective persuader displays conviction about the subject. Some people show conviction through considerable animation. Others show it through a quiet intensity. Maintaining eye contact is a key for all speakers. However it is demonstrated, though, your conviction must be perceived by the audience.

Refuting Opposing Arguments

PRINCIPLE 8

You are more likely to be effective in persuasion if you are able to refute key positions taken by your opposition.

Many times when you want to speak, it is not to propose an idea or plan but to respond to an idea or plan offered by someone else. Further, even without an opponent present, you may often need to counter arguments that your audience has heard in the past. Making the best use of your persuasive potential requires having confidence in your ability to refute.

By definition, *refutation* is the process of proving that a statement is false or erroneous—or, at least, doubtful. Someone says "Steffi Graf will win the match," and you say "No, she isn't even entering the tournament." Someone says "We need more government control of basic industry," and you say "No, according to Milton Friedman, that's about the last thing we need." Each of these replies is a refutation of an assertion. In the following sections, we discuss what can be refuted and how refutation is prepared and presented.

What to Refute. Refutation begins with anticipating what the opposition will say. For any controversial issue, you should know the arguments on both sides. If you have an idea of how an opponent will proceed, you will be in a much better position to reply. If the opponent talks for very long, you should probably take some notes; you do not want to run the risk of being accused of distorting what your opponent has said.

You can base your refutation on the amount of support offered by your opponent, the quality of that support, or your opponent's reasoning. If the opposition's case is built on assertion with little or no supporting evidence, you can refute the argument on that basis. A better method, however, is to attack the quality of the material or the validity of the reasoning. If sheer amount of evidence were the most important criterion in proving a point, the person with the most material would always win. However, there is often no direct relationship between amount of material and quality of proof. For example, a single statement by a judge who has studied the issue of individual right to privacy would be worth far more than several opinions on the right to privacy from athletes, musicians, or politicians who have not studied the subject.

Evaluating Evidence. For every item of evidence that is presented, you should ask the following:

1. *Is the evidence fact or opinion?* As we said earlier, fact is usually worth more than opinion, and expert opinion is worth more than inexpert opinion. When an "expert" opinion is offered, ask yourself whether the supposed expert is actually qualified to judge the point in question. Often people cite the opinions of individuals who are prominent or who are well qualified in one area (say, physics) but who have no special expertise in the subject under discussion (say, medical ethics). Moreover, in some cases, you may be able to counter the effects of expert opinion by citing facts that contradict it.

2. *Where does the evidence come from?* This question involves both the people who offered the opinions or compiled the facts and the book, journal, or source where they were reported. Just as some people's opinions are more reliable than others, some printed sources are more reliable than others. That something appeared in print does not necessarily make it true. (Think of the headlines you see each week in supermarket tabloids.) If data come from a poor source, an unreliable source, or a biased source, no reliable conclusion can be drawn from them, and you should refute the argument on that basis.

3. *Is the evidence recent?* Products, ideas, and statistics often are obsolete as soon as they are produced. You must ask when the particular evidence was true. Five-year-old evidence may not be true today. Furthermore, an article in last week's newsmagazine may be using five-year-old evidence in the story.

4. *Is the evidence relevant?* You may find that the evidence has little to do with the point being presented. This question of relevancy may well lead you into the reasoning process itself.

Evaluating Reasoning. Although attacks on evidence are sometimes an effective means of refutation, the form of refutation that is most convincing is the attack on the reasoning from the evidence. Even if all the facts are admitted, the conclusion fails if the reasoning is unsound.

Each argument presented in a persuasive speech comprises at least three elements: (1) evidence or data from which a conclusion is drawn, (2) the conclusion itself, and (3) a stated or implied link that takes the speaker from the evidence to the conclusion. To refute another's reasoning, first check whether the reasons are relevant to the proposition and are supported; then identify the type of reasoning that describes the relationship between the reason and its evidence and assess its validity. To complete your evaluation, use the information presented earlier in this chapter under "Testing the Validity of Reasons" (pp. 426–428). For additional examples of unsound reasoning, see Five Common Fallacies in Persuasive Reasoning on pages 442–443.

How to Refute. Although you do not have as long to consider exactly what you are going to say, your refutation must be organized nearly as well as your planned speeches. To prepare and present your refutation effectively, think of it as a series of arguments, each of which is organized by following four definite steps:

1. *State the argument you are going to refute clearly and concisely.* Or, as an advocate replying to refutation, state the argument you are going to rebuild.

2. *State what you will prove.* You must tell your listeners how you plan to proceed so that they will be able to follow your thinking.

3. *Present the evidence completely, with documentation.*

4. *Draw your own conclusion.* Do not rely on the audience to draw the proper conclusion for themselves. Never go on to another argument before you have drawn your conclusion.

In the following abbreviated statement, notice how the four steps of refutation are incorporated. For purposes of analysis, each of the four steps is numbered:

> You'll recall that Ms. Horan is supporting the proposition that college students should purchase whole life insurance while they are young. (1) Ms. Horan has said that buying insurance provides systematic, compulsory savings. (2) Her assumption is that "systematic, compulsory saving" is a benefit of buying insurance while you are young. But I believe that just the opposite is true. I believe that there are at least two serious disadvantages resulting from buying insurance when you are young. (3) First, the system is so compulsory that if you miss a payment you stand to lose your entire savings and all benefits. Most insurance contracts include a clause giving you a thirty-day grace period, after which the policy is canceled . . . [evidence]. Second, if you need money desperately, you have to take a loan on your policy. The end result of such a loan is that you have to pay interest in order to borrow your own money . . . [evidence]. (4) From this analysis, I think you can see that "systematic, compulsory saving" is more a disadvantage than an advantage for people who are trying to save money.

Practice in Preparing Presuasive Speeches

By Yourself

1. Prepare a persuasive speech in which you reaffirm, establish, or change an audience belief or move your audience to action. An outline and a bibliography are required. (For an example of a persuasive speech, see "Open Your Eyes," pp. 473–476 in the Appendix.)

2. As an addendum to the outline, you may wish to write a plan for adapting the speech to your specific audience, based on both the predictions you made using the audience analysis checklist in Chapter 11 (p. 275) and the principles discussed in this chapter. The plan should have short sections in which you address the following questions:

a. How will you get, build, and maintain audience interest in your topic?

b. How much background information do you need to present in order to prepare the audience to understand your speech?

c. What reasons will you use and how will you organize your reasons? Find or think of four to six reasons that you could use to support your speech goal. Then, based on your analysis of your audience's attitude toward your topic, select the three or four best reasons and an organizational pattern (logical reasons, problem–solution, comparative advantages, criteria satisfaction, residues, motivational) that you believe is most likely to increase your chance of motivating this audience.

Five Common Fallacies in Persuasive Reasoning

Analyzing the reasoning links in an argument is a key part of both critical thinking and refutation. William D. Gray's examples of common fallacies (unsound reasoning) may provide you with grist for refuting an opponent's argument—and for testing your own.

Normally, when we speak of a fallacy, we mean a notion that's false. Thus, the idea that chocolate causes acne and the notion that a rabbit's foot guarantees good luck are fallacies in this sense. When I use the word *fallacy* in this book, however, I mean a defective argument, one in which the premises do not provide an adequate basis for the conclusion. ...

No one is immune to [fallacies]; we are all, from time to time, taken in by them or commit them ourselves. ... The best way to ensure against them is to become aware of them and develop the ability to spot them when they occur. ...

Ad Hominem

The traditional Latin term for the first fallacy is *argumentum ad hominem,* and it means, literally, "argument against the man." In ordinary English it should be translated "attack the person." It occurs when someone attempts to refute a person's claim by attacking that person rather than the claim. ... It is a fallacy because the person's character has no bearing on the truth or falsity of the claim. No matter how rotten a person's character may be, his or her assertion may still be true. In this argument:

> James Randi says that
> Peter Popoff is a charlatan.
> But only a fool would listen

to Randi, because he's an atheist.

... the speaker tries to refute Randi's claim by attacking him personally. The argument fails from a logical point of view, because even if Randi is an atheist, Popoff may still be a charlatan. ...

Equivocation

Most words have more than one meaning. This fact makes it possible to create fallacious arguments, because a key term is used in one sense in a premise and in another sense in the conclusion. ... We can illustrate this fallacy by the following humorous example:

> The average family has
> 2.5 children, and John's family is very average. So, John's
> family must have 2.5 children.

In the conclusion the term *average* means a mathematical figure (2.5). In one of the two premises, the term *average* means "normal," or "ordinary." The Equivocation Fallacy is being committed because the inference turns on the ambiguity in meaning of this word. Now let's look at an example provided by one of my students:

> What's wrong with taking LSD? It's just a chemical, and the bloodstream is full of

chemicals all the time anyway.

This argument turns on the double meaning of the word *chemical*. The two different senses (meanings) used are:

1. a synthetically produced substance; a drug
2. a naturally produced substance; a hormone. . . .

False Cause

The Latin name for the Fallacy of False Cause is *post hoc, ergo propter hoc,* which means "after this, therefore because of this." The Latin is often abbreviated *post hoc*. We commit this fallacy when we infer a causal connection between two succeeding events when no such connection has been established. . . .

Several years ago, *Life* magazine reported that a man had cured his cancer by eating a strict diet of grain foods for six months. But the mere fact that one event follows another event in time is not enough to prove that the two events are causally related. . . . Although it is true that the man's cancer disappeared after the grain diet, this is not proof that the diet cured the cancer. Any number of other factors could account for the cure.

False Dichotomy

The Fallacy of False Dichotomy is committed when only two options are stated and others are overlooked. . . . Let's listen to one of my students committing this fallacy:

Either I was hallucinating or I actually saw Uri

Geller bend that spoon with his mind. Now, I know I wasn't hallucinating (because other people saw it, too), so Geller actually did bend that spoon with his mind.

The two possibilities offered here are certainly not the only ones. A third possibility is that Geller is a skilled magician using sleight-of-hand to create illusions. . . .

Straw Man

The Straw Man Fallacy occurs when one person misrepresents the view of another person in order to make him or her an easy target. . . . The arguer succeeds, if at all, in knocking down a straw man instead of the real man. . . .

[An] example is:

Penn: Scientists don't take psychic phenomena seriously, because they refuse to consider anything that they don't understand.

Is Penn accurately representing the position of scientists? Would scientists agree with his description of them? Obviously not, because many scientists today are working to understand what they don't, now, understand. For example, some researchers are working hard to find the cause of Alzheimer's disease, and others are trying to understand the braided rings of Saturn. Penn, instead of attacking scientists, is merely attacking a caricature of them. His attack, therefore, is fallacious. ■

SOURCE: William D. Gray, *Thinking Critically about New Age Ideas* (Belmont, CA: Wadsworth, 1991), pp. 52–71.

Persuasive Speech Checklist

Check items that were accomplished effectively.

Specific Goal

_____ 1. Was the specific goal clear?

_____ 2. Was the specific goal designed to _____reinforce a belief? _____ establish a belief? _____ change a belief? or _____ move to action?

_____ 3. Was the specific goal adapted to this audience's interests, knowledge, and attitudes?

Content

_____ 4. Did the speaker present clearly stated reasons?

_____ 5. Did the speaker use facts and expert opinions to support these reasons?

_____ 6. Was the speaker effective in establishing his or her credibility on this topic?

_____ 7. Was the speaker ethical in handling material?

Organization

_____ 8. Did the introduction gain attention and goodwill for the speaker?

_____ 9. Did the speech follow a _____ logical-reasons pattern? _____ problem–solution pattern? _____ comparative–advantages pattern? _____ criteria–satisfaction pattern?_____ residues pattern? _____ motivational pattern?

_____ 10. Was the pattern appropriate for the type of goal and assumed attitude of the audience?

_____ 11. Did the conclusion further the persuasive effect of the speech?

Language

_____ 12. Was the language _____ clear? _____ vivid? _____ emphatic? _____ appropriate?

_____ 13. Did the speaker use emotional language to motivate the audience?

Delivery

_____ 14. Was the delivery convincing?

Evaluate the speech as (check one):

_____ excellent, _____ good, _____ average, _____ fair, _____ poor.

Use the information from your checklist to support your evaluation.

Figure 17.4 *Evaluating a persuasive speech*

d. How will you establish your credibility with this audience?

e. What incentives will you use to motivate and how will you use language to arouse emotions? Identify the emotions that you want to arouse; then determine the places in your speech where you are going to focus your emotional appeals.

3. For one or more of the speeches you hear during a round of persuasive speeches, complete the checklist in Figure 17.4. Then write a two- to five-paragraph evaluation of the speech.

With Another

Working with a classmate, select a debatable proposition, and then clear the wording with your professor. Phrase the proposition so that the first speaker is in favor of the proposal. The first speaker will present a three- to six-minute speech in support of the proposition. The second speaker will present a three- to six-minute speech of refutation. The second speaker should spend the entire time directly refuting the reasons presented. The first speaker will then present a two- to three-minute refutation of the opponent's speech.

Summary

Persuasive speeches are designed to change a belief or motivate an audience to act. They are similar to informative speeches in that both seek to achieve a specific goal, to arouse interest and attention, to ensure understanding and retention, to convey credibility, and to adapt to audience attitudes. Persuasive speeches, however, focus specifically on beliefs and actions.

The principles governing persuasive speeches are similar to those presented for informative speeches, as are the steps of speech preparation.

First, write a clear persuasive speech goal, or proposition, stating what you want your audience to believe or do.

Second, analyze your audience's interest and knowledge levels and attitude toward your goal, and use this analysis to determine the most effective speech strategy.

Third, build the body of the speech with good reasons, statements that answer why the proposition is justified. Support reasons with facts and expert opinion. Five common forms of reasoning are generalization, causation, analogy, definition, and sign.

Fourth, create an organization for the speech that suits your goal and your analysis of the audience. Six organizational patterns for persuasive speeches are the statement-of-logical-reasons pattern, problem–solution pattern, comparative-advantages pattern, criteria-satisfaction pattern, residues pattern, and motivational pattern.

Fifth, motivate your audience by providing incentives that present a favorable cost–reward ratio or satisfy strong unmet needs, and by reworking language to appeal to the emotions, especially in your introduction and conclusion.

Sixth, build your credibility. Especially in persuasive speaking, one of the most important ways of building credibility is to behave ethically.

Finally, deliver the speech convincingly. Good delivery is especially important in persuasive speaking.

In addition to giving persuasive speeches in support of propositions, you may often be called on to reply to persuasion. Refutation can be based on your evaluation of the opponent's evidence or reasoning.

Suggested Readings

Kahane, Howard. *Logic and Contemporary Rhetoric,* 7th ed. Belmont, CA: Wadsworth, 1995 (paperback). An excellent source that gives some outstanding pointers on the use and development of logical argument and places considerable emphasis on identifying and eliminating the fallacies of reasoning.

Larson, Charles U. *Persuasion: Reception and Responsibility,* 7th ed. Belmont, CA: Wadsworth, 1995 (paperback). A solid textbook that places more emphasis on the receiver of the persuasive message than on the persuader.

Packard, Vance O. *The Hidden Persuaders.* New York: Pocket Books, 1975 (paperback). First published in the 1950s but still makes for excellent reading about the problems and excesses of persuasion.

Simons, Herbert W. *Persuasion: Understanding, Practice, and Analysis,* 2d ed. New York: Random House, 1986. An excellent overview of persuasive theory and practice.

Notes

1. Richard E. Petty, Thomas M. Ostrom, and Timothy C. Brock, "Historical Foundations of the Cognitive Response Approach to Attitudes and Persuasion," in Richard E. Petty, Thomas M. Ostrom, and Timothy C. Brock, eds., *Cognitive Responses in Persuasion* (Hillsdale, NJ: Erlbaum, 1981), pp. 11–12.

2. The Yale approach is discussed in detail in Carl I. Hovland, Irving L. Janis, and Harold H. Kelley, *Communication and Persuasion* (New Haven: Yale University Press, 1953), p. 11. For a critical analysis of the Yale approach, see Mary John Smith, *Persuasion and Human Action: A Review and Critique of Social Influence Theories* (Belmont, CA: Wadsworth, 1982), pp. 214–215, 236.

3. Alice Eagly, "Comprehensibility of Persuasive Arguments as a Determinant of Opinion Change," *Journal of Personality and Social Psychology* 29 (1974): 758–773.

4. Herbert L. Petri, *Motivation: Theory, Research, and Applications,* 3d ed. (Belmont, CA: Wadsworth, 1991), p. 3.

5. Richard Weaver, "Language Is Sermonic," in Richard L. Johannesen, Rennard Strickland, and Ralph T. Eubanks, *Language Is Sermonic* (Baton Rouge, LA: State University Press, 1970), p. 205.

6. Petri, p. 185.

7. Eric Klinger, *Meaning and Void: Inner Experience and the Incentives in People's Lives* (Minneapolis: University of Minnesota Press, 1977).

8. Abraham H. Maslow, *Motivation and Personality* (New York: Harper & Row, 1954), pp. 80–92.

9. Speech on euthanasia delivered in a course on persuasive speaking, University of Cincinnati. Portions reprinted by permission of Betsy R. Burke.

10. Kenneth E. Andersen and Theodore Clevenger, Jr., "A Summary of Experimental Research in Ethos," *Speech Monographs* 30 (1963): 59–78.

11. Data taken from surveys conducted over a five-year period in Communication and Society, an introductory survey of speech communication at the University of Cincinnati.

12. David W. Kale, "Peace as an Ethic for Intercultural Communication," in Larry A. Samovar and Richard E. Porter, eds., *Intercultural Communication: A Reader,* 7th ed. (Belmont, CA: Wadsworth, 1995), pp. 438–439.

Public Speaking
Chapters 11–17

What kind of a public speaker are you? The following analysis looks at twelve specifics that are basic to a public-speaking profile. On the line provided for each statement, indicate the response that best captures your behavior: 1, never; 2, rarely; 3, occasionally; 4, often; 5, almost always.

_____ When I am asked to speak, I am able to select a topic with confidence. (Ch. 11)

_____ When I speak, I analyze my audience and occasion carefully before finalizing my speech goal. (Ch. 11)

_____ In my preparation, I know where and how to look for information and what kinds of information to look for. (Ch. 12)

_____ In my preparation, I am careful to be sure that I have developed ideas to meet audience needs. (Ch. 13)

_____ In my preparation, I construct clear main points and organize them to follow some consistent pattern. (Ch. 14)

_____ When I speak, I sense that my audience perceives my language as clear and vivid. (Ch. 15)

_____ I look directly at members of my audience when I speak. (Ch. 15)

_____ My public-speaking voice shows variation in pitch, speed, and loudness. (Ch. 15)

_____ When I speak, my bodily actions help supplement or reinforce my ideas; I feel and look involved. (Ch. 15)

_____ I have confidence in my ability to speak in public. (Ch. 15)

_____ When I give informative speeches, I am careful to use techniques designed to get audience attention, create audience understanding, and increase audience retention. (Ch. 16)

_____ When I give persuasive speeches, I am careful to use techniques designed to build my credibility, prove my reasons, and motivate my audience. (Ch. 17)

Based on your responses, select the public-speaking behavior that you would most like to change. Write a communication improvement goal statement similar to the sample in Chapter 1 (page 24). If you would like verification of your self-analysis before you write a goal statement, have a friend or classmate complete this same analysis for you.

**After you have read
this module, you
should be able to:**

*Form open and closed,
neutral and leading, and
primary and secondary
questions*

*Explain procedures for
conducting an informative
interview*

Interviewing
for Information

"Ramsey, I just got a call from Parker at City Hall saying that the police are planning to extend the experimental program at the Garden Projects—the cooperative program between police and residents for moving drug pushers out of the area. I want you to find out all you can about this. I want to know how well the experimental project is working, what happens to the pushers, what the residents think about the effectiveness of the program, and anything else you can think of."

For getting information in situations like this, the primary source is the interview. *Interviewing* is a form of interaction based primarily on the asking and answering of questions. Interviewing can be a valuable method for obtaining information on nearly any topic. Students interview outside sources to obtain information for papers; people wanting to learn about career and job possibilities interview individuals working in a given field; lawyers interview witnesses to establish facts on which to build their cases; doctors interview patients to obtain medical histories before making diagnoses; and reporters interview sources to get facts for their stories.[1] Interviewing is a valuable skill by which you can get information for interpersonal, group, or public-speaking purposes. Effective interviewing for information involves writing good questions and following a good interview plan.

Questions in Interviewing

An interview differs from other forms of communication in its reliance on the asking and answering of questions. Although we deal here specifically with questions in the interview situation, a knowledge of how to construct good questions can be applied to any communication encounter. Questions may be phrased as open or closed, neutral or leading, primary or secondary.

Open versus Closed Questions

Open questions are broad-based questions that ask the interviewee to respond with whatever information he or she considers appropriate. Open questions range from those with virtually no restrictions, such as "What can you tell me about yourself?" to those that give some direction, such as "What do you believe has prepared you for this job?" Why do interviewers ask questions? Mostly to encourage the person to talk, allowing the interviewer an opportunity to listen and to observe. Through the open question, the interviewer finds out about the person's perspectives, values, and goals. Keep in mind, however, that open questions take time to answer, which means interviewers can lose sight of their original purpose if they are not careful.[2]

By contrast, *closed questions* are narrow-focus questions that require very brief answers. Closed questions range from those that can be answered yes or no, such as "Have you had a course in marketing?" to those that require only a short answer, such as "How many restaurants have you worked in?" By asking closed questions, interviewers can control the interview; moreover, they can obtain large amounts of information in a short time. On the other hand, the closed question seldom enables the interviewer to know *why* a person gave a certain response, nor is the closed question likely to yield much voluntary information.

Which type of question should you use? The answer depends on what kinds of material you are seeking and how much time you have for the interview. Both kinds of questions are used in most information and employment interviews.[3]

Neutral versus Leading Questions

Neutral questions are those questions to which the person is free to respond without direction from the interviewer. An example of a neutral question would be "How do you like your new job?" There is nothing about the wording of the question that gives the respondent any indication of how the question should be answered.

By contrast, *leading questions* are questions phrased in a way that suggests the interviewer has a preferred answer. For instance, "You don't like the new job, do you?" is a leading question. In the majority of interviewing situations, leading questions are inappropriate because they try to force the person in one direction and tend to make the person defensive.

Primary versus Secondary Questions

Primary questions are those questions that the interviewer plans ahead of time. Primary questions serve as the main points in the interview outline—a plan of the major questions and subquestions prepared for an interview. Primary questions may be open or closed, depending on the kind of information being sought; in addition, they may be neutral or leading. As you plan an interview, be sure to include enough primary questions to ensure that you will obtain all the information you want.

Secondary questions, or follow-up questions, are designed to pursue the answers given to primary questions. Secondary questions may be planned ahead if you can anticipate possible interviewee answers. More often than not, however, secondary questions are composed as the interview goes along. To come up with well-worded secondary questions that stimulate the interviewee to provide the information you want, you will need to pay close attention to what the interviewee is saying. Some secondary questions encourage the person to continue ("And then?" "Is there more?"); some probe into what the person has said ("What does 'frequently' mean?" "What were you thinking at the time?"); and some plumb the person's feelings ("How did it feel to get the prize?" "Were you worried when you didn't find her?").

The major purpose of secondary questions is to motivate a person to enlarge on an answer. Such secondary questions are often necessary because interviewees' answers may be incomplete or vague, because they may not really understand how much detail you are looking for, or occasionally because they may be purposely trying to be evasive.

Your effectiveness with secondary questions may well depend on your interpersonal skill in asking them. Because probing questions can alienate the interviewee (especially when the questions are perceived as threatening), such in-depth probes work best after you have gained the confidence of the interviewee and when the questions are asked within the atmosphere of a positive interpersonal climate. We discuss these aspects of interviewing in the next section.

The Interview Plan

Interviews are more likely to achieve the desired result if they are carefully planned. Creating and implementing an interviewing plan involves clearly defining the purpose of the interview, selecting the best person to interview, planning a procedure for the interview, and conducting the interview.

Defining the Purpose of the Interview

Too often, interviewers go into an informative interview without a clearly identified purpose. A clear purpose is a specific goal that can be summarized in one sentence. Without such a statement of purpose, the interviewer's questions more than likely will have no direction, and the information derived from the interview may not fit together well.

Suppose you wish to obtain information about the food service in your dormitory. Possible specific purposes would be:

1. To determine the criteria for selecting the food catering service.

2. To determine the most efficient means of setting up a cafeteria line.

3. To determine the major elements a dietitian must take into account in order to plan dormitory meals.

Notice that each of these covers an entirely different aspect of food service. Your choice, then, would depend on the nature of the information you wish to get.

Selecting the Best Person to Interview

Somewhere on campus or in the larger community there are people who have or who can direct you to the information you want. How do you find out whom you should interview? If you are pursuing the third purpose, "To determine the major elements a dietitian must take into account in order to plan dormitory meals," one of the kitchen employees can tell you who is in charge of the dining hall. Or you could phone your student center and inquire about who is in charge of food service. When you have decided whom you should interview, make an appointment; you cannot walk into an office and expect the prospective interviewee to drop everything just to talk to you. Be forthright in your reasons for scheduling the interview. Whether your interview is for a class project, for a newspaper article on campus food, or for some other purpose, say so.

Before going into the interview, research the topic. If, for instance, you plan to interview the dietitian who creates menus and orders food, make it a point to find out what a dietitian's job is and what some of the problems of ordering and preparing institutional food are. Interviewees are more likely to talk with you if you appear informed; moreover, familiarity with the subject will enable you to ask better questions. If you must go into an interview uninformed, at least approach the interviewee with enthusiasm for and apparent interest in the subject.

Planning a Procedure for the Interview

The heart of the interviewing plan is a list of questions that have been selected and refined to meet the specific goal of the interview. Some interviewers try to conduct the entire interview spontaneously. Even the most skilled interviewer, however, requires some preplanned questions to ensure coverage of important areas.

To generate your list, begin by writing down all the questions you can think of. The topics of the questions are determined by the purpose of the interview. Background, responsibilities, and procedures, for example, would be relevant to the goal of determining the major elements a dietitian must take into account in order to plan dormitory meals. Then revise your questions until you have worded them clearly and concisely and put them in the order that seems most appropriate. Make your questions a mix of open and closed questions and phrase them to be neutral rather than leading. Leave enough space between questions to fill in answers as completely as possible. Also leave enough space for answers to the secondary questions you decide to ask during the interview.

How many primary questions should you have planned? The answer, of course, depends on how much time you have for the interview. If, for example, you have thirty minutes, about ten questions would be a reasonable number. Why ten? In a thirty-minute interview, that would leave about three minutes per question. Remember, for some of your questions you will need one or more secondary questions to get the information you want. If most of your questions are closed, you can ask more than ten; if nearly all of your questions are open, you may want fewer. Keep in mind that you never know how a person will respond. Some people are so talkative and informative that in response to your first question they answer every question you were planning to ask in great detail; other people will answer each question with just a few words.

In the opening stage of the interview, plan to ask some questions that can be answered easily and that will show your respect for the person you are interviewing. In an interview with the head dietitian, you might start with background questions such as "How did you get interested in nutrition?" or "I imagine working out menus can be a very challenging job in these times of high food costs—is that so?" If the person nods or says yes, you can then ask about some of the biggest challenges he or she faces. The goal is to get the interviewee to feel at ease and to talk freely. Because the most important consideration in this initial stage is to create a positive communication climate, keep the questions simple, nonthreatening, and encouraging. Hard-hitting questions that require careful thought come later in the interview, after you have established a rapport. For instance, in an interview with the cafeteria dietitian, the question "What do you do to try to resolve student complaints about the quality of the food?" should come near the end of the interview.

The body of the interview includes the major questions you have prepared. You may not ask all the questions you planned to, but you don't want to end the interview until you have the important information you intended to get. The questions are designed to get the information necessary to achieve your goal. The following is an example of a question schedule you might construct if you were planning to interview the head dietitian and your goal was to determine the major elements a dietitian must take into account in order to plan dormitory meals:

Background

What kind of background and training do you need for this job?

How did you get interested in nutrition?

Have you worked as a dietitian for long?

Have you held any other food-related positions?

Responsibilities

What are the responsibilities of your job besides meal planning?

How far in advance are meals planned?

What factors are taken into account when you are planning the meals for a given period?

Do you have a free hand, or are there constraints placed on you?

Procedures

Is there any set ratio for the number of times you put a particular item in the menu?

Do you take individual preferences into account?

How do you determine whether you will give choices for the entree?

What do you do to try to answer student complaints?

How do your prices compare with those at a commercial cafeteria?

Conducting the Interview

By applying the interpersonal skills we have discussed in this book, you'll find that you can turn your careful planning into an excellent interview.

1. *Be courteous during the interview.* Start by thanking the person for taking the time to talk to you. Remember, although the interviewee may enjoy talking about the subject, may be flattered, and may wish to share knowledge, that person has nothing to gain from the interview. Try to develop a good rapport with the interviewee, be patient at all times, and encourage the person to speak freely. Most of all, respect what the person says regardless of what you may think of the answers.

2. *Listen carefully.* You will want to incorporate those skills related to attending, understanding, and remembering, with special emphasis on asking questions, paying attention to nonverbal cues, and paraphrasing. Remember that a paraphrase is a sentence that states in your own words what you perceive the idea or feeling the person has communicated to be. By paraphrasing, you can assure yourself that you have correctly understood what the interviewee has said.

3. *Keep the interview moving.* You do not want to rush the person, but when the allotted time is ending, you should call attention to that fact and be prepared to conclude. Although some people will get so involved that they will not be concerned with the amount of time spent, most people will have other important business to attend to.

4. *Make sure that your nonverbal reactions—facial expressions and gestures— are in keeping with the tone you want to communicate.* Maintain good eye contact with the person. Nod to show understanding, and smile occasionally to maintain the friendliness of the interview. How you look and act is likely to determine whether the person will warm up to you and give you an informative interview.

5. *If you are going to publish the substance of the interview, as a courtesy, offer to let the person see a copy of the article.* At the least, tell the person exactly when it will be published. Under some circumstances, you may want to show the person a draft of your report of the interview before it goes into print. If the interviewee does wish to see what you are planning to write before it is published, send a draft well before deadline to give him or her the opportunity to read it and to provide yourself with an opportunity to deal with any suggestions. Even if the person doesn't want to see a draft, you will want to double-check the accuracy of direct quotations. Although this practice is not followed by many interviewers, it can help build and maintain your own credibility.

Practice in Interviewing for Information

By Yourself

Conduct an interview outside of class, and submit a written report or deliver a speech based on the interview.

With Another

Conduct an in-class interview with a classmate on a subject with which he or she is familiar.

Notes

1. An excellent source for information interviewing is Shirley Biagi, *Interviews That Work: A Practical Guide for Journalists,* 2d ed. (Belmont, CA: Wadsworth, 1992).

2. Craig D. Tengler and Frederic M. Jablin, "Effects of Question Type, Orientation, and Sequencing in the Employment Screening Interview," *Communication Monographs* 50 (September 1983): 261.

3. For more information on asking questions, see Charles J. Stewart and William B. Cash, *Interviewing: Principles and Practices,* 6th ed. (Dubuque, IA: Wm C. Brown, 1991).

**After you have read
this module, you
should be able to:**

*Explain procedures used by
job interviewers*

Write a résumé

*Explain how to participate in
a job interview*

Job Interviewing

"Glenn Carter. How are you? I'm Julia Garson, Assistant Personnel Director here at Powell's. I have already looked at your résumé, but to get us started, tell me a little about yourself—you know, those kinds of things that one can't really understand by reading a résumé alone."

So begins Glenn's interview for a position in the marketing division of Powell Enterprises. Although interviewing for a job is often a traumatic experience, especially for those who are going through it for the first time, applicants for nearly every position in nearly any field will go through at least one interview, and possibly several. At its worst, an interview can be a waste of time for everyone; at its best, an interview can reveal vital information about an applicant as well as allow the applicant to judge the suitability of the position, the company, and tasks to be performed.

A skillfully conducted interview can help interviewers determine the applicant's specific abilities, ambitions, energy, ability to communicate, knowledge and intelligence, and integrity. Moreover, it can help the interviewee show his or her strengths in these same areas.

The job interview is a special type of communication situation with specific demands. Let's consider some of the procedures and methods that an interviewer uses in conducting an interview, as well as those that an interviewee can use in taking part in one.

Responsibilities of the Interviewer

As an interviewer, you represent the link between a job applicant and the company. Much of the applicant's impression of the company will depend on his or her impression of you, so you will want to be able to provide answers to questions applicants may have about your company. In addition to the obvious desire for salary information, applicants may seek information about opportunities for advancement, influence of personal ideas on company policy, company attitudes toward personal life and lifestyle, working conditions, and so forth. Moreover, you are primarily responsible for determining whether this person will be considered for the position available or for possible future employment with the company.

Determining the Procedure

The most satisfactory employment interview is probably a highly to moderately structured one. In the unstructured interview, the interviewer tends to talk more and to make decisions based on less valid data than in the structured interview.[1] Especially if you are screening a large number of applicants, you want to make sure that all have been asked the same questions and that the questions cover subjects that will be most revealing of the kind of information you will need in order to make a reasonable decision.

Before the time scheduled for the interview, become familiar with all available data about the applicant: application form, résumé, letters of recommendation, test scores if available. Such written data will help determine some of the questions you will want to ask.

Conducting the Interview

A well-planned interview has an opening, a body, and a closing.

The Opening.   Open the interview by greeting the applicant warmly by name, shaking his or her hand, and introducing yourself so that he or she can use your name. Be open with applicants. If you plan either to take notes or to record the interview, let the applicant know why you are doing so.

A major concern of many interviewers is whether to begin with "warm-up" questions to help establish rapport or whether to move right into the question schedule. A good interviewer senses the nature of the situation and tries to use a method that is most likely to encourage applicants to talk and provide adequate answers. Although warm-up questions may be helpful, most applicants are ready to get down to business immediately, in which case warm-up questions may be misinterpreted.[2] Applicants may wonder about the motivation for such questions, and the questions may make them even more nervous. Unless you have good reason for proceeding differently, it seems advisable to move into the question schedule right away in as warm and friendly a manner as possible.

The Body.   The body of the interview consists of the questions you are planning to ask. Let's begin with some guidelines for presenting yourself and your questions.

1.   *Be careful of your own presentation.* Talk loudly enough to be heard. Try to be spontaneous. Interviewees are not going to respond well to obviously memorized questions fired in machine-gun fashion. Be sensitive to your own nonverbal communication. Interviewees are going to be looking for signs of disapproval, and any inadvertent looks or unusual changes in quality or rhythm of your speech may give a false impression. Remember, too, that you can load a question by expressing it in a particular tone of voice.

2.   *Do not waste time.* You have available a wide variety of information about the candidates from their résumés, application forms, and so on. Ask questions about things you already know only if you have some special reason for doing so. For instance, if an applicant indicates employment with a particular organization but does not give any detailed account of responsibilities, questions relating to that employment period would be appropriate.

3.   *Avoid trick or loaded questions.* Applicants are always leery of questions that may be designed to make them look bad. Moreover, if candidates believe that you are trying to trick them, the suspicion may provoke a competitive rather than a positive atmosphere. Anything that serves to limit the applicant's responsiveness will harm the interview by limiting the information needed to get a fair impression.

4.   *Avoid questions that violate fair employment practice legislation.* Congress created the Equal Employment Opportunity Commission (EEOC). In subsequent years, EEOC has written detailed guidelines that spell out the kinds of questions that are lawful and those that are unlawful. For example, questions directed to a woman about her plans for marriage or, if she is married, about her plans to have children are not only irrelevant but illegal. Actually, any questions about marital status, family, physical characteristics, age, religion, or arrests are illegal unless this information is deemed to be a bona fide occupational qualification. By and large, the interview should focus on questions that are relevant to the person's capabilities in fulfilling the job requirements.

5. *Give the applicant an opportunity to ask questions.* Usually, near the end of the interview, you should take the time to see whether the applicant has any questions.

Now let's look at some of the specific questions that interviewers usually ask. The following list was compiled from a variety of sources and is only representative, not exhaustive. It sets no limitations on your own creativity but is intended to suggest the kinds of questions you may wish to ask. Notice that it focuses questions on personal interests; relevant educational background; and job-related attitudes, goals, and skills—three areas of information that are relevant to making a decision on a candidate. You might use this as a starter list or as a checklist for your own wording of questions. Notice that some questions are open and some are closed, but none is a yes-or-no question.

School

How did you select the school you attended?

How did you determine your major?

What extracurricular activities did you engage in at school?

In what ways does your transcript reflect your ability?

How were you able to help with your college expenses?

Personal

What are your hobbies?

How do you work under pressure?

At what age did you begin supporting yourself?

What causes you to lose your temper?

What are your major strengths? Weaknesses?

What do you do to stay in good physical condition?

What kind of reading do you like to do?

Who has had the greatest influence on your life?

What have you done that shows your creativity?

Position

What kind of position are you looking for?

What do you know about the company?

Under what conditions will you be willing to relocate?

Why do you think you would like to work for us?

What do you hope to accomplish?

What qualifications do you have that make you feel you would be beneficial to us?

How do you feel about traveling?

What part of the country would you like to settle in?

With what kind of people do you enjoy interacting?

What do you regard as an equitable salary for a person with your qualifications?

What new skills would you like to learn?

What are your professional goals?

How would you proceed if you were in charge of hiring?

What are your most important criteria for determining whether you will accept a position?

The Closing.   Toward the end of the interview, you should always tell the applicant what will happen next. Explain the procedures for making the decision. Answer any questions about who has the authority for the hiring decision, when the decision will be made, and how applicants will be notified. Then close the interview in a courteous, neutral manner. Avoid building up false hopes or seeming to discourage any given applicant.

Responsibilities of the Job Applicant

Interviews are an important part of the process of seeking employment. Even for part-time and temporary jobs, you will benefit if you approach the interviewing process seriously and systematically. There is no point in applying for positions that are obviously outside your area of expertise. It may seem a good idea to get interviewing experience, but you are wasting your time and the interviewer's if you apply for a position you have no intention of taking or for which you are not qualified.

When you are granted an employment interview, remember that all you have to sell is yourself and your qualifications. Recall from our discussion of self-presentation in Chapter 4 how much your nonverbal behavior contributes to the impression you make. You want to show yourself in the best possible light. Take care with your appearance; if you want a particular job, dress in a way that is acceptable to the person or organization that may—or may not—hire you.

Preparing for the Interview

Of course you'll want to be fully prepared for the interview. Two important tasks you must complete before the interview itself are writing a cover letter and writing a résumé. Although they do not get you jobs, "they advertise you for interviews."[3]

Cover Letter.   The cover letter is a short, well-written letter expressing your interest in a particular position. Always address the letter to the person with the authority to hire you (and not, for example, to the personnel department). If you do not have the appropriate person's name, you can probably get it by telephoning the company.

Because you are trying to stimulate the reader's interest in you, the applicant, take care that your cover letter does not read like a form letter. The cover letter should include the following elements: where you found out about the position, your reason for being interested in this company, your main qualifications (summary of a few key points), how you fit the requirements for the job, items of special interest about you that relate to your potential for the job, and a request for an interview. Keep the letter to one page if possible, and include a résumé with the letter.

Résumé.   Although there is no universal format for résumé writing, there is some agreement on what should be included and excluded.[4] In writing your résumé, you should consider including the following information:

1. *Contact information:* Your name, address, and telephone numbers at which you can be reached

2. *Job objective:* A one-sentence objective, focusing on specific area(s) of expertise

3. *Employment history:* Paid and nonpaid experiences beginning with most recent

4. *Education:* Degrees, schools, and years, with focus on courses that are most directly related to the job

5. *Military experience:* Include rank, service, and achievements, skills, and abilities

6. *Professional affiliations:* Memberships, offices held

7. *Community involvement:* Offices, organizations, dates

8. *Special skills:* Foreign languages, computers

9. *Interests and activities:* Only those that relate to your objective

10. *References:* Include only a statement that references are available on request

Notice that the list does not include such personal information as height, weight, age, sex, marital status, health, race, religion or political affiliation; nor does it include any reference to salary. Also note that although you need not include references, you should already have permission of people whom you will use as references.

In addition, you should consider what format your résumé will follow—how wide your margins will be, how elements will be spaced and indented, and so on. The résumé should be no more than three pages, preferably one or two, because your goal is to make an immediate impact. Be sure to make the résumé neat, proofread carefully, and reproduce it on good-quality paper. Try to determine what to include from the employer's point of view. What you have to present is something that can help an employer solve his or her problems. Think in terms of what the company needs, not personal characteristics of your own that are irrelevant to the job. Think creatively, but foremost, write your résumé from an ethical position. You want to emphasize your strengths without exaggerating facts, which is both deceptive and unethical. Figure B.1 shows a sample résumé of a person who has just graduated from college.

JOYCE M. TURNER

Temporary Address:
2326 Tower Ave.
Cincinnati, Ohio 45220
513-861-2497

Permanent Address:
914 Market
Columbus, Ohio 43217
614-662-5931

PROFESSIONAL OBJECTIVE	A challenging position in sales or public relations with a medium-sized corporation. Geographic preference for the Midwest.
EXPERIENCE 1995	Internship WLW-TV. Received 3 cr. hr. for working 10 hours per week Spring quarter. Worked with sales force selling commercial time.
1994	Sales. Lazarus Department Store. Full-time summer and Christmas vacation; part-time during school year. Experience in clothing, appliances, and jewelry.
EDUCATION 1988–1996	University of Cincinnati, Cincinnati, Ohio Candidate for B.A. degree in June, 1996. Major in Communication with minor in Business (Marketing). Overall grade point average of 3.3.
ACTIVITIES	C.A.S.E. (Communication Arts Seeking Excellence) An undergraduate organization for Communication Majors. President, Senior year. Planned a series of programs featuring talks by former majors who hold positions in business.
INTERESTS	Sports (tennis and racquetball); travel
REFERENCES	On request

Figure B.1 *Sample résumé*

Rehearsing the Interview. For most of us, job interviews are at least somewhat stressful. To help prepare yourself so that you can perform at your best, it is a good idea to give yourself a practice interview session. Try to anticipate some of the questions you will be asked, and think carefully about your answers. You need not write out or say answers aloud; before the actual interview, however, you can anticipate key questions and give careful thought to such subjects as your salary expectations, your possible contributions to the company, and your special skills.

The Interview

You are likely to make a favorable impression in your interview if you follow these guidelines:

1. *Do your homework.* Know about the company's services, products, ownership, and financial health. Knowing about a company shows your interest in that company and will usually impress the interviewer. Moreover, you'll be in a better position to address how you can contribute to the company's mission.

2. *Be prompt.* The interview is the company's only clue to your work behavior. If you are late for such an important event, the interviewer may well conclude that you are likely to be late for work. Give yourself plenty of travel time to cover any possible traffic problems, with a little left over to catch your breath, comb your hair, and so on.

3. *Be alert and look at the interviewer.* Remember that your nonverbal communication tells a lot about you. Company representatives are likely to consider eye contact and posture as clues to your self-confidence.

4. *Give yourself time to think.* If the interviewer asks you a question that you had not anticipated, give yourself time to think before you answer. It is better to pause and think than to give a hasty answer that may cost you the job. If you do not understand the question, paraphrase it before you attempt to answer.

5. *Ask questions about the type of work you will be doing.* The interview is your chance to find out if you would enjoy working for this company. You might ask the interviewer to describe a typical workday for the person who will get the job. If the interview is conducted at the company offices, you might ask to see where you would be working.

6. *Show enthusiasm for the job.* The interviewer is likely to reason that if you are not enthusiastic during an interview, you may not be the person for the job. Employers look for and expect applicants to look and sound interested.

7. *Do not engage in long discussions on salary.* If the company representative tries to pin you down about your salary requirements, ask "What do you normally pay someone with my experience and education for this level position?" Such a question allows you to get an idea of what the salary will be without committing yourself to a figure first.

8. *Do not harp on benefits.* Detailed questions about benefits are more appropriate after the company has made you an offer.

Practice in Job Interviewing

By Yourself

1. Prepare a cover letter and a résumé for a position such as you might seek in the foreseeable future.

2. Think of a job interview that you have had. What parts of the interview were most difficult for you? Why? If you were to engage in that same interview again, what would you do differently?

If you have never had a job interview, talk with someone who has. Find out what parts of the interview were most difficult for that person and why.

In light of this information, where are you likely to put your greatest emphasis in preparation for your next job interview?

With Another

Select a partner in class and interview each other for a particular job for which a résumé has been prepared. Try to follow the guidelines suggested for employment interviewing.

Notes

1. Richard D. Arvey and James E. Campion, "The Employment Interview: A Summary and Review of Recent Research," *Personnel Psychology* 35 (1982): 281–321.
2. John W. Cogger, "Are You a Skilled Interviewer?" *Personnel Journal* 61 (1982): 842–843.
3. Ronald L. Krannich and William J. Banis, *High Impact Resumes and Letters,* 4th ed. (Woodbridge, VA: Impact Publications, 1990), p. 21.
4. There are many up-to-date books on résumés and cover letters at most bookstores, including Marian Faux, *The Complete Résumé Guide,* 5th ed. (New York: Macmillan, 1995).

After you have read this appendix, you should be able to:

Analyze an interpersonal encounter

Analyze an informative speech

Analyze a persuasive speech

Samples and Analyses

S amples can be useful means for studying the principles of any speech communication format. Each of the following is a sample that was presented by students much like yourself to meet a communication assignment. The first is an interpersonal conversation; the second is an informative speech; the third is a persuasive speech. Each contains enough examples of successful applications of principles to make them worth analysis. Your goal is not to copy what others have done but to read and analyze in order to better test the value of what you are planning to do.

In each case, read the sample and then make your own judgments about which parts are good, bad, or indifferent. After you have made your analysis, read the critique and compare it with your own.

Interpersonal Conversation and Analysis

Dating

Sheila and Susan talk about the advantages and disadvantages of dating exclusively within one's own religion. Read the conversation aloud in its entirety. After you have considered its merits, read it again, this time noting the analysis in the right-hand column.

Conversation

Susan: How are you and Bill getting along these days?

Sheila: Not too well. I think you could say our relationship is coming to an end. The feelings just aren't there, and so many problems have been building up.

Susan: I get the impression from the expression on your face that you're having problems. Is there one specific problem?

Sheila: Well, there are a lot, but one that I didn't think would make such a difference at the beginning of the relationship that's made a difference now is the fact that we're from different religions. I'm Jewish and he isn't, and at first I never thought it would affect me, but it does make a difference.

Susan: I think I was kind of lucky, well, lucky in the long run. When I was in high school, my parents wouldn't allow me to go out with anybody who wasn't Jewish. I really resented that at first, but now I'm kind of glad since I'm thinking about the future now. And as my parents said, you don't know what could come out of a high-school relationship.

Analysis

Susan introduces the subject with a question.

Sheila's answer is neither as specific nor as concrete as it could have been.

Susan responds with a perception check *wording; she's responding both to Sheila's spoken words and to what she is implying. A* feelings paraphrase *wording would be better: "From the way you're talking, I get the impression that you're very sad about the outcome of the relationship."*

Sheila says, "It really does make a difference," but she doesn't go on to say what the difference is. We would expect Susan to ask about the difference.

Susan assumes she understands. She needs a question or a content paraphrase here. Instead, she changes the emphasis to her own experience. Now, apparently, the conversation will focus on Susan and an implied contrast in upbringing.

SOURCE: Conversation presented in Interpersonal Communication class, University of Cincinnati. Reprinted by permission of Sheila Slone and Susan Lautman.

Conversation

Sheila: It seems like you were a little upset at first, but now you're pretty happy with the whole situation.

Susan: Yes, now that I look around, I'm not in the predicament that you are of having to get out of a relationship for something that's not what you want.

Sheila: I can see what you mean, but I'm also happy that my parents didn't restrict me because I think I would have felt a lot of pressure just to always . . . I wouldn't have had a choice of whom to go out with, and I wouldn't have felt very independent. But I feel I have to make my own choices. As long as I know what I want, I feel it's all right.

Susan: That was my problem—having to pick and choose. My parents would say, "Oh, is he Jewish?" "I don't know, should I ask him?" They wanted me to say, "Are you Jewish? Oh, you're not? Well, you can't go out with me, then."

Sheila: I can see how you feel—that's a tough situation, but I see now that I feel pretty frustrated because I want to date people who are Jewish, but I'm not going to go around picking on them saying this one is and this one isn't. It's too hard to do that. You can't turn your feelings on and off. You have to be interested in someone. So I get pretty frustrated a lot of times.

Susan: Are you saying that you are kind of glad that your parents didn't restrict you in that manner, or are you saying that you're glad they didn't but wish they had?

Analysis

Although Sheila's paraphrase is satisfactory, the wording could be even more specific: "It seems like you were a little upset at first, but now that you're older you have a better understanding of your parents' position."

Susan's response has a slightly condescending ring to it. Note the connotation of the word predicament. *Susan needs to empathize with Sheila more directly.*

Sheila's reaction is to defend her parents' policy. Then she makes a statement about the value of independence.

Notice that even though the statements are at odds, Sheila and Susan seem to be maintaining a good climate.

Sheila says "feel," but she's not really describing feelings.

Susan begins a response to the subject of the last sentence: choices. But then she returns to her parents' policy. Good, clear statement of position.

Sheila's acknowledgment of Susan's feelings is in the right direction, but her wording appears a bit half-hearted. She needs a good paraphrase of feelings. In the midst of her response, she switches to a description of her feelings. The rest of the sentence is well worded. She needs a clearer division between her response to Susan and her description of feelings.

This is probably one of the best responses in the dialogue. Although it is cast in question form, it is still a good attempt at seeking clarification of Sheila's feelings.

Conversation	Analysis
Sheila: I guess I'm glad they didn't, but maybe it would have been better if they had. I would have been more conscious about it.	
Susan: In the long run, I feel it's best to start early to get an idea in your mind of what you really want to do. I never thought a relationship in high school would go anywhere, but the man I'm dating, it's been four years already. That's a long time.	*Notice the use of the word* feel *when* believe *or* think *would be more appropriate.*
Sheila: You seem happy together. I saw you the other day and that's really nice. I wish I could find somebody that . . .	*A nicely phrased personal feedback statement—a nice compliment.*
Susan: I saw you start shrugging Bill off and just ignoring him.	
Sheila: Yes, that's a hard situation. I get pretty depressed about it, too. I just never thought religion could make such a big difference. But it means a lot to me, and that's why it makes such a difference.	*Sheila again describes her feelings quite well.*
Susan: What are you planning on telling him?	*Here's one of the few times when Susan focuses her attention on Sheila. Good question.*
Sheila: Well, I guess I'll just say that it won't work out. It depresses me to think about that, too.	*Sheila states her plans and continues to describe her feelings.*
Susan: You should really try to go easy—don't let it upset you too much. It's what you want, right?	*Susan gives advice that is meant to be supportive of Sheila's predicament.*
Sheila: I guess so. I'll have to try to do the best I can.	

In trying to help Sheila deal with her problem, Susan probably spent too much time talking about her own background and situation. Although some of her remarks show that she heard what Sheila was saying, some of her comments did not deal directly with Sheila's problem. Because the dialogue began as a response to Sheila's problem, Sheila's attempts at directing conversation to her problem are in order.

Both speakers made satisfactory attempts at paraphrasing and describing feelings; however, there were few good examples of perception checking. Still, the conversation was friendly (nonverbal responses were very supportive, but you can't see that on paper), and no major barriers developed.

Informative Speech and Analysis

In Search of Noah's Ark

Speech

In 1916, during the First World War, in the Russian-occupied sector of eastern Turkey, a Russian airman, W. Roskavitsky, swore that while flying over one of the slopes of Mount Ararat he saw a large vessel. This amazing report was taken all the way to the czar, who himself organized an expedition to climb Mount Ararat, and this expedition brought back the description of just such a large vessel half-submerged in the glacial lake. The czar's commission believed that they had found Noah's Ark. Could this be? Is it possible that Noah's Ark is real? In this speech, I'd like to examine with you some of the historical documentation supporting the statement that an ark, vessel, or boat is on top of Mount Ararat—and that the vessel is in fact Noah's Ark.

First, and probably most familiar to us, of this historical evidence is the biblical account of Noah's Ark and the Flood. In Genesis 8:4 it says that the Ark came to rest upon Mount Ararat. Second, Flavius Josephus, the Jewish historian, wrote in his history, *Jewish Antiquities,* in 37 A.D., that it had been reported that the Ark had been found on top of Mount Ararat. Finally, more than one thousand years later, in 1300 A.D., Marco Polo wrote in his book called *Travels* that on his way through Turkey to China, he had heard that the Ark was on top of Mount Ararat. For a long time historians had held this information suspect. First, it was difficult to believe

Analysis

The speech opens with a good historical narrative designed to get the attention of the class.

Notice the use of rhetorical questions to lead into the speech goal.

In this case, the speech goal is stated at the end of the speech introduction and leads into the body of the speech. If you are going to state or paraphrase your speech goal, this is the place to do it.

Here the body of the speech begins. The first main point—that historical writings suggest the presence of a real Ark—is implied rather than stated directly. Although you should probably state each main point clearly, in this speech the method fits well with the historical narrative approach—an approach that is designed to draw you into the resolution of the mystery.

Here the speaker confuses the date of Josephus' birth, A.D. 37, with the date of the writing of The Antiquities of the Jews, *which was A.D. 93 or 94.*

SOURCE: Speech given in Fundamentals of Speech class, Miami University. Printed by permission of Thomas Grossmann.

Speech	Analysis

Speech

that a boat was on top of a mountain; second, all the documentation was hearsay. Proof in the way of verifiable sightings was needed.

But these actual sightings did come. On two separate occasions, expeditions on Mount Ararat have seen the prow or side of a large wooden vessel sticking out of the glacial ice pack. First, a Turkish expedition in 1840 sent to Mount Ararat to build barricades against avalanches came back and reported that a large prow or side of a vessel was sticking out of the glacial ice pack. In 1952, more than 100 years later, an almost identical sighting was made by an American oil pipeline mining expedition. This expedition, headed by George Jefferson Green, also found the large prow or side of a vessel sticking out of the glacial ice pack.

Even though these sightings were documented, no one had actually been able to bring a piece of this supposed Ark back for study. And often in history supposed firsthand observations had proved to be wrong. With this goal of getting tangible evidence, Ferdinand Navara, a French explorer, climbed Mount Ararat in 1955, and at an elevation of 14,000 feet, he dug down into the glacial ice pack and found an estimated 50 tons of wood. He was able to bring back some of this wood to France, where it was analyzed by the Prehistory Institute of the University of Bordeaux on April 15, 1956. The conclusion of this report said that it was definitely wood, it was white oak, it was more than 5,000 years old, it was covered with pitch, and the wood was hand hewn. The wood was also studied by the Forestry Institute of Research and Experimentation in Madrid, Spain,

Analysis

Here again a main point is stated differently from what we usually expect. In outline form, the main point would be stated: Actual sightings of the Ark have been reported.

Here and throughout the speech the content is excellent. You should keep one criticism in mind, however. Because the source of this material is important and perhaps necessary for building and maintaining speaker credibility, the speaker should have introduced the sources of the various facts with a statement such as "As Jones pointed out in his book on ____." The speaker presented a good bibliography in his outline of the speech, but he did not introduce enough of the sources directly in the speech. Still, the examples are good, and the use of the examples helps to gain and hold attention.

Here we get into the third main point, that recently actual material has been brought back from the source.

The speech continues with specific details.

This speech fits together particularly well. The speaker draws the audience into the investigative process.

Speech

and they reached the same conclusions. This finding of wood may not appear to offer support for the presence of an Ark until another aspect is considered—this wood was found on Mount Ararat at a height some 300 feet higher than the highest tree in the entire world! Moreover, Mount Ararat itself is 300 miles away from the closest living tree.

So, let's see what we've discovered. Historical documentation dating back as far as 1000 B.C. has said that an Ark or boat rests upon Mount Ararat. Three separate expeditions—one Turkish, one Russian, and one American—have all found something that looks like a boat on top of Mount Ararat. A Frenchman by the name of Ferdinand Navara has actually found more than 50 tons of wood on top of Mount Ararat 300 feet above the highest tree line and 300 miles from the nearest tree. What does this mean? In eastern Turkey, in the area of cold Armenia, on top of a volcanic mountain named Mount Ararat, there rests a very large boat-like object—an object that many believe to be Noah's Ark.

Analysis

This is an excellent summary. It states the three main points of the speech— points that were only alluded to in the speech itself. Moreover, the rhetorical question and the last statement leave the speech on a high note—a note of mystery and speculation.

Although there are a few problems with this speech (and as you'll discover, there are some problems with almost any speech), it is a good one.

Persuasive Speech and Analysis

Open Your Eyes

Speech

Would all of you close your eyes for just a minute. Close them very tightly so that all the light is blocked out. Imagine what it would be like to always live in a world of total darkness such as you are experiencing right now,

Analysis

Much of the strength of this speech is a result of the speaker's ability to involve members of the audience personally and get them to feel what she is saying. This opening is a striking example of audience involvement. She does not

SOURCE: Speech given in Fundamentals of Speech class, University of Cincinnati. Printed by permission of Kathleen Sheldon.

Speech

though only for a moment. Never to see the flaming colors of the sunset, or the crisp green of the world after the rain— never to see the faces of those you love. Now open your eyes, look all around you, look at all of the things that you couldn't have seen if you couldn't have opened your eyes.

The bright world we awake to each morning is brought to us by two dime-sized pieces of tough, transparent, semielastic tissue: these are the cornea, and it is their function to allow light to enter the lens and the retina. Normally, they are so clear that we don't even know they are there; however, when they are scratched or scarred either by accident or by disease, they tend to blur or blot out the light. Imagine peering through a rain-slashed window pane or trying to see while swimming under water. This is the way victims of corneal damage often describe their vision.

"To see the world through another man's eyes." These words are Shakespeare's, yet today it can literally be true. Thanks to the research by medical workers throughout the world, the operation known as a corneal transplant or a corneal graft has become a reality, giving thousands of people the opportunity to see. No other generation has held such a profound legacy in its possession. Yet, the universal ignorance of this subject of cornea donation is appalling. The operation itself is really quite simple; it involves the corneas of the donor being transplanted into the eyes of a recipient. And if this operation takes place within seventy-two hours after the death of the donor, it can be 100 percent effective.

Analysis

just tell the audience what it would be like—she has them experience the feeling. The speaker very successfully lays the emotional groundwork for total audience reception of her words.

Here the speaker begins the body of her speech by telling us about the role of the cornea. Notice throughout the speech the excellent word choice, such as "The bright world we awake to each morning is brought to us by . . ."

Here again she does not just tell us what it is like but asks us to imagine for ourselves what it would be like if. The "rain-slashed window pane" is an especially vivid image.

The speaker continues in a very informative way. After asserting that corneal transplants work, she focuses on the two key points that she wants the audience to work with: The operation works, but it must be done within seventy-two hours.

Notice that there is still no apparent direct persuasion. Her method is one of making information available in a way that will lead the audience itself to thinking about what effects the information might have on them personally.

Speech

No one who has seen the human tragedy caused solely by corneal disease can doubt the need or the urgency. Take the case of a young woman living in New Jersey who lost her sight to corneal disease. She gave birth to a baby, and two years ago, thanks to a corneal transplant, she saw her three-year-old baby girl for the first time. And no one who had seen this woman's human tragedy caused solely by corneal disease nor her great joy at the restoration of her sight can doubt the need or the urgency. Or take the case of the five-year-old boy in California who was playing by a bonfire when a bottle in the fire exploded, flinging bits of glass, which lacerated his corneas. His damaged corneas were replaced with healthy ones in an emergency operation, and no one who has seen this little boy's human tragedy caused solely by corneal laceration nor the great joy to his young life of receiving his sight back again can doubt the need or the urgency. Or take the case of Dr. Beldon H. Scribbner of the University of Washington School of Medicine. Dr. Scribbner's eyesight was damaged by a corneal disease that twisted the normally spear-shaped cornea into cones. A corneal transplant gave Dr. Scribbner a 20/20 corrective vision and allowed him to continue work on his invention—the artificial kidney machine. And no one who has seen this man's tragedy caused solely by corneal disease, nor the great joy brought not only to Dr. Scribbner but to the thousands of people his machine has helped save, can doubt the need or the urgency.

Analysis

In this segment of the speech, she launches into emotional high gear. Still, her approach remains somewhat indirect. Although we stress the importance of directness in language, in this speech the repeated use of "no one" in the examples is by design. Although a more direct method might be effective, in this case the indirectness works quite well.

The real effectiveness of this section is a result of the parallel structure and repetition of key phrases: "no one who has seen . . . human tragedy . . . great joy . . . can doubt the need or the urgency." As this portion of the speech was delivered, the listeners were deeply touched by both the examples themselves and their own thoughts about the examples.

Also note how the examples themselves are ordered. The first two represent a personal effect, the final one a universal effect.

Speech

There are many philosophies behind such a gift. One of them was summed up by a minister and his wife who lost their daughter in infancy. They said, "We feel that a part of her goes on living." Or take the case of the young woman with this explanation: "I want to be useful; being useful brings purpose and meaning into my life." Surely if being useful is important, there are few better ways than to donate your eyes to someone who lives after you. But no matter which philosophy you do adopt, I hope each of you will consider donating your eyes to another who will live after you and who otherwise would have to survive in the abyss of darkness. It will do you no good to leave your eyes in your regular will if you have one, for as I mentioned earlier, there is a 72-hour critical period. If you wish to donate your eyes, I would suggest you contact Cincinnati Eye Bank for Sight Restoration at 861-3716. They will send you the appropriate donor forms to fill out, which should be witnessed by two of your closest friends or by your next of kin so that they will know your wishes. Then, when you die and no longer have need for your sight, someone who desperately wants the chance to see will be able to.

Will all of you close your eyes again for just a moment? Close them very tightly, so that all the light is blocked out. And once more imagine what it would be like to live always in a world of total darkness such as you are experiencing right now, never to see the flaming colors of a sunset, or the crisp green of the world after a rain—never seeing the faces of those you love. Now open your eyes . . . Won't you give someone else the chance to open theirs?

Analysis

At this point in the speech, the audience should be sympathetic to the problem and encouraged by the hope of corneal transplants. Now the speaker must deal with the listeners' reaction of "That may be a good idea for someone else, but why me?" In this section, she offers reasons for our acting. If the speech has a weakness, it may be here. A little further development of the reasons or perhaps the statement of an additional reason would have been helpful.

Here she brings the audience from "Good idea—I'll do something someday" to "I'd better act now."

She reminds them of the critical time period and tells them how they can proceed to make the donation. In this section, it might be worth a sentence to stress that the donation costs nothing but a little time.

Here the speaker brings the audience full circle. Although she could have used different images, the repetition of those that began the speech takes the emphasis off the images themselves and focuses it on what the audience can do about those who are in these circumstances.

The last line of the speech is simple, but in the context of the entire speech, it is direct and quite moving.